MANAGEMENT
Theory and
Practice

Michael J. Misshauk

Management
THEORY AND PRACTICE

LITTLE, BROWN AND COMPANY

Boston   Toronto

Book Editor: Tina Samaha
Text Designer: W. P. Ellis
Cover Designer: Steve Snider
Illustrator: Oliver Kline
Art Editor: Tonia Noell-Roberts

Copyright © 1979 by Little, Brown and Company (Inc.)

All rights reserved. No part of this book may be reproduced in any form or by any electronic or mechanical means including information storage and retrieval systems without permission in writing from the publisher, except by a reviewer who may quote brief passages in a review.

Library of Congress Catalog Card No. 78–70456

First Printing

Published simultaneously in Canada
by Little, Brown & Company (Canada) Limited

Printed in the United States of America

To my parents

Foreword

Modern management is constantly changing. Basic theories and research are being applied to areas of business that affect not only the individual but society as well. Today's student should be aware of the forces that shape decision making, thereby gaining a better understanding of the function of management. This was Michael Misshauk's thesis, a philosophy of teaching widely accepted not only among academics but by industry leaders as well. By developing a better understanding of the tools needed to become a successful manager, today's student will have an impact on tomorrow's business community.

The manuscript was completed and in production when Dr. Misshauk died. We greatly appreciate the effort not only of his colleagues at USC, but especially the work of Luke Novelli in the final stages of production.

Roy Herberger

Associate Dean, Graduate School of Business
University of Southern California

Preface

The subject of this book is management and organizations. The purpose of the book is to provide the reader with an understanding of how organizations function and how individuals behave within these organizations. It is also hoped that the reader will gain some thoughts, ideas, and insights that will be useful in managing modern organizations. In fact, the overriding objective of the book is to help the reader to be an effective manager.

The book takes a practical approach, using theory and research only as vehicles for providing the background to practical knowledge and insight. Here again the prime objective is information that can be applied to the work environment.

In addition to the traditional areas of management and organizations, the book focuses on some significant social issues now facing modern managers. These issues include business ethics, social responsibility, and executive stress.

In keeping with the concept of a practical approach to management, each chapter opens with a recent article from a business-oriented periodical which discusses the topic covered in the chapter.

Most chapters are followed by a Case for Discussion which describes a situation or dilemma related to the subject of the chapter; these are designed to provoke thought about the practical implications of the material covered in the chapter. All chapters are accompanied by Discussion Questions and Selected References.

The book is designed for basic management courses, management development programs, or simply as an aid to self-study.

The author is grateful to those who provided help and support in completing this text, in particular Jack Steele, Dean of the School of Business, and Colin MacLeod, Vice-President, Finance, both of the University of Southern California. Special thanks to Charles Summer, University of Washington, Ed Duerr, San Francisco State University, and the many colleagues whose comments on the manuscript were invaluable.

Contents

16 Contingency Theory and Organizational Development

Part VI
QUANTITATIVE TECHNIQUES

17 Quantitative Techniques in Planning and Controlling

MANAGING IN TODAY'S ENVIRONMENT

Part I

Introduction

In recent years both academicians and practicing administrators have become increasingly aware that the field of management is growing more complex. Some of this complexity has come about by changes in organizational structures and authority-responsibility relationships, but much is due to changes within the environment of today's executive. The public and the government are demanding more and more from corporate leadership. Their expectations are directed not only toward products and services, but also toward social issues and corporate ethics. Managers are expected to make decisions in light of increasing awareness and acceptance of social responsibility by the corporation. Defining socially and ethically responsible behavior is difficult and confusing; often top level executives spend as much, if not more, time dealing with these matters as with production or marketing goals.

At the same time, the corporate environment is being recognized as an important source of stress for the individual. Stress generated by the organization is no longer dismissed simply as part of the job, but is recognized as a major component of executive health problems and turnover (and as a possible pressure toward ethical compromises).

Social responsibility, ethics, and stress have become important elements in executive decision-making and in understanding the role of management in today's society. We will introduce the study of management by developing a framework which attempts to provide some insights into these key issues in the world of today's managers.

Major Themes

Social Responsibility:
The evolving role of the corporation

Ethics:
Management as a profession

Stress:
Its impact on today's managers

Social Responsibility: A New Challenge for Business

1

How Union Carbide Has Cleaned Up Its Image

Five years ago, Union Carbide Corp. was close to being tagged Environmental Enemy No. 1. Its Anmoore (W. Va.) plant was the target of a class-action suit for environmental damages. When Carbide threatened to lay off 625 workers at its plant in Marietta, Ohio, to offset pollution control costs, Ralph Nader charged it with "environmental blackmail." And to make matters worse, environmentalists dubbed its Alloy (W. Va.) ferroalloy plant "the smokiest factory in the world."

Today, the company's environmental record invites more kudos than wrath. But the turnabout has been an arduous and costly task for Carbide. Since 1971 the company has been striving to perfect a computer-assisted plant evaluation system that would spot and correct pollution problems before environmentalists have a chance to scream. As Fred M. Charles, corporate director of environmental affairs, puts it, "We simply got tired of always being the bad guys in the press."

Of course, the wish to avoid bad publicity and environmental regulatory clampdowns is not unique to Union Carbide. By now, most major companies have sizable environmental staffs. And a few have resorted to gimmicks to get their points across. Gates Rubber Co., for example, uses in-house inspectors to spot violations. They then tell plant managers what the fine would have been if a government inspector had come by.

Still, few—if any—companies are as formal and quantified in their approach as Carbide is. According to F. Douglas Bess, assistant manager for environmental protection,

Reprinted from the August 2, 1976 issue of *Business Week* by special permission. Copyright © 1976 by McGraw-Hill Publishing, Inc., New York, N.Y. 10020. All rights reserved.

Carbide knew from the beginning that it wanted its Environmental Impact Analysis (EIA) program, as it is called, to rely on numerical ratings rather than "vague evaluative essays."

Under the EIA, each plant provides Bess and his group with details on every aspect of its products and processes. The corporate group plots these data against various environmental areas (air quality, noise, effect on plant or animal life, and the like), and rates each operation from 0 (no impact) to 4 (major impact with immediate shutdown for correction). The visual result is a matrix that immediately pinpoints trouble spots. Although the plants can set correctional priorities according to the severity of the rating, "any rating above 1.5 means that the plant must come up with an 'action plan' to correct the situation," Bess explains.

The rating categories that Carbide uses provide tangible proof of how badly the company was stung by the unfavorable publicity of the early 1970s. In addition to the cut-and-dried performance ratings, Carbide also rates public opinion. A "0" in this category would mean that even if a pollution problem does exist, neither environmentalists nor residents of the community are overly concerned with it. A "4" means that another onslaught of painful publicity is probably in the making. A rating higher than 1.5 on public opinion requires the same action plan as an imminent health hazard.

Ample Data

A public opinion hazard was one of the first problems Carbide spotted when it first tested the EIA system at its Brownsville (Tex.) acetic acid plant in 1971. Along with process data, it gathered meteorological information, and a look at the prevailing wind pattern indicated that odors from acid storage tanks might be wafting toward the community. "We hadn't received any complaints, but we changed our venting procedures just in case," Bess recalls.

The entire Brownsville EIA was done manually, and spotting the odor problem was a lucky break. Today most of the guesswork has gone out of the program. Although the actual ratings are still arrived at by corporate analysts, almost all of the necessary data reside in an extensive computer bank. Carbide has already put in detailed descriptions of some 600 processes and some 450 products, along with details on environmental rules and results of toxicity studies.

The wealth of data is enabling Carbide to do material balances at all of its plants. "We know how much raw material is used and how much product we come out with, so we know that the difference is waste," Charles explains. The computer can then give an accurate assessment of the concentrations of that waste in stack emissions or effluent.

Other Benefits

Although the main goal of the materials balances remains environmental control, they are also giving Carbide a bottom-line bonus: recovering raw materials from the waste stream. "We always knew we were losing some materials through waste, but we were surprised at the volume," Bess recalls. Although he will not divulge details lest they give away Carbide secrets, he does point to one chemical facility's experience as an example. "In our process, we used a colorless, odorless gas, and we had no idea that we had an extensive fugitive emissions problem," he says. "After doing a materials balance, we realized we were losing upwards of 20,000 lb. of material a day." Carbide tightened some flanges to close off leaks and saved $2,000 a day.

The program has other profitable offshoots. "We've found that our engineers use our data base to find out details about some of our manufacturing processes because it's the most complete source we have," Bess says. Carbide is also using the system as an "excellent mechanism to help plan new plants," he adds. For example, Carbide recently reviewed plans for a new facility and discovered that a process vent that met regulatory requirements might still cause an odor problem. The company redesigned the vent system to pipe the offending gas stream to a thermal odor-destruction unit.

Such quantifiable success stories have made it easier for Bess and Charles to sell the EIA program to plant managers. "We're asking some pretty busy people to collect volumes of data to feed through the system," Charles explains. "When we showed that tangible savings were possible, it gave the EIA system a positive boost."

THE CONTRIBUTION OF American business to the standard of living in our society is perhaps unparalleled in world history. Through the efforts of dedicated entrepreneurs and creative business leaders, and aided by the workings of the free enterprise system, our modern corporations have been able to bring about a level of affluence never before achieved. Since the beginning of this century real national product has increased at a rate such that it has approximately doubled every twenty years. Increases in salary levels and wage rates, along with reduced work hours, have enabled today's worker and his or her family to engage in a wide variety of activities meant to contribute to a rich and meaningful life experience. Today's American has opportunities to acquire food, clothing, shelter, health care, and education on a scale obtainable in no other society. Recreational, entertainment, and cultural activities are now enjoyed by a vast number of Americans. In addition, more time is available for other activities designed to contribute to personal growth and development. In helping to bring about such an affluent standard of living our corporations have themselves grown and developed. The fifty largest United States corporations, for example, now own over one-half of all manufacturing assets; Standard Oil of New Jersey has over 100 foreign affiliates; and General Motors and IBM in 1976 each spent over *one billion* dollars in research and development activities.

In considering facts such as these one might believe that our society would hold the modern corporation in high esteem for its contributions to America's development. Nothing, however, seems to be further from the truth. The corporation is being attacked and criticized on various fronts by a great number of political and citizens' organizations. Many young people accuse the corporation of failing to seek solutions to our varied social problems. Minority groups, and women, contend that many corporations have been guilty of discrimination in hiring and in pay scales. Consumer groups charge the corporation with producing and selling unsafe and inferior products. Environmental organizations accuse the corporation of destroying air, land, and water resources. Finally, federal departments and agencies such as EPA, EEOC, OSHA, and CPSC are involved in a series of efforts to bring about laws and regulations restricting many corporate efforts and activities. A newcomer to our society might indeed be confused by these actions, directed as they are toward the business leaders and corporations primarily responsible for bringing about the wealth and prosperity so many Americans enjoy today.

To understand the nature of this criticism of business one must be aware of a change in the philosophy and attitudes of many living within our society. Ironically, these same business economies and efficiencies that have utilized available resources to meet the needs of the nation have also served to bring about a generation of individuals who have the time and wealth to appreciate and enjoy resources—resources which are no longer as available as they used to be. A "catch 22" seems to have taken hold: a society which was able to achieve a high level of affluence by making use of air, land, water, manpower, and economic resources is now no longer able to enjoy those resources because they were used up or in some way destroyed in bringing about the improved living standard. As Americans ever more comfortable economically become more concerned with the quality of their life-style than with the quantity of their goods and services, they begin to question the allocation and utilization of the resources that still exist. In a very real sense American business has brought about a situation in which most individuals are able to rise above day-to-day economics and look out at the environment in which they live. What they see are social problems: crime, discrimination, pollution, congestion, and a series of illnesses, many of which appear to be directly correlated with the pace and pressures of today's environment. In response to public concern, government at the state and federal level has attempted to deal with these issues through a series of legislative and regulatory enactments. Over a period of years, however, it has become apparent that the government, with its bureaucratic structure, which often results in confusion of authority, overlapping agencies and endless red tape, has been unable to deal with the majority of these problems. It appears that as public frustration grows over government failure to solve our problems, the frustrations turn to the business community, whom the public believes responsible for creating many of these very problems, but whom they also believe to be the best remaining hope for finding solutions to them. According to an authority in the field of management, Peter Drucker, "The new demand is for business to make social values and beliefs, create freedom for the individual and altogether produce the good society."[1] And studies by the Opinion Research Corporation conducted during 1970 show that the public has a fairly broad view of what it considers to be corporate responsibility (see table, p. 8).[2]

The remainder of this chapter will explore some of the ways the modern corporation has attempted to redefine its role within our society, turning its managerial, organizational, and technological talent toward seeking solutions to social problems. First, a discussion

Corporate responsibilities	Percentage of public who agree
Satisfy consumer needs for goods and services	60%
Keep environment clean and pollution free	60%
Hire and train blacks	38%
Support public education, health, and charities	36%
Clean up and rebuild ghettos	29%

of those areas in which business and government have engaged in joint action to develop programs to meet some of these pressing social needs.

Government and Business: Working Together on the Problems of Society

There has been a growing recognition that many of the problems of our society are too complex and far-reaching to be handled exclusively by state and federal agencies. Experience has taught that the bureaucratic structure of many government agencies often creates a mountain of red tape that prevents effective action from being taken. Accepting this situation, government leaders are looking more and more to the private sector for help in dealing with many pressing social problems.

In seeking the aid of corporate leaders, government must clearly define government and business roles. As a republic, whose goals and direction are defined by representatives elected by the people, it is the responsibility of government to develop and define the priorities, goals, and objectives of social action programs. It is the legitimate responsibility of government leaders, for example, to determine the priority that is to be given to problems of unemployment, inflation, and urban development. When these priorities have been determined, government may look to the private sector to draw upon the organizational, managerial, and technological expertise of business leaders in designing and implementing programs with these objectives.

With this role relationship clearly defined and accepted by both parties, it is possible for business and government to work together. The key question is then one of means: how can government induce private business organizations to offer their talents in support of social action programs? To be sure, many business leaders have recognized and accepted responsibility for seeking solutions to so-

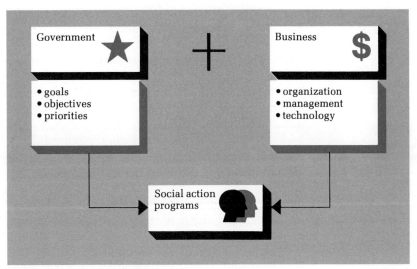

Figure 1.1. *Role Definition*

cial and economic problems. The fact remains, however, that these same people must also maintain financial responsibility to stockholders, employees, and customers. They are not free to assume unlimited activity in the realm of social welfare. Business has traditionally been governed by the balance sheet and profit and loss statement; its leaders must keep as their top priority providing goods and services to the marketplace.

To satisfy the needs of business, government must find ways and means to allow the profit motive, which drives business to operate. Let us examine some of the ways in which business has become involved in social issues. We will discuss some of the incentives that government has used and may use again in order to obtain business involvement in the future. We will focus upon five major areas of business activity: job programs, urban development, pollution control, education, and consumer protection.

Job Programs

To prevent disturbances like those in urban areas in the 1960s government and business leaders cooperated in innovative programs designed to provide greater job opportunities for urban minorities. Three examples of such programs, through which the unemployed have been hired and trained, are described below.

Jobs Now.[3] A program was developed in Chicago after the riots of 1966 sponsored by organizations including the Illinois State Employment Service, the Cook County Department of Public Aid, the Commerce and Industry Association, and the AFL-CIO. This program was directed by the YMCA of Chicago, whose advisory board is made up of some fifty local industrial leaders.

The purpose of the program was to appeal to youth gang leaders to join programs designed to provide job opportunities. The businessmen on loan to the project placed those individuals who responded in suitable jobs within their organizations. In order for these placements to be made, normal hiring standards had to be reduced or waived. After the first year of operation, of 1065 placements, 439 individuals were still working in their jobs.

Opportunities Industrialization Center.[4] Started in Philadelphia in 1964 by the Reverend Leon Sullivan, the OIC has trained unemployed and underemployed men and women in the Philadelphia area. Offering training in such areas as computer maintenance, plumbing, welding, air conditioning and refrigeration, and secretarial skills, the OIC receives input from an industrial advisory board whose members represent business firms that provide equipment and financial support for the program. General Electric, for example, provides equipment, manpower, and publicity for the program in addition to hiring OIC graduates.

JET (Jobs, Education, and Training).[5] This Buffalo, New York, project involved not only vocational training but also development of basic academic skills. Employees hired through this program spent six hours a day in traditional on-the-job training and the remaining two hours studying reading, writing, and arithmetic. The companies in the program are compensated up to $30 a week per person for a period of up to 44 weeks.

These programs are typical of early activities in which government and business organizations worked together to provide jobs for unemployed members of urban communities. In order to make such programs effective business leaders must establish an environment within their own organizations that is receptive to these goals and objectives.

In pursuing such programs, many corporations have had to revise dramatically their traditional approaches to both hiring and training procedures. Less emphasis must be placed upon individual background, references, and education and closer attention must be given to training potential and attitude. A past police record, for example, need no longer in and of itself exclude an applicant from a job opportunity. Job descriptions are being reviewed to determine if some jobs can be broken down to include both skilled components and also components that could be performed by an unskilled employee. In this way jobs can be made available that do not exceed the capabilities of the unskilled. As a result, other employees can be freed to perform more technical aspects of a given job.

Corporations have found that their recruiting procedures must adjust to the types of people they are seeking to attract. Personnel officers find that they must find ways of going out into the community to seek out potential minority employees. In an effort to reach many of these potential employees, several communities (Los Angeles, Chicago, New York City, and Philadelphia, to name just a few) have instituted radio and television shows that announce employment opportunities in the area. Applicants then phone in to the station and speak with interviewers from employment agencies about specific opportunities. In several cities recruiting campaigns have been established within ghetto communities in order to attract the local hard-core unemployed.

As state and federal agencies attempt to gain greater involvement of business in job opportunity programs in the inner city, more and more inducements are being offered as a way of gaining business support. Many of these inducements follow the lines of the federal JOBS (Job Opportunities in the Business Sector) program, in which the Department of Labor contracts with specific corporations to reimburse them for any costs associated with special training or hiring procedures necessary in order to recruit the hard-core unemployed.

Urban Development

As more and more state governments and business leaders recognized the financial and environmental problems faced by many major urban areas, increased attention and support was being given to programs whose objective was to improve the quality of life within these population centers. Typical of these programs is the Industrial Redevelopment Plan for Watts developed by Southern Pacific Company. This program aimed at eliminating substandard housing in Watts as well as developing new industry and commerce within that community. This program was similar to one developed by Eastman Kodak Company for Rochester, New York. Kodak called on local business to develop lists of products that could be supplied by inner-city business. Kodak also proposed the establishment of an organization funded by local business that could supply capital to inner city ventures and offered to provide managerial consulting to local small business enterprise.[6]

The Allegheny Housing Rehabilitation Corporation (AHRCO) was composed of 32 large corporations in the Pittsburgh area who were working to rehabilitate deteriorating housing. The houses to be renovated were made available to low-income families in the community. As this project developed it made available information on rehabilitation methods to other communities; in addition, the project provided on-the-job training in the building trades to many minority workers.[7]

At the national level, the Urban Coalition, made up of leaders from government, business, labor, religion, and civil rights, originated in 1967 to deal with urban problems. The Coalition includes in its goals development of jobs, housing, and educational programs to aid in the reconstruction of our nation's urban areas. A major component of the program is reliance on the organizational and managerial skills of corporate leaders in implementing these programs.

In addition to managerial and organizational abilities, many corporations have utilized new technology, particularly in building construction, to aid in the development of inner-city housing. According to the mayor of one eastern city, "One of the most significant programs to be developed is the housing rehabilitation program of Armstrong Cork, which will provide at least two major benefits: experimentation with housing rehabilitation materials, and the visible involvement of a major industry in hometown problems."[8] Another firm making a technical contribution is the Jim Walter Research Corporation, which is developing acoustical systems to reduce sound levels in high-density living centers. Lockheed Aircraft has developed a system whereby unskilled labor can assemble prefabricated housing units. In addition, prefabricated stairways and chimneys have been developed that have lowered housing costs significantly.

Pollution Control

Perhaps no one social issue has raised so much controversy and attention as the issue of pollution and its impact upon the environment. Business, more than any other institution, has been identified as responsible for the significant deterioration of our nation's land, air, and water resources. While auto emissions and smoke stacks have been feeding tons of pollutants into our air, many corporations have been equally guilty of throwing high quantities of pollutants into our nation's lakes and river systems.

In recent years, activities such as these have been the target of extensive government as well as community action. There has indeed emerged within this country, to quote former Interior Secretary Stewart Udall, "an era of ecology." Legislation such as the Clean Air amendments of 1970 and the Water Pollution Control Act amendments of 1972 have had as their purpose the control of industrial pollution. In addition, the National Environmental Policy Act of 1969 created a permanent Council on Environmental Quality whose function is to advise the President on matters involving the environment. The act provided that the nation might "fulfill the responsibilities of each generation as trustee of the environment for succeeding generations and assure for all Americans safe, healthful, productive, and aesthetically and culturally pleasing surroundings."[9]

Also established in 1970 was the Environmental Protection Agency, which consolidated all major federal pollution control programs including water pollution, air pollution, solid waste, pesticides, and radiation. Previously these areas of responsibility were divided among HEW, the Atomic Energy Commission, the Department of the Interior, and the Department of Agriculture. By its regulatory and financial assistance activity, the EPA is able to exert significant control over the establishment of air and water quality standards. It is this agency more than any other that has been charged with the responsibility of enforcing environmental standards within our nation.

Along with federal regulation, public pressure and an emerging sense of social responsibility have led many major corporations within our nation to become actively involved in reducing environmental pollution. The magnitude of this involvement is evidenced by the fact that in 1974 alone, according to a survey by the McGraw-Hill Company, business planned to invest $7.4 billion in air and water pollution controls.[10] According to this same survey the paper industry would devote 23.7 percent of its capital budget to pollution control and worker safety; for the steel industry the figure would be 22.8 percent.

The costs associated with pollution control are indeed staggering. Table 1.1 represents estimated costs associated with air pollution control in major urban areas. Clearly, in evaluating the economic effects of pollution control, business and government must consider the trade-offs that exist: At what point in reduction of pollution is benefit outweighed by cost? Figure 1.2 provides some insight into control-damage trade-offs.

Despite the vast expenditures required for pollution control, many corporations have issued strong positive statements with respect to the environment. Typical of these is a 1971 statement by the General Electric Company:

> It is the policy of the General Electric Company to contribute
> to environmental protection by eliminating or limiting to the
> lowest practicable levels, and in any event limiting to

Table 1.1. *Estimated Costs for Controlling Air Pollution in 100 Metropolitan Areas (Fiscal Years 1971–1975, Millions)*

Source of pollution	1971	1972	1973	1974	1975	Total 1971– 1975
INVESTMENT COSTS						
Solid waste disposal	$ 17	$ 56	$ 80	$ 50	$ 18	$ 221
Fuel combustion	82	291	443	331	142	1,289
Industrial processes	78	261	410	278	104	1,131
Total investment costs	177	608	933	659	264	2,641
ANNUAL COSTS						
Solid waste disposal	8	35	74	98	107	322
Fuel combustion	107	445	912	1,200	1,330	3,994
Industrial processes	37	147	303	404	443	1,334
Total annual costs	152	627	1,290	1,710	1,880	5,659

Note: Based on requirements under the Clean Air Act as amended in 1967.
Source: Department of Health, Education, and Welfare.

statutorily defined levels, all adverse environmental effects from its products, facilities and activities, and by offering products and processes which will help solve environmental problems.[11]

As further evidence of commitment, many corporations have added to their organizational chart (often at the level of vice-president) a position whose responsibility directly involves environmental quality. In one survey of 174 companies whose products include chemicals, food products, paper, petroleum, rubber, and plastics, 89 respondents indicated that they had given organizational emphasis to the problem of pollution control, either by setting up a corporate unit to be responsible for the problem or assigning pollution control to an existing corporate division.[12] This job description issued by Gulf Oil Corporation (Exhibit 1.1 on page 16) illustrates the responsibilities of such corporate officers.[13]

Education

In its effort to deal with problems of education, government is looking increasingly to the private sector. In 1970 the Office of Economic Opportunity contracted with six private business concerns in a $6.5 million experimental program. The goal of the program was to improve the achievement level in reading and mathematics for the students taking part.[14] Participating firms received $110 for every student whose performance improved one grade level as a result of participating in the program. Such improvement within the time

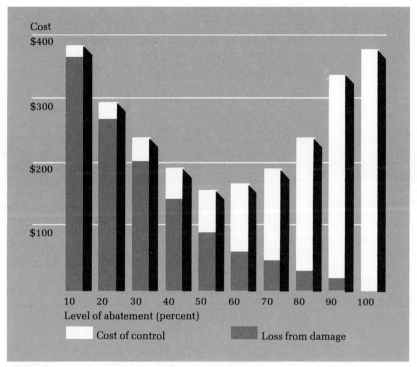

Figure 1.2. *Cost to Society from Pollution Damage and for Pollution Control*

Source: From Azriel Teller, "Air Pollution Abatement: Economic Rationality and Reality," *Daedalus*, Fall 1967, p. 1085. Reprinted by permission of *Daedalus*, Journal of the American Academy of Arts and Sciences.

allotted represented a significant increase over progress in the public educational systems. Corporations such as the Philadelphia Gas Works have provided key executives who served on company time as nonpaid instructors in the public school system. Raytheon Corporation provided staff specialists to classroom teachers in high school physics, chemistry, and mathematics courses.[15]

Within many educational institutions, local business leaders serve as advisors in various curriculum development capacities, providing valuable input in both technical and professional academic programs. For example, the Chase Manhattan Bank Foundation supported a program to develop a high quality economics program within colleges and universities affiliated with the United Negro College Fund. There were also programs designed to motivate students to stay in school and complete their education. The Michigan

Exhibit 1.1. *Job Description*

Gulf Oil Corporation
Air and Water Conservation Advisor

The Air and Water Conservation Advisor is accountable to the Senior Vice President (Technical Advisor to the Executive) and is responsible for the coordination of various technical activities within the Corporation. He is particularly responsible for the coordination of the Corporation's activities in the field of water and air conservation.

The Air and Water Conservation Advisor will coordinate the Corporation's efforts to pursue a realistic and progressive program to ensure that the operations of the Gulf Companies are giving no unnecessary offenses against clear air and water. He will make every effort to obtain governmental and public understanding of pollution abatement problems and appreciation of Gulf's efforts to find solutions to these problems.

To accomplish these activities, the Air and Water Conservation Advisor will maintain such relationships with governmental, technical, and industry societies, and with other industries dealing with such problems so as to achieve effective and sensible control of objectionable air and water pollution resulting from petroleum operations. He shall also be responsible for handling all requests from industry and government in this regard, or for furnishing advice as to how they should be handled at any level of Gulf's operations.

He will also maintain close contact with all operating Officers and Department Heads so as to be fully informed of their activities in this particular field.

Source: Courtesy of Gulf Oil Corporation.

Bell Telephone Company has been active in this work and also on the Higher Education Opportunities Committee, a group of community leaders that has made over 300 scholarships available to colleges and universities in the Detroit area.[16]

Consumer Protection

Consumer protection is another area of public concern. In recent years, government, the courts, and the public in general have taken a position that tends to hold corporations more responsible for the products they market than was the case in the past. In line with this emerging philosophy, the Consumer Product Safety Act of 1972 established the Consumer Product Safety Commission (CPSC) which has rapidly evolved into one of the most powerful regulatory agencies in Washington. The Commission has responsibility for all consumer products, with the major exception of food and automobiles. The Commission has the right of factory inspection and access to company records. Based upon its investigations, it may ban or order the redesign of a product deemed to be hazardous.

The significance of the product safety problem is evidenced by a 1960 HEW report estimating that 20 million Americans are injured each year in accidents involving consumer products other than automobiles. Experts estimate that from 5 to 25 percent of these accidents could be prevented by product redesign.[17] With these statistics in mind, the CPSC has vigorously investigated a wide range of possibly hazardous consumer products, enforcing rules for such products as refrigerator door latches, children's pajamas, and aspirin bottle caps.

The difficulty with the issue of product safety is arriving at an adequate definition of just what constitutes a safe product. The problem involves defining the limits, if any, of the responsibility a corporation bears for the safety of products it places in the marketplace. According to Baron Whitaker, president of Underwriters Laboratories, "If you say 'make it safe' you haven't said anything. Safety isn't an absolute quantity. It represents a compromise on product utility, cost, and choices."[18]

Consumerism

The steady increase in importance of consumerism in our society in recent years is based on the judgment that business has not done its share in protecting the public when it designs, promotes, and advertises its products. As early as 1964, Aaker and Day stated that "as evidenced by consumer agitation at the local-state-federal levels, business has failed to meet the total needs and desires of today's consumers."[19] In answer to this perceived failure, government intervention has evolved responses having an impact on the behavior and philosophy of business organizations. As a result, most business leaders are improving their efforts to meet the needs and desires of the modern consumer.

Advertising

The question of deceptive advertising has been discussed vigorously for a number of years. It is often difficult to define exactly what is meant by an advertisement that deceives those exposed to it. But the problem is serious. The Food and Drug Administration estimates that approximately $1 billion annually is spent on worthless devices, drugs, foods, and cosmetics—purchases induced by advertising claims.[20] Increasing consumer and governmental pressure is forcing corporate marketing programs to monitor more closely statements they make in persuading consumers that their products are desirable. This control has been felt strongly in the advertising of children's cereals. Senate hearings held in 1970 resulted in advertisers improving the accuracy of claims made about the specific nutritive qualities of their cereal products.

**Sales
Promotion**

The mechanisms used to promote products have also come under the gaze of governmental agencies. In the U.S. House of Representatives hearings on fair packaging and labeling an example of doubtful honesty was submitted by a Nebraska housewife.

> In this we have two packages of Baggies. The old one said 150 sandwich bags, 36 cents. The new one is marked still 150 bags for 36 cents, but now the package says "50 Extra Bags Free When You Buy the Box at Regular 100 Bag Price."[21]

It must be assumed that the regular package contains 100 bags at some unstated price but it still contains a total of 150 bags at the 36 cents price, but now there are 50 bags free. Thus the consumer will pay the same 36 cents for 150 bags whichever package is purchased. One package deceptively states, however, that 50 bags are included free.

It is practices such as these that have come under close scrutiny and which corporations have attempted to eliminate from their promotional campaigns.

**Product
Safety**

Let us return to the question of product safety. In the files of the National Commission on Product Safety one can find cases such as that of a 13-month-old boy who hanged himself in his crib with the string of a musical toy designed to entertain babies and that of a 62-year-old woman in California who was electrocuted while standing in a puddle when her electric edger cut its cord.[22]

Are the manufacturers of these products responsible for these accidents? Unfortunately, no adequate definition or standard of safety can be determined by which to hold all corporations responsible, and the major effort toward responsible design and manufacture must come from the corporations themselves. Within recent years, however, the courts have attempted to define the responsibilities and liabilities of the manufacturer in product design, which include:

1. To know and understand the circumstances in which a product is used and to design it so that it will be reasonably safe for such use. This implies performing sufficient research, testing, and selecting adequate materials for applications intended. The designer and manufacturer must also anticipate and allow for the effects of reasonable wear and tear, and must warn of the hazards of use after excessive wear
2. To manufacture the product by the techniques and processes required to assure good workmanship
3. To keep up with advances in science, design methods, standards,

manufacturing techniques, components and materials, and safety requirements

4. To apply the inspection and testing procedures necessary to assure a product "fit for use" by the ultimate user

5. To warn the user of hazards in either the use or foreseeable misuse of the product.[23]

Warranties

The warranty supposedly assures the purchaser of a product that someone will stand behind the product in case something goes wrong. In practice, however, there appears to be significant evidence that in many cases the consumer does not receive the benefits promised by the warranty claim. Even if he receives what is literally promised, the benefits may put him substantially out of pocket.

In one case, the warranty of the Baldwin Piano Company included a promise to promptly repair or replace without charge any part which was found to be defective, provided that the piano was delivered to their factory and all the transportation costs were paid by the purchaser. Under such a provision the consumer might have to spend hundreds of dollars to ship the defective piano back to the factory in order to receive the repair he is entitled to. The Baldwin Company claims to use a "most lenient and flexible" policy when evaluating requests for repair, but the fact remains that many consumer product warranties often fail—as this one does—to meet the rightful expectations of the consumer.

In order to alleviate some of the problems consumers encounter with warranties, there appears to be a need to tighten up the definition of responsibility with respect to the repair and/or maintenance of consumer products. In particular, the obligations of the manufacturer and/or the retailer need to be defined so that the consumer can determine exactly how to proceed with a warranty claim. In addition, there has been a move to eliminate or reduce the legal jargon often found in warranties. Many corporations, some prompted by consumer advocates and some on their own initiative, have simplified the language they use in describing warranty and servicing arrangements. A warranty written in consumers' language is shown in Exhibit 1.2 on page 20.[24]

Affirmative Action

Perhaps no activity has occupied business leaders recently as much as their involvement in developing and implementing affirmative action programs within their organizations. Focusing primarily on eliminating race and sex discrimination, programs of this type have

Whirlpool CORPORATION   ADMINISTRATIVE CENTER • BENTON HARBOR, MICHIGAN 49022

WHIRLPOOL® DRYER WARRANTY

LENGTH OF WARRANTY:	WHIRLPOOL WILL PAY FOR:	WHIRLPOOL WILL NOT PAY FOR:
FULL ONE-YEAR WARRANTY *FROM DATE OF INSTALLATION*	Parts and labor for the repair or replacement of any part that is defective in materials or workmanship.	**A.** Service calls to: 1. Replace light bulbs. 2. Correct the installation of the dryer. 3. Instruct you how to use the dryer. 4. Replace house fuses or correct house wiring or plumbing. **B.** Property damage not caused by a defect in materials or workmanship.* **C.** Repairs when dryer is used commercially or unreasonably. **D.** Pick up and delivery. This product is designed to be repaired in the home. **E.** Damage to dryer caused by accident, misuse, fire, flood or acts of God.

All warranty service must be done by a Whirlpool franchised TECH-CARE® service company. This warranty does not cover damage to the dryer caused by the use of products not approved or manufactured by Whirlpool, such as fabric softeners or conditioners.
This warranty gives you specific legal rights, and you may also have other rights which vary from state to state.
*Some states do not allow the exclusion or limitation of incidental or consequential damages, so the above limitation or exclusion may not apply to you.

MODEL_____

SERIAL_____

DATE OF INSTALLATION _____

The model and serial numbers of your Whirlpool dryer are stamped on the plate shown in the illustration on the back of this warranty. Please record this information in the spaces provided and keep this warranty with your sales slip.

687150D

WE WANT YOU TO BE A HAPPY SATISFIED CUSTOMER
IF YOU NEED SERVICE OR HELP, WE SUGGEST YOU FOLLOW THESE 3 STEPS.

1. Before calling the service technician...*
Check the things you can do yourself. Refer to the Literature furnished with your dryer or contact the dealer from whom you purchased the dryer.

2. If you need service...*

Whirlpool has a national network of franchised TECH-CARE® service companies. TECH-CARE service technicians are trained to fulfill your warranty and provide after-warranty service and maintenance, anywhere in the United States.
Look for the Whirlpool franchised TECH-CARE service company listing in the telephone directory Yellow Pages under:

Should you not find a listing, dial free, within the continental United States except Alaska, the Whirlpool COOL-LINE® service assistance telephone number (800) 253-1301 [when calling from Michigan, dial (800) 632-2243].

3. If you have a problem...*
Call Whirlpool Corporation in Benton Harbor at the COOL-LINE service assistance telephone number (See Step 2) or write:
Mr. Stephen E. Upton, Vice President
Whirlpool Corporation
Administrative Center
Benton Harbor, Michigan 49022

*If you must call or write, please provide: your name, address, telephone number, type of appliance, brand, model, serial number, date of purchase, the dealer's name and a complete description of the problem. This information is needed in order to better respond to your request for assistance.

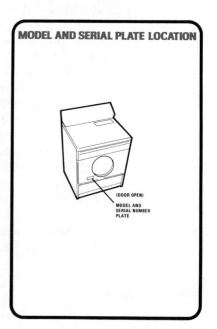

MODEL AND SERIAL PLATE LOCATION

(DOOR OPEN)

MODEL AND SERIAL NUMBER PLATE

Exhibit 1.2. *Warranty*

Source: Courtesy of Whirlpool Corporation.

become an integral part of the planning and operation of business organizations, public institutions, and colleges and universities.

In essence, affirmative action requires not only that organizations not discriminate in hiring and promotion practices in the future *but that they take some affirmative action (positive steps) to eliminate any inequities existing at the present time that may have resulted from past practices or policies.* It is the latter part of this statement that has caused so much concern and controversy. In order to understand the importance and far-reaching impact of affirmative action as a principle governing employment, let us examine the legal framework from which it evolved.

Discrimination and the Law[25]

Fourteenth Amendment. Perhaps the most significant statement concerning discrimination in the United States is to be found in the Fourteenth Amendment of the Constitution (1868). This amendment promises "equal protection of the law" to "all persons born or naturalized in the United States" and goes on to forbid states from adopting a law which would "abridge the privileges or immunities of citizens of the United States."

Although the Fourteenth Amendment would appear to serve to prevent discrimination, its early application was primarily toward blacks, with few or no legal benefits for women. Indeed, women were not given the right to vote until passage of the Nineteenth Amendment in 1920. Thus, although the Fourteenth Amendment has been a part of the Constitution of the United States since 1868 it has had little impact on the overall discrimination based on *sex* that has existed in business organizations.

Title VII. The 1972 amendment of Title VII of the Civil Rights Act of 1964 "prohibits discrimination because of race, color, religion, sex, or national origin in all employment practices including hiring, firing, promotion, compensation, job classification, and other terms, privileges and conditions of employment." In order to insure that the requirements of this act would be carried out, Title VII had also created the Equal Employment Opportunity Commission (EEOC). The EEOC has been given broad investigative powers in order to determine the extent of compliance with Title VII. In the event of noncompliance, the EEOC may make recommendations to various enforcement agencies or seek direct access to the courts.

It should be mentioned that under Title VII interpretation, what is at issue is *not the motivation or intent* of the organization with respect to discrimination but rather the effect or results that have come about. Specifically, it is not necessary that an organization consciously discriminate in its hiring or promotion practices in order to be in violation of Title VII. All that is necessary is that the EEOC produce statistical data demonstrating that minorities or women are not present in the organization in direct proportion to their presence in the community labor force. Such data would be interpreted as prima facie (legally sufficient) evidence of discrimination by the organization and the burden of proof would then rest with the organization to demonstrate that discrimination did not exist. Such a demonstration by the organization would have to be based upon "compelling business necessity," which required the organization to hire and promote based upon criteria that may have resulted in discriminatory practices. The courts have in fact taken a very narrow view of the "compelling business necessity" interpretation, and as a result this argument is not generally successful as a defense regarding violations of Title VII.

Executive Orders 11.246 and 11.375. In 1965, President Johnson issued Executive Order 11.246, requiring all federal contractors including universities that receive federal monies for research or other purposes, to sign an agreement not to discriminate against any employee on the basis of race, color, religion, or national origin. Executive Order 11.375 (1968) extended this coverage on the basis of sex. In addition, these executive orders require that contractors *file a written affirmative action program designed to eliminate any inequities that might exist as a result of past practices.* Failure on the part of an organization to file such an affirmative action program may be interpreted as a failure to comply with the executive order and thus, in and of itself, is grounds for cut-off of federal funds. Affirmative action programs submitted by organizations usually involve a series of "quotas" listing percentages of minorities that will be hired by certain specified dates in the future.

Revised Order Number 4. In order to define more clearly the requirements of an appropriate affirmative action program, the Office of Federal Contract Compliance issued Revised Order Number 4. This order contained a series of instructions to be utilized in developing and implementing affirmative action programs within an organization. Specifically, Revised Order Number 4 requires that a "utilization analysis" be included in any affirmative action program submitted by an organization. This analysis requires "an analysis of all major job classifications at the facility, with explanation of why minorities or women are currently being underutilized in any one or more job classifications (job "classification" herein meaning one or a group of jobs having similar content, wage rates, and opportunities)." "Underutilization" is defined as employing fewer members of minorities or fewer women in a particular job classification than would reasonably be expected by their availability.

As part of its affirmative action program, the organization must include a schedule detailing the procedures which will be utilized to eliminate current inequities, as well as the dates by which these inequities will be corrected.

The above outline represents the current state of legislation regarding discrimination within organizations as well as the affirmative action programs designed to correct the effects of past discrimination. Needless to say, it is the affirmative action component of these antidiscrimination laws that has created the most controversy among business leaders. The key issue in the controversy appears to be that it is not enough for an organization not to discriminate in its hiring practices but that it must show, by statistics, that its labor force is made up of a proportionate number of minorities, based upon their availability in the area. Secondly, the organization must institute positive steps to rectify the effects of past discrimination practices. To rectify past discrimination in one major case, the EEOC signed a consent decree with American Telephone and Telegraph Company in 1974 in which AT&T agreed to pay 38 million dollars in back pay and wage increases to thousands of women and minority employees "whose progress might have been delayed by past employment practices."[26]

Corporate Environment

The significance of the female work force is evidenced by the fact that at the present time 38.6 million women are now working or actively seeking employment; this represents 48 percent of all women in the nation. Within the work environment in general, women earn only 59 percent of what men earn. The average salary for women in secondary schools is 81 percent that of men, while female scientists earn 76 percent of male scientists' salaries and female engineers only 85 percent as much as their male counterparts.[27]

The fact that in the past women have not had the opportunities now available to them is becoming acknowledged by corporate leaders. As part of their affirmative action programs they are adopting various methods and techniques to expand job opportunities for female employees. Recognizing the needs of the potential female employee who may have small children to care for, Xerox Corporation assisted in establishing a day-care center near its Phoenix, Arizona facility. Other corporations, such as Westinghouse, are experimenting with a concept called "flexitime," in which partici-pating employees may work their eight-hour day any hours between 7:00 A.M. and 7 P.M.

Despite implementation of programs designed in response to the affirmative action required by legislation, the fact remains that many corporations are finding that problems with employing women re-main. One is the result of the established male-female role relation-ship that exists in our society. Corporations find that many male employees have difficulty adjusting to the idea that females are holding jobs that have traditionally gone to males. This is particu-larly true in the case of supervisory positions in which a female manager will be supervising male employees. On the other hand, many women, according to psychologist Matina Horner, believe that success on the job may eventually destroy their femininity; the op-portunity to make more money than their husbands or an inability to spend time with children may create a sense of guilt in some women that is difficult to overcome.[28] Clearly, both the legislative and be-havioral implications of affirmative action will make this an issue of continuing importance to business and government leaders in the years to come.

Inducements to Change

We have examined some of the areas in which business organiza-tions have become involved in the design and development of social action programs. We have not attempted to identify in depth the underlying motivations behind such involvement, but we have seen that just as elected government leaders respond to the demands of their constituencies, so have business leaders responded to both government and public inducements with respect to their corporate social responsibility. The many inducements that have been bringing about changes in corporate behavior are noted in Figure 1.3.

It remains for government to set the national priorities and objec-tives that represent the needs and desires of society at any point in time. In order to bring about a shift in the behavior of individuals, institutions, and corporations that is consistent with society's needs and desires, and to insure that all parties adhere equally to these new priorities and directives, the government can legislate and enforce certain rules of behavior. Once legislation and regulation are de-fined, it falls to each individual and organization to seek to achieve the goals implied by the spirit of the legislation.

There can be little question that the behavior of business organi-zations in seeking solutions to social problems is at least in part a

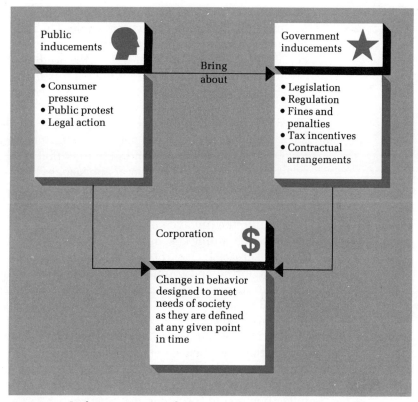

Figure 1.3. *Inducements to Changes in Corporate Behavior*

response to legislative and regulatory action. Government is, however, to a great extent simply defining the issues to which society gives high priority. Modern organizations overall have responded positively to the call of the public for business to take on a larger role in the area of social responsibility.

Social Audit

As corporations become more concerned with their level of involvement in social problems and issues, and as the nature of this involvement becomes more open to public scrutiny, there has developed a need to find new methods to measure the performance of corporations in the social activities in which they may engage. Just as the balance sheet and profit and loss statement measure performance in the financial area of the corporation, so too methods need to be developed to indicate how satisfactorily the corporation is contributing to the needs of society as a whole. The role of the corporation has been changing dramatically, and it is no longer satisfactory for a corporation to concern itself only with production, marketing, and profit. In today's society the corporation is being held accountable for a much broader range of activities and consequences than previously, and it must concern itself with its total impact upon the physical and social environment in which it functions. This broadened responsibility has led many corporations to assess their own involvement in programs and activities that deal directly or indirectly with social issues. Several approaches to describing and measuring this involvement have been developed.

Cost of Social Programs

Insight into the involvement of a corporation in social areas may be gained by obtaining cost data for the expenditures of the corporation in these areas. If a corporation spends $500,000 on a program of minority hiring and training, there is a concrete indication that the corporation is committed to this social responsibility. If this figure of $500,000 is compared with gross sales of the company, yet another measure of involvement can be obtained.

The total cost approach of course merely measures the amount of money that has been spent; it does not provide any indication of the effectiveness of the programs. Put another way, the total cost approach measures *input* to the programs but does not measure *output* (effectiveness) of the programs.[29]

Value of Social Programs

Many corporations have attempted to evaluate their social programs in terms of the value they obtain as a result of active involvement. This approach places a value on the goodwill, loyalty, and trust that is built up in the community and among employees, customers, and suppliers as a result of a corporation's participation in community affairs.

This measurement is of the "good" or benefit to the corporation rather than the good to society that might result from company involvement.

Descriptive Approach

In an effort to avoid the pitfalls of quantitative measurement of involvement in social programs, many organizations have simply listed and described the programs in which they are engaged. The purpose of such a listing is to inform various segments of the public of company activities and programs.

The problem with such an approach is obvious: such an "inventory" provides little information about the extent of the corporation's involvement or about the effectiveness of the programs.

Cost-Benefit Analysis

Perhaps the most ambitious approach to measuring the performance of a corporation with respect to its involvement in social programs lies in the quantitative evaluation of both the costs and the values to be associated with each one. Such an analysis follows an accounting procedure in which "assets" and "liabilities" are listed for each program. It provides the most thorough analysis of corporate performance, comparing both costs and benefits associated with each activity. Here again, the obvious problem is quantifying the benefits from a specific program and then comparing these with accurate estimates of total program costs.

More and more corporations are attempting to develop methods for evaluating their performance in the various social programs they undertake. As the expectations of society continue to expand regarding the nature of the corporation's social responsibility, it can be expected that more and more sophisticated techniques will be developed to measure the social performance of the corporation. The Carson and Steiner model outlined in Exhibit 1.3 on page 28 can be utilized by a corporation wishing to report its activities in the social area.

Discussion Questions

1. Define what is meant by corporate social responsibility.
2. What change has taken place in recent years in the public's perception of the role of the corporation with respect to social issues?
3. Discuss the role of government and business in working toward the solution of social problems.
4. Discuss those areas in which business and government have attempted to deal with social problems.
5. What are the obligations and responsibilities of a corporation with respect to the products it places in the marketplace?
6. To what extent do you believe additional government regulation will be effective in bringing about increased business activity in dealing with social issues?
7. What is meant by a corporate "affirmative action" program?
8. Discuss current legislation in this country aimed at eliminating discrimination.
9. Discuss the concept of "reverse discrimination."
10. What is a corporate social audit?
11. How might a corporation attempt to determine the "value" of its social action programs in order to perform a cost-benefit analysis?

Exhibit 1.3. *The Future of the Social Audit: A Model for Social Auditing/Reporting*

1. An Enumeration of Social Expectations and the Corporation's Response	A summary and candid enumeration by program areas (e.g., consumer affairs, employee relations, physical environment, local community development) of what is expected, and the corporation's reasoning as to why it has undertaken certain activities and not undertaken others.
2. A Statement of the Corporation's Social Objectives and the Priorities Attached to Specific Activities	For each program area the corporation would report what it will strive to accomplish and what priority it places on the activities it will undertake.
3. A Description of the Corporation's Goals in Each Program Area and of the Activities It Will Conduct	For each priority activity, the corporation will state a specific goal (in quantitative terms when possible) and describe how it is striving to reach that goal (e.g., to better educational facilities in the community it will make available qualified teachers from among members of its staff).
4. A Statement Indicating the Resources Committed to Achieve Objectives and Goals	A summary report, in quantitative terms, by program area and activity, of the costs—direct and indirect—assumed by the corporation.
5. A Statement of the Accomplishments and/or Progress Made in Achieving Each Objective and Each Goal	A summary, describing in quantitative measures when feasible and through objective, narrative statement when quantification is impracticable, the extent of achievement of each objective and each goal.

Source: J. Carson and G. Steiner, "Measuring Business' Social Performance: The Corporate Social Audit." Committee for Economic Development, 1974, p. 61.

Case for Discussion

Global Products Inc. is a large, publicly held corporation doing business on an international scale. Its products include a line of agricultural equipment as well as smaller machines and motors for household appliances.

At the annual stockholders meeting of Global Products, much of the agenda dealt with the financial and profit picture for the current year as well as future growth potential.

After the formal financial presentation, the president of Global presented the company's new programs for the coming year. Some of these programs included:

1. A new computerized inventory control system;
2. A feasibility study of expanding the product line into construction equipment; and
3. A new minority hiring and training program.

After these programs were discussed, the floor was opened to questions from individual stockholders. The first question came from a woman who identified herself as an employee of Global Products for over twenty years. The individual inquired "why is Global going to spend money on hiring and training minorities when the employees have needed and requested a prepaid dental program for the last five years. I believe that current employees should have priority in receiving funds rather than using the money to start a minority hiring program."

Before the president could respond, another stockholder objected that funds would be used for purposes that would not provide a dollar return to Global Products. He stated that he strongly believed that the first obligation of the corporation was to its stockholders and therefore those funds which were to be spent upon the minority program should be allocated to increased stockholder dividends. With both stockholders standing waiting for a comment, the president of Global stood and began to reply.

Selected References

Aaker, D. and Day, G. *Consumerism: Search for the Consumer Interest.* New York: Free Press, 1971.

Buggie, F. and Gurman, R. "Toward Effective and Equitable Pollution Control Regulation." In the *AMA Report.* New York: American Management Association, Inc., 1972.

Committee for Economic Development: *Social Responsibilities of Business Corporations.* New York: 1971.

Corson, J. and Steiner, G. "Measuring Business' Social Performance: The Corporate Social Audit." Committee for Economic Development, 1974.

Finley, G. "Mayors Evaluate Business Action on Urban Problems." In *Studies in Public Affairs.* New York: Conference Board, 1968.

Flower, B. "Business Amid Urban Crisis." In *Studies in Public Affairs.* New York: Conference Board, 1968.

Furuhashi, Y. and McCarthy, E. *Social Issues of Marketing in the American Economy.* Columbus, Ohio: Grid Inc., 1971.

Haskell, E. and Price, V. *State Environmental Management.* New York: Praeger, 1973.

Henry, H. *Pollution Control: Corporate Responses.* In *AMA Report.* New York: American Management Association, Inc., 1974.

Hopkinson, R. "Corporate Organization for Pollution Control." In *Studies in Public Affairs.* New York: Conference Board, 1970.

Khare, R., Kolka, J., and Polles, C., eds. *Environmental Quality and Social Responsibility.* Madison, Wisconsin: University of Wisconsin Press, 1972.

Koch, J. and Chizman, J. *The Economics of*

Affirmative Action. Lexington, Mass.: Lexington Books, 1976.

Luthans, F. and Hodgetts, R. *Social Issues in Business.* New York: Macmillan, 1972.

Lyle, J. "Affirmative Action Programs for Women: A Survey of Innovative Programs." In the *EEOC Report.* Washington, D.C.: U.S. Government Printing Office, 1973.

Marx, W. *Man and His Environment: Waste.* New York: Harper & Row, 1972.

Thompson, D. *The Economics of*

Environmental Protection. Cambridge, Mass.: Winthrop, 1973.

U.S. House of Representatives (Report No. 2337), *Report on Public Policy Implications of Investment Company Growth.* Washington, D.C.: U.S. Government Printing Office, 1966.

Weaver, P., "The Hazards of Trying to Make Consumer Products Safer," *Fortune,* July 1975.

"Women at Work." In *Newsweek,* 6 December 1976.

The Question of Ethics

2

How Companies React to the Ethics Crisis

by Carl Burgen and Bureaus

"An overly ambitious employee might have the mistaken idea that we do not care how results are obtained, as long as he gets results. He might think it best not to tell higher management all that he is doing, not to record all transactions accurately. . . . He would be wrong on all counts. . . . We don't want liars for managers."

–Clifton C. Garvin, Jr., chairman of Exxon Corp., in a statement on ethics, 1975

Policy statements on business ethics pour forth from corporations in the wake of almost daily disclosures that some of this country's most distinguished executives were themselves "overly ambitious employees" who did not care how results were obtained, even if it meant breaking the law. Whatever companies do now, the image of America's business elite—shattered by too many illegal campaign contributions made and too many bribes paid—can hardly be repaired quickly. But along with the policy pronouncements, which are not so different from the ones to which corporations have given lip service all along, there are welcome signs of tighter controls, of belated efforts to establish a higher moral tone throughout management and, in a few companies, of a serious grappling with questions of right and wrong that go beyond simple strictures against bribing politicians—questions like whether to buy safety by paying off racketeers or whether to close a plant that is endangering the health of a town.

Reprinted from the February 9, 1976 issue of *Business Week* by special permission. Copyright © 1976 by McGraw-Hill Publishing, Inc., New York, N.Y. 10020. All rights reserved.

At Foremost-McKesson Inc., says President William W. Morison, a special committee consisting of three outside directors is formulating a policy statement that deals with company policies in such areas of social responsibility as equal opportunity hiring and environmental protection, as well as with the conduct of business.

And Allied Chemical Corp. has been running managers through an innovative three-day business ethics seminar in which they discuss the obligations of the company to society at large. (Ironically, Allied has recently found itself under heavy fire for the apparent Kepone chemical poisoning of workers at a contractor's plant at Hopewell, Va.)

Embattled Business

But getting business to own up to its sins and do something constructive about them is a slow process. To much of the public—and, indeed, to many businessmen—it seems that a hard fight still lies ahead merely to establish the principle that bribing politicians and government officials is no longer an accepted business practice. Even now, the most that can be said is that at most companies the problem is no longer being treated as a joke. Executives who have privately contended that there is no other way to do business in many parts of the world than to pay bribes have been forced to look for alternatives as the Securities & Exchange Commission pressures companies for more payoff disclosure, as the Internal Revenue Service adds new procedures to sniff out slush funds, and as company auditors adopt new controls intended to make unauthorized payments difficult to cover up.

Clearly the pressure on executives will not

ease. Shareholders will have their say when annual-meeting time rolls around this spring. Congress, aware that antibusiness sentiment remains at an all-time high, can be expected to try to find a way to legislate ethical practices into boardrooms.

Pressure is also building, from inside business and out, for a national or international code of business ethics. At least two international codes are already in the works, and they could have the advantage at least of prescribing the same principles for U.S. and foreign companies. Most executives, however, put little stock in codes other than the ones companies formulate for themselves. Last May Bendix Corp. Chairman W. Michael Blumenthal proposed that a group of businessmen devise a U.S. business code, but the idea seems to be foundering. "We've had several meetings," says Bendix Executive Vice-President William M. Agee. But those meetings saw the practicality of any national code seriously questioned.

One problem is that any general code would have to be so watered down to gain general acceptance that it would be all but useless. Says Fred T. Allen, chairman and president of Pitney-Bowes Inc.: "Writing a code that would be universally accepted means you would end up with a motherhood sort of thing."

In the final analysis, codes of good conduct—and enforcement of those codes—will be up to individual companies. And the unpleasant truth today is that many corporations, including some that have been in trouble, still seem to be ducking the job. Greyhound Corp., which gave special cash bonuses to executives who made contributions to the 1972 Presidential campaigns of either Richard Nixon or George McGovern (the bonuses were double the amount of the executives' actual contributions), pleaded guilty in federal court to violations of federal election laws. But its 1975 proxy statement concluded its report of the incident by observing, "No steps need to be taken to avoid illegal political expenditures by or on behalf of the company in the future."

Even companies that sincerely want to draft codes of ethics are finding the job difficult. "My primary concern," says Allen of Pitney-Bowes, "is not where to begin but where to stop. It would be fairly easy to draft a general policy and specific guidelines in a given area such as political activity or campaign contributions. But that would be analogous to a nation rearming itself to refight the last war."

Certainly the problem is not insoluble. Enough corporations are taking concrete steps against corruption, real and potential, to demonstrate that the situation can be confronted—and with more than platitudes.

Among the changes that can help restore credibility:

Tighter controls should go into place almost everywhere. Four years ago Exxon discovered that its Italian subsidiary had paid at least $16 million in political contributions over a decade. Although legal, the gifts were not reflected in the company's books. In response, uniform financial controls were instituted throughout the company, and communications among auditors was strengthened (a unit auditor who cannot get satisfaction from his manager can go to higher-level auditors—all the way to the audit committee of the board). Today, an auditor's first task when visiting an affiliate is to make sure that Exxon policy statements are being complied with.

Codes of conduct should be utilized to at least make clear what is expected of employees. Codes, in fact, are coming back into fashion, as they do after nearly every major business scandal. Unlike the proposed U.S. or international codes, the policy statements governing conduct in individual companies receive widespread approval. Heublein Inc. and Pitney-Bowes, for example, are drafting codes of business ethics for the first time. "If you have a formal code," says Wallace W. Booth, president of United Brands Co., a company that paid $1.25-million to Honduran officials before Booth arrived, "you have less chance of getting into trouble unknowingly."

Penalties for unethical conduct should be severe, especially for infractions at the top. Here the credibility gap between corporations and the public is perhaps widest of all. Many companies insist that unethical conduct, such as paying off politicians—both legally and illegally—and covering up with false bookkeeping entries, is grounds for dismissal. Yet many of the chief executives who have admitted making illegal contributions, such as Northrop Corp.'s Thomas V. Jones and Braniff International Corp.'s Harding L. Lawrence, continue at the helm. "I think a few more examples of board action, like at Gulf [where Chairman Bob R. Dorsey was fired last month in the wake of widespread political payoffs by the company] would help," says Thiokol Corp. President Robert E. Davis. "If a few more people like that get axed, people will fall in line."

Prevention

Guidance and direction must come from the top—and so it is at some companies. "You can't legislate morality in a corporation," says William F. Ballhaus, president of Beckman Instruments Inc. "Beyond procedures, it's a matter of climate. I have one simple rule: No one does anything intentionally wrong."

But even where the climate is right, infractions can occur. Accountants at many companies have sharpened their pencils to make sure there are no slips. American Airlines Inc., where George Spater resigned as chairman in 1973 after admitting he contributed corporate funds to President Nixon's reelection campaign, has eliminated procedures that allowed off-the-books cash funds to develop. "Under today's controls, they could not be reestablished," says Senior Vice-President Gene E. Overbeck.

A large number of companies, such as

Pitney-Bowes, have recently demanded that managers sign annual pledges that they have followed the rules in the company's ethics code. Continental Oil Co. has gone a step further. "To detect any possible conduits [for illegal or unethical payments]," says Keith W. Blinn, senior vice-president and general counsel, "we have written to all of our law firms to which we pay more than $2,000 and asked them this year and last year for a certificate that they had not been used in any way as a conduit for the payment of political contributions." Conoco also runs special auditing checks to detect potential sources of slush funds. "We've tried to pick those things we thought were the most fertile fields for this kind of thing," says Blinn. "Law firms are one. Investment bankers, maybe. Suppliers, maybe. Advertisers. Public relations firms."

At Northrop new policies, instituted at the behest of outside directors after the company's illegal campaign contributions came to light, include the elimination of such catch-all expense account labels as "Northrop private," which were apparently covers for entertaining government officials. Special attention was also given to consultants' and agents' fees, an area of abuse in many companies that is coming under increasing scrutiny. Frequently such fees are thinly disguised bribes or are rebated to executives for slush funds outside the company books.

A Blurred Line

The whole question of whether a fee is a legitimate commission or a payoff gets hazy for companies doing business abroad, and most executives who have to deal with the problem say there are no easy answers.

United Brands' Booth says that a problem arises because in many countries where his company does business a "tip" (which is not necessarily a bribe) is simply part of doing business. "We want to identify payments case by case to see if it's proper, legal, and appropriate," he says. If the payment is illegal, it is not made. The "big hangup" is deciding whether it is proper, and Booth knows of no hard and fast rule to determine that.

And that, of course, is the ultimate problem—these gray areas, as opposed to the impropriety of illegal political payoffs by such companies as 3M, Phillips Petroleum, and Goodyear. They were plainly illegal—in violation of even the most rudimentary codes of business conduct. At the very least, the public must be assured that the episode of illegal campaign contributions will not be repeated.

What business must understand today is that the public has a right to demand much more. When executives at the summit of some of the nation's most prestigious and powerful companies fail such an elementary moral test, shareholders, workers, and customers can legitimately wonder what else is going on in the executive suite—whether antitrust laws are being violated, or whether American business is consorting with organized crime. As companies probe their ethical standards, they must accept that the question of illegal political handouts should not be the end of it but just the beginning.

WE ARE LIVING in a time of growing suspicion about the purpose and effectiveness of the major institutions of the United States—business, government, universities, churches, among others."[1] This statement by George Cabot Lodge presents a fairly dark picture of society's attitudes toward some of its most cherished, long-standing institutions. One might ask if such a statement is perhaps too strongly worded and not really reflective of majority opinion in the United States today. The accuracy of Lodge's statement, however, is supported by the findings of pollster Louis Harris, which show a steady and fairly rapid decline in public attitudes regarding many of our professional and governmental organizations. With specific reference to the field of business "only 19 percent of those surveyed expressed 'a great deal of confidence' in the leaders of major companies, the lowest point since Harris began asking the question ten years ago."[2]

In recent years there has been an increasing number of surveys of this type, all of which reflect the public's growing distrust of indi

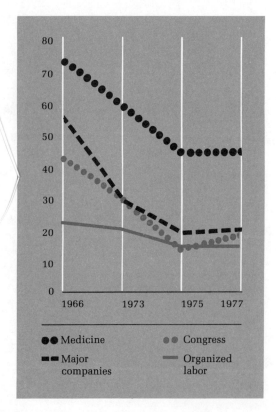

Figure 2.1. *The Confidence Gap*

Source: The Harris Survey, March 14, 1977.

viduals and organizations whose role has traditionally been one of both moral and social leadership. And it is clear to those who keep abreast of current events that this decline in public attitudes is not without some justification, as the public has been made aware of the most serious scandals in business and in our government, in which both elected and appointed officials have been implicated.

1. In the medical field, questions are being raised about allocation of funds for Medicare and Medicaid payments.
2. Within the religious community, there has been widespread division on issues such as the role of women in the church, abortion, and divorce.
3. The campus riots of the late 1960s served to illustrate that all was not well within the university environment. Turmoil and conflict involving rioting students and military forces on college campuses resulted in a serious change in the public's attitudes toward higher education. This decline in approval has brought about a change in many people's attitudes about the role of the university in our system—a change reflected in the reduced level of financial support available to many of our institutions of learning.

These facts serve notice that there is indeed a change taking place within our society. Serious questions are being raised regarding traditional values, ideals, and philosophies. We are concerned here with changes in the public attitude toward business and with attempting to gain insight into the reasons behind the lack of public confidence in our business organizations. We also will examine the concepts of professionalism and ethical behavior as they apply to the modern corporation.

Business Ethics: Past and Present

Some of the practices of American business leaders have been called into question during the history of our economic development. Many people regard the nineteenth century as a period in which a significant number of our business leaders exploited the laissez-faire system of free enterprise for their own personal gain to the great detriment of the public at large. Individuals such as Jay Gould, Cornelius Vanderbilt, Leland Stanford, and John D. Rockefeller have been condemned for engaging in questionable practices in carrying out their money-making activities. Critics point to disclosures surrounding the "Erie Ring," the "Octopus of California," and the "Credit Mobilier" as typical.[3]

In recent years, additional revelations have focused attention on the activities of executives of many of our large corporations. Exhibit 2.1 provides a sampling of some of these corporate practices.[4] The public's attitudes regarding the seriousness of these activities has been such that, according to a recent Conference Board survey,

Exhibit 2.1. *Ten of the Biggest Spenders*

Nearly 40 large American corporations have been accused of paying bribes or questionable "commissions" to win contracts overseas. Ten of the biggest admitted spenders:

Ashland Oil, Inc.	Admits paying more than $300,000 to foreign officials, including $150,000 to President Albert Bernard Bongo of Gabon to retain mineral and refining rights.
Burroughs Corporation	Admits that $1.5 million in corporate funds may have been used in improper payments to foreign officials.
Exxon Corporation	Admits paying $740,000 to government officials and others in three countries. Admits its Italian subsidiary made $27 million in secret but legal contributions to seven Italian political parties.
Gulf Oil Corporation	Admits paying $4 million to South Korea's ruling political party. Admits giving $460,000 to Bolivian officials—including a $110,000 helicopter to the late President Rene Barrientos Orutno—for oil rights.
Lockheed Aircraft Corporation	Admits giving $202 million in commissions, payoffs and bribes to foreign agents and government officials in the Netherlands, Italy, Japan, Turkey, and other countries. Admits that $22 million of this sum went for outright bribes.
McDonnell Douglas Corporation	Admits paying $2.5 million in commissions and consultant fees between 1970 and 1975 to foreign government officials.
Merck & Company, Inc.	Admits giving $3 million, largely in commission-type payments," to employees of 36 foreign governments between 1968 and 1975.
Northrop Corporation	Admits in part SEC charges that it paid $30 million in commissions and bribes to government officials and agents in Holland, Iran, France, West Germany, Saudi Arabia, Brazil, Malaysia, and Taiwan.
G. D. Searle & Company	Admits paying $1.3 million to foreign governmental employees from 1973 to 1975 to "obtain sales of products or services."
United Brands Company	Admits paying a $1,250,000 bribe to Honduran officials for a reduction in the banana export tax. Admits paying $750,000 to European officials. Investigators say the payment was made to head off proposed Italian restrictions on banana imports.

Source: Newsweek, February 16, 1976, p. 76.

"the number one issue with chief executives these days is their own credibility."[5] The fact that some of our largest corporations are involved is, of course, of great concern to those seeking to assess the current state of ethical practice in business. What is perhaps of even more significance, however, is a recent survey conducted by Opinion Research Corporation (July 1975) in which 40 percent of those surveyed agreed that foreign bribes should be paid if such practices were *prevalent* within the country (even if *illegal*).[6]

In another study investigating ethical practices, Archie Carroll surveyed some 238 executives from the Standard & Poor's Executive Register.[7] One question included in the survey asked for a response to the statement

> The junior members of Nixon's reelection committee who confessed that they went along with their bosses to show their loyalty is just what young managers would have done in business.

The executives responded as follows:

Response	Percent
Disagree	24.6
Somewhat disagree	16.1
Somewhat agree	35.6
Agree	23.7

Source: Archie Carroll, "Managerial Ethics: A Post Watergate View," *Business Horizons*, April 1975.

Nearly 60 percent of the executives surveyed believe that young managers in business would have behaved in the same way as the junior members of Nixon's reelection committee.

Results such as those obtained by the Opinion Research Corporation and by Archie Carroll, as well as the payoff scandals enumerated above, indicate that there is indeed some cause for concern regarding the current state of ethical behavior within business. What is of greatest interest is not so much the current state of ethical practice but rather the extent to which the norms, values, and mores of our society may be changing so as to bring about a shift toward less ethical behavior in society in general as well as in business organizations in particular. It is not within the scope of this chapter to examine this question in depth, but we will attempt to investigate some aspects of ethical behavior in business and to focus on factors influencing individual behavior within the corporation.

What Is "Legal" and What Is "Ethical"

The skills, talents, and organizational ability of our business leaders, both past and present, have unquestionably contributed to creating a standard of living for the American people unequaled in any country on earth. American production capabilities, as well as management techniques, have been models for economic development the world over. Modern methods of mass production, scientific advances in aerospace and electronics, and improved service and labor-saving inventions are but a few of the achievements brought about by our modern-day business organizations. Yet there is also no question that in bringing about these advances business has on many an occasion engaged in practices that go beyond, if not legal, then certainly ethical boundaries. Collusion, price fixing, restraint of trade, monopoly, and kick-backs are illegal, and appropriate legislative sanctions exist to prevent such practices. But other activities, such as puffery in advertising, the building of obsolescence into product designs, and the delay of the introduction of product advances that might have a detrimental impact on current product sales, are still considered by many to be a part of doing business in today's corporate environment. Some of these practices not specifically prohibited by law have nevertheless been questioned on ethical grounds by an increasing number of government, community, and business leaders. As one examines some of these practices, it becomes clear that a major part of the problem lies in attempting to define in specific terms exactly what is meant by ethical behavior.

We can see readily that "legally acceptable" behavior can usually be defined in terms of existing legislation and statutes specifying as definitively as possible exactly what may or may not be done. Such definitions are of course not always clear-cut. Recent court rulings, particularly in the area of antitrust, have made it difficult for some corporations to determine exactly what is legally acceptable behavior. Ethically acceptable behavior, on the other hand, simply reflects conduct that is consistent with the norms, values, and mores of society in general as they may exist at any point in time. Because it is most difficult to determine what these ethical beliefs are, many of the activities and behaviors within corporations that are not specifically defined by law simply reflect what has come to be regarded as "accepted practice" within an industry. The key question thus becomes what criteria and guidelines corporations utilize in defining exactly what may be accepted practice in carrying on their business activities.

One definition of "ethical"—"conformity to professional standards of conduct"—does present a useful basis on which to examine corporate behavior. Certain values, ideals, and philosophies normally are associated with professional behavior. It should be clear, of course, that even though we have been discussing the ethical behavior of business organizations, it is not the organizations themselves that behave or do not behave in an ethical manner. It is the individual members of those organizations who, in the course of their daily decision-making activities, are called upon to make determinations as to what is or is not an "acceptable" method of doing business. Ethical behavior is indeed personal; it resides in the individual organizational member and not in the organization. With that point in mind, let us focus on the individual within the corporation and the extent to which there exists a professional standard of conduct that may serve as a guideline for defining acceptable business behavior. The concept of a professional standard of conduct leads us also to examine whether or not the job of "manager," and management in general, does indeed meet the criteria for being considered a profession.

Management as a Profession

For many years, textbooks, articles, and speeches by academicians and business leaders have attempted to examine the extent to which the practice of management meets the criteria necessary for professional status. Writing in 1972, Louis D. Brandeis described a profession as "an area in which the training for its practice was intellectual in character, that it be pursued not for one's own sake, but for others, and that the amount of financial reward not be considered the measure of success."[8] Certain criteria seem to appear over and over again in many of the various definitions we can find of "profession." These criteria include three major components:

An acceptable level of competence in a specified field of knowledge
The placing of the interests of society before personal interests in carrying out the functions of the profession
A code of conduct as behavior imposed upon members and usually enforced internally.[9]

If we examine the field of management in light of these characteristics, there appears to be some doubt as to the legitimacy of characterizing management as a professional field.

Acceptable Level of Competence

There is no question that management as a discipline has developed a body of knowledge which is becoming a more and more sophisticated part of the curriculum in many academic institutions. Research in the field, particularly in the quantitative and behavioral areas, shows promise of making even more significant advances in the future. In addition, more and more academic institutions offering business programs are devoting their primary attention to graduate education in the area of management, with a particular emphasis on both theoretical and practical research. A growing number of business schools are making efforts to integrate faculty more closely with members of the business community so as to apply research findings to actual business problems.

In the area of curriculum, the American Assembly of Collegiate Schools of Business (AACSB), which is the accrediting body for all business schools, has done much to bring about uniformity in the business curriculum. The AACSB has defined a common body of knowledge in the field of business, and any academic institution seeking accreditation in this field must demonstrate adequate coverage of this material. In addition, a wide variety of other criteria must be met—such as number of full-time faculty, degree status of faculty members—if the institution is to be allowed to offer accredited degrees in management.

Finally, there exist professional organizations, such as the Academy of Management and the Society for the Advancement of Management, to name just two, that have as their purpose the development and strengthening of the professional character of this field. Organizations such as these provide for an exchange of thought and opinion as well as the dissemination of research results, all aimed at developing and strengthening a climate of professionalism within management.

In terms of knowledge and competence, then, there should be little question of management's having already achieved, or being very close to achieving, the status of a specific, well-defined, and professional discipline.

Interests of Society

With respect to the second criterion of professionalism, that of placing the interest of society before personal interest in the conduct of activities, the issue is much less clear-cut.

There can be no question that in recent years more and more businesses have become involved in social and ecological programs designed to bring about an improved quality of life, as we have seen in Chapter 1. There is a rapidly growing list of companies working actively with government and community leaders in seeking solutions to many of our problems. Businessmen in general appear to be recognizing that the role of management does include the responsibility of devoting business resources to the common interests of society.

One difficulty facing the manager, however, is determining what is meant by the "interest of society." Many corporations fear that to allocate significant resources to social and ecological programs would raise the ire of stockholders, who would complain that such allocation is not consistent with their own financial interests. Such allocations might put these corporations at a financial disadvantage against competitors not making similar contributions. On the other hand, corporations that fail to allocate stockholder resources for social and ecological purposes find themselves receiving criticism from political and civic groups accusing them of being interested only in profits won at the expense of society and community well-being. Thus, management may find itself in a "damned if you do and damned if you don't" dilemma for which it is often difficult to find a solution.

Corporations that have become involved in social programs have generally done so on the basis of what might be referred to as "enlightened self-interest." That is, many businessmen have taken the attitude that it is simply "good business" for a corporation to assume some degree of social responsibility. The philosophy of these companies is that by attending to problems plaguing society, the corporation is actually helping to bring about a more stable and solid economic environment, an environment not only desirable for its own sake, but necessary for the growth and development of business interests.

Even some of the most severe critics of business would acknowledge that corporate management has become more involved in seeking solutions to social problems. But the question of underlying motivation remains: Is management involved because it fears legislative and community sanctions or because its leaders are becoming more committed to the idea that corporations must assume responsibility in working toward an improved quality of life for all citizens?

One way of looking at the question we have raised is that it is academic: whatever the motivation of a corporation, the results are the results. By this we mean that corporate management is indeed becoming more involved in the problems of society, whether because of self-interest or concern for others. This involvement will almost certainly bring about a more rapid and a more comprehensive set of solutions to the problems. The significant fact—from this standpoint—is that business leaders are indeed becoming more responsive to the issues our society is now emphasizing.

Code of Conduct

It is in the third criterion of professionalism that the case for management is perhaps the weakest. This is the criterion of an internally enforced code of conduct or behavior which serves as a guide to all members of the profession regardless of the specific industry or corporation in which they are employed. With the exception of certain standards that apply to accounting, there are few, if any, professional codes of ethics to serve as universal guidelines for business leaders. Some industries have made attempts at developing industry-wide codes—the National Association of Manufacturers, to cite one example—but for the most part industrial codes of conduct are either nonexistent or have proved to be ineffective and unenforceable. Certainly, the behavior of all businessmen is not therefore unethical. Rather, each person in business must look to his or her own personal code of ethics to determine acceptable behavior in a given situation. Obviously, a wide variety of behavior results, since individuals are likely to view a given situation in slightly different ways, as their personal values, mores, and principles dictate. Diversity of attitudes is shown in a study which appeared in the Harvard Business Review.[10] Executives were presented with the following hypothetical situation:

> The minister of a foreign nation where extraordinary payments are common in order to lubricate decision-making machinery asks you as Marketing Director for a $200,000 consulting fee. In return he promises special assistance in obtaining a $100 million contract which would produce a $5 million profit for your company. What would you do?

Of those executives taking part in the survey, 36 percent said that they would pay the fee, feeling it to be ethical in the moral climate of the country; 22 percent said they would pay the fee but felt it was unethical though necessary to insure the sale; and 42 percent said they would refuse to pay the fee.[11] This simple example, presented within an "ethical" context, reveals the extent to which opinions would vary as to the "ethics" involved in a given situation.

The fact that a code of ethics has not been developed and enforced by business is a matter of increasing concern among many of this nation's top corporate leaders. Treasury Secretary Michael Blumenthal, formerly of Bendix, and Irving Shapiro of DuPont are among several key executives attempting to develop a new ethical code that would provide guidelines for the actions and behavior of all major corporations. In addition, business leaders are becoming much more vocal in their willingness to call for internal reform. A. W. Clausen, president of the Bank of America, has stated, "As of this moment, the public is rightly skeptical of our practices and our preachings. . . . Integrity is not some impractical notion dreamed up by naive do-gooders. Our integrity is the foundation for, the very basis of, our ability to do business."[12] Frank T. Cary, chairman of IBM, has expressed related sentiments:

> When some businesses turn out shoddy products or engage in misleading advertising, or ignore customer complaints, the public gets sour on business as a whole. When some executives have to admit that they bribed foreign officials or illegally channeled corporate funds into political campaigns, the public believes that this is standard business conduct. . . . Some businessmen have tried to excuse themselves by saying that everybody does it. Well, everybody doesn't do it . . . The time has come for those of us in business to put our house in order . . . to restore the faith of Americans in the basic competence and purpose of business.[13]

Statements such as these from top executives are becoming more and more frequent and efforts such as those of Blumenthal and Shapiro more and more common. As leaders become committed to the establishment and enforcement of sound ethical practices within the business environment, there is reason to believe that a code of professional ethics will be forthcoming. Such a code will obviously not emerge without a great deal of debate and discussion. Of particular concern will be methods and procedures by which such codes might be developed, how they would be administered across industries, what body would be responsible for investigating possible violations, and what penalties would be administered for those found violating these codes.

We have been discussing the extent to which management meets the criteria normally associated with "professional" status, and we may conclude that the field is indeed making progress toward this desired goal. At present, however, two major issues still need a more complete resolution: (1) business management must clearly define its role relative to the needs and problems of modern society, determining the extent of its responsibility to involve itself in the major sociological and ecological problems of our day, and (2) management must determine by what means it will govern itself with respect to the behavior and conduct of individual managers. We recognize that each member of our society must answer ultimately to his or her own conscience and that ethical behavior may truly be a function of personal integrity. But it remains for the field of management to develop a position that is consistent with the professional, ethical status of its members.

Factors Influencing Ethical Standards

We will now consider to what extent certain aspects of our society (legal, organizational, social) may have an impact on how businessmen carry on their function. To learn which are the factors most significant in influencing ethical standards in today's corporation, we again turn to the study conducted by Brenner and Molander. They present a list highlighting twelve factors that businessmen taking part in the survey indicated were of importance in influencing either higher or lower ethical standards within the organization. Their findings are presented in Exhibit 2.2. We will not discuss their listing in detail but will examine instead general aspects of our society that seem to account for the most significant influences determining current business practice.

The Social Ethic In his influential book of the 1950s, *The Lonely Crowd*, sociologist David Riesman discusses the changes that have taken place over the centuries with respect to human orientation and frame of reference. According to Riesman, Americans are no longer directed by "tradition" as they were in primitive times, nor are they "inner-directed," as they were during the colonial period of more recent history. Today our orientation is toward those about us. We are "other" directed, and this mentality causes us to be greatly concerned with the attitudes and reactions of others. Psychological and sociological terms such as "reference group," "peer group" and "group norms" have become important in explaining the actions of individuals in a variety of situations. A significant number of research studies have demonstrated the importance of groups in influencing the behavior of individuals. From a somewhat different standpoint we are seen to be moving from the "Protestant ethic" described by the sociologist Max Weber, as a belief that hard work was an individual duty that brought its own reward, to a more "social ethic" in which cooperation within a given group is the dominant force.

To determine the importance of groups in influencing individuals

Exhibit 2.2. *Factors Influencing Ethical Standards*

Factors causing higher standards	Percentage of respondents listing factor	Factors causing lower standards	Percentage of respondents listing factor
Public disclosure; publicity; media coverage; better communication	31%	Society's standards are lower; social decay; more permissive society; materialism and hedonism have grown; loss of church and home influence; less quality, more quantity desires	34%
Increased public concern; public awareness, consciousness, and scrutiny; better informed public; societal pressures	20		
Government regulation, legislation, and intervention; federal courts	10	Competition; pace of life; stress to succeed; current economic conditions; costs of doing business; more business competing for less	13
Education of business managers; increase in manager professionalism and education	9	Political corruption; loss of confidence in government; Watergate; politics; political ethics and climate	9
New social expectations for the role business is to play in society; young adults' attitudes; consumerism	5	People more aware of unethical acts; constant media coverage; TV; communications create atmosphere for crime	9
Business's greater sense of social responsibility and greater awareness of the implications of its acts; business responsiveness; corporate policy changes; top management emphasis on ethical action	5	Greed; desire for gain; worship the dollar as measure of success; selfishness of the individual; lack of personal integrity and moral fiber	8
Other	20	Pressure for profit from within the organization from superiors or from stockholders; corporate influences on managers; corporate policies	7
		Other	21

Note: Some respondents listed more than one factor. There were 353 factors in all listed as causing higher standards and 411 in all listed as causing lower ones. Categories may not add up to 100 percent because of rounding errors.

Source: Steven N. Brenner and Earl A. Molander, "Is the Ethic of Business Changing?" *Harvard Business Review,* January-February 1977, pp. 57–71. Copyright © 1977 by the President and Fellows of Harvard College; all rights reserved.

within the business environment, let us refer to a particular question asked of executives by Brenner and Molander, regarding the extent to which various environmental and personal factors were perceived to be important in influencing decisions regarding unethical behavior. The executives were asked, "What influences an executive to make unethical decisions?" Responses follow on page 48.[14]

Possible influence	Importance as an unethical influence (average rank*)
The behavior of one's superiors in the company	2.15
Lack of company policy	3.27
Ethical climate of the industry	3.34
Behavior of equals in the company	3.37
Society's moral climate	4.22
Personal financial needs	4.46

*1 = most important, 5 = least important.

It seems clear from the responses of the businessmen taking part in the survey that, to a large extent, it is the influence of their environment that has the most significant impact on the behavior and actions of businessmen with respect to making unethical decisions. The survey demonstrates that one's superiors, the policy of the company, the climate of the industry, as well as one's peer group, are all important in determining executive behavior—more important than personal financial gain. One might of course claim that the executives taking part in the survey were expressing excuses for unethical behavior rather than accepting personal responsibility. The respondents, however, were not being asked to explain their own ethical or unethical decisions but rather to explain such decisions in general. Since they had no personal stake in the results, it would seem that the results do indicate valid perceptions. These and other research results suggest that the values, attitudes, and mores of those with whom we associate, particularly our superiors in an organization, are of considerable importance in influencing our patterns of behavior.

Along these lines, it is of considerable interest to note that in the Brenner and Molander study and also in a study by Newstrom and Ruch individuals in a business organization perceived their own behavior to be more ethical than that of their peers. Figure 2.2 presents the results of the Newstrom and Ruch study, in which 121

Figure 2.2. *Frequency of Self-Reported and Perceived Peer Behaviors*

Source: John W. Newstrom and William A. Ruch, "The Ethics of Management and the Management of Ethics," p. 35, *MSU Business Topics*, Winter 1975. Reprinted by permission of the publisher, Division of Research, Graduate School of Business Administration, Michigan State University.

Behavior	At every opportunity (5.0)	Often (4.0)	About half the time (3.0)	Seldom (2.0)	Never (1.0)
1. Passing blame for errors to an innocent coworker			● (peer)	● (self)	
2. Divulging confidential information			● (peer)	● (self)	
3. Falsifying time/quality/quantity reports			● (peer)		● (self)
4. Claiming credit for someone else's work			● (peer)	● (self)	
5. Padding an expense account over ten percent			● (peer)		● (self)
6. Pilfering company materials and supplies			● (peer)	● (self)	
7. Accepting gifts/favors in exchange for preferential treatment			● (peer)	● (self)	
8. Giving gifts/favors in exchange for preferential treatment			● (peer)		● (self)
9. Padding an expense account up to ten percent			● (peer)	● (self)	
10. Authorizing a subordinate to violate company rules			● (peer)	● (self)	
11. Calling in sick to take a day off			● (peer)	● (self)	
12. Concealing one's errors			● (peer)	● (self)	
13. Taking longer than necessary to do a job			● (peer)	● (self)	
14. Using company services for personal use		● (peer)		● (self)	
15. Doing personal business on company time			● (peer)		● (self)
16. Taking extra personal time (lunch hour, breaks, early departure,			● (peer)	● (self)	
17. Not reporting others' violations of company policies and rules			● (peer)	● (self)	

●—— Perceived peer behavior ●—— Self-reported behavior

managers participated. With respect to the individual managers' perceptions of peer group activity, there is clearly an attitude of cynicism. Most managers seem to perceive the worst with respect to the ethical behavior of those with whom they work. Attitudes such as these, in which an individual manager believes that those around him are behaving less ethically than he, can be significant in causing a negative change in the manager's own ethical behavior.

As a result of social pressures to conform, we are becoming more susceptible to the influence of those about us in determining our actions. Ethical and unethical behavior alike will probably be accepted and copied by other individuals. One might say that as our society moves to a greater acceptance of the social ethic, values, attitudes, and behaviors exhibited by various members of a group are likely to spread as if contagious. Combined with the indication that we tend to believe that those around us behave less ethically than we do, this trend can lead to a lower standard of ethical behavior in our business organizations.

The Competitive Environment of the Business World

With the above point in mind, let us examine certain aspects of the business environment. To begin with, let us describe the very foundation of the free enterprise system itself. Our economic system is built on the principle of competition among individuals and groups. In business, competition is essentially the effort of two or more individual parties, acting independently, to secure the business of a third party by offering the most favorable terms. The very essence of the competitive system is to outperform others in achieving certain objectives or goals. In perhaps no other professional area (with the exception of sporting activities) is there such a confrontation between individuals and groups seeking to achieve success, to win out one over another. In recent years, too, our society seems to be placing increasing emphasis on winning as a measure of success. It seems to follow that as individuals become more obsessed with succeeding in their business dealings, they will be more likely to resort to less than ethical practices if such practices are deemed necessary to reach desired goals. Many sociologists believe, in fact, that society's preoccupation with success, along with a trend toward a "winning at any cost" philosophy, may be at least partially responsible for the alienation of so many young people today. Within the business organization, these same preoccupations and trends seem to be important in exerting pressure on executives to find ways of performing successfully. Such pressure may lead to unethical behavior as a means of achieving goals.

To examine how pressures to compete and succeed may be exerted on individuals in an organization, let us consider the concept of decentralization. Decentralization of operations in a large organization has the effect of moving decision-making responsibility further down within the organizational structure. Under a program of decentralization, middle managers may find themselves with increased responsibility. They may now for the first time be held responsible for profits in their cost center. The extent to which they are able to achieve profit goals can be of critical importance in determining their future with the company and the extent to which they will eventually achieve success. This situation clearly can place a great deal of pressure upon these individuals, especially when they are insecure about their abilities to begin with. Such conditions can create an environment in which middle managers perceive unethical practices to be necessary if they are to perform satisfactorily. If indeed unethical practices do lead to success, a climate is created within the organization or industry that influences the behavior of those who come after. Such an environment leads to the proliferation of phrases like "everyone does it" or "it's standard practice in our industry." Over an extensive period of time, individuals may actually lose their perspective on ethical and unethical behavior with respect to a given situation.

It has not been our intent to take a negative or a cynical view of the value of competition in the business environment. Without the spirit of competition that has existed within our society over its first two hundred years we would not be enjoying the standard of living to which we have become accustomed. The point is that this same competitive drive to succeed can be the source of significant pressures that may lead executives at many levels to consider achieving goals to be more important than adhering to ethical means. The potential importance of these pressures is recognized in a statement by Clifton C. Garvin, Jr., chairman of Exxon Corporation: "An overly ambitious employee might have the mistaken idea that we do not care how results are obtained, as long as he gets results. He might think it is best not to tell higher management all that he is doing, not to record all transactions accurately. . . . He would be wrong on all counts. . . . We don't want liars for managers."[15]

The Legal Environment of Business

Finally, the legal and legislative environment in which businessmen function has become increasingly confusing over the last twenty-five years. New legislation, as well as new interpretations of previously existing legislation, have led to a maze of legal entanglements that often make it difficult for the businessman to know exactly what course to take. As far back as 1950, Lowell Mason, then a member of the Federal Trade Commission, stated at Marquette University, "I openly defy the entire university to explain to any businessman what he can or cannot legally do when making up his next season's price list."[16]

In the guidelines recently established by the Securities and Exchange Commission, it was generally acknowledged by those who read them that these guidelines were somewhat fuzzy and key definitions remained vague. In referring to the guidelines, Senator William Proxmire, head of the Senate Banking Committee, endorsed the guidelines stating that they leave "gray areas where both corporations and the Commission must make subjective judgments about what facts need to be disclosed in specific cases."[17]

In a pending case the FTC has charged four leading cereal companies with a shared monopoly. Under the new interpretation of monopolistic practice, firms could be charged with monopoly even though there was no overt conspiracy. According to one lawyer representing the firms, "shared monopoly" was a phrase not found in statute, but rather it was designed and created for this case.[18]

These are but illustrations of the vague, nebulous legal environment in which businessmen are functioning. In recent years, a new series of legislative enactments has established guidelines with respect to areas such as occupational safety and health (OSHA), minority employment (affirmative action), and ecology (environmental impact studies). Each new government statement has created additional confusion in the minds of business leaders; they often cannot determine what constitutes appropriate behavior in a given situation. Since many of the issues have not yet been resolved in the courts, it is extremely difficult for even the most competent corporate legal counsel to give advice on the consequences of a given decision.

The object of this discussion has certainly not been to excuse or condone our nation's corporations. Rather, we have attempted to present and examine a circumstance that can make it difficult for management to make ethical decisions within the competitive environment of business. If the law is not clear, or if interpretation varies, and if the decision does not involve an obvious moral issue, many executives may go ahead with a decision even though they suspect that it may eventually cause them legal difficulties. The rationale behind such an approach is that to behave too conservatively could result in a serious loss in competitive position, particularly if one's competitors choose to take a more liberal point of view with respect to a particular legal issue. The difficulty of interpreting legal issues is compounded, too, by the fact that the law tends to shift with changes in the personnel of the policy-making agencies and also with changes in the economy and the society.

There are those who believe that the real problem with respect to the impact of the law on corporate ethics resides less in the vague interpretation of laws than in the enforcement procedures utilized. In this view, business behavior will become more ethical only when new laws are enacted *and* when existing legislation is more rigidly enforced. Writing in the *Wall Street Journal* in March of 1976, Ralph Nader and Mark Green advocated that the Justice Department create a Division of Corporate Crime.[19] Nader and Green would have such a division investigate activities ranging from mail fraud to illegal political contributions, domestically and abroad. Nader and Green believe that the scope of existing illegal activities together with the lenient penalties normally associated with convictions (average fine paid by firms successfully prosecuted by the Watergate special prosecutor was only about $7,000) warrant such action by the Justice Department.

Nader and Green believe that current enforcement procedures are insufficient to deter unethical behavior in the corporate environment. They cite the "consent decree" (which has often been characterized as a statement by the company that "I did not do it and I promise not to do it again") as a typical example of a current weak enforcement practice within both the SEC and Justice Department's Antitrust Division. They favor far more severe fines, more in line with the $150,000 a day fine Judge William Mulligan levied against IBM Corporation for failing to produce required documents in a recent antitrust proceeding. According to Nader and Green such fines should be consistent with the size of the company and the seriousness of the violation.

Discussion Questions

1. Distinguish between legal behavior and ethical behavior.
2. What do we mean by "accepted practice" within an industry? What is the basis for the evolution of "accepted practices"?
3. Is management a profession? Explain your answer.
4. Discuss the factors you believe to be most important in influencing the behavior of businessmen in our society.
5. Do you see the likelihood of the development of a code of ethical conduct to govern the behavior of all business leaders? Who would develop such a code? How would such a code be enforced?
6. Do you see changes taking place within our society in the next decade that will make currently accepted practices within business unethical? Do you see changes making currently unethical practices

become more acceptable? Give examples of each possibility.

7. How do you feel about the current level of ethical behavior in business? On what criteria did you base your answer?

8. If business behavior is to become more ethical in the future, discuss the role you perceive for each of the following: (a) top management; (b) university; (c) government; (d) church.

Case for Discussion

Harry Johnson was a senior accountant with a large accounting and management consulting firm. He was assigned to audit the accounting records and to provide a management report on overall operations for Jason Electronics Inc., a major electronics and electrical equipment firm doing domestic and international business. The report was commissioned by the president of Jason Electronics and would be used in developing the company's annual financial report and in establishing managerial guidelines for company executives.

After spending three months investigating the Jason's records and interviewing many of the firm's top officers, Mr. Johnson was ready to write his report. Mr. Johnson had uncovered the following information he believed was important, but was not sure if it should be included in the report or even discussed with Jason's president:

It appeared that Jason Electronics had made payments of approximately $2 million to various government officials in foreign countries in which Jason was doing business.

Figures of overall product cost which Jason Electronics had made public during recent union negotiations were significantly higher than actual product costs found in production records and cost analysis reports.

Expense account payments for Jason's top managerial staff, including the president, did not contain receipts or other documentation verifying expenditures.

Jason's president and its director of purchasing had spent a week in Canada on a fishing trip as a guest of the president of one of the firms that sold electronics components to Jason.

In calculating a dollar figure for inventory valuation, Jason included the value of electronic components which used obsolete electronic parts. It was highly unlikely that these components would ever be sold by the company.

In setting up delivery schedules, Jason's salesmen made commitments for delivery which could not be met under current production capabilities.

Mr. Johnson was not sure how each of these revelations should be handled and requested a meeting with his superior before he began to write the report.

Selected References

Andrews, K. "Toward Professionalism in Business Management." In *Harvard Business Review,* March–April 1969.

Baumhart, Raymond. "How Ethical Are Businessmen?" In *Harvard Business Review,* July–August 1961.

Brenner, S. and Molander, E. "Is the Ethics of Business Changing?" In *Harvard Business Review,* January–February 1977.

Brown, S., Keating, K., Mellinger, D., Post, P., Smith, S., and Tudor, C. *The Incredible Bread Machine.* Pasadena, Cal.: Ward Ritchie Press, 1975.

Carroll, Archie. "Managerial Ethics: A Post Watergate View." In *Business Horizons,* April 1975, pp. 75–80.

Cohn, Jules. "Is Business Meeting the Challenge of Urban Affairs?" In *Harvard Business Review,* March–April 1970.

Donhan, Paul. "Is Management a Profession?" In *Harvard Business Review,* September–October 1962.

Griffith, Thomas. "Payoff Is Not Accepted Practice." In *Fortune,* August 1975, pp. 122–125, 200–206.

Henderson, Hazel. "Should Business Tackle Society's Problems?" In *Harvard Business Review,* July–August 1968.

Lodge, George C. "Top Priority: Renovating Our Ideology." In *Harvard Business Review,* September–October 1970.

Marcus, Sumner. *Competition and the Law.* Belmont, Calif.: Wadsworth, 1967.

Nader, Ralph and Green, Mark. "What to Do About Corporate Corruption." In *Wall Street Journal,* 12 March 1976.

Newstrom, J. and Ruch, W. "The Ethics of Management and the Management of Ethics." In *MSU Business Topics,* Winter 1975.

"Payoff Scandals." In *Newsweek,* 23 February 1976.

Riesman, David. *The Lonely Crowd.* New Haven, Conn.: Yale University Press, 1969.

"The Embattled Businessman." In *Newsweek,* 16 February 1976.

Executive Stress: Pressure in the Executive Suite

3

Stress Has No Gender

"I don't know any woman who has an executive position who doesn't have some form of stress or some kind of physical result of it," says Peggy Lancaster, a principal and creative director of Scott, Lancaster & Mills, a Los Angeles ad agency. Heart disease is relatively rare among women, but Lancaster, like a remarkable number of women managers, has a serious heart condition. "I can't imagine what could have caused it other than my work," she says. "You go home, you're still worrying about the problems. You go out, you're worrying over your clients. You walk into a store, you eavesdrop on customers."

As more women become executives, the more they are the victims of heart disease, ulcers, and other ills traditionally associated with men executives. Their health profiles become more like those of male business achievers and less like those of other women.

Because women have entered the corporate world in force only recently, this cannot be proved statistically, says Dr. John P. McCann, medical board chairman of the New York-based Life Extension Institute, which administers annual physical checkups to 30,000 executives of 1,500 major companies. But McCann predicts that Life Extension's own records will produce firm statistical proof of the phenomenon within the next five years.

Heart Attacks

To many executives, female and male, no statistical proof seems necessary. Ethel Narvid, chief regional coordinator for Los Angeles Mayor Thomas Bradley, had her first heart attack certified as work-related 11

Reprinted from the November 15, 1976 issue of *Business Week* by special permission. Copyright © 1976 by McGraw-Hill Publishing, Inc., New York, N.Y. 10020. All rights reserved.

years ago, when the federal government, which then employed her as district representative for a California congressman, ruled her eligible for a pension if she had to quit. Narvid expects to receive workers' compensation benefits for her recent, second heart attack, which led to open heart surgery.

To prevent a third attack, Narvid is trying very hard "to work one day a day instead of two days a day"—a remark that recalls the post-heart-attack resolves of numerous male executives.

Other women managers blame business pressures for their ulcers, high blood pressure, and even cancer, which some researchers are beginning to believe can be related to stress. Even when executive stress does not cause a disease, say some observers, it can obstruct its treatment. Donna Angott, manager of customer relations for Mary Kay Cosmetics in Dallas, recalls a Mary Kay sales director who died of cancer because "she was so busy that she never had time to go for a gynecological checkup until it was too late."

The Dallas case raises a point emphasized by many health experts: It is the executive lifestyle as much as executive stress that causes "executive diseases," in women just as in men. "Women are getting coronaries as never before, but I can't say whether it's because they have been thrown into business situations with the same pressures as the men or whether some of it is due to the lifestyle that goes along with the situation, with smoking and drinking and other things," says Dr. Charles Winterhalter, medical director of Pitney-Bowes in Stamford, Conn. "The alcohol problem is way up among women in the managerial levels, but I can't say whether that is due to stress or social environment."

Lifestyle

Formerly medical director for the corporate staff at Olin Corp. in Stamford, Winterhalter cites an Olin case that obviously sprang from both lifestyle and stress: It was "a woman who underwent a gastrectomy for ulcers after doing a lot of traveling on a job that required intense attention."

Some conditions, he concedes, stem directly from stress. At Olin, he was called upon to treat women who had held nonmanagerial jobs, then suddenly received promotions to posts with executive responsibility. "They'd come in hyperventilating [breathing hard] or with tachycardia [abnormally rapid heartbeat]," he says. "These are stress symptoms."

Historically, such cases represent a temporary aberration, says Tobias W. Brocher, director of the Center for Applied Behavioral Science of the Menninger Foundation in Topeka, Kan. He says that once women executives survive the current, highly stressful period of being conspicuous exceptions in unfamiliar roles, they will probably stand the gaff better than men. Brocher runs the center's executive mental health seminars, which have changed in the past decade from 100% male to 15% to 20% female.

"Women tend to have higher psychological and physical endurance for stress," he says. "They know more about their own feelings and it's easier for them to deal with emotions."

Support System

Moreover, as women continue moving into management, says Brocher, they will find safety in numbers, a great aid to mental and physical health. "Now there is often only one female executive among many males," he observes. "She has no support system. She suffers from isolation. Often her reaction is to outdo her male counterparts constantly, whether in the number of martinis, the number of tough jokes, or whatever. We call

it the 'Annie Get Your Gun Phenomenon.' It creates uncertainty over self-esteem and role perception, and it inevitably ends in depression."

But Jane Voltz, assistant vice-president of personnel at Illinois Bell Telephone Co. in Chicago, comes up with an entirely different prediction of what the future holds for women executives. Tomorrow's women executives will be more rather than less likely to develop executive diseases, she believes.

The women executives she sees today, says Voltz, have excellent health, probably because they attained their positions through outstanding ability and a touch of luck. These women executives were largely untroubled by the pressures of long-range planning. "They didn't look far ahead in their careers because, in the ordinary course of events, the opportunities just weren't there," she says.

"But the woman who will make it 15 years from now is probably a different breed of cat," says Voltz. "Women coming along now know that a woman can become an assistant vice-president. When you know you can, you will drive yourself the way a man does. You're in competition, and that's when the problems may show up."

The Trigger

Voltz's theory dovetails with the opinion that many doctors hold that it is trying rather than achieving that triggers executive diseases. They add that trying unsuccessfully—inevitable for many in a corporate structure with limited room at the top—has the worst effect. They have found that strokes occur more frequently among middle managers than in the executive suite, the doctors note.

"Top executives are among the healthiest people in America," says McCann. "In a sense, they're champion athletes. These people make it in part because they are able to survive stress and, after they've made it, new challenges become stimuli rather than stress. It's the 35-year-old comer who's still in the same spot at 40 who feels a tension he cannot dissipate. He's your likeliest candidate for an executive disease."

Once women have won full acceptance in the corporate world, the formula that McCann describes will apply to them as thoroughly as to men. And in the same way women executives' growing integration into the corporate world subjects them to the same health hazards as their male colleagues, says McCann.

Fortunately for them, he adds, women executives resemble men executives in another respect: Aside from the special risks that are associated with their jobs, the women executives are a sturdy lot. "Both men and women tend to be pretty healthy to begin with," says McCann. "And, as intelligent people with ample means, they usually seek the care that will keep them healthy."

AS THE PACE AND complexity of our society demands more and more from each individual, added pressure is felt within the executive suite. Here, in addition to experiencing the usual mixture of individual successes and failures, both men and women are finding themselves struggling to cope with the tensions and anxieties of corporate life. Executives have reacted to these pressures in a variety of ways. In Chapter 2, for example, we saw how trends in our society may be bringing about a deterioration of ethical practices in our corporations. In this chapter we will explore other ways in which executives react to the pace and pressure of corporate life. In particular we will focus on psychological stress and its effects on the modern manager.

What Is Stress?

Stress is a term finding its greatest application in engineering, where it refers to an object's inherent ability to withstand strain. Steel bridge girders or concrete high-rise pillars, for example, are designed to withstand a specified amount of strain without losing their shape or collapsing. If distortion or collapse does occur, then engineers say that the structure became "overstressed."

As it applies to human biology, *stress* has been defined as "the body's involuntary reactions to the demanding life that we Americans choose."[1] Dr. Hans Selye, one of the pioneers in human stress research, defines stress as the "nonspecific response of the body to any demand made upon it."[2] In his terminology *stress* is the internal response to environmental demands. He called environmental demands *stressors*.

The key phrase in this definition is "*any* demand made upon it" because it suggests that all human beings experience some degree of stress. Existence on our planet requires that the body adjust and adapt to physical conditions, such as atmospheric pressure, which create some degree of stress.

Thus, in understanding stress, we should probably think in terms of a stress threshold for each individual. This threshold represents the capacity of the individual to adapt and cope with whatever stressors he or she encounters, including the pace and pressures of modern society. As pressures increase, they may eventually exceed an individual's stress threshold. At this point, the individual becomes "overstressed," and the body must find some outlet for the excess pressure that has built up. Figure 3.1 is a diagram representing

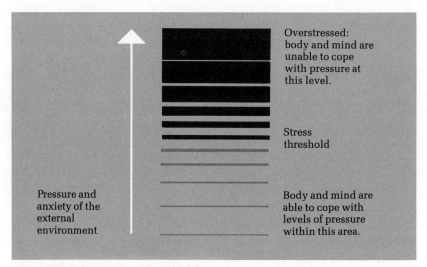

Figure 3.1. *The Stress Threshold*

a simplistic view of this stress situation. One thing we realize is that such factors as personality, temperament, and emotional stability cause each individual to have a different stress threshold. Individuals vary in their ability to cope with pressures.

Reactions to Stress

Once an individual reaches a point at which he or she feels overstressed, the body and the mind react in some way to seek to reduce, avoid, or withdraw from the stressful situation. If the stress continues, there may eventually be a breakdown of some mental or physical component within the body that is simply no longer able to deal with the situation. These are a few of the reactions to stressors we find in our society today:

Withdrawal, avoidance, reduction	Breakdowns
Pills, medication	Mental breakdown
Alcohol	Coronary
Absenteeism	Ulcer
Employee turnover	Hypertension
	Sexual inadequacy

In an effort to reduce, avoid, or withdraw from the high stressor environment, many individuals resort to drugs such as tranquilizers, sleeping pills, or alcohol, in an effort to reduce the functioning of the mind so as to allow the individual to "relax" and be somehow removed from the stressor-producing environment. Many others achieve some degree of stress reduction by withdrawing more directly from the stressful environment: executives may, for example, increase absenteeism or simply leave an organization altogether in order to find an environment which is less stressor producing.

Those individuals who elect to "tough it out" and remain within the high-stressor environment may eventually reach a point of being no longer able to cope with the pressures exerted on them. Once their stress threshold has been exceeded, physical or mental breakdown is likely to occur.

The extent of such physical and mental breakdown in our society

Figure 3.2. *Heart Disease*

Source: U.S. Public Health Service data.

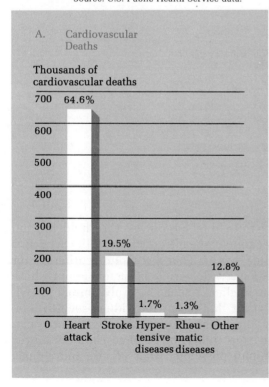

A. Cardiovascular Deaths

Thousands of cardiovascular deaths

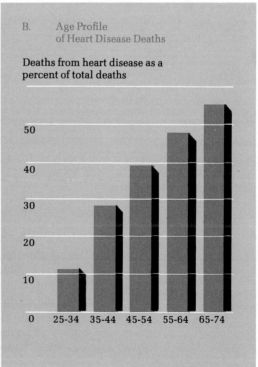

B. Age Profile of Heart Disease Deaths

Deaths from heart disease as a percent of total deaths

is evidenced by some medical facts. Heart attacks and diseases of the blood vessels (a major reaction to overstress) claimed the lives of 183,000 American men under the age of 65 in 1969 (see Figure 3.2). In addition, strokes, another stress reaction, claimed 207,000 lives. We certainly do not mean to imply that all or even most of these deaths were the direct result of individual stress reaction. However, examination of recent trends with respect to those illnesses normally associated, at least in part, with a high stressor environment, yields the information provided in the following table:[3]

Cause of death	1941	1951	1961	1971
Coronary heart disease	805	1,756	2,121	2,603
Cerebrovascular disease	1,228	1,378	1,394	1,309

Crude death rate per million (males) all ages.

In addition, employee absenteeism resulting from illness shows an increase:[4]

	1955/1956	1967/1968
Respiratory disease	27.21	36.41
Digestive disorders	16.29	19.04
Heart disease	11.54	16.59
Mental disorders	5.32	8.29

Millions of days off work due to specific illness (short term incapacity).

Personality and Stress

As we have indicated, each individual has a stress threshold, beyond which the mind and body cannot cope effectively with the pressures and anxieties of the outside world. This threshold is different for each individual. It is based on a wide variety of factors about whose importance and interaction medical science has only limited knowledge. The fact remains, however, that certain individuals seem to demonstrate a greater ability than others to withstand the pressure.

In one theory regarding this ability, medical researchers Meyer Friedman and Ray Rosenman postulated that certain individuals were more prone to heart disease than were others. The researchers proposed that risk of heart disorder was based on a series of factors among the personality characteristics of the individual. The researchers classified those individuals who were likely candidates for heart disease *Type A* and those less likely to experience heart disease *Type B*. Specific behaviors are associated with each type. According to Friedman and Rosenman, the following characteristics distinguish Type A and Type B behavioral patterns:[5]

Type A behavior: High probability of heart attack	Type B behavior: Low probability of heart attack
High degree of drive and ambition Extremely competitive Exhibits a high level of aggressiveness Constantly working against time	High level of patience Takes time to enjoy leisure activities Works at a more leisurely pace Is not preoccupied with social achievement

In 1960 Friedman and Rosenman tested 3,500 males between the ages of 39 and 59. None of the subjects had a known history of heart disease. All were given complete physical examinations. On the basis of observation and interview data, each participant was classified as either Type A or Type B in behavior. One half of the subjects were included in the Type A group and one half were included in Type B. As of 1972, 257 of the subjects had developed some form of heart disease: of these 257, *70 percent were Type A*.[6]

Test results such as these are beginning to show that certain aspects of an individual's personality may be as significant as physical factors such as cholesterol and cigarette smoking in increasing susceptibility to those illnesses that make up a principal reaction to stress.

Stress and the Job of Management

Of key concern in this text is the extent to which business executives are subject to conditions and situations that are likely to bring about high levels of continuous stress. As we have mentioned, the environment in which the executive must function is becoming more complex than it has ever been in the past. As a result of legislative and sociological changes in our society, demands on the executive have become far greater than they were even a few years ago. In addition, the size and complexity of the modern corporation have increased to the point that each decision an executive makes may have a far-reaching impact on the corporation as a whole. When these factors are combined with the growing voice and militancy of consumer groups, minority groups, unions, and environmental groups, one can recognize that modern society has placed today's executive under something of a constant state of siege.

The factors we have just mentioned are primarily *external* forces or pressures—legislation, environmental concerns, minority demands. In addition, there are important internal pressures originating within the corporation and within the individual that may have even greater impact on the level of stress an executive must endure.

To understand these internal pressures and the way they affect human beings, let us examine one of the most basic of our behavioral characteristics, the one referred to by Dr. Wallace B. Cannon of the Harvard Medical School as the flight-or-fight response. Basically, this response represents the reaction of body and mind to a situation perceived as threatening. The flight-or-fight response is characterized by "coordinated increases in metabolism, blood pressure, heart rate, rate of breathing, amount of blood pumped by the heart, and the amount of blood pumped to the skeletal muscles."[7] This response represents the organism's basic reaction in preparing for a fight for survival or for physical flight from a threatening situation. This response to threat has worked equally well for human beings and other animals. However, in modern society, where a wide variety of social norms, role relationships, and rules of behavior hold sway, people must often find alternative ways to deal with a threat; the basic reaction of flight-or-fight is often not appropriate. These alternative methods may place significant strain on the physiological and psychological functioning of the individual.

Threatening situations within the modern organization may be numerous. The individual who aspires to higher management levels must often subject himself or herself to a wide variety of personally distasteful situations, ranging from undesired social contacts with superiors or coworkers to the performance of questionable practices that may be deemed necessary for the good of the corporation. In addition, the route to the top in many large corporations is strewn with "dead bodies" of executives fallen victim to the politics or gamesmanship of the corporate environment. It goes without saying that the pyramid structure of the large corporation offers a narrow funnel through which can pass only a small percentage of those who aspire to the top levels of the organization.

Such a combination of factors creates an environment in which the average executive must respond to a flight-or-fight phenomenon many times during a given day. Within the corporate environment, however, the rallying of the body's defenses often results in fight not against the threat itself but between the individual's mind and body. For example, at the committee meeting in which an executive clearly perceives that his or her position on a particular issue is being attacked by other members of the organization, the normal flight-or-fight defenses of heart rate and blood pressure are activated, but these physical reactions are greatly limited by numerous potent social norms. As a result, the release of the bodily reactions may be prevented and as a result the individual's physical system may become overstressed. According to Dr. Hans Selye, if such unresolved "fight" reactions are continuous and prolonged the human defenses tend to wear down and deteriorate. In effect the body uses up its reserve of energy, and a general deterioration begins to take place. This process, analyzed as the General Adaptation Syndrome by Dr. Selye,[8] has significant application for our understanding of the concept of stress in the organizational setting.

We find pressure, too, coming from society's formula equating such factors as position, salary, power, and title with an individual's overall level of success. Within the American system each individual—regardless of background—is expected to work, to advance, and to take on more responsibility as he or she spends more time as a member of a business organization. Such expectations, often stated or subtly implied by family, friends, coworkers, and superiors, can put significant pressure on an individual. This pressure, likely to create more and more stress as individuals progress into middle age, is especially brutal when they have achieved less than they expected of themselves or than was expected of them by members of the family or the peer group.

The significance of all these stress factors in affecting the health of today's executive is perhaps best expressed by John R. P. French, Jr., a psychologist: "The stresses of today's organization can pose serious threats to the physical and psychological well-being of organization members. When a man dies or becomes disabled by heart attack, the organization may be as much to blame as is the man and his family."[9] This is a sobering reflection on the modern business organization and its possible impact on those who function within it. Figure 3.3 on page 68 summarizes the forces that may be sources of stress in the corporate structure.

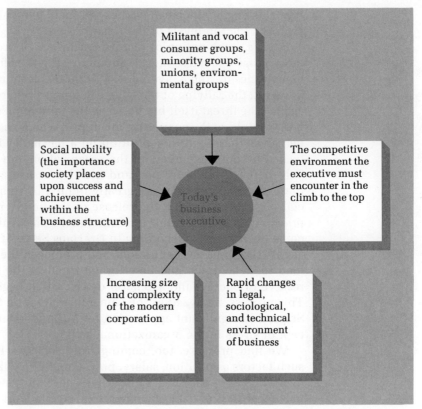

Figure 3.3. *Sources of Stress in the Modern Organization*

Executive Reaction to Stress

Earlier in this chapter we saw some statistics on the increases in physical and mental health breakdowns that have been occurring in this country and in England. In the business community one is likely to find more and more examples of personal tragedy such as those of Eli Black of United Brands, who leaped to his death from a skyscraper in New York City, or James Forrestal, former Wall Street financier and Secretary of Defense who took his life while being treated for a manic-depressive psychosis.[10] Such extreme behavior may be rare in the corporate environment, but the evidence suggests that the stresses endured by today's executive do contribute to both mental and physical breakdowns.

In addition to the physical and mental health problems experienced by executives who remain to fight, there is an increasing trend among many executives and middle managers to a "flight" from the stressor-producing corporate structure. John De Lorean left General Motors Corporation and a $550,000 salary in 1974 because he felt mired in unproductive paperwork and committee meetings. De Lorean, a possible candidate for the GM presidency, was 47 years old at the time; he complained that he was not able to plan or innovate.[11] These stories are not unique. Each day the executive must evaluate in his or her own mind the rewards and punishments that go along with the territory in the corporate structure. More and more individuals are reaching the conclusion that perhaps the price of success in those terms is too high. This conclusion has prompted many to abandon promising business careers in favor of a more relaxed and less stress-producing life-style. James Brown is one who gave up a seat on the New York Stock Exchange and a $168,000 salary in order to become a free-lance photographer in Marblehead, Massachusetts.[12]

Although this phenomenon of midcareer job change is increasing in the business community, there is little doubt that what we see represents only the tip of the iceberg. According to the Department of Health, Education, and Welfare, "57 percent of all white collar workers . . . are unhappy in their jobs and would choose differently if they could start again."[13] For many of these 57 percent, there is little possibility of starting over—at least in their own minds. By the time the average manager reaches the point in his or her career where frustration, anxiety, and stress become overwhelming, this individual must also cope with the financial and emotional responsibilities of children in school, mortgage payments on the house, and sometimes an endless list of other financial and social commitments. Such an environment can often be a trap impossible to break out of. In effect, flight reaction is not an available option. This manager must remain with the organization and cope with the situation as well as he or she is able.

There is no clear-cut formula for coping in this situation, but one method may involve a shift in behavior pattern in order to include certain practices of questionable moral or ethical character. In recent years the media have been filled with stories on a wide variety of unethical practices carried on by some of this country's leading business and government officials. Under less stressful social conditions, such behavior might have been completely out of the question for these individuals. However, in today's corporate society, with its myriad pressures and stressors, these unsavory alternatives might appear as necessary means to goals perceived as desirable or necessary in themselves.

In summary, we might conclude that the organizational environment in which most executives function is one that places many stressors on these individuals over extended periods of time, as a result of which many executives may experience breakdowns in health or moral character, while others may choose to leave the corporate environment altogether and seek satisfaction in a less stressful career. Possible reactions to executive stressors may be summarized as

Physical breakdown: heart disease, ulcers, stroke, mental breakdown, suicide, etc.

Midcareer job change (executive flight): movement from the 'pressure cooker' organization to a new career in a less stress producing environment

Breakdown in ethical standards and practices: performance of questionable and/or unethical practices which often are contrary to the executive's moral character.

Coping with Stress

With increasing recognition of the high-stressor environment of today's executive, there has been a development of methods and techniques for reducing or providing an outlet for this stress. We will examine four approaches to the problem that have as their purpose the release of stress and tensions. These approaches are 1) physical exercise, 2) sensitivity training, 3) executive sabbatical, and 4) relaxation responses.

Physical Exercise

The idea that certain types of pent-up frustration, anxiety, and stress may be released through physical exertion or exercise has long been recognized by medical authorities. The rapid rise in heart attacks and strokes among young Americans has also been an instrumental factor in bringing about a significant increase in physical activity such as jogging, bicycle riding, and tennis. Americans are attempting to improve their physical well-being, and in ever-increasing numbers they are looking to exercise as a way of building physical strength and releasing tension and anxiety.

In an effort to provide an opportunity for business people, who often are not able to exercise when at work, to remain physically fit, more and more corporations are installing gymnasiums, including jogging and basketball facilities, within the company. What is more important, these corporations are not only providing the time but even encouraging their executives to make use of these facilities. For example, Xerox Corporation installed in its management training center at Leesburg, Virginia, tennis courts, a one-mile jogging track, basketball courts, and a swimming pool. According to Don Fredericks, manager of physical fitness for Xerox's Stamford, Connecticut, headquarters, "the gym provides a positive return on investment for the company."[14] Other corporations such as Weyerhauser, Johns Manville, and IBM have also invested in facilities that provide the opportunity for corporate executives to maintain physical fitness and release tension and anxiety.

Facilities such as these, as well as regular health examinations and carefully prescribed and supervised exercise programs, are becoming a significant part of the approach that many corporations are taking to providing sound management. Companies seem to be finding that the cost is justified: "People who exercise regularly seem to be more productive, have better morale, and are ill less often than those who don't."[15]

Sensitivity Training

As early as 1946, Carl Rogers, a pioneer in the development of sensitivity training, was organizing "encounter groups" among returning servicemen.[16] The purpose of these groups was to promote personal growth by encouraging participants to discuss their feelings with other group members. Through the use of such sensitivity training or "T" groups, individuals were brought together and placed in an environment in which they were permitted to pour out frustrations, anxieties, and fears freely. The purpose of this environment was to provide an opportunity for individuals to learn of and accept their own feelings and attitudes, to be aware of why they had such feelings and attitudes, and to see how these attitudes might influence their behavior patterns. Through the use of T-group or encounter-group therapy, each individual attempts to come to terms with himself and as a result to become less susceptible to stress build-up in both mind and body.

Each T-group session was designed to achieve four major objectives:[17]

1. Trust: to encourage the individual to become more trusting of himself and the people around him
2. Openness: to encourage and develop within the individual the ability to communicate openly with others
3. Self-determination: to enable the individual to develop and evolve into the type of person he or she would like to become

4. Interdependence: the ability to live and work with others in an environment that is nonthreatening and growth producing.

The extent of the use of encounter-group therapy is evidenced by the fact that by 1972 over two hundred thousand people had taken part in groups sponsored by the National Training Laboratory alone.[18] In addition, corporations such as TRW have made extensive use of sensitivity training in dealing with the stress, tension, and anxiety of corporate life.

Executive Sabbatical

Another approach that has been receiving more and more attention in major corporations is the concept of the sabbatical leave for executive personnel. In the academic environment, the faculty sabbatical of six months to a year away from normal faculty responsibilities is a time in which the faculty member is free to pursue current research or to develop new areas of research interest. The sabbatical leave has been looked upon as a time to recharge the batteries and renew old levels of enthusiasm and vigor and interest that may have become diminished by the day-to-day pressures of job. This same objective is being applied to executive personnel in the corporate environment. In a survey of some 266 companies, 63 replied that they participated in a program they perceived as "sabbatical" in nature.[19] Of companies that did *not* have a sabbatical program, 41 percent indicated that they thought such a program would be a good idea.

In order to derive maximum benefit from an executive sabbatical program, each corporation should give careful consideration to both the purpose and the timing of a sabbatical leave for its personnel. For most corporations the purpose of the sabbatical leave would not simply be an opportunity for the executive to improve his or her golf game (although this objective need not be eliminated for certain executives who may need an opportunity to get away from it all). In most cases, the purpose of the executive sabbatical, particularly with respect to younger people, is to provide an opportunity for the individual to experience personal growth and development as well as to provide an outlet for tension and stress. Along these lines, academic programs oriented toward executive personnel, such as those offered at Harvard, MIT, and Stanford, may represent one possible objective for the sabbatical leave. In addition, many corporations such as IBM and Xerox participate in federal and state social service programs that allow business leaders to involve themselves in community activities such as the National Alliance of Businessmen or Model Cities programs.

Experiences such as these allow for a certain amount of executive flight from the stressor-producing environment while at the same time providing an opportunity for individual growth and development that will expand the perspective of the individual and improve the future performance of the manager. As organizations become more progressive in their outlook regarding the nature of the work environment, and become more sensitive to the problems of stress faced by executives, it is likely that the concept of the executive sabbatical will become more and more a part of the thinking of corporate management.

Consciousness and Relaxation

There has been a quiet revolution going on in America. Millions of men and women have become involved in a wide variety of techniques, methods, and approaches to becoming "more in touch with themselves" at a different level of consciousness. Unlike sensitivity training, which makes use of the encounter group to have an individual verbalize his or her feelings, thoughts, and ideas, most of the methods of the consciousness revolution seek to provide techniques that enable individuals to turn inward, in private, to find inner peace.

Perhaps the most well known of these approaches is Transcendental Meditation (TM). Other techniques, such as Biofeedback, Arica, Erhard Seminars Training, and Silva Mind Control among others, have attracted many thousands of followers in the United States. The biofeedback technique, pioneered by Leo V. DiCara and Neal Miller of the Yale Medical School,[20] has been used to teach individual participants to control such things their own heart rate, and systolic blood pressure, as well as to modify their brain-wave signals from beta waves to alpha waves, which are associated with a more relaxed state.

Techniques such as these could of course be extremely valuable in teaching corporate executives to remove themselves from the stressor-producing corporate environment and to find internal release from tension, frustration, and anxiety. One Chicago salesman who has tried TM has stated, "When I get back from meditating I'm not only more effective, but I get along better with other people and myself too."[21]

One approach to dealing with stress, advocated by Herbert Benson, is referred to as the "relaxation response."[22] This is an integrated physiologic response used to offset harmful effects of stress by making use of the mental capabilities of the individual. According to Benson, this technique is fairly simple to apply and can be extremely effective in combating stress. The key elements of Benson's technique are described on pages 74 and 75.

A quiet environment. One should choose a quiet, calm environment with as few distractions as possible. Sound, even background noise, may prevent the elicitation of the response. Choose a convenient, suitable place—for example, at an office desk in a quiet room.

A mental device. The meditator employs the constant stimulus of a single-syllable sound or word. The syllable is repeated silently or in a low, gentle tone. The purpose of the repetition is to free oneself from logical, externally oriented thought by focusing solely on the stimulus. Many different words and sounds have been used in traditional practices. Because of its simplicity and neutrality, the use of the syllable *one* is suggested.

A passive attitude. The purpose of the response is to help one rest and relax, and this requires a completely passive attitude. One should not scrutinize his performance or try to force the response, because this may well prevent the response from occurring. When distracting thoughts enter the mind, they should simply be disregarded.

A comfortable position. The meditator should sit in a comfortable chair in as restful a position as possible. The purpose is to reduce muscular effort to a minimum. The head may be supported; the arms should be balanced or supported as well. The shoes may be removed and the feet propped up several inches, if desired. Loosen all tight-fitting clothing.

Using these four basic elements, one can evoke the response by following the simple mental procedure that many subjects have found successful:

1. In a quiet environment, sit in a comfortable position.
2. Close your eyes.
3. Deeply relax all your muscles, beginning at your feet and progressing up to your face—feet, calves, thighs, lower torso, chest, shoulders, neck, head. Allow them to remain deeply relaxed.
4. Breathe through your nose. Become aware of your breathing. As you breathe out, say the word "one" silently to yourself. Thus: Breathe in . . . breathe out, with "one." In . . . out, with "one . . ."
5. Continue this practice for 20 minutes. You may open your eyes to check the time, but do not use an alarm. When you finish, sit quietly for several minutes, at first with your eyes closed and later with your eyes open.

Remember not to worry about whether you are successful in achieving a deep level of relaxation—maintain a passive attitude and permit relaxation to occur at its own pace. When distracting thoughts occur, ignore them and continue to repeat "one" as you breathe. The technique should be practiced once or twice daily, and not within two hours after any meal, since the digestive processes seem to interfere with the elicitation of the expected changes.

The Benson technique is but one of the current methods of dealing with stress to which executives have turned, in this case because it can be learned quickly and practiced in the office.

Discussion Questions

1. Define the terms *stress* and *stressors* as they apply to the corporate environment.
2. What is meant by *overstressed*?
3. What are some typical reactions to stressors?
4. Define the flight-or-fight instinct.
5. Discuss Type A and Type B behavior as they relate to corporate stressors.
6. How would you characterize the job of the executive in terms of its stress potential?
7. List some typical sources of stressors within the corporate environment.
8. What are some possible executive reactions to stressful situations within the organization?
9. Discuss some of the ways in which the modern executive is attempting to cope with stress in his or her job.
10. What are some of the ways corporations are helping their executive employees cope with stress?

Case for Discussion

Bill Robertson is 22 years old, the son of a prominent lawyer in Chicago. He has two older brothers, one a research physicist and the other a physician. Bill grew up in an exclusive Chicago suburb.

After graduation from a midwestern university with a degree in business, Bill became frustrated with the jobs he had been offered by several large corporations. In all cases the job would have required two to three years in corporate training programs designed to prepare Bill for gradual increases in responsibility. Bill believed that his educational background and summer work experience was sufficient preparation for a more rapid assumption of responsibility.

This belief caused Bill to become enthusiastic about an offer from Golden Products Corporation, a medium-sized manufacturing firm. Mr. Brothers, the recruiter from Golden, indicated that should Bill accept the position, he would be placed in charge of a department of twenty-three assembly line and technical workers. On his staff Bill would have a technical foreman who had worked for Golden for seventeen years.

For six months, Bill would be totally responsible for all decisions within the department, including hiring and termination of employees, production scheduling, and profit achievement. At the end of the six-month assignment, Bill's performance would be judged against profit objectives. If

Bill achieved the goals he would immediately be assigned to manage a larger production department within Golden. If, however, Bill was not able to achieve the profit objective within the department, he would be immediately terminated by Golden Products. After listening to Mr. Brothers explain the job, Bill immediately accepted the position.

Selected References

Bartolome, Fernando. "Executives as Human Beings." In *Harvard Business Review,* November–December 1972.

Benson, Herbert. "Your Innate Ability for Combating Stress." In *Harvard Business Review,* July–August 1974.

"Keeping Fit in the Company Gym." In *Fortune,* October 1975.

Goldston, Eli. "Executive Sabbaticals: About to Take Off." In *Harvard Business Review,* September–October 1973.

Jennings, E. *The Executive in Crisis.* New York: McGraw-Hill, 1965.

Kahn, R., Wolfe, D., Quinn, R. and Snoek, J. *Organizational Stress.* New York: John Wiley and Sons, 1964.

Livesey, Herbert. "Second Acts." In *Quest,* July–August 1977.

McQuade, Walter. "Doing Something About Stress." In *Fortune,* May 1973.

————. "What Stress Can Do to You." In *Fortune,* January 1972.

Solomon, L. and Berzon, B., eds. *New Perspectives on Encounter Groups.* San Francisco, Calif.: Jossey-Bass, Inc., 1972.

Steiner, Jerome. "What Price Success." In *Harvard Business Review,* March–April 1972.

Wright, H. Beric. *Executive Ease and Dis-ease.* New York: John Wiley & Sons, 1975.

Zaleznick, Abraham. "Management of Disappointment." In *Harvard Business Review,* November–December 1967.

MANAGEMENT AND ORGANIZATIONS

Part II

Introduction

The purpose of this section of the text is to provide the reader with a survey of the evolution of management thought, as well as to discuss briefly some theories and research studies that have formed the basis for modern thinking in the field of management and organizations.

The reader should not attempt to memorize the dates or details of specific research studies but rather should read the material to obtain a sense of the history of the ideas forming the basis for our modern concept of management.

Major Themes

Management Thought:
An evolutionary process

Management Research:
Some classic studies

A Model of Human Behavior:
Some early theories

Management Thought: Some Contributions to Its Evolution

4

Management: Engine of Progress

After the Arab oil embargo in November 1973, it took only one week to completely reorganize delivery of the world's oil products. Technology was not enough. Management made the difference.

by Theodore Levitt

Ignoring the role of management in the growth of industrial systems *ipso facto* exaggerates the importance of machines and the artifacts of production. Since those machines and artifacts are not presumed to be present or easily usable in service industries today, gloomy conclusions are understandably reached about the future productivity of the expanding service sector, and therefore about the future living standards of the "post-industrial" society.

On the other hand, if the enormous abundance of the industrial age was the product not of new technology but rather of the art of management—that strangely neglected and often rudely dismissed field of activity—then one must consider whether management could also play such a fructifying role in the service economy. I believe that it can—and that evidence on behalf of this thesis is already plentiful.

Management as a practical art originally developed in the conduct of war. Even today, tables of organization and the language of industrial management derive from the military concepts of "line" and "staff." The industrial revolution gradually adapted and

From Theodore Levitt, "Management: Engine of Progress," *The Public Interest*, No. 44 (Summer 1976). Copyright © by National Affairs, Inc. As adapted in *MBA*, November 1976. Reprinted by permission.

expanded these concepts and procedures. Today management is understood and acknowledged as the unique and central characteristic of that revolution, by those who really know the inner workings of modern industry.

Progress

Management is the primary engine of progress, as progress is generally defined. The crucial importance of management has been eclipsed by the historians' almost obsessively childlike fascination with the technological artifacts of nineteenth century industry and the flamboyant entrepreneurs of that era. But the precise story of how those entrepreneurs rendered these artifacts—the machines, engines, tools, and crude instruments—productive has not yet been properly told to this day. Neither Lewis Mumford nor Max Weber—and certainly not Karl Marx—ever bothered to explore the specific details of the functional roles played by industrial organizers and managers.

The significance of management in the creation and development of the industrial age can perhaps best be understood by noting how long it took for the available technology actually to create that age. Technologically speaking, the industrial age began in Milan around 1335, with the gear-driven time clock. It contained all the mechanical hardware and engineerng know-how we associate with the machinery of the industrial revolution in the nineteenth century. But it took Eli Whitney, in New Haven in 1798, to wrest the available technology from the dead hands of isolated medieval craftsmen and put it into the more productive hands of organized unskilled labor. Whitney's contribution was less technological than managerial. To assemble interchangeable musket parts, he created large-scale factories where there had been one-man shops; he organized, directed, and controlled groups of workers to do with existing technologies what had previously been done singly and alone.

It took more than 400 years to go from the clock to the musket factory, and Whitney's contribution was precisely the work of what we call today the "manager." He was also an entrepreneur, but that part of his activity has almost totally obscured a more arduous and encompassing aspect—his role as an organizer and manager.

Henry Ford

Management consists of the rational assessment of a situation and the systematic selection of goals and purposes; the systematic development of strategies to achieve those goals; the marshaling of the required resources; the rational design, organization, direction, and control of the activities required to attain the selected purposes; and, finally, the motivating and rewarding of people to do the work. Whitney's idea of interchangeable parts for manufacturing muskets might be said—in the profundity of hindsight—to have led "inescapably" to the creation of the mass-production factory. But it was hardly obvious then—nor was it, in fact, a century later.

Henry Ford's singular contribution was not that he invented the assembly line. He didn't—he merely rediscovered it while witnessing the operation of Julius Rosenwald's Sears, Roebuck mail-order warehouse in Chicago, where roving clerks assembled orders by picking items off the shelves. Ford's unique insight was that the potential buyer's real problem was getting enough money to buy a car, and he set out to solve the problem by finding a way to make cars more cheaply. (On the other hand Ford might have invented installment credit to solve the problem—a "solution" that came later.) The solution derived largely from Ford's seminal reconceptualization of the engineering of the automobile, making it an assembled rather than a constructed machine. If he had not redesigned the automobile as an assembly of parts, it could not have been manufactured on an assembly line, where the shift from independent craftsmen working alone to unskilled multitudes working together—under highly ordered, closely supervised conditions— helped control quality, productivity, and costs.

Immaculate Conception

The functional rationality which characterizes the cognitive mode of management makes a difference. Technology is not enough. It is one of the great modern mysteries that, although so much is owed by our times to the organizing and productive genius of management, the world must constantly be reminded of this fact, which it seems so obstinately reluctant to learn and believe. And, curiously, it is precisely in the world's intellectual enclaves—in the universities, and among writers and journalists—that this obstinacy reaches its apex. Somehow, results are presumed to happen as if by immaculate conception. It is well to appreciate what the absence of good management can mean in our daily lives. For example, it is a fact now unanimously acknowledged by those who understand that, after the Arab oil embargo in November 1973, it took only one week of intensive around-the-clock work by the managers of the oil industry to rearrange completely the entire sourcing, shipping, pipelining, and delivery of the world's oil and petroleum products to get things back in a new, functioning track. I have been told personally by extremely high-placed government officials in Europe, the United States, and Japan that they viewed this as an almost miraculous achievement that none of the governments themselves could conceivably have accomplished. Compare this to the pathetic logistical blunder in late 1975—by Nigerian government officials well trained in economics at the best British universities—that resulted in a massive glut of 120 cement-laden cargo ships in Lagos harbor with no place to dock and no space or little use for their loads.

Czech Productivity

Or, consider the venerable business of manufacturing textiles and wearing apparel. In 1969, Czechoslovakian labor productivity in these industries was 56 percent above that of Hungary. For every 100 workers needed to do the job in Hungary, only 69 were needed in Czechoslovakia. Each Czechoslovak worker, aided by more machinery than the Hungarian worker, consumed 4,080 kilowatt hours of electricity a year, against 3,108 for the Hungarian worker. But though the Czechoslovak worker consumed on the average 31 percent more electricity, he produced 56 percent more goods. It is not that the Czechoslovak electric machinery was more modern or that there was more of it; it was that the manufacturing process was better managed. Understandably, even though the state rules both economies, the Czechoslovak citizen pays less for his clothes than does the Hungarian. In the end, it is the nature and quality of management that makes the difference.

Genesis of Modern Management

Toward the close of the nineteenth century the Industrial Revolution was having a major impact in the United States. This revolution, with its many commercial inventions and new manufacturing processes, was to launch America into a new era of economic development, bringing with it the beginning of the factory system, mass production, and coordinated work effort. The size and complexity of these new inventions made it necessary to bring many workers together under one roof in order to make efficient use of these new machines and equipment. It also became necessary to coordinate and direct the activities of these workers. It was this need for coordination and direction that was to be the genesis of modern management and administration.

Before the development of inventions such as Hargreaves's spinning jenny and Watt's steam engine, workers could perform their production activities on an individual basis within their own homes. Raw materials could be picked up or delivered to them for application of whatever skill or area of expertise they possessed, and the finished goods could then be delivered to the marketplace. This system was essentially one of individual craftsmen working independently in the production of goods and products. As a result of the greater efficiencies and economies to be derived from the use of large-scale machines and processes, it was no longer possible for workers to perform their tasks on an individual basis. What resulted was the development of central locations with high densities of equipment and machinery to which the workers would come. These centers were the beginnings of our modern factories and assembly plants. It was in these early factories that management as a separate and distinct field was to have its genesis. The individuals responsible for supervising the efforts of the early factory workers were normally the owners of the machinery and they represented some of our first managers.

Prior to 1900, the activities of these early managers were limited primarily to a type of overseer function, concerned mainly with making sure that workers were present at their jobs on time, did not take excessive work breaks, and did not leave their assigned work station until the prescribed time. The tasks of these managers did not generally include activities designed to improve the performance of the workers, either through additional training or improved work methods. As new inventions spurred the pace and complexity of industrial production, however, a greater premium was placed upon the manager's ability to coordinate the efforts of large numbers of workers in order to maximize output. As the size of many firms grew, it became necessary for owners to seek assistance in the coordination of worker activities; the need for such assistance gave birth to the separation of ownership from management of the business enterprise. This separation created the need for a new type of industrial worker, the professional manager, whose job depended upon the ability to supervise and coordinate the activities of others.

Frederick W. Taylor: Scientific Management

Present writers generally credit Frederick W. Taylor with first focusing attention on an analysis of the tasks and responsibilities of the first-line supervisor within the organization.[1] Beginning with his employment in Midvale Steel Works in 1878, Taylor placed new emphasis on the job of the manager. It was his idea that the planning and performance of a task should be separated, the operator being held responsible for performance, while management assumed the responsibility for planning.

The task of planning as conceived by Taylor involved several key points. First, Taylor believed it necessary for management to investigate thoroughly all of the variables and components involved in the performance of each task carried on within the factory. Second, as a result of this investigation, management would be able to select the single most effective method to be used in the performance of a given task. In order to accomplish this objective, management was to use the time and motion study approach to work methods that Taylor was instrumental in developing. This approach is still widely used in industry today. Third, in Taylor's opinion the responsibility of management did not end with the development of a standard method for each job; in addition, it was now necessary for the manager to select workers who were both mentally and physically capable of performing each specific task within the factory. *Finally*, the integration of capable men and most effective method was undertaken by management through the proper training of the workers in the method to be utilized.

As a result of the manager's planning and training activities, Taylor believed it would now be possible for management to achieve lower labor costs as well as increased productivity. This would be possible because the value of the worker's output increased at a faster rate than his piece work wages. This combination would now make it possible for management to provide even higher wages to the workers. In Taylor's opinion, the ability to pay these increased wages would serve to spur worker efforts to increase output to an even greater level and bring about still lower costs and increased productivity.

It seems clear that Taylor's philosophy of motivation was rooted in the concept of the "economic man," and it was therefore mainly through economic incentives that management could appeal to the workers to achieve greater levels of productivity. It should be noted that these assumptions regarding the economic nature of man were consistent with the prevailing religious and social values of the time.

From an examination of the philosophies put forth by Taylor in his two best-known works, *The Principles of Scientific Management* (1911) and *Shop Management* (1903), we see the genesis of many current management tools and techniques. As we have mentioned, Taylor pioneered the development of methods analysis and time study so critical to the job of the modern industrial engineer. In addition, Taylor's ideas on worker selection and training foreshadowed many of the sophisticated forms of these activities found in today's organizations. Perhaps the most important contribution of Taylor, however, was in bringing a specific definition and function to the discipline of management. Based upon the work of Taylor and of other writers of the scientific management school, including Harrington Emerson, H. L. Gantt, Henry Towne, Frank Gilbreth, there began to evolve a set of responsibilities and functions specifically associated with the practice of management. The principles of scientific management may be summarized as follows:

1. Management is a separate and distinct activity.
2. First-line supervision is basic.
3. Management functions include:
   examining variables involved in the task
   developing the most effective methods
   selecting workers according to the psychological and physiological requirements of the job
   training workers in the most effective methods.
4. Productivity increases mean higher wages for the worker.

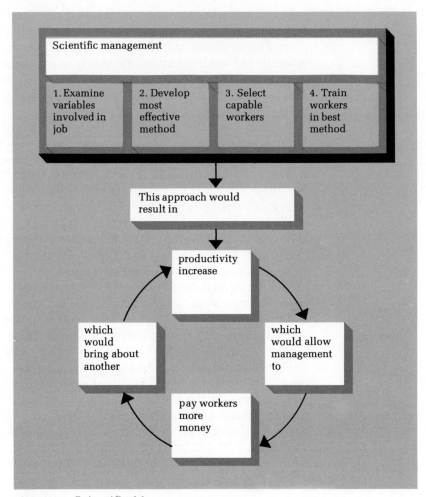

Figure 4.1. *Scientific Management*

Administrative and Functional Management (Classical Theory)

Although Taylor's work provided the framework for much of the original thought regarding the function of management, it was primarily directed toward those management activities normally associated with first-line supervision and other lower-level management positions. Not until the late 1930s did attention begin to focus on management activities normally associated with upper administrative levels. It was at about this time, for example, that the work of Henri Fayol, a French industrialist, was first published in the English language and began to appear in the United States. Fayol and other members of what was to be called the "functional" school of management, including James D. Mooney and A. C. Reiley, Luther Gulick and Lyndall Urwick, Ralph C. Davis, and Harold Koontz and Cyril O'Donnell, provided the impetus for a new approach to the management process. This approach emphasized the administrative activities of a manager as they are performed at all levels in the organization. Their primary focus was on developing a list of functions that must necessarily be performed as part of the overall administrative process. Although the exact number of functions to be performed will vary from author to author, those of *planning, organizing,* and *controlling* are considered to be classic, and in general they will be found in the writings of all members of this school of thought. It was the objective of these writers to examine the organization as a separate entity, to analyze the basic functions a manager must perform, and from these to develop a series of principles that could be utilized to guide management behavior in all organizational situations. These principles provided direction for managers in areas such as authority and responsibility relationships, line and staff organization, business policies, span of control, leadership, and division of labor. Following is a representative listing of management principles drawn from the writings of several well-known thinkers in this area:

1. Clear lines of authority must run from top to bottom in the organization.
2. No one in the organization should report to more than one line supervisor.
3. The responsibility and authority of each supervisor should be clearly defined in writing.
4. Responsibility should always be coupled with corresponding authority.
5. The responsibility of higher authority for the acts of its subordinates is absolute.
6. Authority should be delegated as far down the line as possible.
7. The number of levels of authority should be kept at a minimum.
8. The work of every person in the organization should be confined as far as possible to the performance of a single leading function.
9. Whenever possible, line functions should be separated from staff functions, and adequate emphasis should be placed on important staff activities.

10. There is a limit to the number of positions that can be coordinated by a single executive.
11. The organization should be flexible, so that it can be adjusted to changing conditions.
12. The organization should be kept as simple as possible.[2]

It was generally advocated by members of this school of thought that these principles had application to all forms of organization in all environments. This being the case, they believed that it would be possible for a manager to improve the effectiveness of his organization by a conscientious application of these principles. Several writers of this period did, however, discuss the need to give adequate consideration to each situation when applying these principles to a given organization.

This school of thought has had a most significant effect on management practice, for it represented the first major attempt to develop and apply guidelines to be utilized in the administration of *all* levels of the organization. It created a body of knowledge that could be studied and then applied to the business organization so as to bring about a more effective and efficient utilization of resources.

Although this school of thought has been severely criticized in recent years because it tends to disregard the human element within the organization, it still represents a major milestone in the development of a systemized body of knowledge regarding the practice of management. The contributions of administrative and functional management were to:

Focus attention on administration and upper levels of management within the organization

Develop a series of "functions" that must be performed by every manager within an organization (planning, organizing, controlling)

Develop a series of "principles" believed to have application to all organizations (unity of command, span of control, delegation of authority, division of labor, etc.).

Max Weber and "Bureaucracy"

Although not considered to be a member of the functional school of management theory, Max Weber, whose work was first published in Germany in the 1920s and appeared in the United States in 1946, was consistent in concept and approach with many of the writers we have discussed. Weber used a military analogy to develop what he considered to be the most appropriate approach to developing effective organizations. This approach is referred to as bureaucratic. It is based on the assumption that "the objective discharge of business primarily means a discharge of business according to calculable rules and without regard for persons."[3] According to Weber, this bureaucratic form of organization should be characterized by the following features:

1. A clear definition of duties for each position within the organization, this definition to be based upon the specific functional area of responsibility
2. A clearly defined chain of command extending throughout all levels of the organization
3. Well-defined rules, regulations, and procedures which specify the rights and responsibilities of individuals as well as how they are to function within the work situation
4. An organization which functions in an impersonal manner without regard to individual personality
5. An organization in which promotion is based solely upon technical competence.[4]

According to Weber, the main reason for the increasing use of such bureaucratic organizations is their "purely technical superiority over any other form of organization."[5] When examined in conjunction with the principles of organization developed by writers of the functional school of thought, Weber's concept of bureaucracy provides a framework for understanding the initial development of organizational structure and management practice as first applied to business organizations.

Chester Barnard One writer of this period who deviated somewhat from the strictly classical approach was business executive Chester Barnard. During his years as president of New Jersey Bell Telephone Company, Barnard formulated many theories regarding the function of management. In his now classic work, *The Functions of the Executive,* published in 1938, Barnard used research results of sociology and psychology to further his theory of organization and of executive functions. With his awareness of work in sociology and psychology, Barnard was perhaps the first to recognize some of the implications of the human element in the business organization. In particular, Barnard focused on the potential impact of this human element on communication, decision making, and leadership in the organizational environment. He was perhaps the first also to consider the organization as a social system, and his "acceptance theory" of leadership places emphasis on the willingness of subordinates to comply with the direction of superiors. This approach makes use of the behavioral implications of leadership principles, largely ignored by most writers up to that time.

Human Relations (Neoclassical Theory)

Beginning in 1927 and extending through 1932 a series of experiments were carried out at the Western Electric Plant in Hawthorne, Illinois. These experiments conducted by Elton Mayo and a group of research associates were to have a dramatic effect on the future of the concept of organizations and the practice of management.

These experiments, known as the Hawthorne studies, had as their initial purpose an investigation of scientific management principles. The researchers were interested in the effect of fatigue and monotony on members of the work force, as well as changes in productivity that result from changes in working conditions. In addition, several other areas were examined, all with the purpose of establishing the nature of the relationship between the work environment and employee output. The results of these experiments, however, were far different from what the researchers had expected; their findings were to have far-reaching impact on management thought in the years to come. A detailed account of the Hawthorne studies may be found in a work published in 1939 by F. J. Roethlisberger and W. J. Dickson, *Management and the Worker.*[6] To provide some insight into the importance of these studies, a brief summary of the results follows:

In one study, designed to determine the effect of work area lighting on productivity, the investigators selected a group of workers, noted the initial level of their output and then divided them into a test group and a control group. For purposes of the experiment, the control group continued to work under a constant level of illumination, while the illumination in the test group area was varied. As was expected, as the intensity of the illumination in the test area was increased, the output of the workers also increased. This result would seem to be consistent with Taylor's views regarding the importance of working conditions. However, when the experimenters began to *decrease* the level of illumination in the work area, expecting to find a corresponding drop in output, they were amazed to find that the overall level of productivity continued to *increase*. In fact, test group output levels continued to increase until the level of illumination in the work area was reduced "to that on an ordinary moonlit night" and even at this point the workers were able to maintain their efficiency. This result did not appear to be consistent with the principles of scientific management as outlined by Taylor.

In another experiment, conducted in the bank wiring room (in which a series of wires were connected to large banks of circuit boards), the experimenters attempted to determine the impact of a wage incentive plan on worker output. In this experiment, the nature of the work was such that each worker contributed to the assembly of an individual completed unit. The output of the group and the corresponding wage incentive to be provided were therefore a function of the number of units completed by the entire group. It was expected that highly efficient workers would bring pressure to bear on less efficient workers in order to increase output and thus take greater advantage of the group incentive plan. These anticipated results did not come about. The researchers found that the group had established its own standard of output or what constitutes "a fair day's work." This standard was enforced within the group by various methods of social pressure and was apparently more important in determining group output than were the economic incentives offered by management. This finding also appeared to be contrary to the guidelines established by Taylor in his appeal to the "economic man."

These and other Hawthorne studies made it apparent that there was a need for some new thinking with respect to the motivation and direction of employees within the work environment. The researchers formulated several theories to explain the results of their experiments. First of all, it seemed clear that, within the organization, psychological and sociological factors acting upon the individual were more influential than economic factors in determining workers' behavior. This conclusion, when accepted as true and valid, had far-reaching implications for the future development and character of management-employee relations. The experimenters also speculated about the possible existence of what they referred to as an informal organization. They hypothesized that informal organization, which existed within the formally defined structure, exhibited characteristics that were a function of the psychological and sociological make-up of the particular work group. The goals and objectives of the work group might, however, be in conflict with those of the formal structure established by management. The result would be work group behavior contrary to management's expectations and, consequently, possible hindrance to the achievement of management goals.

The researchers hypothesized further that in the experiment involving the illumination of the work areas, the workers assumed that they had been selected for the experiment because management considered them to be among the most productive in the plant. The workers were determined to uphold this faith in them by continuing to turn out a high level of output even though working conditions around them had deteriorated to an extremely low level.

In the experiment involving the bank wiring room, the investigators hypothesized that the informal organization within the work group had established a level of output not to be violated. This output level represented the group's perception of what constituted a day's work. This level of output did not place undue stress upon the worker, and it did not incur the antagonism of management. Once this level was established the workers chose not to exceed it, even though by doing so they would increase their income. It seemed clear that the workers feared possible detrimental effects from any increase in output, possibly in the form of lost jobs, layoffs, or increased expectations from management. The researchers found also that the informal organization was able to exert strong social pressures on work group members so as to maintain an acceptable level of output. These social pressures had a greater impact in influencing individual behavior than did the economic incentives offered by management.

As a result of the Hawthorne studies and subsequent research, the psychological and sociological aspects of workers and work groups are now considered to be of prime importance for understanding motivation and work group behavior within the organization. Contributions of the human relations approach to management study include

1. Focusing attention on the human element within the organization
2. Using psychological and sociological concepts and research in analyzing organizations
3. Developing the concept of the informal organization
4. Raising issues relating to work group behavior, motivation, and need satisfaction.

Empirical, Mathematical, and Social Systems

Harold Koontz summarizes several additional approaches to understanding work organizations.[7] Among these, he includes the "empirical school," which emphasizes drawing upon business experiences and case analysis as a means of teaching about business organization. The proponents of this approach use the experiences of others in training individuals in the practice of management.

Koontz also discusses the "mathematical school," whose proponents use operations research and quantitative techniques in their approach to management problems. With the model as their basic tool, the followers of this school of thought express organizational activities and relationships in quantitative terms and mathematical equations that offer unique solutions.

Another approach discussed by Koontz is the "social system" school, which views organization and management as one system of cultural interrelationships. This approach, which draws on sociology, seeks to analyze the workings of the organization in terms of its social groups. Proponents of this school of thought advocate developing an understanding of organizations as total integrated social systems.

Contingency Theory

In recent years increasing attention has been given to what has been referred to as a "contingency theory" of management. This theory recognizes and makes use of the contribution of all approaches to the study of management. Its basic assumption is that the organization itself is so complex—in technology and market environment, in individual members, and in the goals, objectives, policies, and procedures by which it operates—that each organization and situation must be considered independently in seeking solutions to management problems. Contingency theory holds that no single approach to management is necessarily appropriate in all situations and conditions or for all types of business organizations. The effective manager is therefore the individual who is able to analyze and assess a particular situation and then applies the most appropriate techniques to that situation.

The focus of this theory is the manager's ability to recognize, identify, and react to a wide variety of organizational variables. These variables include such factors as the state of the economy, the nature of competition, the level of technology, and the particular characteristics of the individuals who make up the organization. Contingency theory states that only when the interrelationship among these factors has been examined and analyzed can the manager draw conclusions as to the most appropriate course of action for a particular organization.

In analyzing each of the variables mentioned, the manager may make use of tools, techniques, and approaches advocated by the various schools of thought. For example, it will be necessary for the manager to understand the workings of the organization in terms of its planning, organizing, and controling procedures. In addition, the analysis may require psychological and sociological approaches for insight into the behavior of organization members. Further, various mathematical models and quantitative techniques may be used to obtain an exact assessment of a particular condition or situation. The contingency theory, rather than representing another approach to the study of management, seeks to utilize all the current approaches as resources. A review of the research that has led to the evolution of this theory will be discussed in the next chapter.

The purpose of our discussion to this point has been to provide the reader with background material on the evolution of thought with respect to management. Though not all-inclusive, the discussion does represent some of the significant contributions that have had an impact on the way we view and study organizations today.

Discussion Questions

1. Discuss the contributions of each of the following to the study and practice of management: scientific management, functional school, empirical school, mathematical school, social system school.
2. How would you relate the evolution of management thought to the evolution of our economic system within the United States?
3. Taylor's theory relied on an appeal to the notion of "economic man," motivated by the opportunity to obtain monetary rewards. Is this appeal still valid in today's work situation? If not, what do you consider to be the prime motivational factors influencing today's worker?
4. Both the schools of scientific management and functional management have been criticized in recent years for their lack of attention to the human element in the study of management. Discuss.

5. The concept of bureaucracy has come to have a very negative connotation today. Discuss those factors you believe responsible for this negative attitude toward bureaucracy.
6. How would you contrast scientific management with contingency theory with respect to the study and practice of management?
7. Many successful businesspeople have neither attended business school nor been exposed to management teaching. Comment.
8. How does management differ from fields such as medicine and law with respect to the necessity of formal training?
9. What changes have taken place in our society in recent years that have made the job of business management more difficult?

Selected References

Scientific Management

Babbage, C. *On the Economy of Machinery and Manufacturers*. London: C. Knight and Co., 1832.

Emerson, H. "The Twelve Principles of Efficiency." New York: Engineering Magazine Co., 1912.

Gantt, H. L. *Organizing for Work*. New York: Harcourt Brace and World, 1976.

———. "Efficiency and Democracy." In *Transactions*, American Society of Mechanical Engineers, 40 (1918).

Gilbreth, F. B. *Primer of Scientific Management*. New York: Harper & Row, 1912.

Taylor, Frederick W. *The Principles of Scientific Management*. New York: Harper & Row, 1911.

———. *Shop Management* (1903).

Towne, Henry R. "The Engineer as Economist." In *Transactions*, American Society of Mechanical Engineers 7 (1886).

Administrative and Functional School

Davis, R. C. *The Fundamentals of Top Management*. New York: Harper & Row, 1951.

Fayol, H. *Industrial and General Administration*. London: Sir Isaac Pitman & Sons, Ltd., 1949.

Follett, M. P. *Dynamic Administration*, H. Metcalf and L. Urwich, eds. New York: Harper & Row, 1942.

Gulich, L. and Urwich, L., eds. *Papers on the Science of Administration*. Columbia University Press, 1937.

Koontz, H. and O'Donnell, C. *Principles of Management*. New York: McGraw–Hill, 1955.

Mooney, J. D. and Reiley, A. C. *Onward Industry*. New York: Harper & Row, 1931.

Weber, M. *Essays in Sociology*, H. H. Gerth and C. Wright Mills, eds. New York: Oxford University Press, 1946.

Human Relations

Mayo, Elton. *The Human Problems of an Industrial Civilization*. New York: Macmillan, 1933.

Roethlisberger, F. J. *Management and Morale*. Cambridge, Mass.: Harvard University Press, 1941.

——— and Dickson, W. J. *Management and the Worker*. Cambridge, Mass.: Harvard University Press, 1939.

Other References

Barnard, C. *The Functions of the Executive*. Cambridge, Mass.: Harvard University Press, 1938.

Balske, E. W. *Bonds of Organization*. New York: Harper & Row, 1950.

Churchman, C. W., Ackoff, R. L., and Arnoff, E. L. *Introduction to Operations Research*. New York: John Wiley & Sons, Inc., 1957.

Dale, E. *The Great Organizers*. New York: McGraw-Hill Book Co., 1961.

Forrester, J. *Industrial Dynamics*. New York: John Wiley & Sons, 1961.

Mee, J. *Management Thought in a Dynamic Economy*. New York: New York University Press, 1963.

Simon, H. *Administrative Behavior*. New York: Macmillan, 1947.

Research in Management and Organizations

5

The Management Psychologists Have Landed

Feeling lonely in the president's office? Wondering where your next executive vice president is coming from? Want someone to think out loud to? Before you call for professional help, there are some things you ought to know.

by Spencer Klaw

In the vast literature that deals with the behavioral sciences and their application to business there is little information on the rapid growth in recent years of a body of specialists most commonly known as management psychologists. Unlike those industrial psychologists who are concerned mainly with workers and first-line supervisors, the management psychologist works with managers. He may, among other things, advise them on whom to hire and promote, counsel them on how to improve their managerial styles, and even offer them specific suggestions for getting along better with particular associates who are giving them a hard time. The management psychologist may also be called on to do a lot of what is referred to in the trade as handholding. This may consist of listening sympathetically for hours at a time to a company president who feels he has no one else to confide in.

Companies that have psychologists to provide them with such services often treat that fact as classified information. They worry that if word gets around people will conclude that the management is losing its marbles. In the circumstances, management psychologists are well advised to be discreet about their work. This may explain why so

Spencer Klaw, "The Management Psychologists Have Landed," *Fortune*, April 1970. Reprinted by permission.

little has been written about them despite the fact that thousands of companies, including such major corporations as Borg-Warner, Inland Steel, and General Foods, now use their services.

Some people who practice what amounts to management psychology are not psychologists at all. No formal training in psychology (or in anything else) is legally required if one wishes to evaluate executives, counsel them on interpersonal problems, or hold their hands, and some people who regularly perform such services have been trained in, for example, engineering or industrial management. The great majority, however, have Ph.D.'s in psychology, and some teach at colleges and universities.

All together, there are now several hundred part- and full-time management psychologists in the U.S. A few are employed as house psychologists by large corporations. Most work as consultants, however, often in association with one of the dozens of firms that have been established to provide psychological services to business. The oldest and largest of these is the Chicago firm of Rohrer, Hibler & Replogle, which was founded in 1945, and which now has seven hundred clients, offices in twenty-two cities, and a staff of ninety-one professionals, all with doctorates in psychology. Psychological consultants sometimes work on an annual retainer, but more often they charge a flat rate for their time. The usual rate is $40 to $50 an hour, and the principals of a successful consulting firm may clear $40,000 or more in a good year.

Spotting the Spendthrift

The basic stock in trade of Rohrer, Hibler & Replogle and of many of its competitors is the psychological evaluation. They evaluate not only candidates for management jobs with client companies, but managers who are already on a client's payroll. Sometimes a company will conduct a management audit, and put everyone above a given level in the corporate hierarchy through the evaluation mill. Last year, for example, when Atlantic Richfield merged with Sinclair Oil, the Chicago firm of Medina & Thompson was retained to evaluate some 800 managers, up to and including divisional vice presidents. At some companies any manager who is in line for an important promotion will be sent to the company psychologist for evaluation (or re-evaluation). Other companies require that everyone in the upper echelons of management be reevaluated at regular intervals.

Many executives swear by the evaluations they get from their psychologists. J. T. Kenneally, chairman of International Systems & Controls in Houston, recalls being warned by Robert Medina of Medina & Thompson that a certain job candidate was very aggressive, and would get into trouble if he had to handle labor negotiations. "So we decided not to let him get involved in negotiations," Kenneally says. "But we didn't place him properly, and, as it turned out, he did get involved. It also turned out that Medina & Thompson had been absolutely right." In another instance, Medina warned Kenneally that a candidate for a key job was a spendthrift, and the company took the precaution of putting him on a very short tether so far as making capital expenditures was concerned. "But we weren't making proper use of the information we had," Kenneally says. "The first thing we knew, the guy started handing out 40 percent salary raises."

As Kenneally's remarks suggest, evaluations are used for other purposes besides getting a line on whether a man should be hired or promoted. An executive may use an evaluation report both as a guide for tailoring a job to fit a particular candidate, and as a guide for dealing with the candidate after he has been hired. The evaluee himself may also get something out of an evaluation. A job applicant who is evaluated but not hired seldom has a chance to learn how the psychologist sized him up. But successful applicants, and people who are already working for a client company, are customarily entitled, at company expense, to what is known as a feedback session, at which the psychologist describes what he sees as the evaluee's strengths and weaknesses, and discusses their implications with him.

There is little evidence that pencil-and-paper tests—except, perhaps, standard tests of intelligence and computational skill—are of much use in predicting managerial performance. Most management psychologists, however, base their evaluations on tests plus an interview that may last several hours. And some psychologists using this technique have been able to beat the law of averages (though not always by a wide margin) in predicting how well people will do in particular management jobs.

Nevertheless, psychological evaluations are often of doubtful value, and can easily do more harm than good. For one thing, psychologists by no means invariably deliver on their promises to be specific and unambiguous. Too often their reports read as if they had come out of a weighing machine, containing statements like—to quote an actual example—"Mr. Sloan gives evidence of having an alert and probing mind, is both practical and realistic and has his feet firmly on the ground." Reports may also be sprinkled with irrelevancies—"Mr. Donaldson believes he is better than his brother at conceptualizing, and is also more of a humanist"—and with trenchant observations such as "He can profit from criticism if given in an appropriate manner."

Evaluations are also frequently misused. Management psychologists are quick to point out that the way they see a man is just one of many factors that an executive must take into consideration in deciding whether to hire or to promote him. But some executives are so grateful for anything that promises to reduce the uncertainty of business life, and so ignorant of the limitations of psychology, that they are disposed to take the psychologist's word as law. And while there are many psychologists who staunchly resist this sort of dependency, there are others who, not surprisingly, indulge themselves in the heady delights of corporate king-making.

Evaluation reports are misused, too, by executives who look on them as sheets of instructions for handling people. "Suppose I have a new guy in charge of all our data processing," says a senior executive of an apparel-manufacturing firm. "The tests and interview might show that he's very creative in benign situations, but that when he's under pressure he pulls in his horns, gets cautious, and only goes with tried and true solutions. Well, if he's this kind of guy, and we've got a problem that requires real imagination, I'll take him out to lunch and talk it over with him in a very low-key way. But if I know that the guy really works best under pressure, I'll just go storming into his office." Manipulation of this kind, needless to say, is a shaky foundation on which to build a productive working relationship.

What Psychologists Shouldn't Tell

Another thing wrong with having people evaluated is that they may resent being judged by a stranger on the basis of a few tests and a morning's conversation. Frederick Jaicks, president of Inland Steel, a company that has its upper-level managers evaluated periodically, says, "I think the situation is better than it was years ago, when people had all kinds of traumatic concerns because an outside party was taking a reading on them. I think people recognize now that this is just one element in the picture of how we move people, and how we broaden them, and

that has tended to dispel many of those fears. But I wouldn't begin to say that everything is sweetness and light. Given a referendum, people still might say, 'Let's not have that sort of thing.' "

Moreover, the evaluation process can put the psychologist in a compromising position. He may promise not to disclose anything that is told him by the evaluee, but what he learns in confidence may well have an important bearing on the recommendation he turns in to the evaluee's employer, or prospective employer. A good many psychologists insist, therefore, that any manager who is sent to them for evaluation must be given a chance to see his report before it goes to his boss, to argue with its findings and conclusions, and to attach a written objection to anything that he thinks is misleading.

There are psychologists who think this does not go far enough. They point out that a manager's abilities are usually well known already to his superiors, and that the main reason for evaluating him is to give the man a little better insight into himself. They go on to argue persuasively that evaluations should be voluntary, and that the evaluee should have the final say as to what, if anything, the psychologist can pass along to his superiors.

At least one psychologist, Dr. Charles C. McArthur of the Harvard University Health Services, believes that even the man who is not yet on the company payroll is entitled to pretty much the same veto power. McArthur, forty-nine, who lectures on executive selection at the Harvard Business School and is active as an industrial consultant, treats job applicants who are sent to him for evaluation as though they were collaborators. "You have to let the man himself control his own destiny," McArthur explains. "Like, look, he's a homosexual. You know it, he knows it, the company doesn't know it. All right, what I say is, 'Now look, friend. How are you going to play this game?' He'll say,

'Well, they won't hire me if they know.'
I'll say, 'Nuts, they won't hire you; they've
hired six. Want me to name them?' Quite
often in the end he says, 'Oh, hell, I'll talk to
the personnel man about it; don't you do it,
I'll do it.' " McArthur adds, "Now suppose
the man says, 'I can't bear to have anyone
know this. I can hardly bear to know it
myself.' What am I going to do? Obviously
I'm not going to hurt him. I'll say, 'All right.
You tell me how much of what we've
covered I should share with the company.'
And he lays down the ground rules. Usually
we come out that I can tell the company
everything that I think will matter in the
least bit to what he's going to be like on the
job from nine to five. If I thought he was
going to be cruising at the water cooler at
ten-thirty in the morning, I might have to
draw the line. But you just don't get that.
There are just certain things a company
needs to know, and most applicants are very
willing to have the company know these
things."

The Case for Handholding

There are psychologists who think the most
useful thing they can do for a company is to
help it find good managers and hang on to
them. Dr. Roy A. Doty, fifty-six, a Chicago
consultant whose clients include American
Hospital Supply Corp. and a number of
consumer finance companies, says, "If you
can get good people, you don't have to hold
their hands. And with all due respect for
some of my colleagues, there's not really a
hell of a lot I can do to make a really
competent executive out of an incompetent
one."

But Doty's is a minority view, and most of
his competitors spend a good deal of time
counseling managers on problems related to
their jobs. An engineering manager, for
example, may go to the psychologist for
advice on whether he might be happier and
more effective in technical sales. Or a
manager who has just been through a formal

evaluation may suggest at his feedback
session—with or without nudging from the
psychologist—that he could stand some help
in understanding better his own and other
people's motivations.

A manager may also ask for counseling
because his boss has urged him to give it a
try, or because he himself thinks it might be
useful. Sometimes this thought may arise in
the course of an informal talk with the
company psychologist. The vice president for
personnel of a large food company recalls
that several years ago, just after he had been
promoted to a new job as a division manager,
the company's psychological consultant
dropped in for a get-acquainted chat, and
that this led to a number of subsequent
meetings. "We talked about what a man can
do to motivate a group," he says. "And to
demotivate it. Specifically, he helped me
identify a tendency on my part—I know
people find this hard to believe now—a
tendency to be quiet and not say very much.
His coaching and encouraging helped me to
be more open, to express myself more freely,
both upward and at the peer level."

More often an executive's difficulty is that
he talks too much, not too little. Not long ago
the new president of a bank asked Dr.
Richard Porter, a Pittsburgh consultant, to
help him figure out how to get more out of
his weekly meetings with the bank's vice
presidents. "We taped some of the meetings,
and analyzed what had happened, and then
went over the whole thing privately with the
president," Porter says. "When he protested
that it wasn't true that he did 99 percent of
the talking, we could prove it to him by
playing the tape."

Another client of Porter's, William A.
Suiter, group vice president for chemicals
and plastics at Borg-Warner, says gratefully
that on occasion Porter has been able to
straighten out intramural quarrels that had
become so fierce and so chronic that Suiter
was considering firing one or both parties.

Porter's approach to such situations is decidedly old shoe. "Let's suppose the head of manufacturing is in a big fight with the guy in charge of marketing," he says. "I'll go to him and say, 'Look, you're being criticized by marketing because they say you're not doing the job. What are you doing about this?' He'll say, 'We're doing a hell of a lot better job than people around here realize.' I'll say, 'Why aren't you making that point? All you do is to get in there and pound on the table, and neither of you gets anywhere.' He'll say, 'Well, the damn fool won't listen to me.' I'll ask if *he's* listening to the other guy, and he'll say, 'Hell, he doesn't say anything worth listening to.' I'll say, 'How do you know? What really *was* he trying to say yesterday?' You try to get him to tell you. If he can't, he says, 'Well, maybe you've got a point there.' So I say, 'All right, why don't you give him five minutes next time and see what he's got to say?' And then you go and do the same thing with the other guy."

A Talk in the Parking Lot

Sometimes, as noted, an executive will use a psychologist mainly as someone to think out loud to. Once a month, for example, George Murray, a consultant who lives in Stamford, Connecticut, pauses on his way home after a day in Manhattan to pick up the president of a large company that is one of his clients. "We drive out to Greenwich, where his car is parked at the station," Murray explains. "We talk all the way out, and then we sit in the parking lot for an hour. He just talks about what's on his mind: not technical problems, but organizational problems, problems with his directors, that sort of thing. Occasionally I react. But mainly I'm his sounding board." The senior vice president of a $300-million-a-year company, who has lunch from time to time with his company's consulting psychologist, says, "The psychologist can help by throwing things back at you. He can say, 'This is what you said; do you really mean it?' "

An executive may also want quite specific advice. The president of a company may ask, for example, how he can learn not to blow his stack every time he sits down with the financial vice president, who seems to think he is running the company. Or he may want the psychologist's views on who should be moved into an important new job, and how that job should be structured. Robert Keith, chairman and chief executive officer of Pillsbury, invariably consults Pillsbury's resident psychologist, Dr. Seymour Levy, on matters of this kind. Levy, forty-six, whose title is manager of personnel research and manpower development, has been with Pillsbury twelve years. "Sy Levy knows our people in depth," Keith says. "When a man has to be selected for a key job, he can be very instrumental. We had a job to fill not long ago, and there wasn't a soul except Sy that I could talk to about it. I said, 'Here are the candidates that I see. Write me a memorandum discussing them.' And he wrote just a terrific memorandum. In fact, his recommendation carried the day."

Occasionally a psychologist will be called on to mediate a quarrel among the principal officers of a client company. The controller of a family-owned firm recently recalled the services rendered by a psychologist—who will be identified here as Pete—at a time when the company's founder was reluctantly turning over the management to his son: "The old man was always slamming down the ash trays and breaking them, and the son was screaming at the father. One or the other was always rushing out of the room and swearing he was never coming back. Pete was terribly helpful, because both of them respected his judgment. They would call him up all the time. Sometimes it was just to sound off. But often they got specific counseling—though Pete would never use that word with them. Actually, someone like the old man, someone who has had the drive and determination to take $20 and run it up into a $20-million business, won't respect a man who just lends an ear. The psychologist must feed back, he must interpret."

An executive may demand repeated assurances that he is doing well. The psychologist, for his part, may feel impelled to lay on the assurances with a trowel. This sort of handholding may be illustrated by a recent telephone conversation between the president of a fair-sized New England industrial conglomerate, and the company's New York consultant. Not long before, at the suggestion of the consultant, the president had turned over some of his responsibilities, including planning, to a younger man named Harry. During the conversation the president complained that he was having a hard time holding himself in check at the weekly planning meetings that Harry had instituted. The consultant, who visits the company's headquarters regularly to talk with its top executives, said, "Why, I understand you've been marvelous at these meetings, Steve. The reports I get are that you just sit back, looking benign, and then maybe when there's been a lot of talk about how everything at the company has to be changed, you'll rear up and say, 'Goddam it, things weren't all *that* bad in the past.' That makes sense. After all, you're a gatekeeper of the past, at the same time you're letting the future in. For my money, you're handling things well." A few minutes later the president said he just couldn't understand why Harry and the other vice presidents wasted so much time holding meetings. "It's like a children's game," the consultant said soothingly. "Until they get a sense of their power, they keep running to meetings to massage their egos."

Why Does Jim Think Paul Is Too Secretive?
Some of the work that management psychologists do is hard to distinguish from the work of the specialist in organization development—OD, as it is commonly known—who is retained to introduce into a company the ideas and techniques of participative management. In general, the OD specialist, who sees his job as changing organizations, not people, is concerned with group processes rather than individual behavior. But a management psychologist, too, may spend a fair amount of time working with groups.

Usually his aim is to help the members of a management team—the head of a division, say, and the people who report to him—work more effectively together. Sometimes, as in a T-Group, members will be encouraged to talk about how they see, and are seen by, one another. David Thompson of Medina & Thompson, for instance, often begins a session by speaking about the value of criticism when it is given properly. He will call for a volunteer, and ask everyone else to write down what he thinks are the volunteer's chief assets and liabilities in his job. Thompson may then start the discussion by saying, "Jim says that Paul is too secretive. How do you feel about this, Paul?" Thompson believes this sort of exercise helps Paul learn to accept criticism, and helps his associates learn to offer it more freely. The psychologist's main task, as he sees it, is to rephrase criticism so as to avoid arousing angry defenses.

A management psychologist, like an OD specialist, will sometimes pay more attention to the process of decision making in a group than with individual managerial styles. At one large conglomerate, for example, groups of ten or twelve managers regularly go off together, with two consultants in attendance, to spend a week working intensively on some major problem confronting them. At the same time, they work on the *way* they are working on the problem. Their sessions are recorded on videotape, and from time to time the tape is played back so that they can see what they are doing right, and what they are doing wrong. At Pillsbury the managers of each division get together every year or so specifically to take a look at how well (or badly) they are working together. Seymour Levy is present at these meetings to act, in his words, as "a kind of kibitzer, a kind of a consultant, a kind of a resource, a kind of a conscience, a stimulus, a perspective provider, a commentator on some situations that I may see happening that aren't being touched on."

The Shadowy Image Behind the Boss

The warmth with which so many businessmen have embraced the management psychologist has both its comic and its depressing aspects. The mind boggles, for example, at the thought of the executive committee of Standard Oil (New Jersey) going through the "Jim says Paul is too secretive" exercise. Moreover, as already suggested, many companies are making improper use of psychological evaluations, and others have become foolishly intoxicated with psychology. Alan Marsh, a management consultant in Cambridge, Massachusetts, cites as a case in point a company where he had been formerly employed as vice president for personnel. "Some of the psychologists were kind of pushy," he says. "They weren't formally making decisions, yet they *were* in a way. Another danger when managers become dependent on the psychologist is that they become sort of psychologically oriented themselves. I had some horrific cases of managers asking psychologically slanted questions like, you know, 'Why did you hate your father?' " Marsh also felt there was too much psychological counseling. "In nine cases out of ten," he says, "if a man has a problem that's not a deep psychological one, he should be able to sort it out with his boss. At this company if there was anything that smacked at all of anything difficult, they brought the psychologist in. It was crazy. It made the psychologist into a sort of shadowy image behind the boss."

It is nevertheless plain that the managers of a company may benefit by having access to a knowledgeable confidant who stands a little apart from the life of the organization, and who can therefore analyze and comment on its strains and conflicts with a certain detachment. The trouble is that the observer and analyst, if he is to do more good than harm, must be discreet, totally honest, and heavily armored against the temptation to engage in manipulation and intrigue. The mere possession of a Ph.D. in psychology is obviously no guarantee that a man will meet these requirements, and the executive who thinks that he and his company need a management psychologist should choose one with great care.

It goes without saying that there are no infallible tests for intellectual and emotional integrity. But one useful indicator is a seemly modesty—a humility on the part of the psychologist about what he *doesn't* know. For there are no miracle cures for interpersonal conflict, alienation, fear of speaking out, autocratic rigidity, and other ills to which organizations are prone. And any psychologist who suggests otherwise is either a knave or a fool.

BEFORE UNDERTAKING the study of individuals and organizations in detail, let us examine the evolution of research that has shaped current thinking about the way organizations carry on their activities. We will not present a complete picture of research activity in management but rather will select a series of studies by organizational researchers that provide the foundation for current thought. These studies were conducted both in the United States and the United Kingdom over a period of approximately twenty-five years.

James C. Worthy:
Sears Roebuck Studies

James C. Worthy has presented a series of findings based on research conducted within Sears Roebuck and Company.[1] During a twelve-year period Worthy studied employee attitudes and morale in surveys covering over 100,000 employees. These employees worked in several hundred different company units both in Sears Roebuck and in other organizations. The survey at Sears was primarily a device used to assist local executives in doing a better job of handling problems within the organization. Analyzing the results, however, Worthy was able to formulate a series of hypotheses regarding the nature of certain organizational problems.

According to Worthy, "The overcomplexity of organizational structure is one of the most important and fundamental causes of poor management-employee relationships in our modern economic system, and until that problem is faced and corrected no substantial improvement in those relationships is likely to be possible. Worthy goes on to state: "One has the feeling of division of labor having gone wild, far beyond any degree necessary for efficient production."[2] Worthy's evidence suggests that where jobs are broken down too finely there is likely to be low output and low morale. Conversely, the most sustained efforts are exerted by those groups of employees who perform the more complex sets of tasks (e.g., salespeople, supervisors, mechanics), and these employees likewise exhibit the highest level of morale. Worthy notes that the trend toward overspecialization is not limited to individual jobs but has also found its way into the overspecialization of the functions of entire departments and subdepartments within organizations. This results in expansion of the administrative unit in the organization and an almost complete destruction of the meaning of the job for the employee. In addition, the overspecialization requires closer and more constant supervision with a greater need for coordination between different units within the organization. Worthy finds that "much of industry's present vast scale of operation is required not so much by economic or technical factors as by an unhappy and unnecessary principle of organization."[2] To achieve the necessary degree of coordination and cooperation between administratively separated functions, management is thus forced not only to build up an elaborate hierarchy of many supervisory levels but also to institute a wide variety of formal controls. These controls may also result in organizational conflict as individual supervisors seek to make a good showing against a specific set of rules, possibly at the expense of other departments within the organization.

Worthy makes the point that the overcomplex, overspecialized organization structure is likely to require the type of leader who drives others; the over-use of pressure as a tool of supervision is thus related primarily to the nature of the structure and only secondarily to the character of the individual at the head of it.

In comparing various organizational structures, Worthy found that in the more elaborate and complex organizations the individual supervisor is more likely to be subjected to constant control and direction and has less opportunity to develop initiative and self-reliance. On the other hand, in organizations characterized by management decentralization, more emphasis is usually placed upon the development of personal initiative. And since there is a lack of detailed supervision and formal controls, executives who function in these more decentralized organizations are more likely to be judged on their ability to get results.

Worthy concludes that the trend toward increasing size of the administrative unit and the trend toward increasing complexity of organizational structure are major contributors to the progresssive deterioration of management-employee relations. His suggestion is that flatter, less complex structures, with a maximum of administrative decentralization, tend to create a potential for improved attitudes, more effective supervision, and greater individual responsibility and initiative among employees.

For Worthy, then, overspecialization is the single most important factor leading to poor management-employee relations because:

1. It destroys the nature of the job by eliminating satisfaction.
2. It requires more coordination and layers of management.
3. It requires a "driver" leader who uses pressure to achieve work standards.

Burns and Stalker

In a study reported in 1961, Tom Burns and G. M. Stalker conducted extensive interviews of key organizational members within twenty industrial firms in the United Kingdom.[3] The firms were involved in a wide variety of activities including electronics, rayon manufacture, and engineering. The purpose of the study was to examine how the pattern of management practice in these companies was related to various elements in the external environment. Specifically, the authors focused on the rates of change in scientific technique and markets in the industries studied.

During the course of their study the authors began to recognize the emergence of two entirely distinct management approaches. They concluded that the particular approach utilized was a function of the stability of the environment in which the firm was functioning. According to the authors, environments characterized by rapid change in technology and market condition required one set of managerial practices, whereas environments remaining relatively stable will bring about another approach to management within the firm.

In the rayon manufacturing plant, which was characterized by having long production runs and an extremely stable environment, management tended to follow classical principles and procedures. Jobs were tightly defined and work was carried on in specialized, independent units. Interaction was primarily vertical, between superior and subordinate, with information flowing upward and with decisions made at the higher levels and then filtering down to subordinates. Coordination of effort took place according to classical hierarchical structure, with each individual responsible for those directly below him. This type of management organization was labeled by Burns and Stalker "mechanistic." According to the authors, a "mechanistic" approach was appropriate for those firms which operated in a relatively stable environment with respect to technology and market conditions.

At the other extreme, Burns and Stalker examined an electronics development firm characterized by rapid changes in environment, particularly with respect to technological advances. In these conditions the authors found a totally different approach to management practice. Jobs were rather free-flowing, with individuals interacting according to the nature of the problem rather than in terms of the organizational hierarchy. Communication flowed in all directions; each individual was more concerned with giving and receiving input in problem solving than with position within the hierarchy. Far less emphasis was placed upon classical principles and greater concern was given to the organization's ability to react quickly to new conditions and situations. This type of management, which Burns and Stalker referred to as "organic," they found appropriate in the more unstable and changing environmental situations.

As a result of their study, Burns and Stalker defined some characteristics of "mechanistic" and "organic" management. These include:

Mechanistic Management

1. Use of the formal hierarchy for coordination
2. Hierarchical structure of control, authority, and communication
3. High level of specialization with jobs highly defined and not necessarily related to the organization as a whole
4. Well-defined job descriptions in terms of rights, obligations, and technical methods to be associated with each position
5. High value placed on individual loyalty to the organization
6. Tendency for information to flow upward to superiors and decisions to flow downward to subordinates (vertical interaction).

Organic Management

1. Less well defined job descriptions, with greater interaction among individuals concerned primarily with problem solving
2. Jobs more clearly related to the needs and goals of the organization as a whole
3. A network structure of control, authority, and communication, with information flowing in all directions
4. Decisions more likely to be made based on expertise than on organizational position
5. An orientation toward the utilization of organizational skills wherever they were found to implement the problem-solving process.

Richard H. Hall

Richard H. Hall conducted a study of ten organizations to determine if the nature of the activities performed in a given department would have an impact on the structure of that department.[4] Hall was interested also in whether variations in structure at different levels in the organizational hierarchy would have an effect on the overall structure of the organization.

Specifically, Hall hypothesized as follows. First,

> Organizational divisions or departments that specialize in
> tasks that are not uniform or are difficult to routinize will be
> significantly less bureaucratic in all dimensions than those
> departments specializing in more uniform or routinized tasks.

Second,

> Those hierarchical levels (typically the executive levels) whose
> tasks are less uniform and routinizable will be significantly
> less bureaucratic in all dimensions than the hierarchical levels
> (typically the non-executive) in which tasks are uniform and
> easily routinized.[5]

In measuring the degree of bureaucracy in a given department or
organization Hall made use of six bureaucratic dimensions previously defined by Max Weber:

1. A well-defined hierarchy of authority
2. A division of labor based upon functional specialization
3. A system of rules covering the rights and duties of positional
   incumbents
4. A system of procedures for dealing with work situations
5. Impersonality of interpersonal relationships
6. Selection for employment and promotions based upon technical
   competence.[6]

In order to measure these variables Hall developed a questionnaire containing a series of statements relating to each dimension.
The measurement technique used was designed to reflect the participants' own perception of their organization. The six scales were
then administered to a random sample of personnel from the ten
organizations (five of which were profit-making and five governmental organizations).

Hall tested his first hypothesis by classifying the departments in
each of the ten organizations into those having uniform (traditional)
tasks and nonuniform (nontraditional) tasks. In this way a total of
sixteen departments were analyzed. Hall's results indicated that on
three dimensions—*hierarchy of authority, division of labor,* and
specified procedures—nonroutine departments were perceived as
being significantly less bureaucratic. No significant differences were
found in the other bureaucratic dimensions.

In testing his second hypothesis, Hall first classified the respondents into executive and nonexecutive categories. This classification

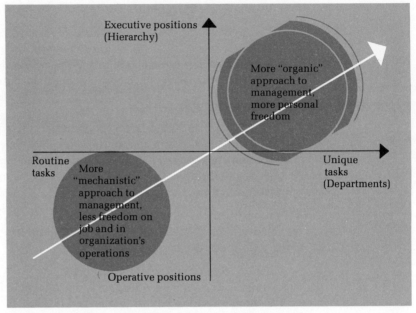

Figure 5.1. *Relation between Nature of Tasks and Bureaucratic Behavior*

was based upon the respondents' own listing of their hierarchical position. The executives from all ten organizations were then combined into one category and the nonexecutives into another. Hall's second hypothesis was substantiated in four of the six dimensions; the executives functioned in less bureaucratic fashion when less emphasis was placed upon the *organizational hierarchy,* the *division of labor, formal procedures,* and *impersonality of relationships.*

Joan Woodward

Joan Woodward and her research associates carried on a study of approximately 100 firms in the area of South Essex, England.[7] The firms ranged in size from 100 to 8,000 employees and were involved in a wide variety of business activities. Each research team collected data by means of interview, observation, and analysis of company records. The researchers were interested in the following information about each firm:

1. Its history, background, and corporate objectives
2. Manufacturing process and methods used
3. Organizational structure and operating procedures
4. Cost data giving indication of overall profitability
5. Type of labor structure.

Preliminary analysis of the data indicated wide fluctuations in such characteristics as number of managerial levels and spans of control. The researchers were interested in learning the causes for some of these variations. Their first approach in analyzing the firms was to group them by level of profitability. The initial results here, however, indicated that few organizational similarities could be found among those firms classified as above average in success. Likewise, there were few similarities among firms classified as below average.

At this point the researchers sought a new basis for classifying the firms. The method adopted was based on the complexity of technology used within each firm, which resulted in classification into three types along a scale of technological complexity:

1. Unit and small batch production
2. Large batch and mass production
3. Long-run process production (for liquids, gases, and chemicals, etc.).

With this classification the researchers found a significant relationship between organizational structure and success for each level of technological complexity. Common organizational elements were found among successful unit and small batch production firms. Successful mass production firms had characteristics in common, also, and so did long-run process production firms. The researchers noted that successful firms in both unit and small batch production and long-run process production exhibited organizational similarities. These characteristics closely approximated those of the "organic" organizational structure described by Burns and Stalker: (1) less emphasis on clearly defined duties and responsibilities; (2) more permissive management; (3) higher level of delegation of authority; (4) more flexible organization; and (5) more emphasis on verbal than written communication.

Woodward found that in the mass production and large batch operations, successful firms displayed—again in the terminology of Burns and Stalker—a more "mechanistic" approach to organization. They followed more closely the classical principles of organization with respect to such points as definition of duties, span of control, definition of line and staff, and unity of command. It was, however, *only within this midrange of technology (large batch and mass production) that these classical principles appeared to be correlated with success.* As we have mentioned, in both the unit and small batch production and the long-run process production, successful organizations were characterized by a more organic structure.

In interpreting the results of the study, Woodward examined the need for coordination and integration of basic functions in each of the three types of technological operations. She found that in the unit and small batch production firms there was a critical need for direct and rapid communication at all levels of the hierarchy. This need was less significant in the mass production firms; here, the product output was less dependent on a close working relationship between

Figure 5.2. *Management Responses to Technological Complexity*

Technological complexity

Successful firms (organic)	Successful firms (mechanistic)
• less emphasis on written definition of duties	• greater definition of duties and responsibilities
• more permissive management	• more rigid management
• greater delegation of authority	• less delegation of authority
• more flexible organization	• more emphasis on written communication
Unit and small batch	Large batch
Long-run production process	Mass production

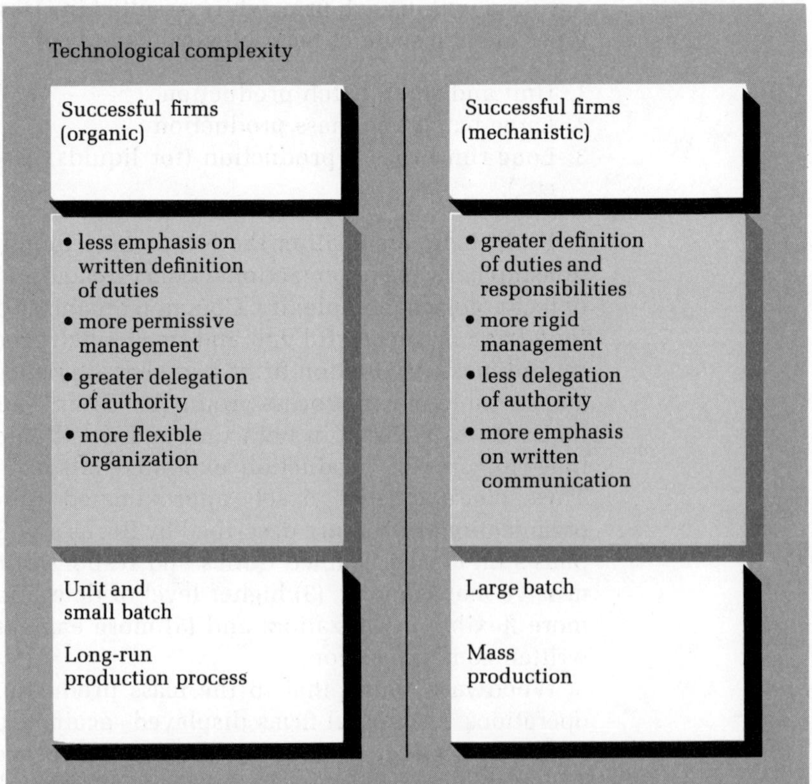

major business functions. She concluded that the type of operation at both the unit and small batch firms and the long-run process firms made rigid organization unfeasible, whereas the mass production type of organization could accommodate it.

Woodward states that the requirements of the situation are more rigid at the two extremes of technological complexity and thus allow for fewer alternative modes of organization. In addition, an inappropriate choice of structures at either of these two extremes leads more quickly to a reduction in success. Woodward suggests that classical principles of organization may be applied successfully only within a fairly limited range of technology (large batch and mass production). Outside of this range, the type of technology involved may well require a different approach to management and organization.

Lawrence and Lorsch

P. R. Lawrence and J. W. Lorsch, recognizing the inadequacy of existing organizational theory, attempted in a study conducted in 1967 to understand what kind of organization it takes to deal with various economic and market conditions.[8] Lawrence and Lorsch asserted that much of the confusion and conflict in existing theory resulted from the fact that researchers usually focused on only one small segment of a given organization and were often limited to a particular industry. The authors believed that this piecemeal approach interfered with the development of a unified theory. Their response was to investigate the *differentiation* and *integration* in organizational systems.

Differentiation within an organization is the existence of differing orientations, points of view, and interests that develop among members of the organization according to the specific task in which they are involved. According to Lawrence and Lorsch differentiation is "the difference in cognitive and emotional orientation among managers in different functional departments."[9] To gain insight into the exact nature of this differentiation they focused on three variables: (1) differences in goal orientation among managers; (2) differences in time orientation; and (3) interpersonal orientation.

Integration, on the other hand, is the function of developing a state of collaboration such that differing orientations can be overcome and a unified effort be devoted to attaining organizational goals. In the view of the authors, this process of integration does not come about automatically through the management hierarchy.

Rather, each organization must develop its own technique and mechanisms for achieving integration of organizational effort.

Lawrence and Lorsch hypothesized that the environment in which the firm functions will be significant in influencing the nature of the differentiation and the corresponding methods of integration. They focus on two major characteristics of the environment: (1) rate of technological change in products and processes and (2) degree to which dominant demands seem to come from different sectors of the environment (that is, the impact of the market place versus the impact of technical or scientific problems). Utilizing these criteria the authors selected for study firms in the plastics, food, and container industries that exhibited differing degrees of success.

The researchers proposed that as the environment of the firm became subject to greater degrees of change—in factors such as technology and market—the firm would exhibit greater degrees of differentiation among its employees and would require more formalized integration policies and procedures. To supply data, between 30 and 50 middle- and upper-level managers in each organization were interviewed and given questionnaires.

The authors found that with respect to the impact of the environment, the dominant issue in the plastics industry was the ability to innovate; this was true in the food industry also, but to a lesser extent. In the container industry, the dominant issue was the ability to provide customer service.

The goal orientation of managers in each industry correlated closely with their functional area of specialization: manufacturing was oriented toward efficiency and cost reduction, engineering toward scientific issues, and marketing toward competition and the marketplace. In general it was found that the degree of differentiation in goal, time, and interpersonal relations was consistent with the hypothesis that uncertainty of environment would be correlated with greater differentiation. Specifically, Lawrence and Lorsch found that in the high-performing container organization, managers in sales, production, and research shared ways of thinking, and their departments tended to follow similar organizational practices. In contrast, functional managers in the high-performing plastics organizations were quite different in their ways of thinking, and their units were structured to fit the differences in their tasks. Lawrence and Lorsch concluded that high-performing organizations would be differentiated according to the demands of their environment.

With respect to the method of integration for the highly successful firms in each of the three industries, the more highly differentiated plastics industry made use of a formal integrating department, the less differentiated food industry utilized individual integrators, and the least differentiated container industry made use of direct management contact.

In summary, the authors found that the state of differentiation in the effective organizations was consistent with the degree of diversity of the parts of the environment, while the state of integration achieved was consistent with the environmental demand for interdependence.

Organizational Research and Contingency Theory

Based on research studies like the ones just described, a new concept in designing and understanding effective organizations has emerged. The concept is that it may not be appropriate to design all organizations to function in exactly the same way. The idea that organizational principles can be applied to all organizations has given way to the recognition that each organization must fit its internal characteristics and structures to the demands of its market and technological environment. What may be effective for one organization in one environment may not be appropriate for another functioning under a different set of market and technological conditions.

This conclusion leads us to assess organizational effectiveness by how well the organization and its management deal with the environment in which they function. In particular, specific questions of authority, decision making, communication, and job definition within the organization must be evaluated in terms of their effectiveness in meeting organizational needs. The research results indicate that factors such as stability of environment, market conditions, and technology influence the effectiveness of particular organizational designs and operations. The key to effectiveness thus becomes a function of matching organizational characteristics and structures with the demands of the overall environment.

We may formulate a model that provides guidelines for aiding a manager in matching organizational characteristics with a given environment. The research results in this chapter indicate that the arrow contained in Figure 5.3 on page 116 should move upward to the right. That is, as the environment in which an organization must function becomes *less stable,* the overall operating characteristics of that organization would tend to become *more organic* (and less mechanistic) in nature. In industries with unstable environments, such as electronics and plastics, the organization must adopt a less rigid and more free flowing operating posture. In the more stable envi-

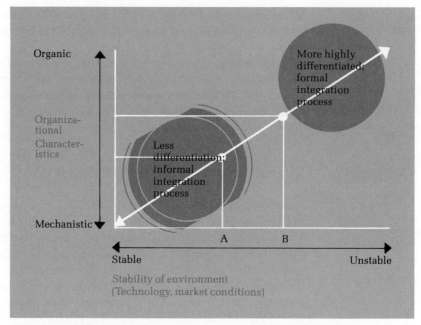

Figure 5.3. *Influence of Environment on Organizational Characteristics*

ronment of rayon manufacturing or the containers industry, the effective organization will be more rigid and well defined in its overall operating characteristics.

No organization will function in a totally stable or unstable environment. The relationship between the stability of environment and organizational characteristics will thus represent a continuum; each situation is unique and requires a slightly different set of organizational characteristics for greatest effectiveness. For example, point A on the graph in Figure 5.3 would require a slightly different set of organizational characteristics than would point B.

A question yet to be answered is the *exact* relationship that exists between a specific set of environmental variables and the most appropriate set of organizational characteristics. Additional research is necessary to determine an accurate scale for both the organizational characteristics and the stability of environment axes in Figure 5.3 as well as to determine the slope of the curve that relates these two variables. If indeed such a determination is eventually achieved, it would provide managers with a set of guidelines with which to form the most effective type of organization for a given set of environmental conditions.

Discussion Questions

1. James Worthy stated that overspecialization is the single most important cause of poor management-employee relations. Discuss this comment in light of your knowledge of scientific management as defined by Taylor.
2. Using the words of Burns and Stalker, Woodward, and others discussed in this chapter as a starting point, where do you see the need for additional research for new insight in the field of management?
3. How would you relate the findings of Burns and Stalker, and others discussed, to the statement, "Once an individual has gained management experience in one industry he may apply this experience to management positions in any industry"?
4. Select industries in which you feel either mechanistic or organic managerial and organizational approaches would be appropriate. Explain your selections.
5. What changes in attitudes toward the practice of management have come about as a result of the work of Burns and Stalker, Woodward, and Lawrence and Lorsch?
6. If "mechanistic" organizations are indeed more likely to bring about high levels of employee frustration, and if these same organizations appear to be the most effective ones in the mass production industries, what might be the future of mass production industries with respect to their ability to attract and hold qualified personnel? What changes, if any, do you see taking place in mass production industries that might make them more satisfying work environments?

Selected References

Burns, Thomas and Stalker, G. M. *The Management of Innovation*. London: Tavistock Publications, 1961.

Hall, R. H. "Intraorganizational Structural Variation: Application of the Bureaucratic Model." In *Administrative Science Quarterly* 7 (December 1962).

Lawrence, P. R. and Lorsch, J. W. *Organization and Environment: Managing Differentiation and Integration*. Homewood, Ill.: Richard D. Irwin, 1969.

Woodward, Joan. *Industrial Organization: Theory and Practice*. London: Oxford University Press, 1965.

Worthy, James C. "Organizational Structure and Employee Morale." In *American Sociological Review* 15 (1950).

A Model of Human Behavior in the Work Environment

6

Worker Unrest: Not Dead, but Playing Possum

by John Hoerr

For the first time in their lives, workers who grew up in the 1950s and 1960s—a generation noted for rebelliousness on the job—have now tasted the bitterness of a prolonged economic slump. A new concern for job security has tamed their restiveness, but underlying generational conflicts remain. Employers and unions must still learn to cope with the markedly different social values of the post-World War II generation.

Unlike workers who grew up in the Depression era, workers of the 1960s were reared in a time of rising prosperity, and their attitudes were formed by the vast social changes of the 1960s. Pouring into the work force in the late 1960s, they demanded new freedoms on the job, scorned authoritarian bosses, clashed with older workers, and generally befuddled management and union officials alike.

But the recession has hit hardest at young workers, who lack seniority, and each year's new crop of high school graduates must compete in a job market where teen-age unemployment remains close to 20%. This has produced a significant change in attitudes.

Blessed Recession

Joseph F. Hegeriche, vice-president of employee relations at Jim Walter Corp., a major building materials producer, feels that the recession "could be a blessing in disguise." Today's young worker "has the real world made more quickly apparent to

Reprinted from the May 10, 1976 issue of *Business Week* by special permission. Copyright © 1976 by McGraw-Hill Publishing, Inc., New York, N.Y. 10020. All rights reserved.

him," Hegeriche says. "I think young people in the next few years will take a different attitude in terms of appreciating the job they have."

"In a large measure," says William P. Drake, president and chairman of Pennwalt Corp. in Philadelphia, "young workers have gotten the '60s out of their system, and they've got their feet on the ground more than the teenagers of a few years ago." Bracy D. Smith, vice-president and comptroller of U.S. Steel Corp., says: "I've been quite surprised at these people vs. those from '68-'69. These people are anxious to get to work."

The personnel director of another major steel company agrees that the inability of dissatisfied workers to change jobs has forced "a slight change" in young workers' attitudes. But he stresses that young workers still assert their independence. "They don't stand there and salute you and say, 'Yes, sir' and 'No, sir.' But if they don't like a job, they're more apt to stay and try to change the situation."

Testing Values

Some authorities on workers' behavior believe that the new stress on job security is only a temporary diversion from the main thrust of the young workers' revolt. The major social and political upheavals of the 1960s—involving civil rights, antiwar protests, women's liberation, and the environment—imbued the postwar generation with cultural values far different from those of the older generations. These values are not reversible. When the job security issue begins to fade as the economy recovers, employers and unions will be confronted once again by demands for more rapid change in the workplace.

Essentially, the young workers want more satisfying jobs, greater participation in decisions affecting their working lives, and an end to authoritarianism. "The society is changing faster than our institutions," says Jerome M. Rosow, a former Labor Dept. official now on leave from Exxon Corp. to head the newly established Work in America Institute Inc. "Unfortunately," he adds, "the workplace has been relatively immutable to these changes. What these young people are saying is that their expectations have gone up, and the response hasn't."

Within a few years the postwar generation will make up a majority of the nation's work force. The pressures for change then may become overwhelming unless corporations and unions find ways to make work more meaningful and rewarding. Research by psychologists Daniel Yankelovich and Raymond A. Katzell has shown that most managers and union leaders believe that, for all the exaggeration of the "assembly line blues," worker dissatisfaction is a reality and that the quality of working life must be improved. They say this can be done with increased productivity, although no single technique will work in all industries.

Absentee Rate

Some employers contend that young workers lack the traditional American work ethic. "Young people don't have the desire to work as hard as their parents," says Henry J. Nave, chairman of Mack Trucks Inc. "The desire to excel just isn't there." William A. Kistler, executive vice-president of Hughes Tool Co. in Houston, adds: "The main problem we have with younger employees is that they have never been trained to work for a living, never had to be at a job every day on time." Kistler complains that the absentee rate for young workers at Hughes averages 14%, vs. only 1% for older workers.

The debate over the supposed decline in the work ethic has been going on for well over a century; each generation claims to see poor work habits in the succeeding

generation. Yankelovich, the social research pollster, has found, however, that the desire to do a good job is "a deeply rooted need" and still very much a part of the work ethic. What has changed, he writes, is that younger workers, in particular, place self-fulfillment—usually in pursuits outside of work—above the striving for material success that motivated older workers. Work for the sake of work holds little value for younger workers if the job is not satisfying.

Given the rapidly rising levels of education, meaningful jobs do not exist in large enough quantities. In 1974 nearly 70% of the work force had completed high school, compared with 43% in 1952. Although workers are becoming more competent, by education, the lack of psychological rewards in work is driving them to seek gratification in a "leisure ethic." In addition, wider travel and long exposure to television have made young workers at all levels—college and noncollege—more familiar with society and its problems. By training, younger workers tend to question their bosses, and this often leads to a generational conflict.

The Question

"Our young people are always asking 'why,'" says a steel executive. "Kids have always asked 'why,' but today they're asking it for a much longer time. If an older supervisor asks a guy to do something, he asks 'why.' Then the boss blows up. It's very difficult for him to handle the 'why' because he's never had to do it before."

Younger workers are also generally more militant about health and safety problems than older employees, and the already high cost of protective measures will rise as more and more of today's teen-agers get jobs. "I'm convinced the young people coming into the labor market are going to want OSHA-plus." says Fred W. Garry, chairman of Rohr Industries in Chula Vista, Cal. "Once our hiring curve starts up again, we're going to have to contend with higher expectations in the work force. Young factory workers will no longer stand for decrepit conditions."

Finally, the relative success of the U.S. economic system has created what Yankelovich calls "the spreading psychology of entitlement." The elevation of living standards, particularly in the 40 years since the rise of industrial unionism, has led young workers to believe that they are entitled to benefits such as a secure retirement, a meaningful job, and health care coverage as a matter of "social right." Union and corporation leaders may fulminate against this belief, but they are not likely to reverse it.

A split within the postwar generation itself also may create dangerous strains for the future. While college graduates have generally been successful in finding challenging work (even members of the "radical generation" of the late 1960s have "turned on" to management jobs, with relish) noncollege youth are being turned off by work. One reason is that although a large minority of workers typically express interest in having more opportunity to use their skills and abilities, jobs are not being upgraded fast enough. This remains a high-priority task if labor-management relations are to become less contentious.

IN RECENT YEARS much attention has been given to improving management's understanding of the *individual* within the organization. Thought and research have been devoted to analysis of the types of leader behavior and organization structures that are most conducive to effective motivation of the work force. In this section a simple model (Figure 6.4, pages 130–131) is put forth to describe and integrate some of the fundamental concepts of individual behavior within the organization. The purpose of this model is to provide the manager with the background necessary to develop and implement programs designed to obtain a high level of motivation from his labor force.[1] To illustrate the model, concepts have been drawn from the writings of three of the major contributors to the *behavioral school* of management thought. Our purpose is to integrate early behavioral theories into a framework that will illuminate how large-scale organizations may affect individuals within them. Admittedly, the model oversimplifies, but it does suggest a way of thinking about the interaction of the individual with the work organization.

Theory X and Theory Y

In *The Human Side of Enterprise*, Douglas McGregor put forth the notion that there are two basic philosophies or ways of viewing human behavior, referring to these as Theory X and Theory Y.[2] The underlying assumption of these two philosophies is that each individual has basic beliefs and expectations about what people are "really like" and how they are likely to behave in any given situation. These beliefs and expectations, in general, have to do with such qualities as the basic honesty of individuals, the extent to which individuals will seek responsibility and initiative, and their willingness to work. The *Theory X* philosophy holds that people have an inherent dislike for work, that they need to be coerced and controlled, and that they will avoid responsibility whenever they can. If a particular individual felt that it was Theory X that accurately described fundamental human behavior, his belief would probably influence his behavior in interactions with others. Specifically, if he or she were a manager, his or her likely leadership style would be to maintain tight controls, close supervision, and strict discipline in order to keep individual members of the work group from avoiding their job responsibilities. Such managers would find it difficult to act on the presumption that workers can be self-motivated, efficient performers without the controls of authoritarian supervision.

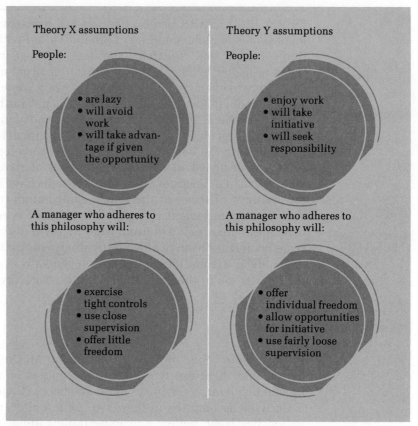

Figure 6.1. *McGregor's Theory X and Theory Y*

Theory Y, in contrast, states that work comes naturally to people, that they can exercise self-control, and that they can, under proper conditions, learn to seek responsibility. A manager holding this point of view would probably behave differently than did our Theory X manager. The Theory Y philosophy would most likely lead to an atmosphere of freedom with few controls and reasonably loose supervision. Admittedly, the Theory X-Theory Y dichotomy is too simplistic, for indeed most peoples' beliefs fall somewhere between Theory X and Theory Y attitudes; however, our general attitude or philosophy about people will tend to influence the way we relate to them and the overall atmosphere we create in our interactions with them.

Maslow's Need Hierarchy

We will leave Theory X and Theory Y for a moment in order to lay additional groundwork for understanding our behavioral model. That groundwork may be found in the writings of psychologist Abraham Maslow.

Maslow hypothesized that each individual has needs that he or she is constantly seeking to satisfy. An individual's behavior at any given time is motivated by a desire to satisfy a particular need, and the needs themselves form a hierarchy. The hierarchy is shown in Figure 6.2.[3] According to Maslow, the basic and most fundamental needs are those that relate to the common physiological characteristics of humankind, including hunger, thirst, and sex. Only after these needs have been satisfied to a certain extent is individual behavior concerned with the next highest need in the hierarchy, security. This process of expansion of needs continues through the social and ego needs until an individual seeks to achieve a state of self-actualization, that is, being or becoming all that she or he is capable of being—reaching full potential as a human being. The fact that the self-actualization need cannot be defined precisely is not terribly important; in reality, most behavior is generally directed toward lower-level needs.

In discussing an individual's attempt to achieve need satisfaction, Maslow makes the key point that a *satisfied need no longer motivates behavior; it is only a need a person is striving to satisfy that motivates a behavior pattern.* It would be easy at this point to become too simplistic and conclude that all a manager need do in order to motivate a subordinate is to determine what specific need that subordinate seeks to satisfy and then provide an opportunity for it to be satisfied in return for desired work performance. But although this approach might appear to be both desirable and effective, we must remember that individuals are individuals; there are virtually an infinite number of ways of satisfying even the same need. To illustrate: some members of the work organization may satisfy the "ego" need by earning more money, with which to acquire possessions our society has come to associate with success—an expensive home or car. For another individual, however, the ego need might be satisfied by increased power in the organization—a title, more subordinates, or more authority. As one moves upward in the hierarchy, toward the satisfaction of higher-level needs, the subtleties of human nature make it more and more difficult to isolate and identify how a given individual may seek satisfaction.

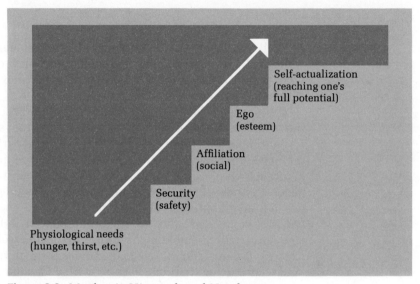

Figure 6.2. *Maslow's Hierarchy of Needs*

The Need Hierarchy and Workers Today

Perhaps the most important use of the need hierarchy concept is in helping management to understand the motivations of workers recently entering the work force. These young people were not exposed to the economic hardships of the Depression, and they may have only a vague recollection of World War II. Many matured during the boom period of the 1960s, and are associated with campus riots and protests of the late 1960s and early 70s. In attitude and philosophy, these workers seem to have as an almost implicit assumption that basic physiological and security needs can be taken almost for granted. It is virtually assumed that these needs will be satisfied. With this assumption, motivation turns toward seeking higher-level need satisfactions through the work environment.

In the past, business organizations have dealt with individuals oriented more toward lower-level needs. The business organization had a very effective method for satisfying these needs, namely, the paycheck. With their earnings, individuals could obtain food and shelter for themselves and their families. Even today, the paycheck is still of primary importance. However, as the worker begins to take the satisfaction of lower-level needs for granted, his wage is no longer entirely sufficient to motivate behavior. The worker is now looking to the organization for satisfactions relating to social needs, needs for esteem, and the self-actualizing goals of the individual. The key question is the extent to which today's organizations are capable of providing the worker with higher-level need satisfactions.

The Need Hierarchy and Individual Frustration

Let us look at the reactions of an individual whose attempts to satisfy a particular need have been unsuccessful. When a person is unable to satisfy a particular need, a state of *frustration* usually results. Frustration is a normal feeling; we all have experienced frustration at some point in our interactions with those around us. What is of concern is how an individual reacts to this state of frustration. Reaction patterns fall into two broad categories, which for lack of a better set of terms we will simply label *positive* and *negative*.

Positive reactions to frustration include behaviors directed toward removing or eliminating any obstacles preventing the individual from satisfying a particular need. For example, a highly qualified engineer who wishes to move into an administrative position but is unable to do so because she lacks certain business or managerial skills might become frustrated. A positive reaction to this frustration might lead the engineer to return to school or attend evening classes to acquire the needed skills. Another type of positive reaction, although one that is sometimes hard to accept, is the recognition that the goal the individual is seeking is beyond his or her capabilities. If this is the case, continued attempts to reach this goal, no matter how sincerely and strenuously attempted, will lead only to increased levels of frustration. It may be necessary to give up this particular objective or to modify goals so that the new goals are more realistic—have more likelihood of being attained. For instance, a student who wants to become an engineer and is more than willing to study very hard may find that he is just not mentally equipped to grasp the principles of engineering and mathematics and is therefore failing these subjects. Once such a student has exhausted all approaches to mastering the material, continued effort would not reduce his frustration level but would more likely only serve to increase it. A positive reaction might be to change goals and perhaps explore a career as a draftsman or technician, where the requirements might be more in line with the individual's capabilities.

Of more concern to management than the individuals who react positively to frustration are those who exhibit *negative* reactions. Negative reactions are likely to cause the organizational and managerial problems with which most managers must deal. Negative reactions include:

Aggression: exhibiting hostility or anger as a means of frustration release

Displacement: directing emotional feelings toward individuals or groups other than the principal source of the feelings (becoming angry with your children after your boss criticizes your performance)

Fantasy: allowing the mind to wander and daydream in order to escape from a frustrating situation

Rationalization: explaining undesired results by finding a less threatening "explanation" for them (after failing to receive a promotion stating that you did not really want the job)

Repression: blocking out of conscious thought feelings or experiences which are threatening to you

Withdrawal: removing yourself physically from the frustrating environment (absenteeism, chronic lateness).[4]

These are behavior patterns that can make an employee uncooperative and a poor performer. It is precisely this type of employee that management must try to motivate if the organization is to function effectively.

Personality Development: Chris Argyris

Chris Argyris, an organization theorist, added to our understanding of behavior.[5] Argyris draws on personality development theory as he describes a series of changes that take place as an individual grows from immaturity to maturity and adulthood. Some of these transformations are represented in Figure 6.3.

The figure indicates that as individuals grow and develop into mature adults their behavior patterns change in ways that create a more active and independent individual, one who requires a deeper and broader involvement in the activities in which he or she participates. The mature adult is a multifaceted entity capable of a wide variety of behavioral patterns who often seeks satisfactions that are complex. As such an individual moves toward the satisfaction of higher-level needs in Maslow's hierarchy, this complexity increases. What results is greater difficulty in understanding the nature of individual behavior.

Argyris focuses on the importance of considering immature and mature behavior patterns in understanding the impact of the organization on the individual. According to Argyris, if we examine the majority of modern organizations we find their structure to be influenced by certain principles or guidelines:

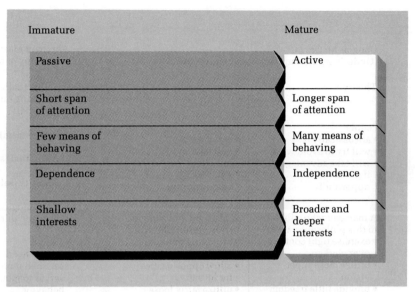

Immature	Mature
Passive	Active
Short span of attention	Longer span of attention
Few means of behaving	Many means of behaving
Dependence	Independence
Shallow interests	Broader and deeper interests

Figure 6.3. *Argyris's Concept of Personality Development*

1. The *division of labor,* with its need for specialization
2. The *scalar* and *functional* process, which defines authority relationships and specific functional responsibilities
3. The *structure* itself (organization chart), which defines each person's position in the organization
4. *Span of control* within the organization, which determines the number of subordinates who report to a given supervisor.

The very term *organization* implies formal structuring by a well-defined set of policies, procedures, rules, and regulations governing the behavior of individuals throughout the system.

Applying the Model to the Work Situation

When an individual is brought into an organization, he or she is usually placed in a particular department, given a specific job assignment, told with whom he or she will work (work group), to whom to report (supervisor), with whom to communicate (channels of communication), and how he or she will be evaluated (control procedures). Such a description may be an exaggeration for more

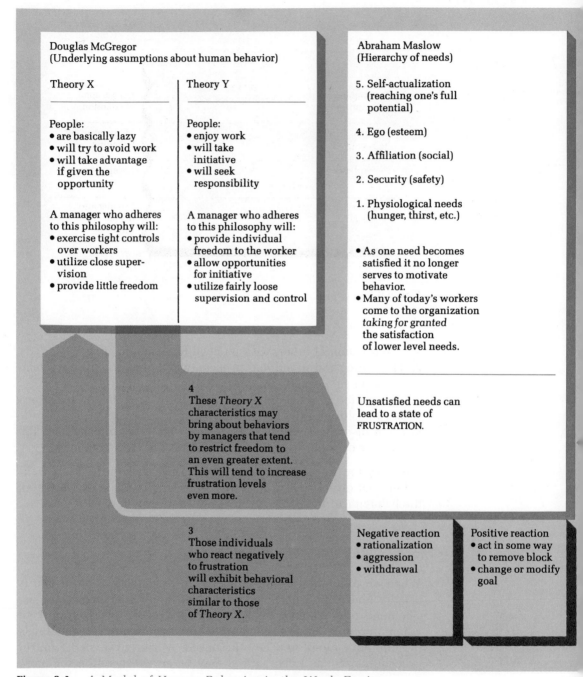

Douglas McGregor
(Underlying assumptions about human behavior)

Theory X	Theory Y
People:	People:
• are basically lazy	• enjoy work
• will try to avoid work	• will take initiative
• will take advantage if given the opportunity	• will seek responsibility
A manager who adheres to this philosophy will:	A manager who adheres to this philosophy will:
• exercise tight controls over workers	• provide individual freedom to the worker
• utilize close supervision	• allow opportunities for initiative
• provide little freedom	• utilize fairly loose supervision and control

Abraham Maslow
(Hierarchy of needs)

5. Self-actualization (reaching one's full potential)

4. Ego (esteem)

3. Affiliation (social)

2. Security (safety)

1. Physiological needs (hunger, thirst, etc.)

• As one need becomes satisfied it no longer serves to motivate behavior.
• Many of today's workers come to the organization *taking for granted* the satisfaction of lower level needs.

4
These *Theory X* characteristics may bring about behaviors by managers that tend to restrict freedom to an even greater extent. This will tend to increase frustration levels even more.

Unsatisfied needs can lead to a state of FRUSTRATION.

3
Those individuals who react negatively to frustration will exhibit behavioral characteristics similar to those of *Theory X.*

Negative reaction
• rationalization
• aggression
• withdrawal

Positive reaction
• act in some way to remove block
• change or modify goal

Figure 6.4. *A Model of Human Behavior in the Work Environment*

Chris Argyris
(Personality development)

Immature	Mature
Passive	Active
Few interests	Many interests
Short attention span	Long span of attention
Few means of behaving	Many means of behaving

2
This will tend to prevent the individual from achieving higher level need satisfactions and thus increase levels of frustration.

1
Because of the way they are structured, many of today's organizations appeal to the *immature* side of the individual's personality.

Today's Organization

- structure (span of control, well defined hierarchy, division of labor)
- specific communication channels
- authority, responsibility relationships.

progressive organizations, but the "bureaucratic" foundations of many businesses may appeal more to the *immature* rather than the *mature* side of the personality.

When business organizations could rely upon the paycheck to motivate individuals, rigid structure was less of a problem. Today, however, most entering workers are looking beyond the paycheck and evaluating the organization's ability to satisfy high-level needs. We recall our discussion of Maslow: a satisfied need no longer is a motivator of behavior. Today's organizations, if they are to attract and motivate effective employees, must find ways to satisfy higher-level needs.

It seems at least unlikely that the highly bureaucratic organization would provide opportunity for workers to satisfy higher-level needs, and we would expect to find large numbers of frustrated employees in such a work environment. Indeed, the potentially frustrating work environment is clearly exemplified in the automobile assembly lines of Detroit.

Here needs of the worker and the requirements of the job may come into greatest conflict. Short cycle times, highly repetitive work, and little, if any, variety in the job cycle often create significant levels of frustration. The problem has been compounded in recent years as more highly educated workers enter into this job environment. The result is often some form of frustration release behavior in which the worker seeks to "strike out" at some part of this environment. Assembly-line workers have been found, for example, to be welding screwdrivers into the fenders of cars to give the motorist an eternal, unlocatable rattle.[6] The same report told of a sign that appeared near one of the assembly plants that read, "I spend 40 hours a week here, am I supposed to work too!"[7] Cases like these can be understood in the light of our discussion of frustration.

Frustration is not confined to assembly lines, however. It may result *whenever* a need is not satisfied, and thus it may occur at any level of an organization when workers are unable to satisfy certain needs.

Let us take a closer look at the term *satisfaction,* which may be defined as the difference between a person's *expectations* and *perceptions* of, or about, a situation. Simply stated:

$$\text{Satisfaction} = \text{Expectations} - \text{Perceptions}$$

If expectations about a given situation are greater than perceptions, an individual will be likely to experience dissatisfaction, the degree of dissatisfaction being related to the extent of the difference between expectation and perceptions. To illustrate, suppose that two workers, each earning $25,000 a year, are both offered promotions to new jobs at a salary level of $35,000. Let us assume that worker A perceives that this new job will make many demands on her time and force her to change her life style; as a result, her expectations regarding an appropriate salary might be more like $45,000. Worker B, on the other hand, perceives the new job as not significantly different in terms of time commitment, and as a result he has a salary expectation of $30,000 a year. The same job offer at the same salary level ($35,000) would create two totally different levels of satisfaction for Worker A and Worker B, the difference being due to variations in perceptions and expectations on the part of the two individuals.

We can see that as individuals become better educated and more aware of the opportunities in the world around them, they tend to change their perceptions and expectations. These changes usually increase the overall expectation level of a worker, and it is this change that can lead to dissatisfaction and frustration even for individuals in important positions in an organization.

One point to emphasize is that for a manager to understand and deal with worker needs and frustrations, the manager must deal not with the situation as *he* perceives it, but rather from the point of view of the individual concerned. Managers are often guilty of making statements such as, "I don't understand Joe. He has a good job, a secure future, and yet he's not putting forth his best effort." What this manager is really saying is that according to *his own value system*, Joe has a good job with a secure future. This may not be Joe's perception of the situation.

Once again referring to our model on pages 130–131, if indeed many of today's work organizations do have a greater likelihood of bringing about high levels of frustration among employees and this in turn results in more examples of negative frustration behavior (as was mentioned on the Detroit assembly line) these same negative reactions closely approximate those behaviors associated with McGregor's *Theory* X. That is, under the *Theory* X philosophy, behavior such as aggression, withdrawal, uncooperativeness, etc., would be fairly typical individual behavior patterns. According to our model the managerial response brought about by such behavior patterns would likely be one of closer supervision, tighter controls, and strict discipline. This in turn would tend to reduce even further the ability of the individual employee to satisfy higher level needs within the work environment, thus increasing his frustration level and bringing about greater negative reactions, which in turn may lead to tighter controls, even closer supervision, etc. *Thus, it may be that the cycle tends to reinforce itself,* creating an overall environment in which the employee is not able to achieve higher level need satisfactions and consequently remains frustrated.

Professional employee need satisfaction presents management with a special challenge. There does appear to be, however, a growing recognition on the part of management that new approaches must be taken in order to attract and hold the highly qualified and extremely mobile professional employee. College recruiters as well as managers are finding that the questions being asked by potential employees deal more and more frequently with the relationship of the organization to its environment (social responsibility goals and/or programs) and with the relationship of the particular job to the total organization. Of less importance is the specific monetary compensation associated with the job.

A second comment sometimes made by management relates to the eventual impact of the reduced work week. Recognizing that the organization may be a source of individual frustration, management may look to the 32 hour work week as an opportunity to provide the employee with more time off the job to satisfy higher level needs. These needs might be satisfied through increasing employee involvement in such activities as local politics, sports programs, community organizations, etc. If indeed this increased involvement does take place the role of the organization would continue to be one of providing the opportunity to satisfy lower level needs by means of monetary compensation. This philosophy, if generally adopted, would appear to be something of a 'cop-out' on the part of management, in effect admitting that new and creative approaches could not be found that would provide an exciting and challenging work environment for today's employee.

It will be the purpose of the remainder of this text to examine both the individual and the organization to see what developments have taken place or may take place in the future that can serve to bring about a more satisfying and challenging work environment in the organization of the future.

Discussion Questions

1. The term "generation gap" has often been used to describe the inability of one generation to communicate with another. Discuss the generation gap in light of Maslow's need hierarchy.

2. Discuss some of the changes that have taken place in our society that have brought about a new attitude on the part of the worker.

3. In order to understand the relationship of

a particular job to an individual's need satisfactions, one must have an understanding of that individual. Explain.

4. Discuss the impact of a severe economic recession on the attitudes of both management and workers with respect to need satisfactions.

5. What modifications might take place within organizations that could provide a more satisfying working environment for today's employee?

6. If a manager observes an employee behaving as described in McGregor's Theory X, how might the manager determine if this behavior is a negative response to frustration?

Case for Discussion

State University, which prided itself in the development of new curricula and innovative academic programs, had recently instituted a master's degree in entrepreneurial management within its graduate business school. The program was designed for bright students who believed that they would not fit into the rigid organizational structure of the large corporation, but rather wished to pursue a career in individual entrepreneurship.

The program director, Dr. John Vincent, had personally selected the thirty students admitted to the first class from over a thousand applicants. Each applicant admitted had an undergraduate grade point average of 3.7 (of a possible 4.0) or higher and had scored in the top ten percent in the graduate school admission test.

Much of the first year involved each student writing a venture capital proposal which would be evaluated by local businessmen and university faculty. The grade for this proposal would be a major part of the student's overall grade in the program. A full semester was allowed to write the proposal which would be the student's plan for the development of a new product and/or business.

At the end of the class in which the venture capital proposal was discussed, students were allowed to ask questions of Dr. Vincent; a sampling of these questions follows:

"How long should the proposal be?"

"What information should be included in the proposal?"

"Will the faculty be available for periodic review of proposal content?"

"What type of financial analysis should be contained in the proposal?"

"How detailed should the proposal be?"

"Will each section of the proposal be weighted equally in terms of grade?"

"Was a sample of such a proposal available for distribution to the class?"

After the questions, Dr. Vincent returned to his office where he paused to reconsider the nature of the program and the admission policies.

Selected References

Allport, G. W. *Personality.* New York: Henry Holt, 1937.

Argyris, Chris. *Personality and Organization.* New York: Harper and Brothers, 1957.

_____. "The Individual and Organization: Some Problems of Mutual Adjustment." In *Administrative Science Quarterly* 2 (1957).

Berlew, D. and Hall, D. "The Management of Tension in Organizations: Some Preliminary Findings." *Industrial Management Review* 6 (1964).

Brayfield, A. H. and Crockett, W. H. "Employee Attitudes and Employee Performances." In *Psychological Bulletin* 52 (1955).

Friedlander, F. "Motivations To Work and Organizational Performance." In *Journal of Applied Psychology* 50 (1966).

Lawler, E. E. and Porter, L. W. "Predicting Managers' Pay and Their Satisfaction With Their Pay." In *Personnel Psychology* 19 (1966).

Likert, R. *New Patterns of Management.* New York: McGraw-Hill, 1961.

Maslow, A. H. *Motivation and Personality.* New York: Harper and Brothers, 1954.

———. *Eupsychian Management.* Homewood, Ill.: Richard D. Irwin, 1965.

McClelland, D. C. *The Achieving Society.* New York: Van Nostrand Reinhold Company, 1961.

McGregor, Douglas. *The Human Side of Enterprise.* New York: McGraw-Hill, 1960.

Misshauk, M. J. "Supervisory Skills and Employee Motivation." In *Personnel Administration,* July-August 1971.

Scott, William E. "The Behavioral Consequences of Repetitive Design." In *Personnel Psychology.*

Seeman, M. "On the Personal Consequences of Alienation in Work." In *American Sociological Review,* 32 (1967).

Stogdill, R. M. *Individual Behavior and Group Achievement.* New York: Oxford University Press, 1959.

Vroom, V. H. *Work and Motivation.* New York: John Wiley & Sons, 1964.

Walker, C. "Lire in the Automated Factory." In *Harvard Business Review* January-February 1958.

Zalkind, S. S. and Costello, T. W. Perception: "Some Recent Research and Implications for Administration." In *Administrative Science Quarterly* 7 (1962).

THE INDIVIDUAL

Part III

Introduction

This focuses on the individual within the organization. Specifically, the next three chapters discuss group behavior, leadership behavior, and communication. The purpose of the material is to provide the tools and techniques that may aid the reader in understanding how an individual functions within the organizational framework. Our objective is to impart skills that build managerial capability. The areas discussed focus on the behavioral aspects of individual and group interaction within the organizational framework.

Major Themes

Group Behavior:
The individual in group situations

Leadership Behavior:
Using style and power to influence
the behavior of others

Communication:
How the communication process is affected by
individual perceptions

The Behavior of Individuals in Groups

7

Auto Plant in Sweden Scores Some Success with Worker "Teams"

Kalmar unit, which hasn't an assembly line, runs fairly well, Volvo says; good morale but high costs

by Bowen Northrup

The auto plant here, says Volvo AB, is built for the worker. It is light, airy and far less noisy than the usual auto assembly line.

The reason: The Swedish company's Kalmar plant doesn't *have* an assembly line, at least in the conventional sense. In place of the efficacious but notorious device pioneered by Henry Ford, Kalmar has a system of computer-controlled "trolleys" that move about the plant bearing autos. The battery-powered flatbed carriers follow electronic commands from magnetic tapes set into the concrete floors.

The trolleys dramatically change the tedious chore of assembling cars. They are one of many technical and environmental innovations at Kalmar, a prototype plant where Volvo has tried to come to grips with the problem that increasingly bedevils Western industry: As workers' educational levels and general expectations rise, they are less and less inclined to do the dirty or boring jobs that predominate in basic industries. Turnover and absenteeism rates reflect that disenchantment.

Using a flexible production system with a "team" approach, Volvo has tried to provide creativity, responsibility and variety on the job—and still make cars profitably. A steady stream of industrialists, union officials and social scientists has been coming to

Bowen Northrup, "Auto Plant in Sweden Scores Some Success with Worker 'Teams,'" *Wall Street Journal*, March 1, 1977. Reprinted by permission.

Kalmar—from Communist and Third World nations as well as the West—with two chief questions in mind: Does it really work, and is it economically feasible?

Pleased, With Qualifications

Kalmar opened three years ago, so answers ought to be forthcoming by now. A qualified "yes" to both questions, Volvo says. Too expensive and exotic for us, say some big foreign auto makers that haven't any plans to follow Volvo's lead, although a few are using limited amounts of the same technology.

"We have nothing but admiration for Kalmar," says a spokesman for Peugeot in Paris. But the French company sees "no chance whatsoever" that it will emulate Volvo. "Investments in a Kalmar-type plant would be 30% above normal cost, and operating costs would be 30% higher, too," the Peugeot man contends.

George Morris, vice president for industrial relations at General Motors Corp., says, "It's a very attractive plant." But, he adds, "It looks like a helluva waste of space," and he questions whether a plant of similar capacity would be useful to U.S. auto makers. Kalmar can produce only 30,000 cars a year with a single work turn and 60,000 with a double work turn; in contrast, a typical U.S. plant, using the preferred two work turns, can make 200,000 cars a year, and GM's big Lordstown, Ohio, facility can turn out 400,000 a year.

Ford Motor Co. offers this comment: "At best, the impact these experiments might eventually have on our operations will be gradual."

Somewhat More Costly

Volvo acknowledges that Kalmar cost about $25 million, some 10% more than a conventional plant of its capacity, even though the land for it was contributed by the government. The company adds that new technology inevitably raised the price, but it says Kalmar production costs are working out at only $7.74 more per auto than at its other assembly plants—and with fewer flaws to correct after final inspections.

Is Kalmar really that different from an ordinary assembly plant? Its workers, after all, still are putting autos together, and working under the relentless strictures of "method time measurement," under which every movement they make is timed and put into the forecast of their day's production. And all of Kalmar is monitored by computers that flash hourly production rates onto display screens, with new information available every fifth of a second.

"There are limits," says S. A. Ewergardh, Volvo's vice president for production and administration development. "We must have a certain speed of the line." He explains that "the basic idea of Kalmar is flexibility—now people can choose the way they assemble a car." The facility has fewer supervisors than a normal auto plant.

Following the tapes, the auto-bearing trolleys move around the plant in approximation of assembly-line organization. But whereas assembly-line workers would be rooted in position doing a single specialized chore all day, Kalmar's workers are grouped in about 25 teams of 15 to 25 persons each. Each team handles a general area, such as door assembly, electric wiring or fitting upholstery.

Muted Discipline

The rigid discipline of the assembly line is muted. Members of teams can exchange jobs, or change teams when they wish. They also can vary the pace of the work, keeping up with the general flow of production but speeding up or pausing as they wish—because the car-carrying trolleys can be delayed for a while both before

entering and after leaving each team's work area.

One recent morning at 10:30 found half a dozen workers from the door-assembly team lounging against the wall and listening to a radio. "We hurried it up for a while so we could take a few minutes off and hear the news," explained one.

The trolleys make for flexibility, too. If there is a breakdown, or an auto needs special attention, its trolley can be shuttled off into parking position while the others glide by along the line or into unmanned elevators that move them, on computer command, between the two floors of the plant. Problems that could halt an assembly line are solved easily.

The plant also has other work-saving devices. For example, while conventional assembly-line workers must perform operations on the undercarriage by the tiring method of working from beneath, the Kalmar worker presses a button and the trolley rolls an auto 90 degrees on its side, so the work can be done from a comfortable position.

Volvo started thinking about a new kind of assembly plant in the late 1960s, when absenteeism and turnover were becoming serious problems for Swedish employers. The company started by conducting in-depth interviews with its blue-collar workers.

What did they like or dislike about the assembly-line routine? What features would they like to see in a new plant? The answers were collated. Then a group of Volvo officials and outside experts engaged in a prolonged brainstorming session and emerged with plans for a new type of assembly plant.

The resulting building differs markedly from conventional plants. While they tend to be large rectangles, Kalmar consists of four six-sided structures—three of them two stories tall and the other single-story—that fit together, forming the general shape of a cross.

The windows are big, and the workshop is compartmented, so the workers, located along the outer walls, have natural light and the sensation of being in a comfortably small workshop. Stores and supplies are available to all from central depots.

Comfortable Atmosphere

Kalmar is notable for creature comforts. Separate entrances plus elaborate changing and locker rooms with sauna for each team, laundry service for their work clothes (fresh ones in the locker each Monday morning) and a lounge adjoining each work place with coffee facilities, comfortable chairs and tables, and a bulletin board. There also are amenities usually reserved for white-collar workers, such as a toll-free telephone for local calls.

Between managers and the 600 or so workers, the stress is on democracy. "There are only three doors between the plant manager and the boys and girls on the floor, and those doors are always open," a Volvo official says.

Much of this reflects "work enrichment" methods in which the Swedes have pioneered. Volvo doesn't believe that it has gone too far in coddling the workers. "It's supposed to be profitable; it's not a welfare institution," an executive says.

And it is profitable—for an automobile as carefully made as the Volvo (the U.S. price is about $6,600 to about $10,200) and a factory of its size. In a preliminary report, Volvo recently posted a gain in earnings, before taxes and special allocations, to the equivalent of $136.4 million last year from $117.8 million in 1975; sales rose to $3.69 billion from $3.22 billion.

Doubts at Fiat

For a mass maker of autos that are cheaper than the Volvo, the Kalmar system might not be economically desirable. At Fiat of Italy, a spokesman notes the large capital outlay required for space at the Kalmar plant. The Kalmar idea, he says, "needs further studies to lower production costs."

GM's Mr. Morris observes that while Kalmar produces about 15 autos an hour, U.S. plants turn out 40 to 60 cars an hour. Building a Kalmar-style plant for 60 cars an hour, he says, "would take a building 10 miles long" (because of the central core at Kalmar that is accessible to all workers).

An interesting aspect of Kalmar is the personal chemistry produced by the team concept. Volvo has found that natural leaders emerge—and that some workers resist the idea of responsibility to the team that is implicit in the arrangement. Some have left to go back to more routine work.

Some time ago, six U.S. auto workers came to Kalmar for a tryout. Five reportedly didn't like it, one reason being that it required constant attention and thought. On a conventional assembly line, a worker can do his routine job and daydream, blocking out the drudgery of the work, a United Auto Workers official suggests. The auto union itself has its reservations about the Kalmar system, although Leonard Woodcock, its president, called the facility "the cleanest plant I've ever seen" after a visit a couple of years ago.

Learning to Love Computers

At Kalmar, blue-collar workers have come to feel at ease with that exotic instrument, the computer. While it keeps tabs on their work all the day, it also responds to their commands, and, through the display terminals, keeps them informed of the rate of production.

On the root problems of absenteeism and turnover, Volvo hasn't made dramatic progress, though the results aren't conclusive. Sweden's social-benefits system, providing almost full pay for a worker claiming illness, makes an occasional brief holiday all too attractive.

Absenteeism at some Volvo installations runs as high as 20%. At Kalmar the figure has been lower, around 12%, but the staff is young, carefully chosen and well motivated. Similarly, turnover, at 10% annually, has been lower than the norm—just under 15% at Volvo plants—but jobs are hard to find in the Kalmar region.

Morale seems high, but not euphoric, on the work floor at Kalmar. "It was fun at first," says Margit Hjalmarsson, once a housewife but now among the 10% of the workers who are women, "but now it has gotten routine."

Lars-Erik Morin, the production manager, echoes that thought—"It isn't an experiment any more; it's just a plant for building cars"—but his main interest now is to get the factory at full production. Due to sluggish demand for cars, it is operating at only two-thirds of capacity.

MODERN SOCIETY virtually requires each individual to become a member of, and function within, a variety of group environments. Regardless of individual orientation, attitude, or philosophy, each of us from time to time has probably participated in some activity in groups—groups of childhood friends, school companions, sports teams, clubs, or work groups. Throughout our lives, a large part of our time is spent interacting with others. It would seem to follow that much of our success and satisfaction in life will be derived from our ability to understand and function effectively within various types of group environments.

In the world of business, the organizational structure of modern corporations is based on the concept of groups of individuals working together in some coordinated fashion to achieve some goal or objective. The purpose of this chapter is to discuss the nature, function, and behavior of individuals as they exist within the group environment, especially in terms of groups working within business organizations.

What Is a Group?

Let us define exactly what we mean by *group;* many definitions of this term exist in the literature.

Since group activity has been the subject of much research by psychologists and by sociologists, two distinct categories of group definition have emerged. The first emphasizes the individual within the group and limits its focus to small groups, or what are called "primary" groups. Homans, for example, defines a group as "a number of persons who communicate with one another often over a span of time, and who are few enough so that each person is able to communicate with all the others, not at second hand, through other people, but face to face."[1] Schein offers a similar definition: "any number of people who (1) interact with one another, (2) are psychologically aware of one another, and (3) perceive themselves to be a group."[2] These authors limit their definition to include only those situations in which individuals are aware of and can interact with all members of the group. Leonard Sayles, however, in a discussion of work groups within the large organization, emphasizes other characteristics: individuals may belong to a variety of groups, including

1. *command* groups (superior and subordinates)
2. *task* groups (employees responsible for accomplishing some job)

3. *friendship* groups (individuals who have some affinity for each other)
4. *interest* groups (employees who share a common economic interest).[3]

It is unnecessary for all members of such groups to be able to interact with every other member; not all members of a given department (command group), for example, may interact. What is necessary is only that the individuals work together in some manner to achieve a common objective. We will define a group here as *any collection of individuals who interact, directly or indirectly, as a result of some common interest or in order to achieve some common goal.* This broad definition includes both small and larger groups within the organizational setting.

The Function of Groups

In most cases, individuals come together into groups in order to satisfy some need by means of group interaction. Viewed with respect to Maslow's hierarchy of needs, the group may provide an opportunity for individuals to satisfy needs at all levels. These are some ways individuals may achieve need satisfaction through group interaction:

Exhibit 7.1. *Need Satisfaction in Groups*

Need	Group activity
Safety	Individuals may join together to protect each other from harm or injury (against enemies, natural disasters, hazardous work conditions)
Security	Individuals may join together to provide each with greater personal security resulting from the strength of numbers (the development of trade unions and trade associations industry)
Social	Individuals may join together to enjoy some common interest or activity or simply to interact with those whose company they enjoy (social clubs, tennis or golf clubs)
Esteem	Individuals may derive certain status from membership in activities or organizations (fraternities, country clubs, sports teams)
Self-actualization	Individuals may join with others whose activities they may perceive to be enlightening, challenging, or interesting (research departments, art or craft groups).

A given group of course often provides an opportunity for individuals to satisfy more than one need. For example, a worker's membership in a trade union may be the basis for financial *security* as well as for *social* interaction through union activities, and it also may bestow a certain status or *esteem*.

The fact that group membership can provide opportunities for individual need satisfaction does not, in and of itself, explain why individuals become members of groups. Individuals can often satisfy needs on their own. Group membership does become a desirable alternative, however, when a person perceives that the group will provide *better* satisfaction. For certain types of tasks and problems, in which the *size* of the problem, the *complexity* of the task, or the *skills* required for analysis are such that a single individual would not be able to achieve completion, it is often necessary for individuals to join together. In general, individuals join together in group activities when they perceive that joint activity will be an appropriate and effective method of satisfying individual needs.

Types of Groups

Let us now examine some of the different groups in the organizational environment. The work of Leonard Sayles will help us identify various group types: the command group, the task group, the friendship group, and the interest group.[4]

The Command Group
1. Consists of a superior and immediate subordinates
2. Relationship of members defined by organizational structure
3. Responsible for performing some specific task or activity
4. Formal reward and punishment based on individuals' contribution to objectives.

This type of group could be represented by a department within an organization in which the manager had direct authority over a number of subordinates and was responsible for the performance of specific organizational tasks.

The Task Group
1. Usually smaller than the command group; made up of individuals who must interact in order to accomplish some *specific* task
2. Relationships of members are usually defined by the organization; may involve superior and subordinate roles as well as different degrees of authority and responsibility within the organization

3. Usually involves individuals working in close proximity to each other
4. Duration of group membership may depend on the nature and complexity of the task.

This type of group comes together in order to perform some specific task. The nature of the task may be ongoing (assembly line work group) or temporary (special committee); group membership is limited to those directly involved in task completion.

The Friendship Group
1. Usually based on age, ethnic background, marital status, sex, or other social characteristics shared
2. Members join together for satisfacton derived from interaction
3. Membership is informal and not defined by organizational structure
4. May have goals contrary to formally defined organization goals
5. Structure of the group (leadership, etc.) may not resemble that of a formal organizational hierarchy.

Examples include parties and other social groups. Formation of such groups is usually based on human needs to associate and interact.

The Interest Group
1. Usually based on the perception that a common interest or desire can best be obtained through group action
2. May be based upon "strength in numbers" concept
3. Goal or objective is usually to bring about a certain state or condition within the organization (wage rate, work standards, etc.)
4. May be formal (trade union) or informal (a committee of workers).

This group comes together as a result of some common interest. The group works as a unit in order to bring about a mutually desired goal or objective.

Concepts in Analyzing Group Behavior

In order to understand group behavior, we must be familiar with some terms and concepts that are used in describing group process. We will define and discuss three basic components of the group interaction process: *group norms, role relationships,* and *group cohesiveness.* These provide a framework for analyzing individual behavior in the group environment.

Group Norms   When an individual accepts membership in a group, one of the first things he or she may recognize is that it may no longer be possible to behave with complete freedom. Each group, whether because of its goals or because of the characteristics of the individuals in the *group,* will establish what the *group* considers to be *acceptable patterns of behavior.* These acceptable behavior patterns are referred to as *group norms.* They define the ways in which group members ought to behave in given situations.

Behavior covered by group norms may include style of dress, type of language used, areas of interest, type of work in which one may be engaged, amount of output that is acceptable, or categories of people with whom one may associate. In general, the norms define a pattern of behavior which the group deems acceptable. Once a series of norms have been adopted by a group, an individual's failure to comply will usually bring about some form of group *sanction.* This may take the form of derogatory comments from group members, the withholding of certain types of benefits, or perhaps even the complete ostracizing of the offending group member. Compliance with group norms is a requirement that an individual must fulfill in order to remain a member in good standing of the group. Because of this, most group norms are well accepted by the group members.

If at some point an individual no longer believes that he or she can fully accept a group norm, the individual usually has two alternatives available: the individual could simply leave the group and relieve himself of the responsibility to conform, or he could seek to change the norm.

Sometimes the attraction which the group may have for an individual ceases to be sufficient for that individual to continue to conform to a norm that seems unacceptable. Membership in a political group may terminate, for example, if the group establishes norms advocating violence.

If, on the other hand, an individual continues to find a group attractive but simply does not wish to conform to a particular norm, the individual may seek to have the group change its policies or attitudes. In such cases, the group may be faced with the decision of whether the norm or the individual is more important to it. If the group feels that the norm is too important to give up, pressure will likely be brought to bear on the individual to comply. If this fails, the individual may be asked to leave. If, on the other hand, the group perceives the individual to be more important to its overall objectives than the norm in question, the group may make changes. In either case, the group is faced with weighing the "costs" and "rewards" associated with the individual's membership in the group and those associated with the norm at issue.

In determining whether to leave a group or to try to bring about a change in it, an individual will normally consider such factors as how important is continued group membership to him, how unacceptable the norm is, how much influence the individual perceives he or she may have in the group, and what alternative groups may be available.

Role Relationships

As individuals come together to form a group, each person's behavior in some way contributes to the overall functioning of the group. Over a period of time the group comes to expect certain types of behavior from each member. This behavior is defined as the *role* a person plays within the group, and it refers to behavior exhibited when interacting with others. The interaction pattern between two individuals can usually be described in terms of the role relationship between them. For example, father and son each have a role superior and subordinate in a relationship, as do coach and player. In these situations, each individual is expected to behave in a certain way. This expectation is based on the role that one person occupies relative to the other. In the course of day-to-day living, most individuals find themselves in a wide variety of roles. One person may be both father and son in a family setting, both a superior and a subordinate in the work environment. The individual will change his role—his behavior pattern—according to the person with whom he is interacting.

Within the group, each individual will usually play a particular role. That role will partially be a function of the status the person has in the group. In most cases status more or less defines a person's position, and position determines how individuals with whom the person interacts develop expectations. An exchange of expected behavioral responses occurs. The combination of behaviors and behavioral responses received forms an individual's role relationship with each member of the group. In any given group one can expect to see a variety of roles being played. The role of leader is usually associated with the person who gives direction to the group, who has power to issue rewards and punishments to individual members, and who generally dominates each interaction with individual group members. The group may also have a scapegoat to whom it looks whenever blame is being placed for problems the group has encountered. There may also be a group comedian whose behavior can release group tension.

In summary, in order to understand the behavior patterns or roles of a given individual, it is necessary to investigate the group with which he or she is interacting at the time as well as the status of the individual within the group. With this information, it is possible to anticipate the behavioral expectations of that individual toward the group and to be aware of the behavioral responses he or she may receive in turn.

Once an individual has assumed a given role within a group, it is often difficult for either the individual or the group to adjust to a change in the established role relationship. This situation becomes apparent in the business environment when a member of a work group is promoted to a supervisory position. Since the new supervisor was previously a member of the work group, fellow workers have come to expect certain behavior patterns and are accustomed to responding in certain ways. Once the individual has been promoted, she or he may find it necessary to change behavior patterns with respect to the work group. It is often difficult for the members of the group to recognize that their former peer is now functioning in a very different role. If so, they may find it difficult to adjust to the changing role relationship. Such a situation can often result in hostility between the supervisor and members of the work group as each side tries to adjust to the new relationship.

We can readily see that multiple role relationships exist in the business environment. For example, an individual will interact with superiors, subordinates, and peers. In each of these situations the behavior of the same individual will likely be very different. Group members will usually play roles filling three main functions; they may be called task roles, maintenance roles, and personal roles.

Task roles. These roles are carried on in order that the group can successfully complete a job or project. The person or persons fulfilling this role will be continuously moving the group in the direction of task completion; they will be providing guidance and direction—leadership—to the group in the performance of its job or task.

Maintenance roles. The second of these functions is called a maintenance role. This is the job of keeping the group working together, performing those functions necessary for keeping the group functioning as a working unit—smoothing over friction between group members or reinforcing the need for the group to work together to accomplish its goal. The person who performs this function well is skilled in human relations.

Personal roles. These roles are the ones that satisfy personal needs of group members, whether or not they are related to the needs or goals of the group. A group member may be functioning in such a way as to satisfy his own individual needs through his activities within the group. The satisfaction of his needs may or may not serve to aid the group in achieving its goals.

Group Cohesiveness

The cohesiveness of a group is the strength of attraction that exists among the members. The strength of this attraction will vary from group to group and is usually a function of the extent to which the norms and values of the group are shared by all. As identification with norms and values increases, the overall cohesiveness of the group also increases. Thus, sharing something in common is a significant factor in influencing the level of cohesiveness that exists within the group.

In the work situation, one can frequently encounter groups that maintain a high degree of cohesiveness. Cohesiveness must be taken into consideration when making decisions involving one or more members of the group. The greater the level of group cohesiveness, the greater will be the impact of the decision on all members of the group. For example, if management makes a decision to transfer or lay off a member of a group in which there is a high degree of cohesiveness, then it is likely that other members of the group will react negatively. The remaining group members may bring pressures to bear upon management in order to show their displeasure with the decision. These pressures may take the form of lowered efficiency, reduction in overall quality of work, or an increase in the time spent away from the job on breaks.

The fact that a highly cohesive work group may take collective action to demonstrate their feelings about a management decision is significant. It indicates the need for managers to give careful consideration to the impact of their decisions, not only on the individual or individuals directly involved but also on the groups to which these individuals belong. If management perceives a high degree of cohesiveness, it should be prepared to deal with the reaction of the group, positive or negative. The degree of group reaction to management's decision will be a function of the status of the individual directly affected by the decision. The higher the status of the individual within the group, the more pronounced will be the group reaction.

There are identifiable factors in the work situation that create an environment in which cohesiveness is relatively high. For groups that work together in the same geographical area in the plant, physical proximity is likely to result in a high level of personal interaction.

Personal interaction is a strong factor serving to increase the level of cohesiveness within a group. Individuals with similar backgrounds or interests, too, will generally tend to be cohesive. Their common factor tends to form a bond that results in a high level of group cohesiveness. This is often true for various ethnic groups in the work environment. And individuals who have rallied around a common purpose generally tend to be bound in a very cohesive unit. Once that goal is achieved, each member may choose to go his or her own way. This is often the case with political and social issues.

In summary, cohesiveness is the extent to which a group tends to stick together. It is a measure of the degree to which individuals identify with a group. Group cohesiveness will directly influence the strength of a group reaction to events that impact individuals within the group.

Theories of Group Behavior

In this section let us examine two of the theories that have been advanced to analyze group behavior in what is a particularly "group process."

The Homans Model

In *The Human Group,* George Homans developed a conceptual framework to aid in understanding the complex workings of group behavior. His model is based on three concepts: activity, interaction, and sentiment.

Activity. The physical activities in which individuals engage include such behavior as walking to work, assembling a machine, inspecting a component. In considering the activities of a group, Homans makes the point that we should focus on such features as the efficiency with which an activity is performed and the similarity of activities performed by various members of the work group as well as simply evaluating the output or result of the activity.

Interaction. The mutual responses of individuals in carrying on group activities may be verbal or nonverbal. Interaction may involve two or more individuals. The interaction between individuals is simply the extent to which individuals come into some form of contact during the group process. Interaction represents the behavior of one individual toward another.

Sentiments. The feelings, attitudes, and values each individual brings into the group environment make up the group sentiments. Unlike interactions and activities, sentiments are not directly observable in group interaction; rather, they must be determined subjectively by inference from ongoing group activity.

Homans uses these three basic elements of *activity, interaction,* and *sentiment* to define and describe two basic systems that exist within the group. Homans calls them the *required system* and the *emergent system.*

The *required* system includes all activities, interactions, and sentiments that are a necessary part of the group function. Workers in a group may be responsible for producing a particular product. To produce it, certain jobs must be performed (activities); certain individuals must work together on some aspects of the job (interactions); and each individual in the group will exhibit certain attitudes, ideas, and values in connection with the work (sentiments). Together, these required activities, interactions, and sentiments form the required system in the group. They include the ways the organization specifies the group *must* behave to accomplish its specific task.

The *emergent* system includes activities, interactions, and sentiments that emerge or evolve as a *result* of the required group function. For example, it is likely that in working together within the required system, the members of the group will evolve their own social structure. This social structure will most likely have its own hierarchy and status levels, its own norms of behavior (such as agreed-upon acceptable levels of work output), and its friendships and hostile interaction patterns. These elements are the emergent system within the group. The emergent system is made up of all of the *activities, interactions,* and *sentiments* that are not part of the required system but emerge as a result of the group function.

Homans makes the point that the specific features of a group's required and emergent systems will be influenced by a wide variety of background and environmental factors. These will differ in each situation. The political, cultural, and economic environment, the nature of competition, the technology utilized, the specific nature of the job design, the organizational structure, and the specific layout of the workplace will all affect both systems. It is the interaction of these background factors influencing both the required and emergent systems that will determine levels of group output in three important areas: *productivity, satisfaction,* and *personal growth.* The Homans model is summarized in Figure 7.1 (page 154).

Exhange Theory (Thibaut and Kelly)

This theory of group behavior was developed by social psychologists John Thibaut and Harold Kelly.[5] Exchange theory rests on the idea that each individual evaluates an interaction relationship in terms of its rewards and its costs. An individual will choose to continue a

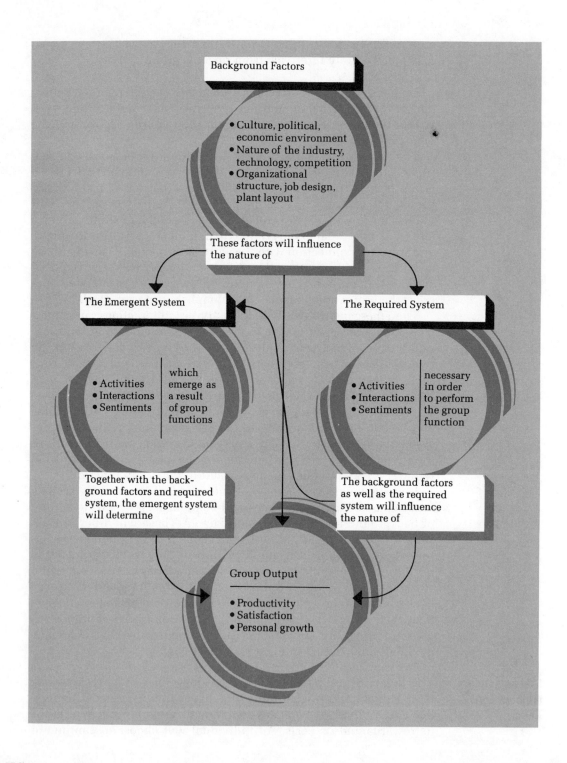

Figure 7.1. *The Homans Model*

relationship as long as the perceived rewards to be derived from it exceed the costs associated with continuing the relationship. The concept is expressed in Figure 7.2.

Although this model presents a simplified view of exchange theory, it makes the key point that the individual's decision to remain involved in an interaction situation is a rational one, based on an evaluation of the rewards and costs associated with the relationship.

What are some rewards and costs that might be associated with a particular interaction? In order to understand these concepts let us look at some examples that illustrate the nature of exchange theory.

An individual finds that to continue a particular interaction would require a time commitment that would keep her from other activities. In addition, she would have to give up some of her freedom of behavior for a period of time. Against these "costs," she must compare the rewards or benefits, either certain or expected, to be derived from this involvement. These rewards take the form of monetary compensation (payment for a service), increased position (job promotion), and the satisfaction of helping someone. If, in this person's perception, the desirability of the rewards outweighs the costs, she will enter into the relationship. This is what might happen if a worker takes time away from her job to help another worker with a job-related problem.

In order to understand the exchange theory concept we must be careful to define reward or benefit in its broadest possible terms.

Figure 7.2. *Exchange Theory*

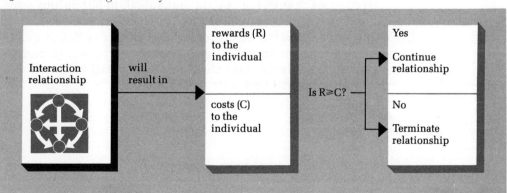

Thus, the reward to be derived may simply be the personal satisfaction that comes from helping others or it may be the esteem or ego satisfaction that comes from displaying one's ability. Then again, the reward may be the expectation that the person being helped will in some way provide a tangible reward—such as inviting one out for lunch.

Another example of the reward-cost consideration might be the case of the person who continues to associate with someone he finds extremely distasteful. To continue the association represents a significant psychological cost to the individual, for he would much prefer to dissociate himself from the relationship. However, if the person with whom he is associating is perceived as being able to provide some benefit or reward, either now or in the future, the individual may well choose to continue the relationship.

In both of our examples, the individual providing help or choosing to maintain the relationship will continue to do so as long as the *perception of the rewards* to be derived from the relationship is that they will exceed or equal its costs. Should this situation no longer be true, it is likely that the relationship would be terminated.

In summary, both interactions would continue as long as

Perceived rewards $>$ perceived costs.

This simplified equation does provide a framework for thinking about an individual's decision on continued group membership. In utilizing the equation, we must remember always to interpret rewards and costs in both the psychological and tangible sense.

In formulating how individuals evaluate rewards and costs in relation to exchange theory, Thibaut and Kelly define the following relationships:

CL *(comparison level)*: relationships which fall above CL are perceived to be "satisfying" by the individual. Relationships which fall below CL are perceived to be "unsatisfying."

CL *(alt) (comparison level for alternatives)*: this is defined as the lowest level of outcomes a group member will accept and still maintain the relationship. Should outcomes fall below CL (alt), the individual will terminate the relationship.

Studying Group Behavior

Several techniques have been developed to provide a tangible approach to understanding group behavior. Two in particular enable the observer of group interaction to classify individual behavior patterns within the group and obtain a profile of the group structure with respect to such areas as leadership and role relationships.

Interaction Process Analysis (Robert Bales)

Robert Bales has observed groups in a wide variety of settings and situations.[6] During his observations records were kept of interaction patterns between group members. Specifically, Bales observed which individuals would interact and, more importantly, the nature of the interaction. As a result of his analysis, Bales developed a list of twelve interaction patterns involving both *task-related* and *interpersonal* processes. Figure 7.3 on page 158 shows the *interaction process analysis* categories in chart form.

The *interaction process analysis* scheme can be a valuable tool for use in observing and identifying particular group processes. Figure 7.3 provides a framework with which to analyze interaction patterns within the group. By using these concepts the observer can focus readily and with some exactness, on *what* is said, to *whom* it is said, and how that individual *reacts* to what has been said. After observing the group interaction over a period of time the observer will normally find that the statements or comments of certain individuals tend to fall into specific categories: social-emotional positive, task neutral, or social-emotional negative. As these observations are made and classified, the observer will be able to make some judgments regarding the *role* that each individual may be playing in the group. The observer can analyze the group behavior in terms of individual role relationships. Such an analysis can provide insight into the leadership of the group, the way in which decisions are made, the status of each member of the group, and antagonism and friendship cliques that may exist.

Sociometric Analysis

Another technique for studying group interaction is the *sociometric analysis* developed by the psychiatrist J. L. Moreno.[7] The idea behind sociometric analysis is to chart and classify the nature of the interaction patterns that take place between individuals within a given group. To use the technique in its simplest form, an observer of group interaction would place an arrow between the names of those individuals who interact. If this process is carried out over a period of time, the number of arrows between any two individuals will provide an indication of the frequency of their interaction. In addition, the direction of the arrows would indicate who initiated the interaction. Figure 7.4 on page 159 provides an example. We note that Member 2 was the individual most often involved in the conversation. The direction of the arrows indicates that it was Group Member 3 who initiated the greatest number of comments to Member 2.

Figure 7.3.
*The System of
Categories
Used in
Observation
and Their
Major
Relations*

Source: Redrawn
from Robert F. Bales,
*Interaction Process
Analysis* (Chicago:
University of Chicago
Press, 1951), p. 9.
Copyright 1951 by
The University of
Chicago. All rights
reserved.

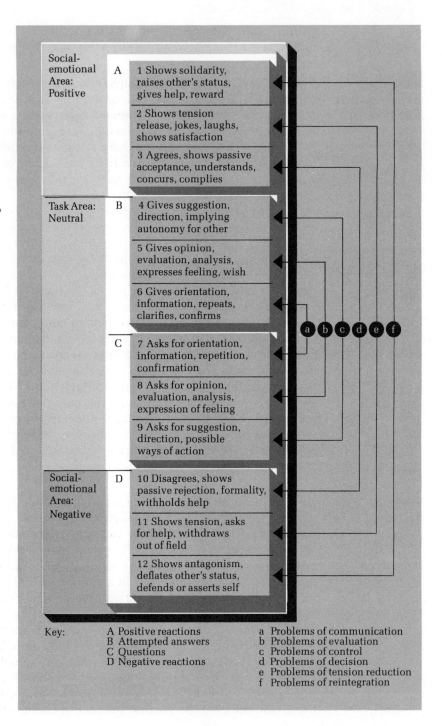

Key:

A Positive reactions
B Attempted answers
C Questions
D Negative reactions

a Problems of communication
b Problems of evaluation
c Problems of control
d Problems of decision
e Problems of tension reduction
f Problems of reintegration

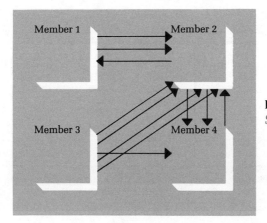

Figure 7.4.
Sociometric Analysis

A sociometric analysis of this type can be expanded to classify not only the frequency of comments but also the nature of these comments—whether they are questions, criticism, or praise, for example. The information obtained based on such an analysis would provide insight into such interactions as group leadership, friendships and hostility, and role relationships.

Another approach to sociometric analysis developed by J. L. Moreno and H. H. Jennings makes it possible to obtain additional information regarding the nature of the group process.[8] Questionnaires are given to each member of the group. Each is asked to select the individual with whom they would most like to interact (first, second, and third choice). They may also be asked with whom they would least like to interact. When the resulting data are analyzed statistically, information is obtained regarding "isolates" (individuals not chosen), reciprocating pairs (those individuals who chose each other), and other relationships. A picture develops of the nature of the group. This picture normally reveals four types of individual behavior patterns:

1. *Group Leaders:* are "popular" with members of the group, conform to group norms, and exert influence over group members
2. *Deviates:* do not adhere to the norms and behavior patterns of the group
3. *Isolates:* are not involved in the normal group process; are rarely chosen as partners by other group members
4. *Members:* appear to hold a middle position within the group. Are accepted by the group but in general do not exercise a great deal of direction over group activity.

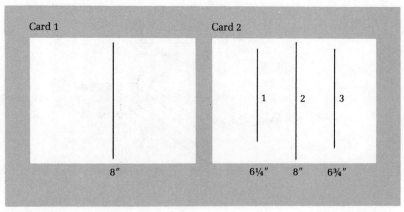

Figure 7.5. *Group Pressure*

Group Pressure

In a classic experiment, Solomon Asch demonstrated the effect of group influence on the judgment and behavior of individuals within the group.[9] Asch asked groups of college students to compare lines on white cards. The individuals participating were asked to select the line on card 2 which was the same length as the line appearing upon card 1 (see Figure 7.5); the lines were drawn to appear almost the same in length.

The groups ranged in size from seven to nine members. All but one individual in each group was told secretly to select one of the two *wrong* lines on card 2. The individual who was not aware of the situation was always the last to be asked to select the appropriate line. In the cases in which an uninformed individual would make a selection in isolation, a mistaken choice would be made approximately one percent of the time. But when exposed to the "planted" wrong answers, the uninformed member of the group made the wrong choice 36.8 percent of the time. The Asch experiment revealed, in addition, that the number of individuals who disagree with the uninformed subject had an impact on the accuracy of selection. These results appear below:

Number who disagree	Wrong selection by uninformed member
1	0%
2	13.6%
3	31.8%

Results of the Asch experiment, as well as the Crutchfield study and the Sherif study, demonstrate the importance of group pressure in influencing individual behavior.[10] As individuals were placed in a situation in which others disagreed with their own perceptions, there was a strong tendency to abandon their own judgment and to "agree" with other members of the group. As Cruchfield discovered in his experiment, the extent to which a given individual will yield to "pressure" will be a function of his or her own personality characteristics and feelings of security. The fact remains, however, that each of us, in our interactions with others, will be likely to have our judgments modified to some extent by group pressures.

Committees

Perhaps one of the most common formalized groups within the organization is the committee. Attending committee meetings "is probably one of the most popular avocational pursuits in American business today."[11] For all of their popularity within the organizational framework, committees have long been the subject of criticism as well as the butt of many jokes. These are some of the key problems associated with committee operation:

Within the committee system it is often difficult to pinpoint specific responsibility. Since the committee is usually made up of several individuals, it is easy to pass the buck in decision making.
In order to reach agreement within the committee structure it is often necessary to develop compromise solutions which may not be satisfactory to anyone.
The time spent in discussion within committee may often exceed the importance of the issue itself.

These are typical criticisms of committees in large organizations. The fact that committees are often criticized, however, has not seemed to diminish their presence in the modern organization. A study reported in the *Harvard Business Review* was based on data received from 1200 readers:

There existed regular or standing committees in over 80 percent of the firms surveyed.
The average executive spends 3½ hours a week in committee, with an additional 9½ hours in informal consultation with other executives.
Sixty percent of the responding executives reported that they were

now sitting on *at least* one committee, with the average being three committees.[12]

The substantial amount of time spent in committee by corporate executives indicates that, despite its shortcomings, the committee process does have a use in the corporate environment:

1. The committee system provides a hearing for a true cross section of ideas and points of view on an issue or decision alternative.
2. Since a position or statement by a committee represents the input and participation of a number of individuals, there is often greater commitment by each individual to the committee position.
3. The fact that many individuals have been involved in the committee discussion often results in improved communication of results throughout the organization. (This can sometimes be a disadvantage if the work of the committee is confidential.)
4. The committee can be a valuable training ground for young managers. Within the committee structure a manager has an opportunity to test thoughts and ideas with other members of the organization.

Committee Effectiveness

The effectiveness of a committee will generally be strengthened if consideration is given to some important factors in setting up of the committee.

Individual Background and Experience. Groups may develop better solutions to problems if members come from a wide variety of backgrounds and possess a wide range of skills and experiences. If groups are made up of individuals having similar views and ideas, all members may approach a problem in much the same way, with each individual being able to contribute little that is new to the group effort. In this situation much of the value of group problem solving is lost.

Status Differentials. To provide an environment in which individuals can bring up ideas openly, status (formal) differences in the group should be minimized. The environment in which a group is asked to function will have an effect on its ability to solve problems. A significant part of this environment is the structure existing within the group.

If there is a strong formal hierarchy within the group, lower-status members may be reluctant to bring up new ideas, especially those ideas which contradict group members of higher status. When this occurs, one of the main advantages of group effort is greatly diminished.

Involvement. To be most effective, the group will require the active participation of all members. Many so-called group interactions actually involve only a few members. Whether due to the personality characteristics of the members or simply to a lack of interest in the group activity, the resources of one or more members of the group go untapped.

Under these conditions, what may outwardly appear to be a group effort may in reality be a single individual's approach to the problem with other members simply giving passive acceptance. The main value of group problem solving is the ability to bring many different ideas and viewpoints to bear in a given situation. If all group members are not involved in the process, then the main advantage of group effort will be lost.

Specific Charge. In most cases, the group should be given a well-defined area of responsibility. (Though in the next section we will discuss creative problem-solving groups which may not be given a specific charge.) The group should be aware of the expectations of management regarding its output. Specifically, the group should know whether it is responsible for producing recommendations, a specific decision, or merely an evaluation of some issue or activity. Unless the group is specifically aware of its responsibility, it is often difficult to obtain effective performance.

The Use of Groups in Creative Problem Solving

In recent years several new ideas have been developed for obtaining more creative output from small groups. Most readers are probably familiar with the concept of brainstorming as a means of developing creative results from group efforts. Companies such as General Electric, IBM, and General Motors have found this approach effective in certain group situations.

The "group" approaches to creative problem solving are based on certain assumptions regarding human behavior:

1. Each individual has some creative ability
2. The values and mores of our social system may inhibit an individual from freely expressing some of this creativity
3. In order to bring out creativity in the individual, an environment must be established in which ideas and suggestions are both desired and sought by the group.

There are two basic approaches to establishing an atmosphere of creativity in which the group may function:

Brainstorming, developed by Alix Osborne for application in the advertising industry

The Gordon technique, developed by William Gordon of the consulting firm, Arthur D. Little, Inc.

Although these techniques are quite similar, the Gordon technique places a greater emphasis on the role of the group leader in the problem-solving situation. Both techniques seek to establish a positive attitude in the group; criticism of ideas or negative comments are virtually prohibited. In addition, each group member is encouraged to contribute novel ideas or suggestions to the discussion. A summary of both techniques as well as suggestions for implementation follows.

OSBORN BRAINSTORMING

Rules:
1. Judicial thinking or evaluation is ruled out.
2. Freewheeling is welcomed.
3. Quantity is wanted.
4. Combinations and improvements are sought.

Suggestions for the Osborn technique:
1. Length: 40 minutes to one hour; sessions of 10 to 15 minutes can be effective if time is short.
2. Do not reveal the problem before the session. An information sheet or suggested reference material on a selected subject should be used if prior knowledge of a general field is needed.
3. Problem should be clearly stated and not too broad.
4. Use a small conference table which allows people to communicate with each other easily.
5. If a product is being discussed, samples may be useful as a point of reference.

GORDON TECHNIQUE

Rules:
1. Only the group leader knows the problem.
2. Free association is used.
3. Subject for discussion must be carefully chosen.

Suggestions for the Gordon technique:
1. Length of session: two to three hours are necessary.
2. Group leader must be exceptionally gifted and thoroughly trained in the use of the technique.

GENERAL SUGGESTIONS THAT APPLY TO BOTH TECHNIQUES
1. Selection of personnel: a group from diverse backgrounds

helps. Try to get a balance of highly active and quiet members.

2. Mixed groups of men and women are often more effective, especially for consumer problems.
3. Although physical atmosphere is not too important, a relaxed pleasant atmosphere is desirable.
4. Group size: groups of from 4 to 12 can be effective. We recommend 6 to 9.
5. Newcomers may be introduced without disturbing the group, but they must be properly briefed in the theory of creative thinking and the use of the particular technique.
6. A secretary or recording machine should be used to record the ideas produced. Otherwise they may not be remembered later. Gordon always uses a blackboard so that ideas can be visualized.
7. Hold sessions in the morning if people are going to continue to work on the same problem after the session has ended; otherwise hold them late in the afternoon. (The excitement of a session continues for several hours after it is completed, and can affect an employee's routine tasks.)
8. Usually it is advisable not to have people from widely differing ranks within the organization in the same session.*

Formal and Informal Organization

Concepts such as division of labor, span of control, and departmentation are central to the formal structuring of organizations. *Formal structure* defines the way an organization will operate in accomplishing its primary objectives. In terms of our current discussion, the formal structure of the organization (formal organization) represents the *required system* as defined by Homans. This is the mechanism utilized by management to coordinate and direct the activities and interactions of members of the organization. The formal organization is the one that appears on paper, so to speak, defining the way individuals should interact with one another. Specifically, the formal organization defines communication patterns, rank and position, and areas of responsibility.

Figure 7.6 presents a typical formal organizational structure that

*Source: Reprinted by permission of the publisher from Charles S. Whiting, "Operational Techniques of Creative Thinking," *S.A.M. Advanced Management Journal*, October 1955, © 1955 by Society for Advancement of Management, p. 28. All rights reserved.

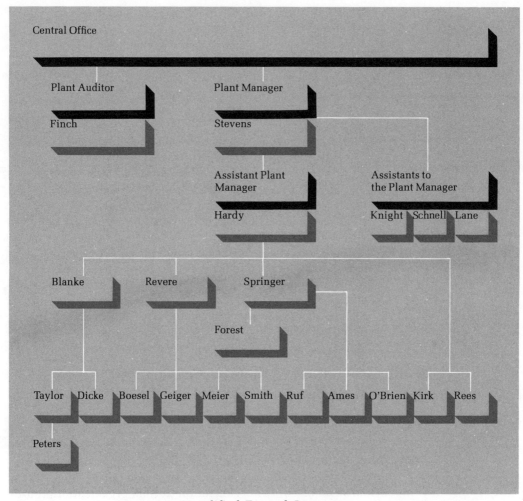

Figure 7.6. *Simplified Formal Structure*

Source: M. Dalton, *Men Who Manage* (New York: John Wiley & Sons, 1959).

might be found in a medium-sized manufacturing organization. A formal structure like this would be designed to facilitate accomplishing the goals of the organization. One goal might be to produce a product efficiently so as to generate profits. The formal organization of the company would define the way various individuals interact so as to attain the goal.

During the course of these interactions (brought about by the required system) there develops, over a period of time, an emergent

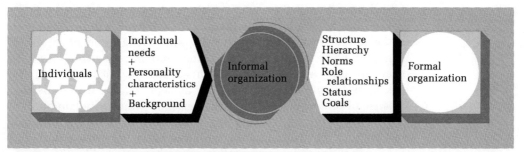

Figure 7.7. *Individuals and the Informal Organization*

system (see Figure 7.7). This is sometimes referred to as the *informal organization;* a group of individuals who interact over a period of time will develop their own informal, social structure. This structure will exist apart from the formal structure defined by management and will include its own hierarchy, with specific norms of behavior, leadership, status among members, role relationships, and goals. The reality of the informal organization should be clear to any reader who has been a member of some childhood club or gang, or who has worked for a period of time in a large organization.

The informal organization represents the evolution of a structural environment that develops a certain character according to the *needs* of the members of the group as well as *personality* and *background* characteristics of those members. As individuals come together in a group environment, each brings needs, personality characteristics, and background which combine to make each individual unique. When these individuals interact, these factors blend to form a social structure which in turn will eventually define the position and role of each individual within that group. This social structure is the informal organization of the group and has a strong influence on actual behavior. It is called "informal" because it has not been defined by some outside agency but rather has evolved on its own.

Let us examine some of the personal factors that may influence the nature of the informal organization. Each member of a group seeks to play a role that satisfies some personal need. For example, the individual who has a high need for *power* may seek to become the leader of the group. In this situation the personality and background of that individual, in combination with other group members, will determine if the individual's desire to become a leader will, in fact, be fulfilled. Factors such as intelligence, age, experience, and self-confidence will partially determine an individual's success.

Each member of the group will be seeking to satisfy some set of needs. The extent of the satisfaction of each need will be a function of the interaction of the personality and background of all group members. For example, one individual may have a strong desire to be accepted by all the others, but this desire may be a function of a lack of self-confidence or a feeling of dependence. It may be that because of other personality characteristics (inferiority complex, timidity) or background factors (sex, education, race) this individual is rejected. In such a situation the individual may leave the group or, if this was not possible, continually seek to be accepted by the others.

From interactions such as those just described, the group will evolve its own social structure, in which each individual plays a particular role and through this role seeks to satisfy individual needs.

Within the work organization the social structure resulting from the interaction of group members (informal organization) may be far different from the structure defined by management. For example, Melville Dalton, in a classic study of informal organizations, analyzed an organization whose formal structure is shown in Figure 7.6.[13] Dalton analyzed the role each individual played, regardless of his or her actual position in the formal structure. Dalton used such factors as

1. Member dominance in meetings
2. Voice in promotions
3. Leadership in challenging staff projects
4. Force in emergencies
5. Knowledge of subordinates
6. Position in firm's social and community activities

to determine the nature of the informal organization of the company. Shown in Figure 7.8, this informal organization reflects the actual status, power, and influence of each individual; the resulting picture is quite different from that of the formal structure of the same organization.

A comparison of the formal structure (Figure 7.6) with the informal (Figure 7.8) clearly demonstrates that individuals often play roles informally within a group that are far different from those that might be expected from looking at the formal organization. Their status, power, and influence in the work situation may be significantly different. Individuals who appear to be able to influence group attitudes and behavior, even though their formal position does not appear to be significant, are referred to as *informal leaders.*

Informal leaders derive their power not from the formal structure

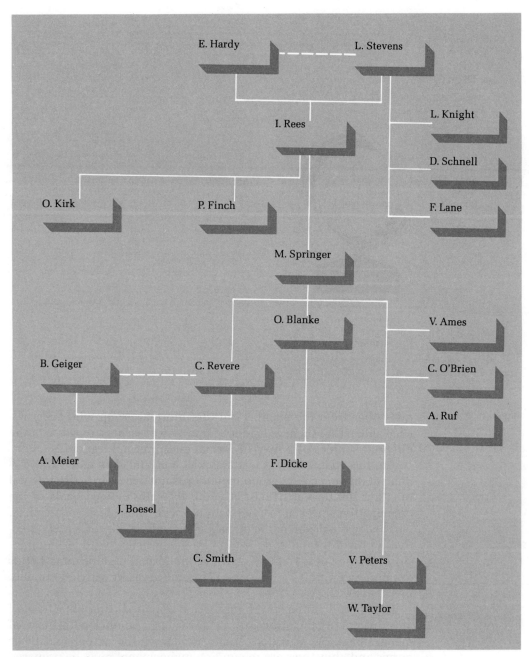

Figure 7.8. *Informal Structure*

Source: M. Dalton, *Men Who Manage* (New York: John Wiley & Sons, 1959).

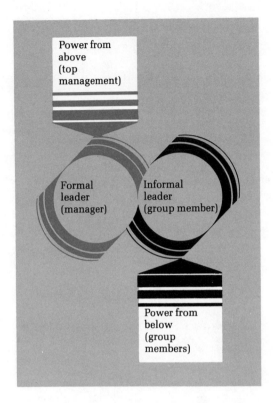

Figure 7.9. *Different Sources of Power of Formal and Informal Leaders*

but rather from the members of the informal group who acknowledge and accept them as leaders. Figure 7.9 presents a diagram of the different sources of power of formal and informal leaders.

The fact that informal leaders exist and that they may exert significant influence over group members is not necessarily detrimental to either the formal structure or the formally defined goals of the organization. Informal organizations, with their accepted leaders, will become a problem for management only if the goals and objectives of the informal organization are inconsistent with, or in opposition to, the goals and objectives of the formal organization. Let us examine in Exhibit 7.2, on page 171, some areas in which there may be conflict.

The chart is not meant to imply that the norms and objectives of all informal organizations are necessarily in conflict with those of management. What it does imply is that, to the extent that these norms and objectives are in conflict, management must be prepared to deal with informal leaders within the organization in order to

Exhibit 7.2. *Goals and Norms as Defined by Formal and Informal Organizations*

The formal organization	The informal organization
1. Maximum production of products based upon predetermined standard.	1. Production of product based upon perception of a "fair day's output."
2. Identification of those individuals who fall below accepted production levels.	2. Protection of all members of work group. Aiding those workers who are not able to meet production standards.
3. Work activity to include a full eight-hour period.	3. Work activity to include some informally accepted time period, with unauthorized work breaks.
4. Work to follow well-defined procedures based upon safety and quality criteria.	4. Work to follow informally defined procedures based on ease of effort and time reduction.
5. Promotion and pay raises based upon productivity and performance.	5. Promotion and pay raises based upon seniority and informal influence within the group.
6. Work layout and job definition based upon production needs.	6. Work layout and job definition based upon interaction and cohesiveness needs of the informal organization.

obtain desired group effort. The greater the discrepancy between the goals of management and the goals of the informal organization, the greater will be the conflict between management and work group members. This will be particularly true if the members of the informal organization have a strong feeling of unity (cohesiveness).

In a study of some 300 work groups in the corporate environment, Leonard Sayles defined four types of informal groups and indicated some of their characteristic modes of activity:

1. *Apathetic groups:* usually made up of low-paid, low-skill employees who exhibited low levels of cohesiveness and vague informal leadership.
2. *Erratic groups:* semiskilled workers working on jobs in which they frequently interact (assembly line or job shop). They tend to be fairly cohesive and usually select autocratic leaders.
3. *Strategic groups:* skilled workers whose jobs were generally important within the organization. Their jobs usually were responsible and required judgment and decision making. Leaders were usually high-performing members of the group.
4. *Conservative groups:* the most highly skilled workers in the organization. They are secure and powerful and could significantly

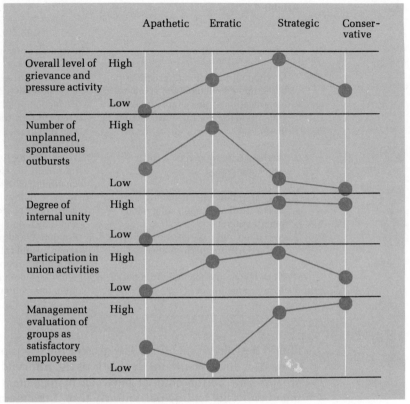

Figure 7.10. *Summary of Work Group Differences*

Source: Leonard M. Sayles, *The Behavior of Industrial Work Groups* (New York: John Wiley & Sons, 1958).

disrupt activities if they so chose. They are usually master crafts-men who operate independent of union activities. Their leaders are normally highly skilled members of the group.[14]

Sayles's research is reflected in Figure 7.10.

In summary, management must recognize and accept that within the formally defined structure, there will exist an informal organization with its own hierarchy, status, norms, and role relationships. This informal organization may help or hinder management in reaching its formally defined goals and objectives. The role that the informal organization will play will be a function of the goals and objectives of the informal structure, the cohesiveness of the group, and the type of members who make up the informal organization.

Discussion Questions

1. Define what is meant by *group*.
2. Discuss the different types of groups found in the organizational environment.
3. Discuss some of the reasons that individuals may join together in a group environment.
4. Define group *norms*, *roles*, and *cohesiveness*.
5. What are some of the differences between the Homans model and the Thibaut and Kelly model of group interaction?
6. What are the *required* and *emergent* systems within the group?
7. How would you use the *Bales interaction process analysis* chart to study group behavior?
8. Discuss various techniques for creative problem solving within the group environment.
9. What are some of the factors that can contribute to a more effective committee environment?
10. What is an informal organization?
11. Discuss the role of the informal organization in the overall corporate environment.
12. Discuss some areas in which the goals of the informal organization may be in conflict with those of the formal organization.

Case for Discussion

Professor Jackson, a member of the management faculty at a large university, divided his class into small groups which were to work together on a class project. This project would last the full semester and was to result in a 75–100 page team paper which would make up 30% of the students' grade; each student would receive the same grade based upon the quality of the paper.

The members of one team included Jack Wilson, Mary Barnett, Sally Jones, Mike Pearson, and Tony Barett. At their first meeting they decided that Jack Wilson would be group leader. His responsibilities included assigning tasks to each team member, scheduling meetings, and coordinating the overall effort.

Six weeks into the semester Jack, Mary, Sally, and Tony met again to discuss the progress of the project. Following are some excerpts from the conversation:

Jack Wilson: Has anyone seen Mike Pearson? As you know, he has not attended our group meetings and has not turned in his section of the group assignment.

Sally Jones: I saw Mike in my history class and asked him why he has not been coming to our meetings. He said he had been sick and was now trying to catch up on his other work.

Mary Barnett: I don't know when he was sick. He went skiing with some of my friends two weeks ago.

Tony Barett: I spoke with Mike last Tuesday at a party and he said he didn't think he was going to be able to get his share of the work done. He said he needed to pick up his grades in his other classes because he's currently on probation and in danger of losing his scholarship. He said that without the scholarship he would have to drop out of school.

Jack Wilson: Well, what do we do? We can go to Professor Jackson and tell him about Mike and ask to have him given an 'F' for the paper or we can pick up Mike's work among the rest of us and go ahead and get the job done. Does anyone else have any other suggestions?

Selected References

Asch, S. "Effects of Group Pressure Upon the Modification and Distortion of Judgments." In *Group Dynamics: Research and Theory,* D. Cartwright and A. Zander, eds. New York: Harper & Row, 1960.

Athos, A. and Coffey, R. *Behavior in Organizations: A Multi-Dimensional View.* Englewood Cliffs, N.J.: Prentice-Hall, 1968.

Allen, L. "Making Better Use of Committees." In *Management Record,* December 1955.

Cartwright, D. and Zander, A. eds. *Group Dynamics: Research and Theory.* New York: Harper & Row, 1960.

Crutchfield, R. "Conformity and Character." In *American Psychologist* 10 (1955).

Dalton, M. *Men Who Manage.* New York: John Wiley & Sons, 1959.

Davis, K. *Human Relations at Work.* New York: McGraw–Hill, 1967.

Hare, P., Borgatta, E., and Bales, R. *Small Groups.* New York: Alfred A. Knopf, 1962.

Hampton, D., Summer, C., and Webber, R. *Organizational Behavior and the Practice of Management.* Glenview, Ill.: Scott, Foresman and Co., 1968.

Homans, G. *The Human Group.* New York: Harcourt Brace and World, 1950.

Ivancevich, J., Szilagyi, A., and Wallace, Marc. *Organizational Behavior and Performance.* Pacific Palisades, Calif.: Goodyear Publishing, 1977.

Moreno, J. L. *The Sociometric Reader.* New York: The Free Press, 1960.

_____ and Jennings, H. H. "Statistics of Social Configurations." In *Sociometry,* 1938.

Olmsted, Michael. *The Small Group.* New York: Random House, 1959.

Portes, D., Applewhite, P., and Misshauk, M., eds. *Studies in Organizational Behavior and Management.* New York: International Textbook, 1971.

Powell, R. "Race, Religion, and the Promotion of the American Executive." Columbus, Ohio: College of Administration, Ohio State University, 1969.

Sayles, Leonard. *The Behavior of Industrial Work Groups.* New York: John Wiley & Sons, 1958.

_____. "Work Group Behavior and the Larger Organization." In *Readings in Management,* M. Richards and W. Nielander, eds. Cincinnati, Ohio: South-Western Publishing Co., 1963.

Schein, Edgar. *Organizational Psychology.* Englewood Cliffs, N.J.: Prentice-Hall, 1965.

Sherif, M. and Sherif, C. *Reference Groups.* New York: Harper & Row, 1964.

_____. "A Study of Some Factors in Perception." In *Archaeological Psychology,* 1935.

Stogdill, Ralph. *Individual Behavior and Group Achievement.* New York: Oxford University Press, 1959.

Tillman, R., Jr. "Problems in Review: Committee on Trial." In *Harvard Business Review,* May-June 1960.

Thibaut, J. and Kelley, H. *The Social Psychology of Groups.* New York: John Wiley & Sons, 1959.

Leadership: Style and Power

8

Mastering Management in Creative Industries

In Gulf & Western Industries Inc.'s modern New York City offices, Martin S. Davis, a conservatively clad executive vice-president, rides up in an elevator with a man wearing jeans, a sweater, and a big political button. Davis, pointedly, says nothing. "He was a Paramount Pictures executive," Davis explains. Would he have commented about the strange attire if the man had been, say, a corporate financial officer? "Probably," Davis says.

Managing people in the so-called creative industries—moviemaking, recording, mass-market publishing, and the like—simply calls for different rules, not the least of which is making people in the creative end of the business feel that Big Brother is not watching. These are industries where computerized market research does little good, where an idea session in someone's living room takes the place of a research and development laboratory, and where long-term growth and sales projections are often little better than a shot in the dark. Whether the company is an independent, freewheeling studio or part of a giant conglomerate such as G&W or Transamerica Corp., B-school training simply falls short of what is needed. Some prerequisites for the successful manager:

The courage to act on gut feeling and a nebulous sense of the public's tastes when assigning top dollar to film production or book promotion.

The ability to stroke people whose egos are outsized, and whose work habits are peculiar at best.

A willingness to bury any latent Napoleonic instincts and persuade, rather than order, creative staffers and artists to follow a profitable path.

A strong business sense that can attend to details such as keeping warehousing costs down, improving distribution, and holding budgets in line without interfering with the creative process.

The odds against success are sobering. Hundreds of books are published for every one that hits the best-seller list, only one of five movies ever turns a profit, and probably less than 5% of all single records and only 20% or so of all record albums ever break even. Unfortunately, there is no surefire formula or discernible pattern. *The Godfather* pulled in $129 million on an initial cost of $6.8 million for Paramount, while *The Great Gatsby*, an $8 million endeavor for which the movie company had similarly high hopes, netted only $24 million.

Even in hindsight, most of the more truthful heads of creative companies admit that many of their biggest successes were surprises to them. "Who could have really predicted that *Bubbles* [Beverly Sills' autobiography] would sell 130,000 copies?" asks Stanley Sills, who, in addition to being Beverly's brother, is group general manager of ITT Publishing, an International Telephone & Telegraph Corp. group that includes Bobbs-Merrill Co. among its holdings. "I told my sister that if she sold 25,000 copies, she'd be an institution."

Keeping Protected

Sills recalls that about the same time Bobbs-Merrill put out *Bubbles*, it also pub-

Reprinted from the May 29, 1978 issue of *Business Week* by special permission. Copyright © 1978 by McGraw-Hill Publishing, Inc., New York, N.Y. 10020. All rights reserved.

lished a book by Aleksandr Solzhenitsyn's wife, giving an inside view of what the world-famous Russian author was really like. "This was something we felt certain that people would want to read," Sills says. "I think we sold all of 8,000 copies, and we would have had to sell at least 15,000 just to break even. I guess to some extent, this business is a gamble in which you throw the dice and hope."

Of course, most of these companies have found ways to hedge their bets, at least partially. Publishing houses have sizable backlists of books that bring in respectable incomes each year—how-to books, textbooks, and the like. Film studios have lucrative incomes from their film libraries, which bring a pretty penny from television networks, as well as from their made-for-TV series and movies. And in the case of those companies that are part of conglomerates, a corporate financial cushion helps them keep at least the semblance of an even keel. "This is a cyclical industry where you can't predict your upsides, and having a company like G&W behind you lets you protect your rear end in case of a downside," explains Barry Diller, chairman of Paramount Pictures Corp.

Diller's comment might surprise anyone who caught the full-page advertisement that ran in *Variety* magazine earlier this year condemning conglomerates as the ruination of all things creative. The ad ran shortly after the much-publicized defection of five high level executives at Transamerica's United Artists subsidiary. Although neither Transamerica nor UA would discuss that debacle with BUSINESS WEEK, Diller and other G&W creative executives quickly came forward to cry foul for the record.

"There is zero corporate participation in deciding which books we buy," notes Richard E. Snyder, the flamboyant and feisty head of G&W's Simon & Schuster Inc. publishing subsidiary, who adds that the editorial board at S&S serves to make sure that individual editors do not get carried away

on bad acquisition decisions. "I retain 99.9% of decision-making authority," Snyder says.

Diller claims an equal degree of freedom at Paramount. "We'll tell G&W we expect to put, say, $60 million on the line for film production and plan to distribute maybe 16 films this year, but we aren't expected to get more specific than that," he explains.

Turning Around

As long as their creative instincts are left unfettered, such executives seem to welcome corporate "meddling" into their businesses. Prior to G&W's purchase of Simon & Schuster in 1975, "we didn't even have a purchasing department," Snyder recalls. "We had inefficient warehousing and dingy little offices all over the city," he says. Now G&W has moved S&S into plush offices in New York's Rockefeller Center, where it is paying less total rent than it did three years ago and has slashed its accounts payable tally for supplies.

G&W gave similar help to Paramount, recalls Davis, who was with the foundering movie studio for eight years prior to its purchase by G&W in 1966. He claims that the conglomerate modernized the film distribution system, systematized methods for deciding how many prints of each movie were needed, and formed a huge and efficient foreign distribution network as a joint effort with MCA Inc., the consistently profitable entertainment conglomerate that recently made it big with *Jaws*.

Possibly most important, G&W had the foresight to cut Paramount's excess staff and take a $29 million early write-off on money-losing films. It was also G&W's influence that got the film company into the lucrative television business, helping it acquire Desilu Studios. "We had one red year, in 1969—a bad year for the entire industry. But we've been in the black ever since," Davis claims.

The Talent Search

Still, even Paramount's Diller concedes that "financial controls are not going to make our picture choices any better." So the quest for managers who feel equally at home with creative decisions and with balance sheets continues fast and furious in these industries. Most of these managers grew up in the business. "I'd never buy bringing a guy from a lumber company into the entertainment business," notes Sidney S. Sheinberg, president and chief operating officer of MCA. Although an attorney by education, Sheinberg points to his work as a radio announcer in his youth, his marriage to actress Lorraine Gray, and his 19-year tenure with MCA as proof that he has paid his dues as far as sensitivity to the creative process goes. Similarly, most heads of record companies have been in the music industry since they were teenagers, and most chief editors in book and magazine companies rose through the editorial ranks.

Companies have been putting out fewer movies and books over the last few years, however, and the supply of potential managers may be slowly drying up. Raiding among rival companies for top people is increasingly common. "The musical chairs in the movie industry are incredible," notes G&W's Davis. "In the days of second features you could build up a stable of talent, but now we just don't have a training ground." Adds Simon & Schuster's Snyder: "I spend at least 30% of my time looking for people to bring into S&S who are disciplined, almost compulsive workers and who can deal with intangibles."

Not surprisingly, money is a prime motivator for keeping top managers. Two of the three best-paid executives in the U.S. last year were with American Broadcasting Cos., with both of them grossing more than $1 million in total compensation. And industry scuttlebutt has it that the defecting United Artists executives left as much because of discontent over compensation as they did over disagreements with parent Transamerica on UA's artistic freedom.

Art for Money's Sake

But nowhere is the importance of money more apparent than with the salaries and advances paid to big names in these industries. "Creative artists" may be non-conformist, but apparently they are as interested in their own bottom line as any businessman. "I used to think artists signed contracts based on personal relationships they have with the company, but I've concluded that it almost always comes down to money," notes Arthur Mogull, president of United Artists Records Co. Companies are willing to pay top dollar because it usually comes back in higher profits, Snyder at S&S explains. "Our safest bet is the book that we pay a $1 million advance for, because the author has a brand-name image and we can be pretty sure he'll sell."

But money, while definitely necessary, is nonetheless not sufficient. All of the industry executives BUSINESS WEEK spoke with say they spend inordinate amounts of time coddling, nurturing, and otherwise "managing" creative people. "Employees may be out until 2 a.m. and not make it to work until 11, but you just have to accept certain eccentricities," notes UA's Mogull, who adds that as much as 90% of his time goes to personnel relations. "When someone hits a writing block, you have to be almost like a therapist to get him out of it," notes the manager of a five-person department of magazine writers. "You simply cannot separate being sensitive to the people from being sensitive to their work."

Artists' Relations

Handholding and persuasion are important in bringing together the artist's conception of his own best interest and the executive's gut feel for what the public wants. Dee Anthony, whose Bandana Enterprises Inc. manages such rock stars as Peter Frampton, notes that he deliberately shied from talk about record sales when he persuaded one of his singers to team up with a new band recently. "I had to convince him that there would be a chemistry that could work," he says. Anthony notes that many recording companies are beefing up artists-relations departments to shape subtly performers' careers toward salable records.

The recording companies seem to have the mix of good business sense and good personal relations down pat. Superficially, they are as informal as the offices of an underground newspaper. At RSO Records Inc., for example, the blue-jean-clad receptionist yells questions to executives in neighboring offices, a vice-president interrupts a meeting to look for a pen that turns up in his own pocket, and Albert E. Coury, the slender 43-year-old president, who sports frayed blue jeans, a football jersey, and scruffy suede cowboy boots, looks more like a disc jockey than the head of a company that projects sales of $130 million to $150 million this year. Yet he obviously knows what he is doing: RSO, with a relatively small stable of 14 acts under contract, boasts 4 of the top 10 single record hits in the country as well as 4 of the top 50 albums. "I help the artists pick their songs, but I'm aware of their temperaments, so I don't offend them," Coury says. "They like to feel like they're the only act on the label."

Even the staunchest supporters of the "business is business" theory of managing creative industries admit that flexibility and a bit of psychology are absolute necessities. "It is very important for creative types to be as informed as possible about business, and vice versa," says MCA's Sheinberg. "But you'd better not try to run by a set of hard and fast rules, because by definition you would squeeze out the very elements of creativity that make it work." And Dennis C. Stanfill,

chairman and president of Twentieth Century-Fox Film Corp. but also a veteran of such "noncreative" posts as corporate finance specialist with Lehman Bros., adds that even he will let a film go over budget when artistic demands are justified. "We have strict financial controls but administer them with a degree of flexibility," he says. "You have to give quality creative people your confidence."

A Delicate Balance

That does not necessarily mean letting them run the show, of course. RSO's Coury recalls a time when he was with Capitol Records Inc. and had to persuade Paul McCartney of Beatles fame to change the song mix on a new album. "He accepted my argument," Coury says. Result, according to Coury: The album took off in the U.S., but in Britain, where it went with McCartney's original choices, sales were substantially lower.

Similarly, studio chiefs adhere to common-sense rules of thumb—holding off release of a potential big hit until Christmas or Easter, or until a current blockbuster has peaked. Still, they will grant directors and other creators consultation privileges on ad campaigns and distribution decisions, if for no other reason than to assuage insecure artistic egos. "The narcissus factor is much bigger than in other businesses," sums up Samuel Z. Arkoff, chairman and president of American International Pictures Inc., a small independent studio known both for its willingness to take chances on new talents and for Arkoff's somewhat autocratic managerial style. "Committee decisions haven't worked in this field, and I'm not particularly renowned as a handholder," he says. "But even I have to be more tolerant than if I were in some other business."

IN THIS CHAPTER we will discuss the concept of leadership in the organizational framework. Few areas of management or organizational behavior have received as much attention from researchers and writers as this. We will view some of the ideas and concepts that have served to shape current thinking with respect to leadership behavior. Specifically, research and theory will be discussed in order to formulate and develop a framework by which the student may analyze and understand the concept of organizational leadership.

The chapter will focus on two basic dimensions of leadership. The first of these is *leadership style* and the variations in style that may be appropriate for different situations. The second dimension is the *sources of power* that a leader may draw on in carrying out the leadership function (see Figure 8.1).

What Is Leadership?

Let us begin by defining the term *leadership*. During the years in which leadership has been studied and analyzed there have evolved many ways of describing the leadership function.

One of the best known of the early researchers in the field, Ralph Stogdill, defines leadership as "the process (act) of influencing the activities of an organized group in its efforts toward goal setting and goal achievement." Another well-known researcher, Fred Fiedler, has defined leadership as "a process of influencing others for the purpose of performing a shared task." Finally, Tannenbaum, Weschler, and Massarik express the definition of *leadership* as "interpersonal influence, exercised in a situation and directed through the communication process toward the attainment of a specific goal

Figure 8.1. *Leadership Style and Sources of Power*

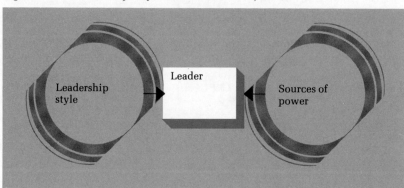

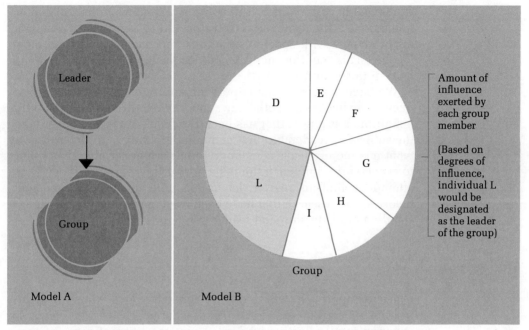

Figure 8.2. *Leadership and Group Influence*

or goals."[1] From these and other definitions, certain basic components or characteristics of leadership emerge:

1. A leader is one who, through some method or means, is able to
   influence the behavior of others.
2. The purpose of this influence is *directed toward the achievement
   of some task or goal.*

While defining the leadership function as the ability to influence
group behavior toward a specific goal, recent research in group dynamics has brought about a shift in thinking about this function. In
most group situations *one does not find a single leader who exists
apart from the group* to provide total direction and guidance to the
group (Model A, Figure 8.2). Current thinking suggests that within
any group it is likely that more than a single individual will exert
some degree of influence on overall group goals and direction. This
simply means that within a given group, each group member will
probably have *some influence.* With this concept in mind, we will
say that the individual whose influence is *most* significant in determining group behavior is the one we may designate as the leader
(Model B, Figure 8.2).

Viewed in this manner, leadership is a somewhat fluid phenomenon in which the leadership itself (the ability to influence behavior) might change with specific situations and changes in group membership. This "contingency" idea of leadership is discussed in depth later in this chapter.

We have defined leadership as the ability of an individual to influence the behavior of others in some desired direction. Beyond this definition, a problem that has been the focus of research ever since the subject of leadership first came under study is to determine by what method or means some individuals are better able than others to successfully influence the behavior of those around them. In an attempt to find an answer, let us examine some of the concepts, theories, and research that have been used in the quest for an understanding of leadership and leader behavior.

Trait Approach

One early approach to the study of leadership focused on the identification of certain specific *traits* or characteristics that might be common to all effective leaders. It was the hope of some of these early researchers to identify certain specific leadership traits so that testing procedures in the organization and classroom could be utilized to determine the presence of these traits in individuals, thereby identifying individual leadership potential. This approach can be found in a research project carried on by Edwin Ghiselli, whose results were published in 1963.[2] To identify those traits that might be associated with effective leader behavior, Ghiselli selected for study 416 workers representing eleven different types of jobs. Ghiselli divided these jobs into four major categories representing both man-

Category		Jobs
Management employees	I. Top management	District managers Personnel officers
	II. Middle management	Office managers Supervisors: Food processing plant
	III. Lower management	Foremen: Oil refinery Foremen: Metal plant
Operative employees	IV. Nonmanagement jobs	Mechanics Office workers

agement and operative level positions. Ghiselli administered a series of tests to measure five key characteristics of each individual taking part in the study:

1. Intelligence
2. Supervisory ability
3. Initiative
4. Self-assurance
5. Perceived occupational level.

As a result of the study Ghiselli concluded that "as a group, those individuals who hold management positions stand higher in intelligence, supervisory ability, initiative, self-assurance, and perceived occupational level than do those who hold line (operative) positions."[3]

Studies like Ghiselli's formed the basis of the trait approach to the study of leader behavior. In order to better understand this approach, as well as the results obtained by the researcher in the field, let us look at a summary by one of the foremost researchers in the field of leadership, Ralph Stogdill.

From the research that focused on identifying leadership traits, Stogdill concluded that factors normally associated with leadership would fall in the following categories:

1. *Capacity* (intelligence, alertness)
2. *Achievement* (scholarship, knowledge)
3. *Responsibility* (dependability, initiative)
4. *Participation* (activity, cooperation)
5. *Status* (socioeconomic position, popularity)
6. *Situation* (needs and interests of followers, objectives to be reached.)[4]

More recent research in the area of leadership trait identification caused Stogdill to add such factors as

1. Strong drive for responsibility and task completion
2. Originality in problem solving
3. Self-confidence and sense of personal identity
4. Readiness to absorb interpersonal stress
5. Willingness to tolerate frustration and delay.[5]

Recognizing the complexity of the interrelationship among leadership traits, Stogdill concluded that, although in isolation each trait may be of little value in predicting leadership qualities, "in combination ... they interact to generate personality dynamics advantageous to the person seeking the responsibilities of leadership."[6]

Problems with the Trait Approach

Although much of the research involving the search for specific leadership traits gave positive results, it soon became clear that (1) there was some conflict in the results of various research studies, (2) many of the "traits" identified were so general in nature as to be almost meaningless in interpretation, and (3) the list of identified leadership "traits" was becoming so lengthy as to include almost all human characteristics. With growing perception of these problems, emphasis on the trait approach to the study of leadership became less significant as a research activity.

This is not to say that the trait approach was useless. The many studies that did take place provided insight into leadership characteristics. For example, while recognizing the difficulty in identifying specific traits associated with leader behavior, Keith Davis does present a series of four general traits that he believes are characteristic of successful leadership:

1. *Intelligence:* Leaders tend to have somewhat higher intelligence than their average followers. The difference may not be great, but it usually exists.
2. *Social Maturity and Breadth:* Leaders are emotionally mature and have a wide range of interests and activities. They are not easily frustrated and maintain a fairly high level of self-assurance and self-respect.
3. *Inner Motivation and Achievement Drives:* Leaders seek responsibility as a way of satisfying a strong personal need to accomplish and achieve. Leaders constantly seek self-actualization as defined in Maslow's hierarchy of needs.
4. *Human Relations Attitude:* Leaders realize that they accomplish goals as a result of the cooperation of their followers. Consequently, leaders possess a high degree of respect for people, as well as a great deal of empathy and understanding for those around them.[7]

In general, researchers seeking to isolate and identify specific "leadership traits" have been unable to provide much insight into those characteristics that are associated with leadership behavior. As we have said, the "traits" that can be identified appear to be so general and so numerous as to be almost useless in gauging leadership potential in a specific individual.

Leadership Style

The research results of another group of investigators have suggested an approach to leadership that recognized that effective leader behavior might well be different for different individuals and for different situations. That is, one leader might exhibit a particular *style* of leadership in one situation and utilize a different *style* in a different situation. The recognition that leadership styles might vary from individual to individual and from situation to situation led researchers to investigate the dimensions or characteristics that might be associated with various styles of leader behavior and their resulting efect upon both the individual and the group. Let us examine some of the results of those who focused their attention on an analysis of leadership style.

Throughout this next section the reader is asked to consider each of the research studies in terms of two broad orientations: a particular leadership style may be oriented toward (1) individuals—human beings—or toward (2) production and tasks—a more material approach. Individual researchers whose work will be discussed utilize somewhat different terminology in describing their research activity. The emphasis of each study, however, is to identify the extent to which a leader utilizes a *style* that focuses upon the *individual* in a given situation or a style that focuses upon *production, task* or some other nonhuman aspects of the situation. The objective of the various research studies is to determine the probable impact of one

Figure 8.3. *Leadership Styles*

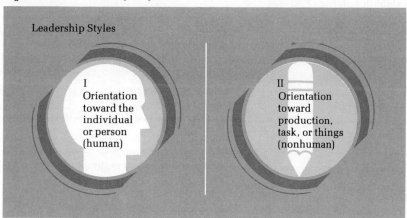

leadership style as opposed to another (human versus nonhuman) in a variety of situations.

The studies that have been selected represent a cross section of some of the most significant research in the area of leadership style.

White and Lippitt

In a now classic study conducted by White and Lippitt, the researchers used four groups of ten-year-old boys who were engaged in hobby activities.[8] The groups were considered to be approximately equal in personality characteristics, intelligence, physical, and socioeconomic criteria. For the purpose of demonstrating the impact of various leadership styles upon group behavior, four adult leaders were trained in three different styles of leadership. (These styles and their corresponding characteristics are described in Exhibit 8.1.) The leaders were moved to a new group every six weeks. Each leader changed his style for each new group. Thus each group experienced a different leader style with a different leader.

Having observed group behavior and individual member reactions under each style of leadership, White and Lippitt arrived at a series of conclusions regarding the effectiveness of leadership styles:

1. "Laissez-faire" was less efficient than "democracy." In the democrat group there was more work and higher quality work than in the laissez-faire environment.
2. Although there was more work done in the "autocratic" groups than in the "democratic," overall worker motivation and originality were higher in the democratic groups.

Exhibit 8.1. *Leader Styles*

Authoritarian	Democratic	Laissez-faire
All determination of policy by the leader.	All policies a matter of group discussion and decision.	Complete freedom for group or individual decisions.
Techniques and activities dictated by leader.	Activities arrived at during group discussions. Alternatives suggested by the leader.	Materials supplied by the leaders, who would provide information if asked.
Leader dictated individual job task and work companion of each individual.	Members were free to work with whomever they chose. Division of task left up to the group.	Complete nonparticipation of leader.
Leader was "personal" in praise and criticism of group work. Tended to remain aloof.	Leader was "objective" in praise and criticism and tended to be a member of group.	Infrequent comments on member activities. No attempt to regulate the group.

3. Autocratic leadership can bring about a high level of hostility and aggression among group members; this behavior became evident when groups moved to a new style of leadership and often exhibited some type of "release" behavior.
4. There is more dependence and less individuality under autocratic leadership. Member reactions were more submissive and less individual under the autocratic leader.
5. There was more friendly behavior and a higher level of group-mindedness in the democratic environment.

The study by Lippitt and White indicates that the *autocratic* style of leadership may generate more *output* than either *democratic* or *laissez-faire,* but the higher level of output may be obtained at the sacrifice of morale and motivation within the work group. In addition, the hostility created in the autocratic environment might well have far-reaching negative implications for the organization. This being the case, it appears as though the autocratic style may be more effective than other styles for only a short period of time, after which the high levels of hostility and low morale within the work group would tend to bring about a serious deterioration in overall group performance.

Ohio State Leadership Studies

In 1945 the Bureau of Business Research of Ohio State University initiated one of the first major scientifically designed research efforts into the type of behavior that leaders exhibit.[9] The research team of psychologists, sociologists, and economists believed that no satisfactory definition of leadership was available at that time and that prior research in the field of leadership had not sufficiently distinguished between the *concept* of leadership and the *effectiveness* of the resulting leadership behavior. In other words, "leadership" was too often confused with "good leadership."

The researchers at Ohio State decided not to concern themselves with an exact definition of leadership but rather to concentrate their attention on determining how successful leaders carry on their activities. To accomplish this objective the researchers developed the Leader Behavior Description Questionnaire (LBDQ), which they believed had wide application across many organizational settings. This questionnaire was administered to Air Force commanders and bomber crews and included among respondents commissioned and noncommissioned officers as well as civilian personel within the Navy Department. In addition, the LBDQ was distributed to college administrators, principals, teachers, school superintendents, manufacturing foremen, executives in regional cooperative associations, and leaders of various student and civilian organizations and groups.

The questionnaire focused on the following leader dimensions, or behaviors:

1. Initiation: Frequency of originating, facilitating, or resisting new ideas.
2. Membership: Frequency of mixing with the group, stressing informal interaction between himself and members and interchanging personal services with members.
3. Representation: Frequency of defending the group against attack, advancing the interest of the group, and acting on behalf of the group.
4. Integration: Frequency of subordinating individual behavior, encouraging pleasant group atmosphere, reducing conflicts between members, or promoting individual adjustment to the group.
5. Organization: Frequency of defining or structuring his or her own work, the work of other members, or the relationship among members in the performance of their work.
6. Domination: Frequency of restricting the behavior of the group in action, decision making, or expression of opinion.
7. Communication: Frequency of providing information to members, seeking information from them, facilitating exchange of information, or showing awareness of affairs pertaining to the group.
8. Recognition: Frequency of engaging in behavior which expresses approval of the behavior of group members.
9. Production: Frequency of setting levels of effort or achievement, or prodding members for greater effort or achievement.[10]

The Ohio State studies revealed highly consistent patterns of behavior with respect to how leaders carry out their leadership function. Analysis of the emerging patterns exposed two basic types of behavior:

Initiating Structure: Behavior concerning the degree to which the leader organized and defined tasks, assigned the work to be done, established communication networks, and evaluated work group performance.

Consideration: Behavior that involved trust, mutual respect, friendship, support, and a concern for the welfare of the employee.

The leaders studied did not exhibit equal amounts of each type of behavior, but on a comparative scale the types serve to describe the style of leadership that might be exhibited by a particular individual. This style could be represented by the grid shown in Figure 8.4. Depending upon the degree to which a manager made use of "ini-

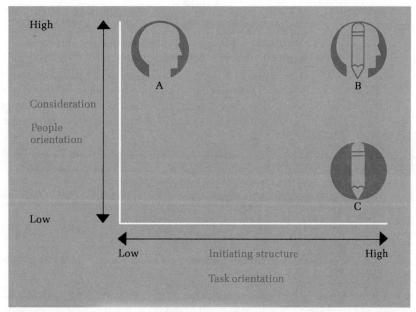

Figure 8.4. *People and Task Orientations*

tiating structure" and "consideration" in carrying out his or her activities, that person's "style" could be represented by some point on the grid scale. For example, with respect to a given individual's leadership style, Point A in Figure 8.4 indicates a high concern for people (consideration) and a low concern with task (initiating structure). Point B indicates high concern with task and low concern for people. Point C indicates high concern for both.

Although it was at first assumed by the researchers that the most effective manager would be the one who ranked high in both initiating structure and consideration (point C in Figure 8.4), more recent research indicates that certain types of organizational settings may require differing leadership styles. For example, a study by House, Filley, and Kerr conducted among research and development personnel in an "airframe" manufacturing company, a business machine company, and a petroleum refinery showed wide variations in the relationship between the perceived consideration of the leader and the satisfaction of subordinates.[11] These variations seemed to indicate that differing organizational environments will call for different leadership styles in order to maximize the satisfaction and performance of subordinates.

The Managerial Grid

Another approach that utilizes a grid to identify and classify various leadership styles has been developed by Robert Blake and Jane Mouton.[12] Blake and Mouton identify the axes of the grid as representing concern for production and concern for people. Using the grid shown in Figure 8.5, Blake and Mouton describe five basic leader styles. The numbers that preface each of the five styles of management describe where the style would fit on the grid. For example, (1,9) Management would indicate high concern for people (9 on the

Figure 8.5. *The Managerial Grid*

Source: From Robert R. Blake and Jane Srygley Mouton. *The New Managerial Grid* (Houston: Gulf Publishing Company. Copyright © 1978), p. 11. Reproduced by permission.

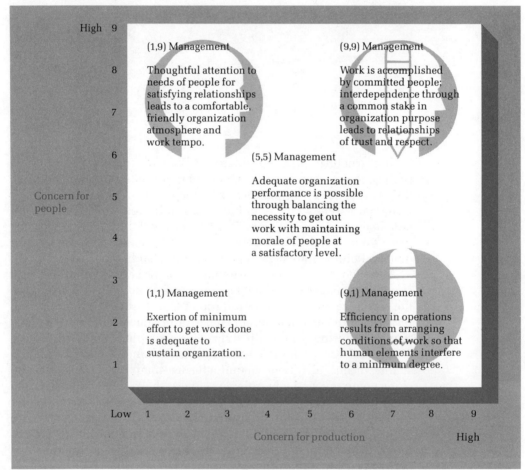

"people" scale) and low concern for production (1 on the "production" scale).

Blake and Mouton used answers to a series of questionnaires to identify the specific leadership style normally utilized by a given manager. Their analysis defines the extent to which a particular individual is oriented toward either task (9.1 Management) or people (1.9 Management) in carrying out leadership activities. Once the style of a particular leader is understood, the analysis is then used as the basis for a training program designed to bring about some change in the leadership style exercised by that individual. Such training techniques usually make use of case discussion as well as small group simulation and role playing in order to give all individuals the opportunity to analyze and understand where their style of leadership fits within the grid. Once individual managers have some awareness of their style of leadership it is possible for them to attempt to change or modify their style in future situations.

Situationist Approach

To aid managers in selecting the most appropriate leadership style for a given situation, Tannenbaum and Schmidt designed a continuum of leadership behavior that includes seven specific types of managerial action (leadership styles).[13] Each type represents a different degree of authority that a manager would exercise in dealing with subordinates. The continuum of leader behavior is shown in Figure 8.6 on page 191. The extreme left side of the scale represents a highly autocratic style of leadership. The right side of the continuum, on the other hand, characterizes a style of leader behavior that is essentially democratic.

Tannenbaum and Schmidt make the point that the key to successful leader behavior is the ability to determine accurately what leadership style would be most effective for a given situation. The major issue they address is thus the identification of those factors a manager should consider in determining the most appropriate leadership style for a given situation. Prior to the selection of a particular style, according to Tannenbaum and Schmidt, three major factors should be considered and evaluated: factors in the manager, factors in the subordinate, and factors in the situation (see Figure 8.7).

Factors in the manager. Managers must consider their own attitudes regarding the sharing of authority. In addition, they must evaluate their overall confidence in subordinates' ability as well as their own feelings of security.

Factors in the subordinate. The manager should consider the needs of subordinates for freedom and independence. In addition, an

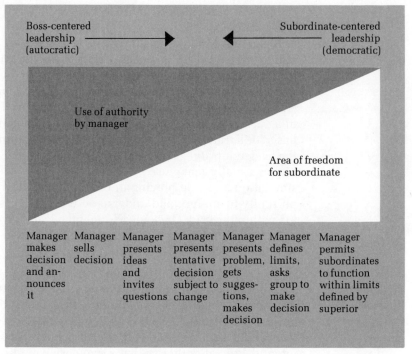

Figure 8.6. *Continuum of Leadership Behavior*

Source: Robert Tannenbaum and Warren H. Schmidt, "How to Choose a Leadership Pattern," *Harvard Business Review,* March–April 1958. Copyright © 1958 by the President and Fellows of Harvard College; all rights reserved.

evaluation should be made of their abilities and interests in the particular problem area, as well as the extent to which they may identify with corporate objectives or goals.

Factors in the situation. Finally, the situation itself will play a large part in determining what may be an appropriate leadership style. The type of organizational structure as well as the extent to which policy statements and defined procedures exist within the company may well influence the choice. The effectiveness of subordinates in working together on a common problem and also the time available for problem solution will usually provide additional guidance for developing an effective style of leadership.

Choosing a Leadership Style

Up to this point we have attempted to present some of the research that has focused on analyzing leadership style. In addition, factors about the leader, the subordinate, and the situation that may influence the appropriate choice of a leadership style have been discussed. We will now discuss some of the elements that should be

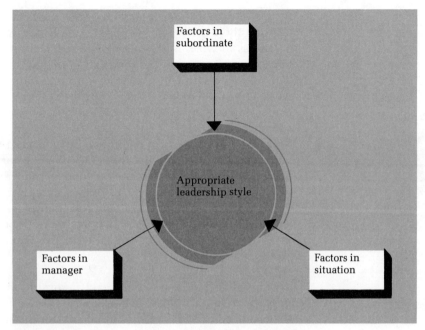

Figure 8.7. *Factors in Selection of Leadership Style*

considered in deciding upon the most appropriate style of leadership for a given situation.

Perhaps the most important thing to remember about leadership style is that *no single style is appropriate for all situations*. The truly effective leader is the one who is able to assess a particular situation and select the style of leadership that will be most effective. Just as there is no one set of leadership traits peculiar to all leaders, there is no one style of leadership that is effective in all situations.

Let us take a moment to discuss some of the situational and behavioral factors that may affect the style of leadership utilized within a given situation. For purposes of illustration we will speak in terms of the three styles defined by White and Lippitt—the authoritarian, the democratic, and the laissez-faire.

In the authoritarian style of leadership, all decisions are made by the leader and orders are then issued to subordinates. Little or no input is provided by subordinates; they merely follow the leader's policies and procedures. In examining some rationales for this style of leadership, we can consider the following points:

1. With respect to the manager's own attitudes, an authoritarian style of leadership might well reflect a "Theory X" philosophy

regarding subordinate behavior. You recall that under this philosophy the manager lacks confidence in the willingness of subordinates to work independently to reach desired goals.

2. Lack of confidence in the motivation of subordinates might well lead a manager to feel it necessary to maintain tight control over work group behavior. Tight control itself reflects an autocratic leadership style in which very little freedom would be allowed to subordinates.

3. This style of leadership might also be exhibited by an individual manager who is somewhat insecure in his or her own abilities or position. Insecurity may make the manager feel that it is necessary to rely on formal authority to obtain compliance. For example, newly appointed managers unsure of their position may affect an authoritarian style until they become more familiar and comfortable with the nature of the task and the make-up of the work group.

In general, subordinates will react favorably to an authoritarian leadership style only if they themselves exhibit relatively high dependency needs or are unsure about job requirements or manager expectations. To the extent that subordinates need a high degree of security within their job environment they may depend on the leader (manager) to define their job and work habits and provide restrictive guidelines governing work group behavior. The authoritarian style normally provides very little freedom for initiative on the part of subordinates, but it does provide a relatively well-defined, unambiguous environment for the employee. The need for a well-defined work group environment may be particularly strong in large work groups or in the performance of tasks that are unstructured in nature. Certain employees, too, may lack confidence in their skill or ability. Lack of confidence may create frustration if the subordinate is left to make many decisions. As a result, the more closely the job and all its parameters are defined, the more secure the environment and the less frustrated this type of employee. To some employees this environment is more desirable than one in which the decision making is required or one in which the manager provides complete freedom.

The second leadership style is democratic. Its effectiveness is based on the assumption that a higher level of motivation will be achieved if employees are given the opportunity to participate in the various decision-making processes, the theory being that employees will work harder to achieve goals that they themselves have had a part in establishing. This style therefore involves the active participation of subordinates in establishing policies and procedures within the work situation. Subordinates take an active part in discussions regarding alternatives, and their opinions are considered by the manager. It is still the leader (manager) who is ultimately responsible for making the decisions, but in making them the manager seeks input and advice.

To utilize this style of leadership effectively, the manager should feel a high level of confidence and security. This is necessary so that the manager will not be threatened by the input and recommendations of subordinates. In addition, the manager should have respect for the skill and competence of subordinates; the manager should believe that the employees possess the knowledge and ability to deal with job-related problems and make responsible recommendations. In order to be an effective democratic-style leader, the manager must be willing to spend a little extra time in the overall leadership process. This is necessary in order to actively seek and evaluate input from subordinates. It is hoped that this style of leadership will result in a higher level of employee dedication to the objectives established. The higher level of dedication may then reflect itself in increased performance and work group satisfaction.

The third leadership style, laissez-faire, prevails in an environment where significant independence is given to subordinates by the manager. This style of leadership finds its application almost exclusively among professional employees. Its effectiveness is based upon the assumption that the goals or objectives to be reached are known and accepted by subordinates and that they themselves are motivated and skilled enough to determine the most effective method of reaching those goals with a minimum amount of leadership and direction. Here again leaders must have a high degree of confidence in the skill and dedication of subordinates. The manager's function is usually that of providing information as it is needed and facilitating the supply of resources required by the work group. A key point is that for this method of leadership to be effective, the manager must take added time and effort to insure that the desired goals are known and accepted by the subordinates. This is necessary since the manager will be less involved in general with subordinates.

Justification for the laissez-faire style rests on the idea that a group of highly skilled professionals who are aware of objectives to be reached are most effective if left on their own to evaluate a situation and decide how to proceed. Significant interference from the manager would create frustration in the work group; it might be considered an infringement on professional competence. For this reason, skilled professionals are perhaps the most difficult group to supervise, since the manager must constantly walk a fine line between "overmanaging" and maintaining control of the work situation. When dealing with skilled professional employees, the manager's responsibility lies mainly in overall guidance with respect to general goals and provision of necessary resources. The specific actions to be taken will generally fall within the purview of the individual employees. This type of leadership style finds its widest application in research and engineering facilities where the individual skill level of subordinates in a given area may well exceed that of the manager.

In summary, we have presented some criteria that may lead a manager to choose one style of leadership over another. The points that have been made should not be taken as absolute or all-inclusive, since to a certain extent they represent an oversimplification of the leadership style issue that does not take into account the complexities of the real world environment. In an appendix to this chapter we will examine some contingency models that attempt a more sophisticated examination of leader behavior.

Leadership Style and Group Performance

So far we have focused on some theories and models designed to explain the leadership function. Only a few of these theories suggested that one particular style of leadership is more effective than another for a given situation. With the varied situations and conditions examined for each study, it is often difficult to draw meaningful conclusions. There do, however, appear to be certain consistencies across a substantial number of studies regarding the effectiveness of leader behavior. Here are some recurring general conclusions:

1. Current research does not show any consistent relationship between leadership style and worker *productivity*.
2. Overall work group *satisfaction* does appear to be more clearly associated with a democratic, participative style of leadership than with an autocratic style.
3. Overall work group *productivity* tends to be higher if the leader maintains some psychological distance from subordinates.
4. Overall group *cohesiveness* tends to be higher in groups in which the leader uses a democratic or participative style of leadership.

In summary, if we group the varied leader styles discussed into two major categories—person-oriented and work-oriented—the following conclusions seem reasonable:[14]

1. Person-oriented patterns of leader behavior are not consistently related to productivity.
2. Among the work-oriented patterns, only those behaviors that maintain role differentiation and let followers know what to expect are consistently related to group productivity.

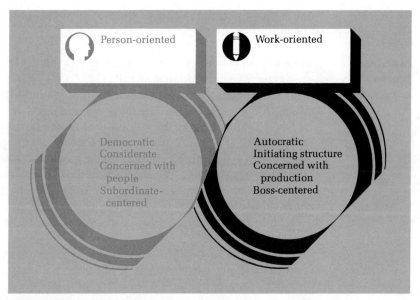

Figure 8.8. *Person-Oriented and Work-Oriented Behaviors*

3. Among the person-oriented behaviors, only those providing free-dom for member participation in group activities and showing concern for followers' welfare and comfort are consistently related to group cohesiveness.
4. Among the work-oriented behaviors, only the pattern that structures member expectations is uniformly related to group cohesiveness.
5. All the person-oriented behaviors tend to be related positively to follower satisfaction.
6. Among the work-oriented behaviors, only those that structure expectations are more often than not related positively to follower satisfaction.

Leader Behavior and the Sources of Power

In our discussions of leadership we have been analyzing leadership styles and the factors that may make one style more appropriate than another for a particular situation. There is one aspect of leadership we have not yet mentioned, however. That is *power*. Many leadership techniques depend on the effective and appropriate use of power in bringing about some desired behavior on the part of others.

Let us now examine some of the ways various bases of power can be used within the organizational setting.

Power in Today's Organization

The key to success for every manager is the ability to influence the behavior of subordinates effectively. One of the major jobs of any successful manager is to select a style of leadership that will accomplish this objective. The ultimate success of each manager rests on the ability to influence the behavior of others so that they accomplish given tasks. It is important to note that we use the phrase "influence the behavior of others" and not the more "authoritarian" concept that has traditionally been associated with the management function. This change in orientation for management has become more apparent in recent years as managers are dealing with subordinates who have different needs and attitudes than those of several years ago.

To be sure, the traditional sources of power, such as the ability to reward and punish, still have a place in the organizational environment, but these are no longer sufficient to insure managerial success. In many cases, they may only serve to alienate many of today's workers. The traditional concept of a single leader or manager directing the efforts of a mass of subordinates has given way to the recognition that, within any group, including the work situation, many different individuals may influence the overall attitudes and behavior of group members. Thus, the manager must act in such a way that subordinates perceive they will satisfy their needs most effectively by behaving according to the wishes of the manager. The manager must create an environment conducive to subordinate need satisfaction. It is by means of this environment that the manager will be effective in motivating subordinates to behave constructively. With this refined concept of managerial leadership and power as our reference point, we will discuss some of the power bases a manager may draw on.

Sources of Power

According to J. R. P. French and B. Raven, there are essentially five bases of social power that are instrumental in eliciting some desired behavior from another individual. Their analysis of the bases of power as *reward, coercive, referent, expert,* and *legitimate* will be the foundation of our discussion. [15]

Reward Power. The first power base a leader may draw on is the ability or potential ability to bestow some *reward* upon the person whose behavior he or she is attempting to influence. The idea of influencing another's behavior by means of reward is certainly not new. What is somewhat new is our understanding that in order to be

Exhibit 8.2. *Bases of Social Power*

Power base	Source	Comment
Reward	Ability to provide something of value in exchange for some desired behavior	Manager must determine exactly what an individual perceives as a reward and be able to convince subordinates that she or he can deliver the promised reward.
Coercive	Ability to punish undesired behavior	Can be effective, but leadership based solely on this base may eventually lead to loss of morale and destruction of work group.
Referent	Charismatic personality	Highly effective but usually cannot be acquired; individual manager may or may not have this power base available.
Expert	Acknowledged expertise in a given area	Highly effective but only in the limited area in which individual is perceived to be an expert.
Legitimate	Formal position or title	Based on internalized values within society and normally associated with formal position. This power base is becoming less significant as an effective method of influencing individual and group behavior.

effective the reward must be properly applied. The person attempting to use reward power must be sure to be sufficiently aware of the value system of the person to be influenced in order to determine what that person considers a reward. Too often a manager inadvertently imposes his or her own values on others and attempts to influence through rewards based only on the manager's own value system. To repeat a typical case previously mentioned, a manager who finds it hard to deal with a given employee may be heard to say, "I just don't understand Joe. He has a good job with a good future and yet he still doesn't seem to want to produce." In fact, what the manager is saying is, "*I consider* that to be a good job with a good future." In this situation, the manager is imposing a value system on the employee, rather than trying to determine what Joe expects from his job or what motivates Joe.

To use reward power effectively, the manager must give careful consideration to the needs of the individual whose behavior he or she is attempting to influence. The manager must consider a complete spectrum of rewards that would satisfy a wide variety of needs. For example, an employee who was entitled to a new office as a result of a recent promotion was denied this office because of remodeling in the plant. This same employee began arriving approximately one-half hour late for work each morning. When questioned by his superior he always had some excuse for his lateness, even though tardiness had not been a problem in the past. Eventually it came out that the employee considered the one-half hour to be his legitimate right because he was not able to move into his new office. In this case, even though the employee knew that he would have the office in time, he *felt* that he had earned a reward that was being denied to him. In order to compensate, the employee felt entitled to a substitute reward for the promotion. It is clear that the use of rewards to motivate behavior may indeed be full of complications and therefore should be studied closely by the manager.

Aside from the reward itself, an employee's behavior will be influenced by the probability he or she attaches to actually receiving the reward for behaving in the desired manner. According to the *expectancy theory* of motivation (see Appendix), an individual's behavior will be influenced according to the following formula:

$$\text{Amount of influence (motivation)} = \text{Desirability of reward} \times \text{Probability of receiving the reward}$$

This probability value will be a function of the trust that a subordinate has in the manager, as well as the employee's perception that the manager not only wants to give the reward but has the *power* to provide it. If a manager promises a promotion for performing in a certain manner, the behavior of the subordinate will be influenced (1) by the extent of the subordinate's belief that the manager actually means to give him the promotion and (2) by the subordinate's perception that the manager has the power to grant promotions. If the subordinate believes all this and if the subordinate considers the promotion to be highly desirable, then his or her behavior is likely to be significantly influenced by the desires of the manager.

Coercive Power. The concept of coercive power is similar to that of reward power, but it is located at the opposite end of the scale. Coercive, or punishment, power refers to the manager's ability to withhold rewards or to punish an employee in some way for failing to perform in the desired manner. The threat of punishment may have significant impact on the behavior of an individual, but a manager should give careful consideration to influencing the behavior of others through an *extended* use of threat or punishment.

Extensive use of coercive power may create a situation in which the subordinate feels more comfortable withdrawing from the threatening environment (quitting the job, absenteeism) than being constantly exposed to the negative feelings brought about by threats or punishment. In addition, the overall effect on morale and frustration levels in the work force created by the constant use of coercive power will in many cases lead to a breakdown of authority and structure within the group. This breakdown may lead to a reduction of performance by all members of the work group through subtle but effective application of group norms. The group draws upon its own ingenuity to create an environment in which problems invariably occur. The manager is often helpless to deal with these problems; it is often impossible to isolate the cause and identify those responsible. In one department in which the manager was constantly threatening individuals who did not reach performance goals, a large number of this department's employees fell victim to "strange and unique illnesses" that did not seem to be affecting other departments. These "illnesses" caused overall performance within the department to drop significantly over a period of time. In this case, the work group had joined together to reduce performance and in this way strike back at the manager for creating employee frustration by using coercive power.

Referent Power. This refers to the ability of one individual to influence the behavior of another because of the latter's desire to "identify" with the former. This identification does not necessarily relate to influencing the individual's ability to reward or punish. It relates more to the feelings of admiration or respect that one person may have for another. These feelings result in a person's attempt to emulate the individual he or she admires and respects. The world of advertising capitalizes on the referent concept by having well-known athletes and sports personalities endorse consumer products. These personalities, although certainly not able to reward or punish behavior, are able to exert significant influence over the behavior of others simply because many people identify with them or wish in some way to be like them.

This desire to identify with another may be due to some accomplishment on the part of the individual, as in the case of the sports personality, or it may simply be a function of the magnetism of personality. In the latter case, the individual is said to possess *charisma* and is often able to influence behavior by the strength of this charismatic quality. One example of a charismatic leader would be John F. Kennedy. In his speeches and interactions with others, President Kennedy was able to create in those around him a strong feeling of identification. As a result, Kennedy could influence the attitudes and behavior of many.

This referent or charismatic power base is not one that can be readily acquired. It is usually inherent in personality and behavior, and is either present or not present in a given individual. Managers fortunate enough to project referent or charismatic qualities may use them as tools of influence. Managers who do not must cultivate other bases of power.

Expert Power. This form of power is based upon the perception, accurate or not, that a particular individual has superior skill or knowledge. Attempts to influence the behavior of others in the area of expertise are generally successful.

There are two key points here. First, there must be the perception that a person does possess superior knowledge in a particular area. Second, influence attempts based on expert power will be successful only in those areas in which the individual is perceived to be an expert. Thus the person using "expert power" to influence behavior should limit influence attempts to the areas in which she or he is considered to be an authority. Attempts to influence behavior in other areas may be ineffective. They may even create a reduced perception of expertise in *all* areas.

The concept of expert power is very much in evidence in our specialized society. We are all influenced to behave in certain ways by a wide variety of "experts," including lawyers, doctors, accountants, and mechanics. The degree of influence in which expert power may be applied is of course limited; we would probably be unwilling to put much faith in advice on our health from a tax accountant even though we would be most willing to follow his recommendations on our tax return.

Legitimate Power. This base of power derives from society's expectations and attitudes regarding certain roles and positions. Perceptions regarding the way we *ought* to act toward a given position or office are influenced by our cultural background. Legitimate power gives an individual the ability to influence the behavior of another *simply because of the position he or she occupies.* Because it is a function of a value system, this kind of power carries varying degrees of influence, depending on the values of the social group with which we are dealing.

In recent years there has been a dramatic decline in the ability of individuals to influence others solely on the basis of the legitimate power of their position. We see all around us challenges to the authority of parents, law enforcement officers, political leaders, and college professors. Society is serving notice that the position, in and of itself, is no longer sufficient to serve as a basis for influence. Thus, an individual in a *position* of leadership may find it difficult to influence another's behavior if legitimacy of position is the sole basis for influence. As today's worker becomes better educated and more aware of the social and political environment it becomes more necessary for the manager to take the time to explain the rationale behind a given request or directive. Being "the boss" is not enough. The manager should not think of this as relinquishing power or authority; rather, it is an adjustment that needs to be made to deal effectively with the changing character of the work force.

Review of Leadership Style and Power

We may conclude that the behavior of a leader is made up of two basic components: (1) the *leadership style* exhibited as a means of influencing the behavior of others and (2) the *source of power* that the leader draws upon.

To understand the dimensions of leadership within a given group situation, we need to determine the leadership style and source of power that are most appropriate for a particular group and situation. Exhibit 8.3 suggests some generalizations about some leadership styles and sources of power that tend to appear—and to be effective—in combination:

1. *Autocratic* leaders *may tend* to rely upon *reward, coercive,* and *legitimate* power bases.
2. *Democratic* leaders *may tend* to draw upon an *expert* and *referent* power base.
3. *Laissez-faire* leaders *may tend* to utilize a more *legitimate* base of power.

Exhibit 8.3. *Relation of Sources of Power to Leadership Styles*

Source of power	Autocratic	Democratic	Laissez-faire
Reward	X		
Coercive	X		
Legitimate	X		X
Expert		X	
Referent		X	

Appendix—Theories of Leader Behavior: The Development of Contingency Theory

In addition to those who have studied leadership in terms of leadership styles and sources of power, there is a group of researchers who believe that to understand leader behavior one must give more careful consideration to the contingencies that may exist with respect to a given situation at a particular time. (In management, "contingency" means the necessity to adjust leadership style to fit specific conditions that exist at the time.) These contingencies, which may involve the manager, the task, the subordinates, or the environment, are considered to be key variables in analysis of the leadership function. In an effort to place a greater emphasis on these contingencies, several researchers have developed models or theories that make use of this dimension in analyzing the leadership function.

Expectancy Theory (Victor Vroom)

In essence, the Vroom model states that an individual's *motivation* to behave in a particular manner is a function of two factors: (1) the *expectation* that a particular behavior will lead to a desired goal and (2) the *strength of the desirability* of the goal. (The degree of desirability of a given goal is called its *valence*).[1] Motivation to behave in a certain way can be stated in terms of these two factors as follows:

$$\text{Motivation} = \text{Valence (desirability of goal)} \times \text{Expectancy (expectation that behavior will lead to goal achievement).}$$

If a student wanted a grade of "A" for a particular course, for example, his or her *motivation* to study would be a function of how badly the student desired the grade *(valence)* and the level of *expectancy* that study would result in achieving it.

Path-Goal Analysis (Robert House)

Starting with this expectancy theory as a base, Robert House has defined a path-goal theory of leadership made up of two components:

1. Leader behavior is acceptable and satisfying to subordinates to the extent that the subordinates see such behavior as either an immediate source of satisfaction or as instrumental to future satisfaction.
2. Leader behavior will be motivational to the extent that (a) such behavior makes satisfaction of subordinates' needs contingent on effective performance and (b) such behavior complements the en-

vironment of subordinates by providing the coaching, guidance, support, and rewards necessary for effective performance.[2]

According to House, the behavior of a leader should (1) clearly define goals to be reached, and (2) remove obstacles that could stand in the way of the employee's achieving these goals.

The leader can most effectively accomplish these functions by selecting an appropriate style of leadership from among the styles House defines:

1. *Directive leadership:* an authoritarian style of leadership in which goals and direction are clearly spelled out by the manager with no involvement or participation by subordinates.
2. *Supportive leadership:* the manager is concerned with subordinates and interacts with them in a free, friendly, and open manner.
3. *Participative leadership:* subordinates participate and provide input, aiding the manager in the decision-making process.
4. *Achievement-oriented leadership:* causes subordinates to strive for higher standards of performance and to have more confidence in their ability to meet challenging goals.

The key to successful leadership behavior, according to House, is the ability of the manager to recognize and identify certain *contingency factors* that will dictate the use of one of these leadership styles over the others in a specific situation. House identifies two major contingency variables:

1. Personal characteristics of the subordinates
2. Environmental pressures and demands with which the subordinates must cope in order to accomplish work goals and to satisfy their needs.[3]

These contingency factors have been investigated in various research activities carried on by House as well as other researchers in the field. They found that

1. *Supportive leadership* will be most effective in bringing about satisfaction for subordinates who work in high-stress, frustrating and dissatisfying tasks.
2. *Directive leadership* will be most positively related to satisfaction and expectations of subordinates who perform unclear and ill-defined tasks, but directive leadership will be negatively related to satisfaction and expectations of subordinates performing clear tasks.
3. *Achievement-oriented leadership* in unclear task situations in-

volving nonrepetitive work will be as effective as the leader's commitment to goal achievement; the greater the achievement orientation of the leader the greater the confidence of subordinates that their effort will result in desirable performance.

4. *Participative leadership* will have a positive effect on both satisfaction and motivation of subordinates when subordinates are highly ego-involved in a decision or task and the decision or task is ambiguous.[4]

Fiedler's Contingency Model

Fiedler's model was developed from his research activities involving managers and supervisors in a variety of organizational settings.[5] Fiedler used a series of tests to obtain data on the values and attitudes of each manager. The tests provide a measure of leadership style, yielding information in two basic areas:

1. *Assumed similarity between opposites (ASO)*. This measurement determines the degree of similarity between a leader's perception of his most preferred coworker and his least preferred coworker.
2. *Least preferred coworker (LPC)*. This score measures the degree to which managers are favorable in their perceptions of least preferred coworkers. This score relates to the ASO and likewise attempts to determine the perceptions of a manager with respect to his least preferred coworker.

These test scores indicate which of two basic leadership styles a particular individual prefers:

1. The *human relations style* is typified by the individual who does *not* differentiate significantly between his most preferred and least preferred coworker (ASO) and who has a fairly *favorable* attitude toward his least preferred coworker (LPC).
2. The *task-oriented* leaders perceive a *wide differential* between the characteristics of most preferred and least preferred coworker (ASO) and have *unfavorable* perceptions of their least preferred coworker (LPC).

According to Fiedler, the leader who uses the human relations style is concerned about the feelings of others and derives satisfaction from a good relationship with coworkers. The task-oriented individual is concerned primarily with the task or job and directs efforts toward productivity rather than interpersonal relations.

Fiedler makes the point that a leader's ability to influence the behavior of others is a function of selecting the *appropriate* style of leadership. The appropriate style may well be different for different groups in different situations. Thus Fiedler presents three contingency factors that he believes will have the most significant impact in determining the appropriate style of leadership for a given situation:

1. *Leader-member relations:* the extent to which the leader is personally attractive to group members and is respected by them
2. *Task structure:* the extent to which the task is defined and structured in terms of goals to be achieved and means for achieving these goals
3. *Position power:* the extent of power inherent in the position of the leader (reward and punishments).

Fiedler developed a continuum identifying different possible states of each of the three contingency factors. This scale represents a series of conditions ranging from "extremely favorable" to the leader to "extremely unfavorable" (see Figure 8.A1.). He concluded that in

Figure 8.A1. *Continuum for Contingency Factors and Leader Style*

Source: Fred E. Fiedler, "Engineer the Job to Fit the Manager," *Harvard Business Review,* September–October 1965, p. 119. Copyright © 1965 by the President and Fellows of Harvard College; all rights reserved.

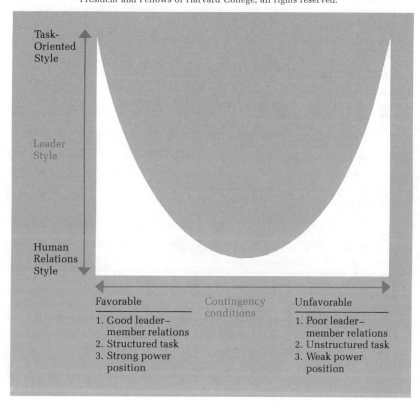

207

very "favorable" or in very "unfavorable" situations for getting a task accomplished by group effort, the autocratic, task-oriented management style works best. In situations intermediate in difficulty, the nondirective, permissive leader is more successful (see curve in Figure 8.A1.).

Discussion Questions

1. Define the concept of leadership.
2. What is meant by the trait approach to a study of leader behavior?
3. Discuss the current status of the trait approach in the study of leadership.
4. What is meant by leadership style?
5. Discuss the leadership styles defined and studied by (a) White and Lippitt, (b) the Ohio State leadership studies, and (c) Robert House and associates.
6. Discuss the situationist approach to leadership.
7. Discuss the relationship between leadership style and (a) group performance, (b) group satisfaction, and (c) group cohesiveness.
8. What is meant by a base of leadership power?
9. Define and discuss the bases of power mentioned in the text.
10. Based upon what you have read in the text, discuss current thinking regarding the concept of leadership as it is applied to business organization.
11. Select a leadership position with which you are familiar and analyze (according to the matrix format) the leadership style and base of power utilized by the leader you have in mind.

Case for Discussion

At a planning meeting held by the directors of Multi-Products Corporation, each director presented his approach to profit and budget planning within their divisions. Two of the directors, James Winters of the Construction Products Division and Joseph Hardy of the Chemical Products Division, spent about twenty minutes each in describing how their budgets and profit projections were determined.

Below are excerpts from their presentations:

Mr. Winters: As division manager I believe I have the best picture of the capabilities of the whole division. So I set the target profit and sales goals for my managers. These goals represent my expectations and I simply call in each of my managers and give them the sales and profit goals for their departments. Their performance is then measured against the goals I have set. If a manager has a question about the target, we discuss it and I explain my reasons for setting the goal at a particular level.

Mr. Hardy: I feel my managers should determine the goals for their departments. I ask each manager to submit to me his projections for sales and profits. Once I receive these targets I increase them by fifteen percent to "force" creativity from my managers in order to achieve these modified goals. In this way I can identify my truly creative managers.

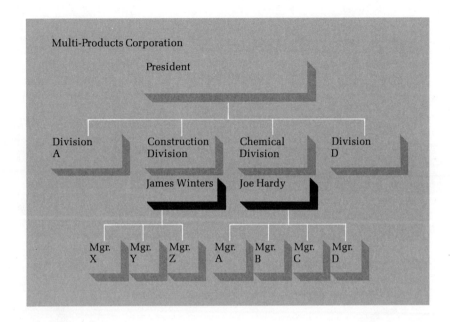

Multi-Products Corporation

Selected References

Blake, R. and Mouton, J. *The Managerial Grid*. Houston, Texas: Gulf Publishing Co., 1964.

Davis, Keith. *Human Relations at Work*, 3rd ed. New York: McGraw–Hill, 1967.

Fiedler, Fred. "Engineer the Job to Fit the Manager." In *Harvard Business Review*, Vol. 43, No. 5 (1965).

———. "Personality and Situational Determinants of Leadership Effectiveness." In *Group Dynamics: Research and Theory*, D. Cartwright and A. Zander, eds. New York: Harper & Row, 1968.

Filley, A., House, R., and Kerr, S. *Managerial Process and Organizational Behavior*. Glenview, Ill.: Scott, Foresman and Co., 1976.

French, J. R. P. and Raven, B. "Basis of Social Power." In *Group Dynamics: Research and Theory*, D. Cartwright and A. Zander, eds. New York: Harper & Row, 1964.

Ghiselli, E. "The Validity of Management Tracts in Relation to Occupational Level." In *Personnel Psychology*, Summer 1963.

House, R., Filley, A., and Kerr, S. "Relation of Leader Consideration and Initiating Structure to R & D Subordinates Satisfaction." In *Administrative Science Quarterly*, March 1971.

——— and T. Mitchell. "Path-Goal Theory of Leadership." In *Journal of Contemporary Business*, Autumn 1974.

Likert, R., *The Human Organization*. New York: McGraw–Hill, 1967.

Luthans, F. *Contemporary Readings in Organizational Behavior*, 2nd ed. New York: McGraw–Hill, 1972.

Porter, D., Applewhite, P., and Misshauk, M. *Studies in Organization and Management*, 2nd ed. New York: International Textbook Co., 1971.

Stogdill, Ralph. *Handbook of Leadership*. New York: The Free Press, 1974.

_____, Coons, A., eds. *Leader Behavior: Its Description and Measurement.* Columbus, Ohio: Bureau of Business Research, 1957.

_____. *Individual Behavior and Group Achievement.* New York: Oxford University Press, 1959.

Tannenbaum, R., Wecshler, J., and Massarik, F. *Leadership and Organization: A Behaviorial Science Approach.* New York: McGraw-Hill, 1961.

_____ and Schmidt, W. "How to Choose a Leadership Pattern." In *Harvard Business Review,* March–April 1958.

Vroom, Victor. *Work and Motivation.* New York: John Wiley & Sons, 1964.

_____ and Yetton, P. *Leadership and Decision-Making.* Pittsburgh, Pa.: University of Pittsburgh Press, 1973.

White, R. and Lippitt, R. *Leader Behavior and Member Reaction in Three Social Climates.* In *Group Dynamics: Research and Theory,* D. Cartwright and A. Zander, eds. New York: Harper & Row, 1960.

Communication:
Process and Perceptions

Teaching the Boss to Write

It may be old news that "Johnny can't write," but to legions of U.S. executives the problem is no longer in the schools but right next door in the executive suite. So appalling is the quality of written reports in some companies that senior executives are sending their managers—and sometimes themselves—through writing courses intended to put some point back into the reports that cross their desks and to eliminate the extraneous material that increasingly obscures that point.

"It's hard for me to believe grown men write the kind of things I see in some client organizations," says Jack Shaw, a partner in the accounting firm of Touche Ross & Co. and the head of the New York office of its management services department. To head off such trouble on his own team, Shaw and some of his senior managers this week went through a writing and logic course offered by one of the writing consultants who are themselves becoming a mini-industry.

Report-writing courses are being treated with a new seriousness in industry. Companies are having to learn to cope not only with supervisors and first-line managers who have trouble communicating, but also with senior research scientists, B-school graduates, and otherwise bright top executives who cannot turn out a clearly written, logically organized interoffice memo—and often do not realize it.

Seeking Conclusions

Unfortunately, education and intelligence offer no guarantees. "Those with PhDs may be the worst of all," says Albert Joseph, president of the Industrial Writing Institute, whose tape-and-slide and personally

Reprinted from the October 25, 1976 issue of *Business Week* by special permission. Copyright © 1976 by McGraw-Hill Publishing, Inc., New York, N.Y. 10020. All rights reserved.

conducted courses have been given at hundreds of companies. "The higher the education, the worse the writing they've been exposed to."

Some of those who are most skilled in their own field are among the poorest writers. "Many people who are good on their feet can't put together four good sentences in a row," says Joan Griewank, director of market planning for CBS Records Div., who put herself and those working under her through the course of Barbara Minto, a London-based writing consultant whose week-long course, stressing logic more than style, costs $4,300 (for groups up to 10).

The most common complaint of managers about the reports they receive is that the conclusions of the writer are either buried or missing altogether. But there is a whole catalog of other sins: excessive wordiness, poor grammar and sentence structure, atrocious spelling, and general confusion. "I see an erosion of writing skills in a lot of the young people we bring in here who are very bright," says Pepsi-Cola Co. President Victor A. Bonomo. He believes that since some 100 of his managers took Minto's course in the past three years, Pepsi's internal communication has significantly improved.

The payoff is that Bonomo himself spends much less time today going through reports, and he can grasp their point immediately. "And it avoids mistakes," he says. "We have had instances where material was completely misinterpreted." In one case, a Pepsi executive's reorganization plan that was turned down before he took the writing course was approved when he rewrote it after the course two weeks later.

Time savings can be significant. American Telephone & Telegraph Co., which started using Joseph's tape-and-slide course this spring, finds that managers who take it can cut a 300-word report to 100 words. The time it takes to produce the report is reduced from one hour to half an hour, and reading time shrinks as well. Du Pont Co., which has a similar course, also puts managers through a writing seminar that shows them how to trim the size of reports by half.

Impressing Clients

The writing consultants say a course must include top executives if it is to have maximum impact in a company. "The people we train in business are mostly managers and professionals," says Joseph. "They're highly educated, but educated people left to their own devices gradually pick up an academic style. It's slow and it causes misunderstanding. And most of them don't know beans about organizing. They never heard of putting the conclusion first."

Some of those who are supposed to know the most about writing reports really know the least. "Management consultants tend to be the frothiest and most pompous, perhaps to impress their clients," says consultant Pauline E. Putnam, whose own writing clinic clients include such companies as Standard Oil Co. of California and Pacific Gas & Electric Co.

Many executives feel that until the schools begin to rethink their own role in teaching students to write, the corporate efforts will amount to little more than skirmishes with the problem. "My course is really for people reading the reports, not the writers," says Minto. "You don't give the course unless somebody is complaining. I'm teaching an elite course for a small group of people, and yes, the impact is limited."

Wider Impact

But there are signs that the impact is widening. Those who learn to write better reports tend to become more demanding in what they expect of the reports they receive. "When 800 people took my course at Standard of Ohio," says Joseph, "they began to ridicule the reports that still were written in the old style. The environment has changed."

But there still is much to be done. Edward F. Howard, chairman of Schorr & Howard, a public relations company that produced an elaborate guide to better written communications for one of its clients, gives a recent example. An executive of one of the largest corporations in the world was so insecure about a letter the company was sending to an American ambassador that he hired Schorr & Howard to compose the one-and-a-half pages that would go out above his signature.

THE ABILITY OF individuals to communicate with each other is affected by such factors as individual personality traits, values, systems, attitudes, and perceptions. In a business organization, the relative position of individuals in the organization may also affect their success in communicating. Research has been conducted to provide insight into the most effective methods of communicating within groups and organizations, and in this chapter we will examine some of these investigations.

The Meaning of Communication

The ability to communicate is often taken for granted. Too often one assumes that if he or she has spoken or written to another, a message has been communicated. Unfortunately, however, for a variety of reasons, the message we *intend* to communicate is often not the same message that is understood by the receiver. As a result, our attempt to communicate may lead to misunderstandings and misinterpretations — in other words, communication breakdowns. Many people simply are not aware of all the factors involved in the communication process.

What exactly do we mean by "communication"? For purposes of our discussion, "communication" will be defined as the ability to transmit a message to another so that the meaning and intent are accurately interpreted and understood. It is clear that the communication process goes far beyond simply "sending a message to another," for if we simply send the message we have no guarantee that its meaning has been accurately understood. Our language is filled, for example, with words which may be defined and interpreted legitimately in a number of ways. According to one study "for the five hundred most commonly used words in our language there are 14,070 different dictionary definitions."[1] In the business environment words such as *management, administration, model, control, decentralization,* and *policy* may all be subject to more than one definition or interpretation.

Since the words in our language bear such a wide variety of meanings, it is no wonder that readers and listeners often misinterpret what is written or said. Since individuals are exposed to a wide variety of experiences and situations, different individuals may interpret words in a given context in different ways. For example, the author knows of a secretary who had worked for a stockbroker. According to the broker, the secretary's typing ability and general performance were excellent. When the secretary decided to take a new job, the broker gave an excellent recommendation to a lawyer who was interviewing the secretary. The lawyer hired the secretary and after a few weeks called the broker to complain that the secretary's typing was "horrible" and full of errors and asked how the broker could have given such a high recommendation. During the course of the conversation it became clear that the broker had evaluated the secretary on the *speed* with which she could type stock transactions during busy trading sessions. On the other hand, the prime concern of the lawyer was the *accuracy* of legal documents. In this situation the evaluation of *excellent performance* was based upon two entirely different frames of reference—speed and accuracy. These differing frames of reference led to a breakdown in communication when the secretary's typing ability was being discussed.

Differing frames of reference can cause genuine misinterpretation of words. Individuals may, however, *choose* to give meanings to words that they would *like* the words to have. A person's own desires or values may cause him or her to associate meanings with a word that were not intended by the sender of the message. For example, this author was present at a meeting called by the president of a large manufacturing company. As a result of an expansion of its activities the company was planning significant changes in its plant layout. The meeting was called to give various manufacturing groups a chance to provide "input" to the design of the new layout. The word "input" was used in the memo that was sent to each manufacturing group containing the agenda. As the meeting progressed, however, it became clear that each group interpreted the word "input" to mean "getting their own way" regarding the new layout. At the end of the meeting, when it was necessary to make compromises, several group representatives stated that it was obvious that they had not been given the chance to provide "input" in the final decision. The result was that a meeting originally called to seek advice from a wide variety of individuals regarding an important management decision, ended by creating ill will toward management.

Thus, the communication process involves far more than simply sending a message to another individual or group. It also involves the need to determine if the meaning has been accurately interpreted by those receiving the message. By accurate interpretation we do not mean to imply that the persons receiving the message necessarily *agree* with or *accept* what has been communicated. It is very possible to communicate effectively with another and yet have that person disagree with, or disregard, the message. This does not necessarily represent a failure to communicate. If the message has been interpreted accurately, then communication has taken place, even though the person receiving the message may choose not to allow the message to influence his or her attitude or behavior. Just as we must guard against giving meanings to words simply because we would like the words to have them, so also we must be careful not to confuse communication with our ability to convince others that what we are communicating is correct. If we communicate to someone the idea that $2 + 4 = 5$, our statement may be *interpreted* correctly but nevertheless justifiably disagreed with.

Individual Perception and Communication

One of the major difficulties individuals experience in attempting to communicate with one another is not so much a function of the language they use but rather of a whole series of psychological and sociological factors acting on them. These factors tend to influence our interpretation of what we see and hear and may cause us to reach conclusions or make judgments that are inaccurate or inappropriate. In this section we will focus on some of these factors, examining their potential impact on our ability to communicate and to interpret communication. At first glance, the process of communication might appear simple enough. It might be described as in Figure 9.1. From this simplistic diagram it might be difficult to understand how individuals can fail to communicate effectively.

This model does not take into account, however, the fact that both sender and receiver are human beings, each with individual *perceptions* of the meaning of the world around them. Because we are all unique, each of us perceives and interprets a message in a slightly different way.

It is this concept of individual perception that is so important for understanding the process of communication. As human beings, we are not so much "receivers" of messages as "perceivers" of these messages. The difference can be significant, for as perceivers we are affected by our personality characteristics, our ego (with its various needs and defense mechanisms), and our past experiences. Factors such as nationality, cultural background, sex, and education all blend to form our individual perceptual frame of reference, and this will determine the degree to which we may be psychologically threatened by the behavior of those around us or secure in our abilities. Personality characteristics we carry with us will affect how we perceive a message. All of the factors we have mentioned serve to

Sender
Message medium (oral, written, etc.)
Receiver

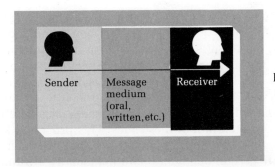

Figure 9.1. *Communication*

create a unique filtering mechanism for each of us. It is possible that no two individuals will perceive and interpret a given message in exactly the same way. In short, words are merely symbols; the meaning we attach to these symbols is in ourselves.

Let us now modify our model in Figure 9.2 to reflect the psychological and sociological factors that influence the way we perceive and interpret messages communicated to us.

Stereotypes

To understand the way our individual frame of reference may influence our perceptions with respect to the communication process, we must analyze the way we interpret messages we receive. The full meaning of these messages comes to us not only through the words

Figure 9.2. *Factors Influencing Perception of Messages*

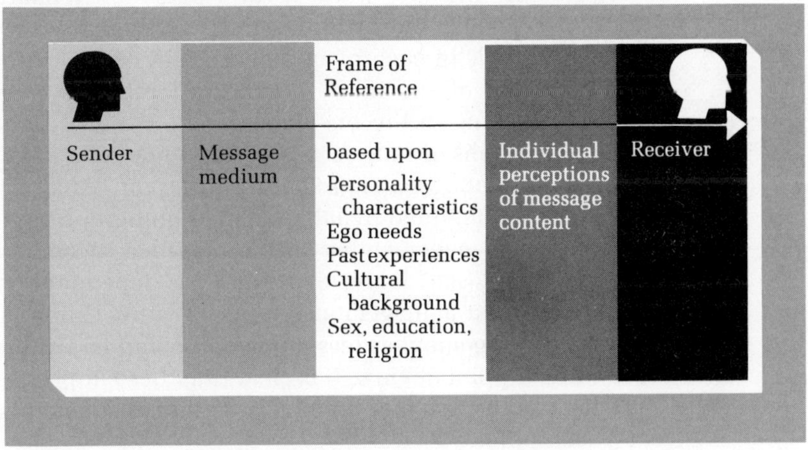

Sender
Message medium
Frame of Reference
based upon
Personality characteristics
Ego needs
Past experiences
Cultural background
Sex, education, religion
Individual perceptions of message content
Receiver

that may be spoken or written but also by means of many other cues that we perceive as part of the total communication process. These cues fill out the message; we use them in completing our interpretation of the messages we receive. Specific examples of such cues include the clothing, hair style, and accent of the sender of the message, as well as that individual's position, title, or status. Our frame of reference will make us tend to associate specific attributes and behaviors with certain of these cues. This process is known as stereotyping. *Stereotyping* simply means that we have a tendency to associate certain behavioral and personality attributes to particular individuals because of some preconceived ideas we may have regarding age, appearance, ethnic background, etc. In our society the image of a young man with a beard, long hair, and Levi's may bring to mind an individual with whom we would associate a particular set of values and attitudes. The image of an individual with short hair, a three-piece suit, and a clean-shaven face may create a totally different stereotype. Perhaps our most familiar example of the process of stereotyping is the television character Archie Bunker. Archie lives in a world of stereotypes; he judges each individual simply on the series of cues presented to him.

We can find this concept of stereotyping in the business environment. Impressions of people are often based upon characteristics associated with certain skills, occupations, and positions. Readers may wish to investigate their personal stereotypes by listing those attributes or personality characteristics that come to mind when they think of an accountant, a public relations executive, an engineer, an assembly-line worker, or an advertising executive. Each of us would probably bring to mind certain personality characteristics, intelligence levels, and attitudes that we would tend to associate with individuals in each of these occupations.

In one of the most well-known research studies dealing with stereotyping in the business world, Mason Haire found that when photographs of individuals were shown to members of labor unions and to managers, significantly different reactions and impressions could be obtained by labeling the photograph as either a representative of management or a union leader.[2] Members of management tended to "see" labor leaders as less dependable and as less able to understand management's point of view. Union members tended to see *management* as less dependable and less able to understand the *union's* point of view. It is clear that these impressions were based on the stereotypes that both labor and management had with respect to each other.

In an unpublished piece of research conducted by this author, thirty individuals were used as judges to evaluate the qualifications of individuals who were theoretically applying for a variety of jobs within a corporation. Each judge was given the résumés of five different applicants and the judge was asked to rank them in the order in which he considered each as qualified for the job. The résumés contained information on past experience, education, and references. After each judge made his decision regarding the qualifications of each of the applicants, new information was provided to the judge. This new information contained data on sex (male vs. female), ethnic background, and the applicant's age. After this new information was provided, the judges were asked to reevaluate each applicant and to again rank them according to qualifications. The information was controlled so that it was possible to determine the impact of certain data on the judge's evaluation. The results of the data showed clearly that factors such as sex and ethnic background had a significant impact on the judge's evaluation of a given applicant. Clearly, many of these judges had a stereotype of certain characteristics associated with these factors, and these stereotypes seemed to influence their decisions.

This tendency to stereotype is often difficult to overcome because it is often deeply imbedded in an individual's frame of reference. In some cases the individual is not even fully aware of the fact that he or she may be associating certain attributes based upon a stereotyped image. In the business environment, the potential problems associated with stereotyping of others can result in significant loss of coordination and cooperation among the various disciplines and departments—we have already briefly discussed the research by Haire relating to perceptions of management and labor.

In an effort to offset some of the effects of stereotyping, several organizations have attempted to bring together members of various groups in order to work on problems and projects apart from the specific discipline they represent. The objective of such interactions is to reduce the adversary relationship that might exist between individuals and replace it with one in which the individuals find it necessary to cooperate in order to find a solution to a common problem. The nature of the problem assigned should be such that no individuals will perceive a threat to themselves as a result of cooperation with others. When individuals are brought together in this environment, the need to cooperate can often bring out skills, expertise, and personal attributes which each individual finds impressive in the other. As these skills and attributes are recognized, they tend to offset some of the stereotype images the individuals may have had of each other. The hoped-for result of such an interaction is for the individuals involved to begin to question the stereotype images they may have for certain occupations, positions, or coworkers.

Halo Effect

Closely associated with the concept of stereotyping is that of the *halo effect*. This phenomenon also affects our ability to evaluate objectively and accurately. According to researchers Thibaut and Kelley, the halo effect can be defined as the "tendency for one's general attitude toward a person to influence more specific evaluations of him."[3]

Research evidence has indicated, for example, that we are more likely to agree with a statement made by someone we like than by someone we dislike. In a classic study by Asch, significantly different impressions were found of individuals who were described as being "warm" than of individuals described as being "cold" but possessing otherwise the same characteristics.[4] There is a great deal of research to indicate that we do indeed generalize about the nature and character of individuals, and once a specific impression has been formed this impression seems to permeate all our future judgments about them.

In the work environment, the halo effect can have a significant impact on employer-employee relations. We are all familiar with expressions ranging from "the boss is out to get me" to "he is one of the boss's boys." These are expressions of the perception that certain individuals may be regarded by their supervisor as being able to do no wrong—and others, to do nothing right. Once a supervisor forms an impression of a subordinate, there will be a tendency for the supervisor to evaluate that subordinate according to the initial impression. If a supervisor perceives an employee to be honest, this impression will probably influence his other attitudes toward the employee's productivity, willingness to cooperate, and intelligence.

The halo effect would seem to be derived from our need to seek consistency in the environment. Our cultural background may indeed have led us to believe that certain personality traits tend to go together. If this is the case, it is very easy for us, once we observe one of these linked traits in an individual, to assume that the others are also present. We may draw this conclusion even if we have no evidence to justify it. Our tendency to make such leaps of judgment is based on our need to view and understand our environment in terms of a consistent and integrated whole. To do this, it is often necessary for us to fill in the blanks, so to speak, so that we can complete our information about a particular individual, situation, or object. In filling in these "blanks" we tend to supply data that we consider to be consistent with whatever information we may already have. The fact that human beings tend to function in this way is a reason why it is often possible to form wrong impressions about others or to misunderstand communication attempts.

One final factor that tends to influence our perception of others, and as a result to have an impact on the communication process, relates to the *situation* in which interaction takes place. In light of our previous discussion it is clear that we tend to make rather sweeping assumptions about others, often basing them on limited information. One piece of information that can have a great deal of importance in our initial impression of another is the situation in which we first interact with that individual. The environment in which the interaction takes place provides us with the background from which we may then engage in stereotyping or "halo" assumptions. Our initial impression of the driver who bangs into the back of our car, for instance, may be far different from our impression of the selfless person who gives us a ride to the service station. Again, our impressions of the person we meet at the opera may differ from our initial impressions of the person we meet at the bowling alley.

Here again we may recognize our tendency to generalize about individuals on the basis of some limited amount of information. And in the business environment, the importance of the situation in helping us form impressions of others is critical. Our society has tended to associate certain symbols with success in business practice—symbols such as a plush office, country club membership, a private plane. If our initial interaction with a businessperson were to take place in his plush office, at a country club luncheon, or aboard his private plane, our impression might be far different than if we were to meet this same man at a party at a friend's home. Because of the association of certain symbols with success in business, corporations put a lot of effort into creating interaction situations in which the surroundings are designed to form favorable impressions.

With these ideas in mind, let us again modify our model of communication to include additional psychological and sociological factors in the communication process (Figure 9.3, page 222).

This model shows that the process of communication is significantly influenced by various psychological and sociological factors that tend to filter, distort, or in some way modify communication attempts between individuals. The accuracy of communication between individuals will, in many cases, be a function of the extent to which each individual is aware of the presence of these factors and is able to compensate for them.

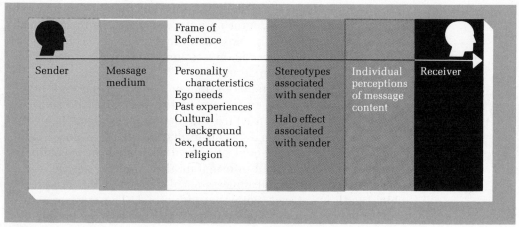

Figure 9.3. *Additional Factors Influencing Perception of Messages*

The Effectiveness of Communication Networks

A number of researchers have investigated the effectiveness of various communication networks in problem-solving situations. Bavelas, Smith and Leavitt, and Guetzkow and Simon conducted some of the earliest research along these lines.[5] In much of this research, communication patterns were set up so as to define the way information could flow between various group members in a problem-solving situation. The researchers could then examine the effect of the communication networks on such performance factors as speed of problem-solving, morale of group members, leader emergence, and accuracy of solution. From these initial research studies there emerged some general guidelines about the attributes of various patterns of communication flow. Perhaps the best known of the studies is the work of Smith and Leavitt, whose results were published in 1951. Smith and Leavitt conducted a series of experiments in which groups of five people were used, each member of the group being given a cup containing five marbles of different colors. Only one color was common to all members; the task was for each member to determine that common color as quickly as possible. Communication between group members was in written form only and was restricted to a particular pattern or flow (circle, chain, or wheel, as shown in Figure 9.4). In Figure 9.4, the lines represent the particular direction of information flow for each of the three groups. The results of the experiment are summarized by Bavelas and Barrett in

Figure 9.4.[6] In addition, Leavitt also found that the "circle" network was more effective than the "wheel" for dealing with unique problems or problems requiring creative solutions.

Leavitt's work shows clearly that particular communication patterns will affect group attitude and performance in specific ways. It appears that choosing communication networks for effectiveness would therefore be a function of management. One pattern tends to produce rapid and accurate problem solving, while another might foster a more creative environment with fairly high levels of morale. It would thus be up to management to determine which result was most important in a given situation; once this decision was made, management could then take steps to set up the most appropriate communication network for the work group.

Another significant aspect of Leavitt's research was his mathematical development of an *index of centrality* and an *index of pe-*

Figure 9.4. *Patterns of Communication Flow*

Source: Reprinted by permission of the publisher from Alex Bavelas and Dermot Barrett, "An Experimental Approach to Organizational Communication," *Personnel,* March 1951, © 1951 by American Management Association, Inc.

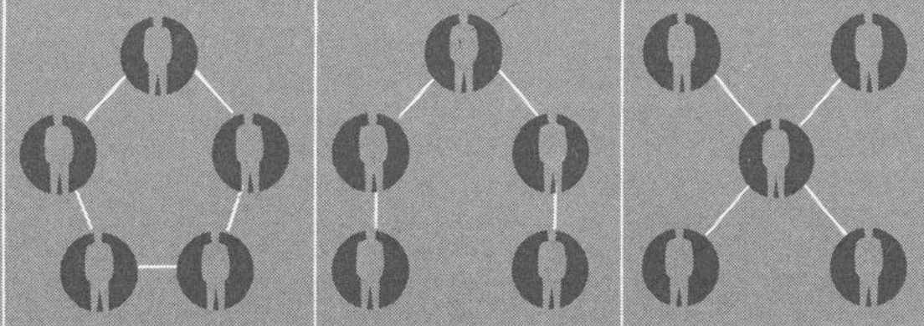

	Circle	Chain	Wheel
Speed of Performance	Slow	Fast	Fast
Accuracy	Poor	Good	Good
Emergence of Leader	None	Marked	Very Pronounced
Morale	Very Good	Poor	Very Poor
Organization	No stable form of organization	Slowly emerging but stable organization	Almost immediate and stable organization

ripherality for each position in a communication network. The index of centrality provides a measure of the extent to which a given individual interacts with others; the index of peripherality gives a measure of the extent to which individuals are precluded from interacting with others. These two indices, as their names imply, provide a quantitative measure of the relative position of each individual with respect to the overall flow of communication within the group. The implications of these indices can be found in the fact that with respect to leadership emergence, the leader of the group was always the individual who possessed the highest index of centrality. In addition, the index of peripherality was directly related to group morale, with those individuals having a high index of peripherality exhibiting characteristics associated with low morale and individuals having a low index of peripherality appearing much more satisfied with group membership (see Figure 9.5).

Figure 9.5. *Centrality and Peripherality*

Source: H. J. Leavitt, "Some Effects of Certain Communication Patterns on Group Performance," *Journal of Abnormal and Social Psychology* 46 (1951).

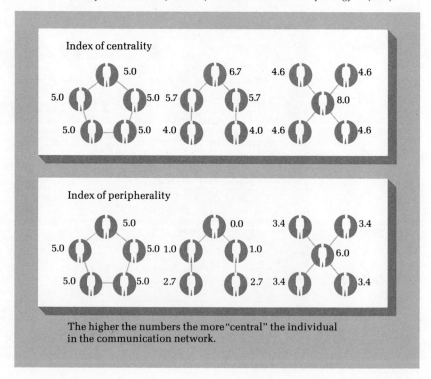

The higher the numbers the more "central" the individual in the communication network.

The concepts of centrality and peripherality seem to have significant implications for management. They suggest possible causes of poor morale within the organization and also determine some factors that give rise to the emergence of informal leaders in a work group.

The Effectiveness of Communication Channels

A study conducted by Dale Level set out to determine the most effective and least effective communication channels for use in specific business-related situations.[7] The channels evaluated were (1) written messages only, (2) oral messages only, (3) written followed by oral messages, and (4) oral followed by written messages. Each method was evaluated by each of 72 supervisors with respect to 10 situations. The situations included communication of information requiring immediate employee action, communication of information on an important company policy change, communication to reprimand an employee for work deficiency, and communication to settle a dispute among employees about a work problem. In analyzing the results of the supervisory survey, Level concluded that the combination of oral communication followed by written is appropriate for most business situations. This method is of particular importance in situations calling for quick action, a need for follow-up, or documentation. Written communication alone is most appropriate for dealing with general information or future action. Oral communication is necessary when immediate feedback is required or when the communication is directed toward bringing about a change in an employee's behavior.

Research on Communication in Organizations

Attention in this section will be given to organizational factors that have proven significant in influencing the flow and patterns of organizational communication, as well as the ramifications of these communication patterns with respect to such areas as leadership development and employee morale.

Perhaps the most dramatic piece of research illustrating the failure of communication within the organizational environment is a study conducted by Maier, Hoffman, Hooven, and Read.[8] The researchers conducted in-depth interviews with 58 middle managers in 5 corporations. The interviews were to determine the extent to which there was agreement between superior and subordinate about the nature of the subordinate's job activities. Each middle manager selected one subordinate with whom he had extensive interaction, and a comparison was made of the 58 pairs as to their agreement about the nature of the subordinate's job activity. The results of this study appear in Table 9.1.

The results show the extent to which communication can break down in an organization even between immediate superior and subordinate. Perhaps most striking is the lack of agreement with respect to the nature of the duties of the job itself, with 54.1 percent of the pairs agreeing on one half or fewer of the duties included in the job. In addition, 68.2 percent of the pairs agreed on fewer than half of the obstacles standing in the way of the subordinate's performance. The implications of this study are significant when considered in terms of the ability of the organization to coordinate resources and unify effort toward objectives. If breakdown in communication is so widespread between immediate superior and subordinate, one can only speculate as to the distortions that take place as one moves a greater distance through the organizational hierarchy. It is apparent, too, that lack of communication, particularly with respect to job duties and obstacles to performance, can be a major source of frustration and anxiety for both superior and subordinate. The person often labeled a reluctant or unwilling subordinate, or an unreasonable and demanding superior, may be simply the victim of a breakdown in communication with respect to the superior's expectations about the nature of the job.

Another study, by Read, investigated the motivational and atti-

Table 9.1

	Almost no agreement on topics	Agreement on fewer than half of topics	Agreement on about half of topics	Agreement on more than half of topics	Agreement on all or almost all of topics
Job duties	3.4%	11.6%	39.1%	37.8%	8.1%
Job requirements (subordinates' qualifications)	7.0%	29.3%	40.9%	20.5%	2.3%
Future changes in subordinates' job	35.4%	14.3%	18.3%	16.3%	15.7%
Obstacles in way of subordinates' performance	38.4%	29.8%	23.6%	6.4%	1.7%

Source: Reprinted by permission of the publisher from Norman R. F. Maier, L. Richard Hoffman, John J. Hooven, and William H. Read, "Superior-Subordinate Communication in Management." AMA Research Study 52, © 1961 by American Management Association, Inc., p. 10.

dunal factors that affect the reliability of communication from one administrative level to another.[9] Of particular interest to Read was the extent to which subordinates would tend to screen or suppress information from their superiors if the subordinates perceived that this information might reflect negatively on them. Read hypothesized that the extent of this screening process would be a function of the mobility aspirations of the subordinate as well as the extent of influence the superior was perceived to have. Specifically, Read hypothesized that "the greater the influence the upwardly mobile subordinate perceived his superior to have, the greater would be the subordinate's tendency to withhold problem-related information from the superior."[10] Read believed, however, that the degree of trust a subordinate had in a superior would tend to modify the amount of screening and suppression by the subordinate. In order to test his hypothesis Read conducted interviews of 52 superiors and their 52 respective subordinates in three major industrial organizations. Measures were obtained of mobility, trust, and influence; correlations were used to determine the significance of the relationships. The results of Read's study generally support the hypothesis that mobility aspiration among subordinate managers is negatively correlated with the accuracy of upward communication. There is some indication that this correlation is also influenced by the degree of influence of the superior as perceived by the subordinate. The correlation is, however, affected by the degree of trust the subordinate has in the superior; as this trust increases, it tends to reduce the extent of screening of information by the subordinate.

This study sheds some light on the impact of psychological factors in influencing the accuracy of communication between superior and subordinate. Subordinates who desire to move upward within the organization are obviously fearful of communicating to superiors information that is perceived as threatening to the future advancement of the subordinates. This attitude is understandable. It creates an extremely difficult situation within the organizational environment, however. In order for effective decisions to be made, it is imperative that accurate information regarding possible or existing problem areas be communicated up through the hierarchy. If this is not done, it becomes virtually impossible for top management to evaluate a situation in order to react appropriately. If accurate information is suppressed, the organization becomes virtually cut off from the operating level and as a result may cease to function effectively.

Since the importance of clean and complete information flow throughout the organization is obvious, it becomes necessary for each manager to take steps to insure that his or her subordinates are not screening or suppressing necessary information to keep from "looking bad" in the eyes of their superior. If subordinates feel threatened in this way, accurate information flow through the levels of the organizational hierarchy will be reduced, and the communication process will suffer.

The Grapevine

Keith Davis identifies the importance of communication in the organization through what he calls the company "grapevine."[11] Davis makes the point that management should not disregard this informal communication route, which may be a useful medium. Management should understand how the grapevine operates so that it may be utilized effectively. In studying the grapevine, Davis utilized data gathered in a study of a single company of 67 employees engaged in the manufacture of leather goods. Davis began his search with the recipient of some specific bits of information and then attempted to trace this information back to its source. He could thus determine the flow of communication for a given piece of information.

Prior to his investigation Davis visualized four possible methods for grapevine communication (Figure 9.6).

1. The *single strand*: A to B, B to C, etc.
2. *Gossip:* A acquired information and tells everyone else
3. *Probability:* A would communicate *randomly* with perhaps two others and these others would then do similarly
4. *Cluster:* A would tell perhaps three *selected* others and then one of these would tell two *selected* others, etc.

When Davis analyzed the *actual* information flow in the organization, the cluster chain was virtually the only one he found.

In analyzing the patterns of communication in the company, Davis found several interesting facts:

1. Information tended to be transmitted primarily by "liaison" individuals. These are the individuals management must identify if communication flow is to be improved.
2. Staff individuals, because of their mobility and the role they play, tend to receive and transmit more information than do line officers.
3. Communication within the grapevine *rarely* followed functional or hierarchical lines; in most cases information flowed across functional areas (marketing, finance, production, etc.), and in the

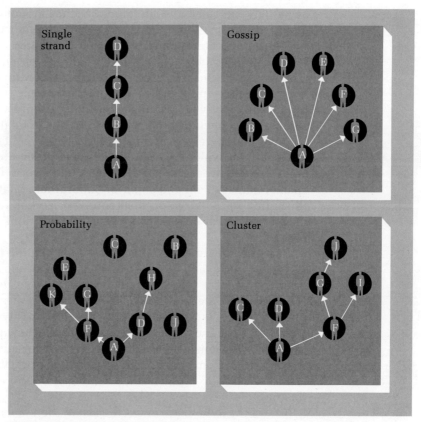

Figure 9.6. *Grapevine Communication*

Source: Keith Davis, "Management Communication and the Grapevine," *Harvard Business Review,* September–October 1953. Copyright © 1953 by the President and Fellows of Harvard College; all rights reserved.

specific instances studied by Davis in only three of fourteen communications did this information follow the chain of command.

4. Certain individuals within the organization—as a result of location, social factors, or job requirements—tend to be isolated from communication flow. As a result these individuals are not always aware of certain information or are not able to transmit information they receive. These factors affect the flow of information through the organization somewhat unevenly.

Aided by Davis's results, management can work with the grapevine to improve the overall flow of information in the organization. By making use of important liaison individuals, staff employees, and cross-communication, management can help the work force to be accurately informed and can minimize the amount of erroneous and distorted information passing through the organization.

The far-reaching communication capabilities of workers in an organization as observed by Davis were reported also in a study conducted by Wickesburg at the University of Minnesota. Analyzing communication patterns of 91 businesspeople enrolled in Minnesota's Executive Master of Business Administration Program, Wickesburg concludes that "the extent of the total communication network and therefore the range of individual contacts in an organization are far wider for both managers and non-managers than one would gather from such traditional concepts as formal structure, span of management and superior-subordinate relationships. This is illustrated in the large proportion of horizontal and diagonal contacts which exist outside the formal prescriptions of structure and procedure."[12]

In a study dealing with the selective perception of business executives, Dearborn and Simon investigated the proposition that executives will be more likely to perceive those aspects of a situation that are directly related to the goals, objectives, and activities of their own departments or discipline.[13] The study involved 23 executives from a single manufacturing corporation, all from approximately the same middle-management level. Six were from sales, five from production, four from accounting, and eight represented areas such as research and development (R & D), legal, public relations, and industrial relations.

To test the hypothesis about the orientation of each executive, the researchers gave the executives a case study typically used in business school instruction. The case consisted of approximately 10,000 words and covered many managerial issues. The subjects was asked to present their views on what was the single most important managerial problem faced by the corporation as discussed in the case. A summary of the findings appear in Table 9.2.

The results of this study suggest how individuals will tend to "filter" information according to their own orientation or function. These executives involved in sales activities tended to focus on sales problems, executives in production focused on organizational problems, and executives in public relations and industrial relations tended to "see" human relations problems as being most significant. This tendency to perceive certain aspects of information selectively has wide-reaching implications for any discussion of the communication process in organizations. Disagreements about organizational priorities or about the importance of various corporate problem areas should take into account the orientation or discipline of these individuals involved in the disagreement. The concept of selective

Table 9.2. *Identification of Managerial Problems*

Department	Number of executives	Number who mention as the most important		
		Sales	Organization	Human relations
Sales	6	5	1	0
Production	5	1	4	0
Accounting	4	3	0	0
Misc. (R & D, Legal, P.R., I.R.)	8	1	3	3
	23	10	8	3

Source: D. Dearborn and H. Simon, "Selective Perception: A Note on the Departmental Identification of Executives," *Sociometry* (1958): 140–144.

perception may explain the reason why many corporations, in selecting members for a given task force or committee assignment, will include one or more individuals whose background or expertise lies in an area far removed from the particular problem to be discussed. It is hoped that these individuals will be able to examine information without the perceptual bias exhibited by individuals who may be involved with these issues on a daily basis. It is often possible for these noninvolved individuals to develop new approaches to problems since they are not inhibited by their previous experience and orientation.

Improving the Communication Process: The Linking Pin

While director of the Institute for Social Research at the University of Michigan, Rensis Likert carried on research that led to a concept designed to provide a method for improving communication and group effort in organizations. This concept, known as the "linking pin," is based on the idea that "management will make full use of the potential capacities of its human resources only when each person in an organization is a member of one or more effectively functioning work groups. . . ."[14] This idea is illustrated in Figure 9.7.

As we note in this figure, the organization has three hierarchical levels with a span of control of three subordinates at each level. For purposes of illustration, the levels have been designated as top management, middle management, and operations. The linking pin concept would require that individual A be an accepted member of the top management group *as well as* of the middle management

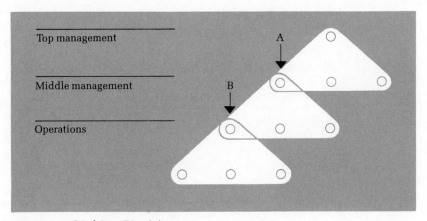

Figure 9.7. *Linking Pin (a)*

> *Source:* Rensis Likert, *New Patterns of Management* (New York: McGraw-Hill, 1961).

level. Individual B would work with both the middle management group and the operations level of the organization. The key point is that these individuals be *accepted* as legitimate members of both groups. This is necessary: Likert's research indicates that as individual identification with a group increases, the individual will cooperate more with the group and will also be more willing to both give and receive communication within the group and support goals and decisions. The linking pin concept could thus be instrumental in bringing about improved organizational communication, not necessarily because more information is being made available but because individuals are more ready to accept this communication, coming as it is from accepted and trusted members of their work group. Under

Figure 9.8. *Linking Pin (b)*

> *Source:* Rensis Likert, *New Patterns of Management* (New York: McGraw-Hill, 1961).

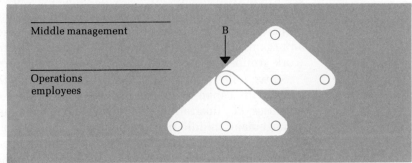

the linking pin concept, for example, individual B would represent both operations employees and middle management (Figure 9.8). As such, B would be considered a trusted supervisor by operations employees within the department. This trust would normally mean that B would be regarded as a supervisor who would represent the best interests of the department in discussions with middle management. As such, B would be a person that operations employees would communicate openly with. B's decisions and direction would be respected. At the same time, B must also be an accepted and trusted member of middle management. In this capacity B would be able to communicate across organization lines to other members of middle management and have this communication considered as coming from a legitimate member of their group. With individuals serving as linking pins in the organizational structure, problems of coordination and integration between various organizational groups could be facilitated.

Carried to its logical conclusion, the application of the linking pin idea would provide a network of communication channels throughout the organization. High levels of trust and acceptance among group members would bring about an atmosphere in which various organizational components would operate in a spirit of cooperation and support (Figure 9.9).

Figure 9.9. *Linking Pin (c)*
Source: Rensis Likert, *New Patterns of Management* (New York: McGraw-Hill, 1961).

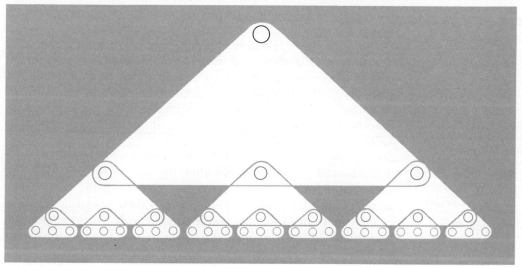

The most difficult obstacle to overcome in implementing this idea is the selection of individuals who can be trusted and accepted by more than one work group. As one crosses functional lines in an organization or moves up or down in its hierarchy, one is likely to find sharp differences in orientation, goals, and attitudes among various work groups. It is often difficult for a single individual to be fully accepted as a member of more than one work group. This difficulty should not prevent management from taking steps toward effective implementation of a linking pin organization. Techniques such as job rotation, T-group training, role playing, and varied committee assignments can all serve to build a more open and receptive environment. This environment, in which organizational members are more aware of each other's problems and goals, can increase the likelihood of an effective linking pin arrangement.

Communication Breakdowns

In an article written in 1953 F. J. Roethlisberger analyzed five fundamental causes of misunderstanding between individuals engaged in communication. The article provides a framework for seeking the underlying causes of failure in communication. Once these causes have been isolated and identified, solutions to problems of misunderstanding may be found. These are the problem areas Roethlisberger identified:[15]

1. *Difference of opinion as to facts:* In this situation two individuals may disagree about facts associated with a given situation. Usually the disagreement can be resolved by referring to records which can establish the accuracy of an assertion.
2. *Personality clash:* Misunderstanding may result from personality characteristics. Feelings of insecurity, inferiority, or aggression may create defense or attack behaviors which come into conflict with the personality and behaviors of another. In this kind of situation it is often impossible to improve the communication process without in some way bringing about a change in the self-awareness of the individuals involved.
3. *Social role conflict:* In this situation we deal with the role of each individual as perceived by another. Because of their occupation, sex, nationality, or other identifying characteristic, individuals may be expected to play certain roles. If their actual behavior is inconsistent with the role, conflict may result. For example, the traditional "role" of women in our society may be inconsistent with the role of a woman as manager of a department employing a

majority of male employees. In this situation it may be difficult for male members of the work group to adjust to the role played by the female supervisor. The result may be conflicts in the interaction and communication process. Conflicts of this type may be temporary in nature, becoming less significant as one individual becomes more accustomed to the new role of the other. The length of time necessary for the resumption of a normal working relationship will be a function of the degree to which a given individual is able to change his or her perception of the other's role.

4. *Struggle for power:* If individuals involved in a misunderstanding represent two different groups, organizations, or affiliations, their failure in communication may be the result of a power struggle in which each party feels it is necessary for the sake of the group not to lose face or suffer reduction in status by giving in. In this situation, each individual perceives that more is involved than a simple misunderstanding. Both sides may believe they must win if they are to maintain their position. Conflicts of this type are common among individuals representing different political parties or religious affiliations, as well as in communication between management and union.

5. *Breakdown in communication:* In some situations there may be a genuine breakdown in the communication process. This may result from the differing perceptions of individuals with respect to a given situation, from a misinterpretation of words or actions, or when one party fails to listen to the other. As a result of the breakdown each individual behaves according to his or her own interpretation of the situation. Since the individuals are operating within differing frames of reference with respect to the interaction, it is likely that conflict will result. To resolve conflicts of this type it is often necessary to retrace original statements and action so that each party is made aware of the actual meaning and intent of the other with respect to the original interaction. Once this is done each individual is able to proceed from the same point of reference and the original communication breakdown will have a good chance of being resolved.

Discussion Questions

1. Define what is meant by *communication.*
2. Discuss some of the obstacles that may cause breakdowns in the communication process.
3. Discuss the concept of frame of reference and apply its meaning to the communication process.
4. Distinguish between *stereotype* and *halo effect.*
5. Select three of the research studies

discussed in this chapter and apply the results of each to the process of communication in the business organization.

6. Define the five fundamental causes of communication breakdowns discussed by Roethlisberger. How might you determine which of these five is at work in a given situation?

7. According to S. I. Hayakawa, "the meaning of words are not in the words but in ourselves." Discuss.

8. What are some approaches that a manager might take to improve the communication process in an organization?

Case for Discussion

Bill Boatwright was called into his manager's office at 3 o'clock on a Friday afternoon for his semiannual performance review. The performance review process at Bill's company was designed to provide employees with feedback as to their performance, to indicate areas in which improvement might be made, and to announce the amount of the next salary increase. At his last review, six months earlier, the manager, Mr. Dale, praised Bill's work highly. He added that if Bill's development continued, he might expect to move rapidly within the company. In the week before his review, Bill heard by way of the grapevine that because of current economic conditions the average raise for the present year would be about eight percent.

The performance review form used by Bill's company is seen opposite (the marks indicate how Mr. Dale rated Bill's performance in each category).

Mr. Dale handed Bill the performance review sheet and asked him to think about it over the weekend; they would discuss it on Monday. Before Bill left Mr. Dale's office, his manager indicated that Bill's pay increase for the coming year would be eleven percent. Bill had not been encouraged by Mr. Dale's

performance rating; however, he perceived the eleven percent pay raise as a positive sign, because he knew that the average raise was only eight percent.

Category	Excellent	Good	Fair	Poor
Quality of work	X			
Quantity of work	X			
Motivation				X
Attitude				X
Accuracy			X	
Cooperation			X	
Initiative	X			
Creativeness		X		
Ability to work with others				X

As Bill left the office that day he ran into two coworkers who told Bill that they were extremely pleased about their own raises of fifteen percent. As Bill drove out of the parking lot that evening he assessed his standing with his supervisor and what he should say on Monday morning.

Selected References

Bavelas, A. "Communication Patterns in Task Oriented Groups." In *Journal of the Acoustical Society of America*, 1950.

———— and Barrett, D. "An Experimental Approach to Organizational Communication." In *Personnel*, March 1951.

Davis, K. "Management Communication and the Grapevine." In *Harvard Business Review,* September-October 1953.

Guetzkow, H. and Simon, H. "The Impact of Certain Communication Nets Upon Organization and Performance in Task Oriented Groups." In *Management Science,* Vol. 1, No. 329 (1955).

Haire, Mason, "Role Perceptions in Labor-Management Relations: An Experimental Approach." In *Industrial Labor Relations Review* 8 (1955).

Leavitt, H. J. "Some Effects of Certain Communication Patterns on Group Performance." In *Journal of Abnormal and Social Psychology* 46 (1951).

Level, Dale. "Communication Effectiveness Method and Situation." In *Journal of Business Communication,* Fall 1972.

Likert, R. *New Patterns of Management.* New York: McGraw-Hill, 1961.

Maier, Norman, Hoffman, R., Hooven, J., and Read, H. "Superior-Subordinate Communication in Management." In *AMA Research Study,* No. 52 (1961).

Read, W. "Upward Communication in Industrial Hierarchies." In *Human Relations* 15 (1962).

Roethlisberger, F. "The Administrator's Skill: Communication." In *Harvard Business Review,* November–December 1953.

Strong, Lydia, "Do You Know How To Listen?" In *Effective Communication on the Job,* M. Dooher and V. Marques, eds. New York, 1956.

Thibaut, J. and Kelley, H. *The Social Psychology of Groups.* New York: John Wiley & Sons, 1961.

Wickesburg, A. K. "Communication Networks in the Business Organization Structure." In *Academy of Management Journal,* Vol. 11, No. 3 (1968).

THE ORGANIZATION

Part IV

Introduction

The next four chapters introduce the basic concepts of organizational structure. Beginning with the most fundamental building block, the <u>division of labor</u>, the chapters focus on basic organizational structures and explore new approaches to understanding the organizational framework. As the title of one chapter indicates, the text provides an outline of the <u>anatomy of an organization</u>. At the conclusion of this Part, the reader should have a broad understanding of the way modern organizations are structured as well as a methodology for analyzing organizations in order to determine structural flaws.

Major Themes

<u>Division of Labor:</u>
Job design

<u>Organizational Structures</u>

<u>Understanding Organizations:</u>
Linear responsibility chart

<u>New Approaches to Organizational Structure</u>

Division of Labor and Job Design

10

Wanted: Ways to Make the Job Less Dull

Against a backdrop of dollar devaluation, soaring costs, and sluggish productivity, worker discontent in the factory and office has suddenly become something of a national issue. A decline in the will to work has been blamed for dulling the nation's competitive edge in world markets and frustrating consumers with products that are shoddily made and services that are arrogantly offered and grudgingly performed.

Worker discontent is basically nothing new. It has been around as long as work. Laborers who built the Pyramids staged a short-lived revolt—perhaps the first strike—over working conditions. Why should job dissatisfaction be so critical a problem now? Workers have the shortest week and the highest pay ever. Technology has eased or even eliminated much of the old manual work. Conditions of work, jealously supervised by unions, are the best ever. Yet increasing numbers of workers seem dissatisfied with their jobs—frustrated, alienated, apathetic, and poorly motivated. Pollsters find evidence of it; corporate managers say they see it in poor productivity, deteriorating quality of work, rebelliousness, growing use of drugs, even sabotage. Unions concede that it exists, though most labor leaders think it is exaggerated as a work factor. They see it as a mere symptom of society today.

Real or Trumped Up?

Social scientists and politicians tend to feel that today's work dissatisfaction is genuine, brand-new, and an urgent problem. Along with labor chiefs, some top executives question its uniqueness to our times.

Reprinted from the May 12, 1973 issue of *Business Week* by special permission. Copyright © 1973 by McGraw-Hill Publishing, Inc., New York, N. Y. 10020. All rights reserved.

The academics see a parallel between the surge of worker dissatisfaction and the spread of dissension on college campuses, in the church, in the armed services, and elsewhere. Discontent, they say, has intensified as a reflection of contemporary society's mood.

The social scientists are getting support in Washington to try to do something about it. The National Commission on Productivity wants to launch experiments on ways to humanize work—a "Quality of Work Program." Senator Edward M. Kennedy (D-Mass.) has introduced a bill to authorize the Health, Education & Welfare Dept. and the Labor Dept. to study the real extent of worker discontent. Among other things, the two departments would be expected to measure the costs of absenteeism, turnover, sabotage, and productivity losses. Last year, a HEW report on "Work in America, prepared under the auspices of the W. E. Upjohn Institute for Employment Research, fueled vigorous debate over worker alienation. It bluntly called for redesign of jobs to increase productivity and improve the quality of life for "millions of Americans at all occupational levels."

Labor historian Thomas R. Brooks delivered one of the sharpest criticisms of the HEW report and of "radical-chic academics and pop sociologists." Says Brooks: "I detect an underlying contempt for working people and a scorn for their unions, as well as the creation of a new myth and a new conventional wisdom."

Businessmen, too, weighed in with denial of HEW's thesis. James D. Hodgson, former Labor Secretary and now a vice-president at Lockheed Aircraft Corp., scoffs at efforts to make job discontent "a contemporary phenomenon." Malcolm L. Denise, Ford

Motor Co.'s vice-president for labor relations, calls the issue "a creation of the pundits."

Chairman Richard C. Gerstenberg of General Motors Corp. takes a more pragmatic view of the job enrichment movement. The "plight" of the worker in the auto industry, and other industries, has been "magnified by political leaders, union officials, and social critics," he says. But he adds that it would be "unwise of us to rationalize inaction merely because the case has been overstated." GM signaled its awareness of the problem when it hired Stephen H. Fuller, a Harvard Business School professor of organizational behavior, a year ago last November to find answers in worker motivation.

With its high rate of absenteeism and its frequent callbacks of defective cars, the auto industry has become a focal point of debate over worker alienation. The auto assembly line epitomizes the idea of reducing work to simple, repetitive tasks, performed under rigorous, continuous supervision. Such an approach, says the HEW report, can lead only to alienation of human labor.

Thus, last year's strike at GM's Lordstown (Ohio) plant became a *cause célèbre*. The plant, built to produce GM's Vega at a rate of 100 per hour, is a showcase of assembly line efficiency. Young labor leaders said Lordstown was struck because workers felt that their jobs were inhumanly dull and the pressure too high.

Ammunition for Both Sides

Behavioral scientists seized on this explanation as support for the point they were making: that breaking work down into simple, repetitive tasks is anachronistic. The technique worked when it was introduced at the turn of the century, because the work force then was largely immigrants with only a grade school education. Now workers are mostly second- or third-generation Americans who average better than a high school education. They will not settle for the way things used to be.

GM officials deny the widespread impression that Lordstown represented a revolt by a new breed of younger, more sophisticated worker against the monotony and pressure of the assembly line. They contend that the strike really was over work standards stemming from the consolidation of two GM arms, Fisher Body Div. and the GM Assembly Div., and the subsequent merging of two union locals.

In Detroit, United Auto Workers officials say that the real issue was the layoff of 700 workers—GM says 400—with no significant drop in assembly-line speed. That amounted to more work at the same pay, they say, and when GM agreed to slow the assembly line, workers returned.

Whatever triggered the trouble at Lordstown, it gave the 30-year-old president of the UAW local there a chance to have his say. "The attitude of young people," he said, "is going to compel management to make jobs more desirable in the workplace and to fulfill the needs of man."

Schools of Thought

In an attempt to carry out this purpose, several companies have turned to the behavioral scientists for help through such techniques as job enrichment and organizational development. The concepts are broad and flexible, yet entrenched attitudes of both managers and workers make them difficult to apply to the work situation.

Psychologist Frederick Herzberg, now a professor of management at the University of Utah, advanced the job enrichment theory in the late 1950s. His idea: Satisfaction and motivation of the worker can be provided by systematically giving him greater responsibility, autonomy, and feedback on his performance.

Organizational development takes a slightly different tack. It is a structured way of fostering communication between worker and supervisor. Groups of employees informally hash over problems, propose solutions, and set mutual objectives with their supervisors. As the theory goes, each will see the other's side more clearly.

In the Phone System

One of the first big companies to redesign jobs was AT&T, which began in 1964. Robert Ford, personnel director for manpower utilization, says: "We had to start by finding out what was wrong with existing jobs. The second step was to organize new jobs, The third step, which we started within the last year, is to design new equipment and the jobs required to operate it."

Ford's department is working with Bell Labs in design of equipment to be used in the 1980s. The goal is to tailor jobs to the new equipment so the workers feel that they are giving a service and are "in charge." Says Ford: "With the more technologically advanced equipment, we have to avoid making the worker feel he is only a machine tender. If we don't, I can guarantee we will have unhappy people. We'll have another of those dumb-dumb jobs."

AT&T may be deeper into job redesign than any other company so far, but an increasing number of companies are experimenting with the idea, including A. B. Dick, Bankers Trust, Corning Glass, General Foods, IBM, Motorola, Polaroid, Prudential, TRW, and Western Union.

Some Skepticism

Not all behavioral scientists are convinced that these experiments are the whole answer, despite their evidence of improved morale. Dr. David Sirota, an associate professor of management at the University of Pennsylvania's Wharton School, for example, thinks management will have to probe deeper into the meaning of work to individuals before basic answers to alienation are found. He does not doubt that redesigning jobs has value—he spent 12 years supervising job enrichment programs at IBM—but he is disturbed when managers seize upon it as a panacea for productivity problems. And he is very annoyed that consultants prescribe it indiscriminately. "Selling job enrichment like soap is bound to create a high failure rate," states Sirota.

Industrial engineer Mitchell Fein is more skeptical. "If job redesign is so wonderful, why have no major unions asked for it?" he asks. "Workers are not stupid. They're not bashful. They'll strike for more money—why not for job enrichment? And if bosses saw any mileage in job enrichment, they'd all be doing it."

Fein does not doubt that many workers are "turned off" by highly routinized jobs. But, he asks, "To what extent is dissatisfaction caused by the work or by insufficient pay? Is it possible they might have a greater interest in the work if their living standards were raised and they could see their jobs as contributing to a good life?"

In the Long Run

Social scientists argue that more pay might produce a brief spurt in job satisfaction but is no long-term answer to the problem. Employees at all levels are saying that they will not accept management's manipulative tactics, says Harry Levinson, president of the Levinson Institute in Cambridge, Mass., and a former visiting professor at the Harvard B-school. "People are willing to put up with a lot when they have no other choice, or a very limited one," he says. Today, when that is not the case, techniques such as job enrichment, worker teams, and participative management will only provide temporary relief, Levinson says.

"The real issue is whether you paste these new techniques on questionable assumptions about people, or do you step back and ask what's really going on?" he says.

As the Labor Dept.'s Neal Herrick, a key member of the task force that wrote the HEW report, sees it, managers must look dispassionately for the key to effective productivity. Says Herrick: "What we have to look at, despite the people who say worker discontent is the creation of pop sociologists, is the gap between what satisfaction from the job is and what it might be. How much could people benefit if changes were made in the way work is structured? How much would productivity improve?"

BEGINNING WITH the work of F. W. Taylor and other members of the scientific management movement, there has been a trend within organizations to emphasize the division of labor into smaller and smaller units.[1] This means, essentially, that the duration of the job cycle—i.e., the task that the worker is required to perform—should be defined by its smallest possible component. Proponents of the scientific management school based this idea on the proposition that smaller units of work require less time to train or retrain a worker to perform the job. In addition, the smaller unit of work usually requires a lower level of skill on the part of the employee; in many cases wage rates could be reduced. Finally, and perhaps most importantly, the smaller the unit of work, the more proficient the worker can become at that job. The worker's motions can become almost machinelike, repeating a process over and over again. It may not even be necessary for the worker to think about the task being performed. Constant repetition will result in rapid and efficient performance.

This high level of human performance is the goal of many of today's industrial jobs. The automobile assembly lines of Detroit are perhaps the best examples of the degree to which the division of labor has developed. Here work cycles of a minute or less are not uncommon; each job is performed hundreds of times per day. The resulting levels of output have made the American automobile assembly plants models for production efficiency.

In recent years, however, these same assembly lines have been the focus of increasing worker unrest and frustration. As workers become more highly educated and economically secure they become more willing to express their dislike for the environment created by these highly efficient assembly lines. More and more, management is forced to deal with problems such as high employee turnover, absenteeism, and work slowdowns. It is becoming clear that there is indeed a series of trade-offs to be considered in the design of individual jobs.

Research results in the behavioral sciences have led many corporations to experiment with new concepts of job design. In these newly designed jobs not only the physiological but also the psychological needs of the worker are taken into consideration. These experiments have grown out of an increasing awareness that today's worker comes to the job environment with values and attitudes significantly different from those of previous generations. The affluent 1960s have led many of today's workers to seek satisfaction to needs beyond those filled by means of the paycheck. Many workers are looking for meaningful experience in the work situation, one that will enable them to leave the job each day with a feeling of satisfaction and accomplishment rather than frustration. Finally, greater education and social awareness have made many workers more co-cerned with the relationship of their individual work to overall corporate goals and objectives.

This recognition of the changing nature of the work force and the high frustration levels that many of today's jobs can create has led many corporations to investigate methods and techniques that might be utilized to increase employee motivation and performance. One of the most often employed techniques has dealt with the basic redesign of the job itself so that the worker has a more satisfying experience. Programs of job rotation, job enlargement, and job enrichment have all been incorporated into the work situation. For the most part, these programs run contrary to the fundamental concepts of the scientific management school of thought. Most have as their objective increasing the variety or complexity of the job itself so as to provide each worker with the opportunity to utilize more of his or her abilities. An objective is to create an environment in which workers may seek satisfaction to a wider variety of individual needs. These programs have met with varying degrees of success. The overall result has been to reinforce the understanding that a very complex relationship exists between the satisfaction of individual needs and the type of work found in the job environment.

The Work Environment and Individual Needs

If we examine the work environment in light of our discussion of individual needs (Chapter 7) we may develop a diagram like Figure 10.1. In this section we will examine the job itself in terms of its ability to satisfy higher-level needs. Figure 10.1 represents an extremely simplistic view of the relationship between the work environment and individual need satisfaction, but it does provide a framework for discussion.

In general, the compensation workers receive for their efforts enable them to satisfy the lower-level needs in the hierarchy—food, clothing, and housing. Through these purchases an individual is generally able to satisfy physiological and security needs. In addition, in some cases the individual is also able to satisfy certain ego needs by acquiring items society associates with success. These "status symbols" include cars, boats, and summer homes. In most cases, however, it is the lower-level needs that can be satisfied most readily by means of the compensation the worker receives.

Satisfaction of social needs in the work situation is generally the

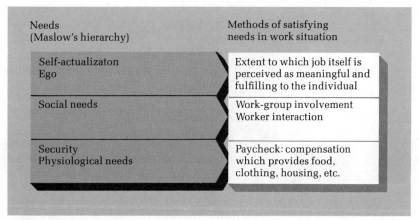

Figure 10.1. *Satisfying Needs in the Work Environment*

Source: Abraham H. Maslow, *Motivation and Personality,* 2nd ed. (New York: Harper & Row 1970).

result of interaction with coworkers. There is much research evidence to indicate that a work group tends to form a close-knit "organization" with its own behavior patterns, norms, and role relationships.[2] These informal organizations can provide the worker with a feeling of belonging that can satisfy social as well as security needs.

When we examine the higher-level needs and the extent to which they may be satisfied in the work situation, we must look to workers' perception of the job and the degree to which it provides them with what they consider to be a meaningful experience. "Meaningful experience" will no doubt be somewhat different for each worker, but research has revealed that certain conditions must be present in the work situation if higher-level needs are to be satisfied. Let us examine some of the research in order to identify these conditions and determine the extent to which they can provide an opportunity for the worker to satisfy higher-level needs.

Herzberg's Two Factor Theory

Perhaps the best known research in this area has been that conducted by Frederick Herzberg.[3] Herzberg and his associates conducted interviews with engineers and accountants in a total of nine corporations. Each employee was asked to describe some of his or her job experiences and the extent to which these experiences may

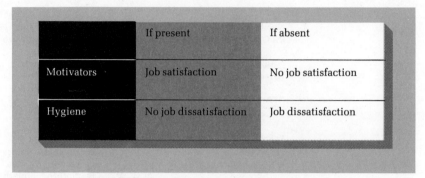

	If present	If absent
Motivators	Job satisfaction	No job satisfaction
Hygiene	No job dissatisfaction	Job dissatisfaction

Figure 10.2. *Relationship between Motivators and Hygiene Factors*

Source: F. Herzberg, B. Mausner, and D. Snyderman, *The Motivation to Work* (New York: John Wiley & Sons, 1959).

have made him or her feel "exceptionally good" or "exceptionally bad." In this way the researchers attempted to focus on specific job experiences and the extent to which these experiences might be tied to overall feelings of satisfaction or dissatisfaction on the part of the worker. As a result of his research, Herzberg postulated that there are *two groups of factors* having an impact on individual satisfactions in the work environment.

Herzberg's research indicates that there is a distinct difference between those factors that can bring about "job satisfaction" and those factors that may lead to "job dissatisfaction." Herzberg defines the factors leading to job satisfaction as being directly related to the job itself. These include achievement, recognition for achievement, the work itself, responsibility, and growth or advancement. According to Herzberg, these *motivators* must be present if an individual is to be satisfied with the job. Herzberg defines another set of variables, called the *hygiene* factors. If present, they will not lead to job satisfaction, but neither will job dissatisfaction result. If, however, these hygiene factors are absent, the result will be a high level of job dissatisfaction. Hygiene factors include company policy and administration, supervision, interpersonal relationships, working conditions, salary, status, and security. Figure 10.2 shows the relationship of both motivational and hygiene factors to overall job satisfaction.

According to Herzberg's theory, the matrix shown in Figure 10.2 would represent the relationship between motivators and hygiene factors in influencing overall job satisfaction for employees. As a result of the work done by Herzberg it became clear that not all changes in the work environment would necessarily lead to an improvement in overall job satisfaction. In order to increase the level of employee satisfaction, management must differentiate between the motivational and hygiene factors as defined by Herzberg. It appears that only the motivational factors are influential in bringing about higher levels of employee job satisfaction. In examining these motivational factors one can note that in almost all cases they deal with aspects of the *job itself* and not with the work environment. This does not mean that the hygiene factors can be ignored by management; these factors must be present if management is to avoid employee job dissatisfaction. Because of the Herzberg research, however, most organizational programs designed to improve the level of job satisfaction within the organization have focused on the motivational factors associated with the job itself. Let us examine some of these programs.

Job Enlargement and Job Enrichment Programs

In an effort to depart from highly repetitive work cycles, many corporations have sought to provide employees with a more satisfying job environment by increasing the variety of their activities. As early as 1944, the IBM Corporation significantly altered the job design in its parts manufacturing department in Endicott, New York. As a result of the redesign, the jobs of tool sharpener, set-up man, machine operator, and inspector were all combined into a single activity. After the changes were put into effect, IBM reported increases in overall worker satisfaction, improvement in product quality, and reduction in production costs. Programs such as this one were generally referred to as *job enlargement*. The programs were approached by corporations in two different ways—*horizontal* and *vertical* job enlargement.

Some companies increased the number of activities that each employee performed. For example, for an employee responsible for placing a series of eight bolts on a machine, job enlargement might provide that the employee would also fit the cover on the machine and secure it in place with another series of bolts. The idea here is one of *horizontal* job enlargement; the employee is given more of the same kinds of activities to perform, with a resulting increase in the *scope* of the job. Other companies, however, such as in our IBM example, approached job enlargement programs from a *vertical* dimension; that is, they increased the *depth* of the responsibility given to each employee. In a program of vertical job enlargement designed to increase the depth of the job, the employee who placed the series of eight bolts on the machine might also be given the responsibility of inspecting the bolts to insure acceptable quality and examining the cover assembly to determine if specifications were met. The worker would also be given the authority to reject components that did not meet specifications. Programs of this type, in which the job is modified so as to increase in overall depth and responsibility, are usually referred to as *job enrichment* programs. In summary, *vertical* job enrichment tends to increase the overall level of responsibility in the job; *horizontal* job enlargement merely increases the number of activities included.

The concept of vertical job enrichment is the one that seems to possess many of the factors that correlate most highly with worker motivation. If we examine the idea of vertical job enrichment in conjunction with the motivating factors defined by Hertzberg, there begins to emerge a series of guidelines for management to follow if job redesign is to maximize higher-level need satisfaction. It seems highly desirable for jobs to be designed so as to allow each employee a greater degree of control over his or her own work situation. This control can take many forms, but it generally includes increasing the worker's power to influence the *planning* and *organization* of the work cycle. Further, it requires the worker to use a wider variety of skills, particularly those skills the worker perceives to be meaningful or important. Jobs designed along these lines allow the worker to become more involved with the job in its entirety. The worker comes to understand not only *how* the job is to be done but *why* it needs to be done in a certain manner and how it fits into the overall work situation. The worker is better able to see the job in relation to the needs and goals of the entire corporation and thus to appreciate the importance of his or her own contribution. It is clear that job redesign programs whose objective is to provide the worker with more opportunities to satisfy higher-level needs must meet these requirements (see Figure 10.3).

1. Attention should focus on ways of increasing the *depth* rather than merely the *scope* of the job, allowing the worker to deal with the job as a complete entity. The worker should be involved as much as possible in all phases, including planning and organizing his or her activities and also having the opportunity to evaluate his or her own performance.
2. The worker should be given the opportunity to recognize how this job relates to those around it and more importantly how it contributes to overall corporate goals. This will permit the worker to

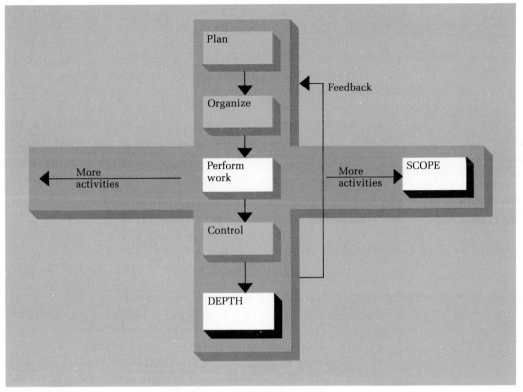

Figure 10.3. *Increasing Job Depth*

recognize his or her contribution to the organization and build an appropriate sense of importance.

3. The job should enable the worker to maximize the use of a wide variety of physical and mental skills; the worker should feel that he or she is reaching individual potential.

4. Finally, the job should provide for individual growth and development, which will lead to increased responsibility in the future. The worker should be made aware of how present performance may lead to recognition for achievement through promotion. This will provide the individual with an awareness of the relationship of this job to future career development.

The reader should keep in mind that not all jobs lend themselves to be redesigned so as to relate directly to overall corporate goals. Many assembly line and component-related jobs may be far removed from the larger company picture. Even so, the worker can develop a sense of how his or her job ties in with those around it and of why it is a necessary component of the overall work flow. To be avoided is the situation in which the worker feels isolated and insignificant with respect to his or her job contribution. Management should take the time and effort necessary to create an environment in which each employee feels that he or she is making maximum use of ability and skills in contributing to the objectives of the work group, the department, and the organization.

Job Redesign: Not for Everyone

Deciding to Redesign Jobs

We have focused on ways and means to redesign jobs so as to provide a more meaningful work experience. The objective we have defined is to create an environment in which employees may satisfy higher-level needs and thus reduce job-related frustration. We have made a series of assumptions which may or may not be true with respect to particular industrial settings. At this point let us examine some of these assumptions. In determining whether or not a job redesign program will be effective in increasing employee satisfaction, management should consider the following points:

Employees' Economic Needs. We have stated that job redesign usually has as its purpose the satisfaction of higher-level employee needs. This assumes that the employees to be affected are indeed seeking satisfaction to the higher-level needs in Maslow's hierarchy; this would mean that they have already achieved some degree of satisfaction with the more basic physiological, security, and social needs. We have suggested that the behavior of many of today's workers does seem to be caused by the frustration of being unable to satisfy higher-level needs in the job environment, but management must not automatically assume this to be the case in all situations. As workers become better educated and more aware of the environment around them they tend also to increase their expectations regarding the material things they desire in life. When these increased expectations collide with the high level of inflation experienced during the early 1970s, the result for many workers is to find themselves economically unable to acquire the goods and services they desire. For example, the tremendous increase in the cost of single-family dwellings during the early 1970s has made it very nearly impossible for many workers to be able to afford this type of housing, while those who do buy homes must continually strive to meet mortgage and higher tax payments. There has also been a significant increase in the cost of higher education. As a college education becomes more and more an apparent necessity, parents are faced with the economic hardships that such an education for their children entails. These are but two examples of the increasing economic pressure being brought to bear on workers. Such pressure has caused many to become increasingly concerned with the economic aspects of their work. In situations such as these, higher-level needs may become subordinate to the more pressing physiological and security needs, and it is once again these lower-level needs the worker seeks to satisfy.

Workers who are experiencing economic hardship would probably strongly resist any attempt to redesign their jobs—regardless of the reason. They might fear that their performance would suffer while they were learning their new responsibilities, with the possible result that their income would be reduced. These same employees might be receiving significant supplements to their income through wage incentive programs. These supplements may be providing the employee with the opportunity to own a home or to send the children to college. Here again, the new job might be seen as threatening the availability of wage incentives, which would result in additional economic hardship. It is clear that for these workers the importance of the lower-level needs will take priority over any desire to achieve a more meaningful work experience. Workers finding themselves in situations of potential economic loss are most concerned with their ability to meet their immediate economic obligations. In a very real sense, some workers are operating at the lower levels of Maslow's hierarchy; they are primarily motivated by economic objectives.

This does not necessarily mean that a program of job redesign should not be undertaken by management. It simply means that management should take precautions in its job redesign programs. No situation should be created in which the program is seen as possibly threatening the economic base of the individual employee. Management must remember that the physiological and security needs are the most basic and that any job change that might threaten workers' ability to satisfy these needs would be strongly resisted.

Work Group Interaction. Sometimes a redesign of the job may require a change in the layout of the workplace. Change in layout may be necessary in order to provide the worker with the additional space, equipment, or machinery needed to perform the redesigned job function. As a result of this change workers may be less able to interact with other members of their work groups. If these workers are now no longer able to satisfy social needs in the work environment, the result may be a less satisfied work force with a corresponding increase in frustration. Management should not underestimate the importance of the work group and its ability to provide satisfaction to individual needs. The informal organization, with its own hierarchy, role relationships, and norms, provides a necessary environment in which workers may satisfy a wide variety of needs. Security and social needs may be satisfied when an individual is an accepted member of a group. In addition, certain ego needs may be satisfied by a particular member's status within the group. If the interaction of the work group is to be significantly affected as a result of a job redesign program, it may have a negative impact on overall worker attitudes and performance. Management must give careful consideration to each individual worker in order to determine the impact of any job redesign on all needs of the hierarchy. Management must determine what set of needs each worker is seeking to satisfy and must evaluate how a redesign of the job would affect these needs.

Worker Attitudes and Abilities. If jobs are to be redesigned so that workers have increased decision making power, management must be certain that each worker is capable of handling this additional responsibility. Does the individual worker have the skill, intelligence, and willingness to perform effectively, given these new job requirements? Here again management should not make the assumption that job redesign is the panacea that will solve all problems of employee performance. Low levels of productivity, as well as other job-related problems, may be due to a wide variety of factors other than the worker's frustration over an inability to satisfy higher-level needs at the workplace. A manager must learn to recognize when a job that may appear to him or her to be routine and monotonous may actually be utilizing *all* the skills and abilities of the worker who is now performing this job. Should such a job be redesigned to build in additional responsibility, it would almost certainly exceed the capabilities of that particular worker. This could well result in a reduction in overall performance. The author can recall a situation in which a certain assembly line job, which required the extensive connection of wire leads, was considered to be extremely undesirable by most members of the assembly line work group. The worker who was eventually assigned to that job was one who was unable to perform satisfactorily on other stations in the assembly line. This job, however, considered highly repetitive and monotonous by most, fit exactly the capabilities of this worker. His performance was excellent and his attitude was favorable; he felt comfortable in this job, which did not exceed his capabilities. The point to be made is that management should not overlook the possibility that low performance may be due to insufficient skill or intelligence of the employee; it may not be at all related to the worker's inability to satisfy higher-level needs.

Another point to remember is that many workers satisfy higher-level needs through activities that are not job-related. These include community involvement groups, local sports, or political activities. Clubs and organizations which have their own hierarchical structure, role relationships, norms, and status levels may offer a great deal of high-level need satisfaction, particularly if the worker-member occupies a high position. Should a worker with responsibilities in organizations outside the workplace experience an increase in responsibility in the job, it might be perceived as taking time away from involvement in some of these outside activities. The extent to which the employee finds these outside activities necessary and satisfying will therefore influence his or her reaction to any job redesign. If the worker believes that the new requirements will reduce or diminish other satisfying activity, any attempt to redesign the present job will almost certainly be resisted.

With respect to the willingness of employees to assume additional responsibility, management must recognize the fact that each of us has a tendency to be somewhat afraid of the unknown. Workers will often have some fear that they may not be successful in dealing with new responsibility. This fear may cause some resistance to the idea of leaving a job experience that is both known and understood for one that is unknown and will require some time to master. Even in the best of circumstances both management and the worker must recognize and accept the fact that some initial drop in employee performance must be expected during this learning phase. Management should place its emphasis on the long-run implications of a job redesign program rather than focus on the short-run resistance that may be expected.

Management Attitudes

If jobs are to be redesigned so that workers are given additional responsibility, management must be willing to delegate authority for decision making. As we have said, the objective of a program of job redesign should be to enlarge the "depth" of the job. This will provide the employee with the opportunity to have input in more aspects of the job environment. Management must be willing to consider inviting this input into its own decision making if the program is to have maximum positive impact on the worker. Otherwise, the negative effect on employee attitudes and corresponding levels of performance may well be significant. In these situations employees will rightly perceive that management is merely playing games with them and is not interested in providing them with an opportunity to assume more responsibility.

As a result of an effective program of job redesign, individual workers will become much more involved in the planning and organizing of their own job activities. When this happens, it is often difficult for management to evaluate input from subordinates objectively without feeling some threat to their own ego and status. Thus, it becomes extremely important for top-level management to consider carefully the impact on all managerial personnel that will result when a certain amount of control and authority moves down into lower levels of the organization. Some members of middle management and first-line supervision may perceive this movement as a loss of status and prestige in their own jobs. To the extent that such a perception does exist these same managers may make subtle attempts to try to prevent the successful implementation of a job redesign program. It is therefore necessary to consider the attitudes and abilities not only of those employees whose jobs will be redesigned but also the attitudes of the managers who will be responsible for supervising these employees. In implementing a job redesign program whose objective is to bring about a greater opportunity for job satisfaction, management must be careful not to create a situation in which either the operative employees or the supervisors will feel threatened or frustrated.

Finally, we must acknowledge that there may be instances where individual workers are so alienated from the work environment that no attempt on the part of management to increase their motivation will have much effect. These workers perhaps reject the work ethic entirely and exhibit behavior that closely approximates that described by McGregor's Theory X. In situations such as these it is unlikely that a program of job redesign will have much impact. In fact, in some cases the disruption may actually result in a long-run decline in performance, especially if the worker experiences increased alienation as a result of the greater demands of the newly designed job.

Discussion Questions

1. Compare Herzberg's two factor theory with Maslow's hierarchy of needs. What implications does each have with respect to the job environment?
2. Discuss the difference between programs of vertical and horizontal job enlargement.
3. What are some of the factors that should be considered before initiating a program of job redesign? Pay specific attention to those factors which might bring about a negative response to a program designed to increase the depth of an employee's job.

4. "Within a given organization it is just as possible for a manager to be frustrated and dissatisfied with his job as it is for an assembly line worker." Comment.
5. Division of labor is viewed differently by scientific management and by advocates of job enlargement and job enrichment. What factors brought about a change in this concept?
6. How can a program of job enrichment be applied to jobs at the middle and upper managerial levels?

Case for Discussion

At a meeting of the production staff of Hawkins Manufacturing Corporation, production manager Mark Barker faced the problem of how best to organize and set up production for a new product.

The product was a bracket and motor assembly that was fairly simple and straightforward, requiring little skill or expertise in assembling. Estimates from the industrial engineering department indicated that the entire operation would require about twenty minutes for each unit assembled.

The work force at Hawkins was unionized and most of it had been recruited from fairly sophisticated aerospace manufacturing and assembly plants on the east coast. Most workers had experience on detailed, complicated assembly operations requiring close tolerances.

After production schedules had been discussed, Mr. Barker asked for suggestions about how to begin the production operation. At this point, the chief industrial engineer suggested the six-person assembly line shown below.

Each person would perform four minutes of work and then pass the component to the next station where the next four minute job could be performed. At the end of the fifth station (total of twenty minutes' work) the component would be finished and the sixth and final station would then test the product. The industrial engineer believed that by giving each station only four minutes to perform each operation, assemblers would become highly proficient in their tasks and overall productivity would be high. Mr. Barker listened to the recommendations of the industrial engineer, adjourned the meeting, and returned to his office to consider these recommendations.

	Assembly station 1	Assembly station 2	Assembly station 3	Assembly station 4	Assembly station 5	Test station 6
start $\rightarrow$	4 minutes of work $\rightarrow$	4 minutes of work $\rightarrow$	4 minutes of work $\rightarrow$	4 minutes of work $\rightarrow$	4 minutes of work $\rightarrow$	completed, assembly tested

Selected References

Davis, L. and Canter, R. "Job Design Research." *Journal of Industrial Engineering* 7 (1956).

Ford, R. N. "Motivation Through the Work Itself." *American Management Association*, 1969.

Herzberg, F., Mausner, B., and Snyderman, D. *The Motivation to Work*. New York: John Wiley & Sons, 1959.

Hulin, Charles and Blood, Milton. "Job Enlargement, Individual Differences, and Worker Responses." In *Psychological Bulletin* 69 (1968).

Kilbridge, M. D., "Reduced Costs Through Job Enlargement: A Case." In *Journal of Business,* October 1960.

Myers, Scott. "Every Employee a Manager." In *California Management Review* 10 (1968).

Nadler, Gerald. *Work Design.* Homewood, Ill.: Richard D. Irwin, 1963.

Scott, William. "Activation Theory and Task Design." In *Organizational Behavior and Human Performance,* August 1966.

Seeman, Melvin. "On the Personal Consequences of Alienation in Work." In *American Sociological Review* 32 (1967).

Trumbo, D. "Individual and Group Correlate of Attitudes Toward Work Related Change." In *Journal of Applied Psychology* 45 (1961).

Turkel, Studs. *Working.* New York: Avon Books, 1974.

Turner, Arthur. "Foreman, Job and Company." In *Human Relations* 10 (1957).

Turner, A. N. and Miclette, A. L., "Sources of Satisfaction in Repetitive Work." In *Occupational Psychology* 36 (1962).

Tyler, William. "Measuring Organizational Specialization: The Concept of Role Variety." In *Administrative Science Quarterly,* September 1973.

The Anatomy of an Organization

11

GE's Jones Restructures His Top Team

General Electric Chairman Reginald H. Jones this week unveiled a sweeping high-level reorganization that "rewrites the position guides" of his job and those of GE's 10 other top officers. Jones' avowed aim: to keep the diversified giant on a profitable growth track by making his vice-chairmen more directly responsible and accountable for the operations they oversee.

True, it is not unusual for a GE chief executive to tailor the top management staff and structure to his own operating style. Jones' predecessors have each put their own distinctive stamp on GE, and they have done it successfully enough to make the company a pacesetter in management structures and procedures.

Ralph Cordiner applied decentralization to GE's operations in the 1950s, an approach copied by company after company. Fred J. Borch, who took over from Cordiner in 1963, created the "office of the president" device in the 1960s. This top-level management structure was designed to spread the president's job among a triumvirate of executives. In the early 1970s, Borch, working closely with Jones, put GE heavily into strategic business planning—a technique that treats the company's vast array of ventures as an investment portfolio, backing the winners and pruning the losers through systematic analysis.

What is startling about Jones's tailoring job is the speed with which he has acted. Explains the 55-year-old chairman, who took over the job only last December: "I've had six months. The transition is over. Now it's time to get on with the job."

Reprinted from the June 30, 1973 issue of Business Week by special permission. Copyright © 1973 McGraw-Hill Publishing, Inc., New York, N. Y. 10020. All rights reserved.

Financial Accountability

At first glance, Jones appears to be scrapping the "team-at-the-top" approach created by Borch as a way to manage the vast enterprise, with its $10-billion in sales, with 10 groups, 50 divisions and 166 departments. While Borch was very much the No. 1 GE executive, he created a phalanx of vice-chairmen who functioned as a corporate executive staff with policy responsibility but no direct financial accountability for the operations they monitored.

Though Jones is keeping the corporate executive staff in place, the three vice-chairmen have significantly different responsibilities now. They are financially accountable for the operating groups reporting to them. And each is involved with line operations.

Vice-Chairman Herman L. Weiss, 56, who previously was in charge of administration and staff, now has three operating groups—special systems and products, components and materials, and industrial products—as his responsibility. Staff and administration now come under the wing of Hershner Cross, a senior vice-president, who reports directly to Jones rather than a vice-chairman.

Jack S. Parker, 55, the vice-chairman with the most seniority of the trio, now oversees the aerospace, aircraft engines and international groups.

Walter D. Dance, 55, emerges as the vice-chairman with the heaviest load. He winds up with the power generation, power delivery, major appliance and consumer groups. Those operations last year accounted for more than half of GE's revenues and earnings.

"The group executives will still be the chief operating officers of their groups," says

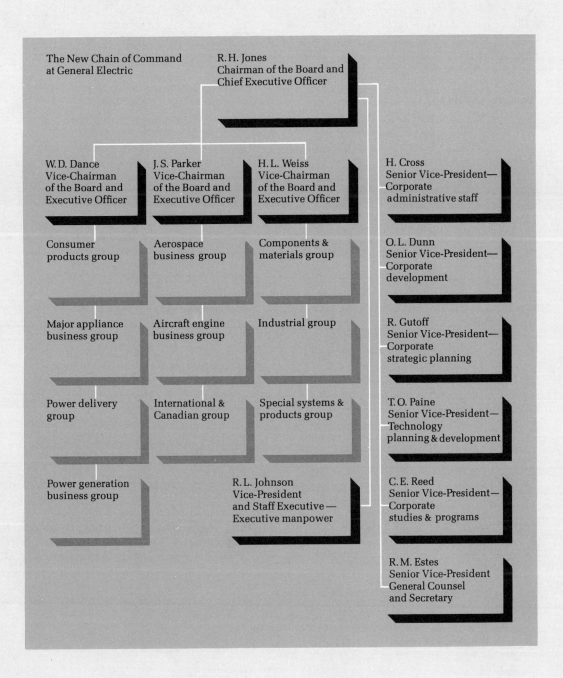

The New Chain of Command at General Electric

R.H. Jones
Chairman of the Board and Chief Executive Officer

W.D. Dance
Vice-Chairman of the Board and Executive Officer

J.S. Parker
Vice-Chairman of the Board and Executive Officer

H.L. Weiss
Vice-Chairman of the Board and Executive Officer

H. Cross
Senior Vice-President— Corporate administrative staff

Consumer products group

Aerospace business group

Components & materials group

O.L. Dunn
Senior Vice-President— Corporate development

Major appliance business group

Aircraft engine business group

Industrial group

R. Gutoff
Senior Vice-President— Corporate strategic planning

Power delivery group

International & Canadian group

Special systems & products group

T.O. Paine
Senior Vice-President— Technology planning & development

Power generation business group

R.L. Johnson
Vice-President and Staff Executive — Executive manpower

C.E. Reed
Senior Vice-President— Corporate studies & programs

R.M. Estes
Senior Vice-President General Counsel and Secretary

Jones, "but now the vice-chairmen are responsible for the overall financial results and planning of the groups assigned to them."

Measure of a Man

In the old alignment, he adds, the vice-chairman "followed the groups, but their accountability was not clearly defined. I feel very strongly that you have to give a fellow a job with clearly defined responsibility and accountability and then, by God, you can measure him."

As part of the reorganization, Jones relinquishes the monitoring function he had over the power generation and power delivery groups. "I want to give myself a little more time to step back from the operating responsibility I had to work on the general thrust of the corporation," he says.

But the British-born GE career man is not moving into an ivory tower. Indeed, his span of control has broadened. In addition to three vice-chairmen reporting to him, he will have six senior vice-presidents on a direct reporting line. They will be responsible for areas that Jones considers vital for GE's growth. The men and their responsibilities are: Cross, administration; Oscar L. Dunn, corporate development; Robert M. Estes, legal and social responsibility; Reuben Gutoff, strategic planning; Thomas O. Paine, technology, and Charles E. Reed, product quality and reliability. Additionally, Jones has put Roy L. Johnson into a vice-president slot on executive manpower development, which will report directly to him.

"I want the views of these executives directly. As the person finally responsible for the financial results and thrust of this company, I want their inputs," says Jones.

Cross, Dunn, Estes, and Reed were already senior vice-presidents but each has now had his responsibilities broadened. Gutoff moves up from a group executive job where he headed the components and materials group and Paine, a former director of the National

Aeronautics and Space Administration, shifts from running the power generation group to his new post.

Replacing the 46-year-old Gutoff in his group executive job is John F. Welch, Jr., who moves up from being general manager of the Chemical & Metallurgical div. At 37, Welch becomes the youngest group executive in GE's history. Paine's replacement to run the power generation group is Edward E. Hood, Jr., 42, who shifts from leadership to the international and Canadian group.

No Indictment

Gutoff and Welch, in Jones' view, have been "outstanding in laying out strategic plans and profitably implementing them." Their ascendancy takes on significance since Jones vaulted to the top at GE by embracing strategic business planning—the approach that led to the spinoff of GE's money-losing computer operation to Honeywell, Inc., in 1970.

The new organizational alignment, Jones insists, is in no way an indictment of the setup Borch built. "There was always a *primus inter pares* in the corporate executive office. We simply have recognized that now and clearly defined responsibilities," he says.

There is another element in the shift away from the office-of-the-president concept, which Jones understandably is not trumpeting. One of Borch's primary reasons for setting up the device was to find his successor among an array of candidates all in the same age range. That reason was wiped out when Jones was tapped as heir apparent last July.

Nor is the new structure an abandonment of GE's vaunted decentralization. There has been no change in any manager's authority, says Jones. "They have all the authority they have always had—to buy equipment, hire people, set rates," he explains.

The difference is in the over-all coordination of the operating division activities. The vice-chairmen will be more heavily involved in making sure that the groups and divisions in their charge are "performing according to the operating plan on which we've all agreed," says Jones. But, with a senior vice-president working directly for Jones on strategic planning, GE is, in fact, centralizing policy and strategy functions. This move should prevent the sort of foulups that can plague a huge corporation.

There is a story around GE that illustrates the need for such centralization. When GE decided, in the mid-1960s, to expand in Europe via acquisition and joint ventures, 70 division vice-presidents scoured the continent looking for candidates for their individual operations. They wound up stumbling over one another. With his overhaul of GE's top structure, Jones thinks he will not have to suffer such cases of bureaucratic bungling.

THE SUBJECT of this chapter is the components of the corporate organizational structure. Up to this point we have discussed only the basic building blocks of organizations—the individual jobs and tasks that must be performed. If these jobs are to be performed efficiently and effectively, there must be some ordering of the relationship between the tasks to be accomplished. This ordering is defined by the structure that each organization employs in carrying out its activities. Three of the major elements of a corporation's organizational structure are its *departmentalization, span of control,* and *line and staff* relations.

Departmentalization

As jobs within an organization begin to grow and multiply it becomes necessary to group various individuals in some rational way so as to insure effective direction and coordination. Since a single individual—the corporate president—is limited in the number of individuals she or he can effectively supervise, some structure must be established that will determine how each individual is to function and relate to others. This structure will define which individuals work together, to whom individuals report, and the position of individuals vis-à-vis other work groups. These groupings are called the organizational departments.

Decisions on how departments are to be formed and their relative position and relationship to one another are fundamental to any organization. These decisions will influence the way the corporation will conduct its business and will have significant impact on decision making, reporting procedures, and planning.

For purposes of this analysis we will focus on the most common forms of organizational departmentalization, discussing some of the advantages and disadvantages of each. Of course, no one type of departmentalization is correct for all situations and business conditions. One of the characteristics of sound management is the ability to recognize the unique circumstances of an industry and then select the type of departmentalization that most closely fits the needs of that industry.

Functional Departmentalization

The first departmental structure to be discussed is the grouping of individuals according to the type of function they perform. When this approach is used, individuals are generally grouped along the lines of the basic corporate functions. These might include areas such as marketing, production, finance, engineering, and legal (Fig-

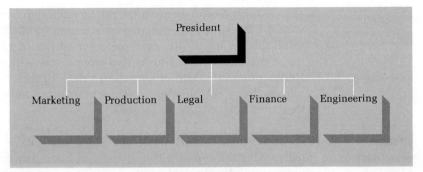

Figure 11.1. *Functional Departmentalization*

ure 11.1). Under the functional structure, all individuals in some way involved in the marketing function would be grouped together in the same organizational department. This does not necessarily mean they would be physically located in the same area. The department concept serves to define channels of communication, lines of reporting, and organizational level; it does not necessarily refer to specific geographical location. An example of departmentalization by function is shown in Figure 11.1. In this example the departments named are all at the same organizational level and all report directly to the president.

Geographical Departmentalization

A second type of departmental breakdown might be by geographical area. This would be used when top management wished to give specific departments responsibility for given geographical regions. Geographical regions might be defined by state, section of the country, or even continent. Figure 11.2 gives an example of such a breakdown.

Figure 11.2. *Geographical Departmentalization*

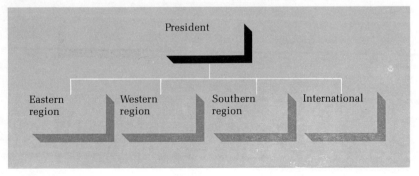

In this type of departmentalization each department (or division) would be responsible for the area under its direction. In order to fulfill this responsibility each department would generally be able to make decisions regarding varied operations within its own region. Geographical departmentalization refers to the area in which individuals have responsibility; it does not necessarily refer to where they themselves may be located.

Product Departmentalization

A third type of departmental structure would be a division by product or product type. In this structural breakdown top management would isolate similar products or product groups for inclusion within the same department or division.

Figure 11.3 shows a departmental structure by product or product line. General Motors is perhaps the best known of those organizations utilizing division by product type. Each division or department within GM operates in essentially an independent manner and is responsible for products that fall within its area.

Layering

Management may choose different types of departmentalization at different levels within the organization. This brings us to the next step in the development of the organizational structure. The layering of departments, one upon another in pyramid fashion, coordinates effort throughout the organization.

Figure 11.4 shows an example of layering. In the figure we observe that the corporation has chosen to departmentalize first by product (level 2), then by function (level 3). With this type of structure, Product A, Product B, and Product C divisions would each have its own marketing department. Each marketing department would be responsible for the marketing effort associated with its own product

Figure 11.3. *Product Departmentalization*

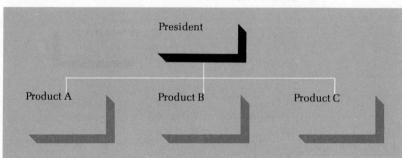

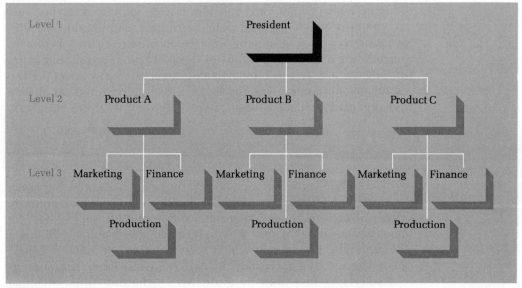

Figure 11.4. *Layering*

line and would report directly to the head of the product division. The same would be true for each of the other functional areas shown (production, finance).

This structure would allow the manager responsible for Product A to maintain close control over the entire product line; this manager would be directly in charge of all of the functions directly associated with the line (marketing, production, finance). In this situation any decision regarding Product A could be handled by the manager of Product A rather than being sent all the way to the president. On the other hand, an organizational structure such as this might result in some duplication of effort: each product division (A, B, C) would in many cases maintain complete and independent functional departments, and as such, there might be activities that overlap or are duplicated in two or more of these independent functional departments. For example, similar types of national demographic studies might be undertaken by each of the divisional marketing departments. This would obviously mean a duplication of effort within the organization as a whole.

As we can see, this type of departmentalization will offer some advantage to the organization but may well have some disadvantages associated with it. In order to decide the most appropriate type of departmental structure to be employed at each level of the organization, top management must consider a wide variety of factors, such as type of products handled, sales territories, competition, stability of industry, and skill of subordinates. In order to gain a better understanding of the implications of these decisions we should examine how various types of departmental structures may affect the way an organization operates. Figure 11.5 illustrates two typical alternative organizational structures.

Departmental Characteristics

In examining Figure 11.5 we note that the structures shown represent two entirely different approaches to the organizational question. These structures would represent different philosophies by top management as to the best way to meet the needs and conditions of the particular industry in which they function. No type of departmentalization is appropriate in and of itself. Each has a set of characteristics that must be evaluated by the individual organization. Certain of these characteristics may be deemed more desirable than others in various situations. Let us examine some of the characteristics of different organizational types as they might be represented in the structures of Figure 11.5.

Centralization and Decentralization of Operations

The degree of centralization within an organization is the extent to which control and decision making reside at the top levels of management. The more highly centralized the organization, the more control and decision making reside at the top. As control and decision-making authority move down to lower levels, the more decentralized that organization becomes. Let us examine the two structures in Figure 11.5 in order to determine how the decision-making process might operate in each. For purposes of discussion we will deal with a single product and note where specific decisions might be made. It is apparent that any problem or decision regarding a product would necessarily be handled quite differently by the two organizations.

In structure A, for example, if a problem were to arise with respect to Product A it would be necessary for product representatives from each of the three divisions (production, marketing, finance) to become involved, with a decision eventually having to be made by the company president. It is to the presidential level in this structure that all three divisions ultimately report. If we examine structure B, on the other hand, we note that problems or decisions regarding a particular product could be discussed by individuals within one division, with the decision ultimately being made by the vice-presi-

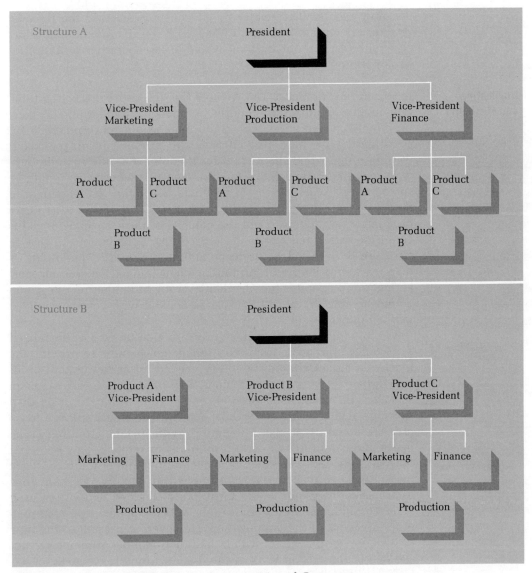

Figure 11.5. *Two Approaches to Organizational Structure*

dent responsible for that product, *one managerial level below the president.* In this situation we can see that the product structure lends itself more readily to a decentralized form of management, while the functional structure would fit more closely with a management that wished to maintain a more centralized control over decision making. The reader might consider whether the regional structure is more closely associated with the functional or product type with respect to management's ability to centralize or decentralize operations.

Duplication and Flexibility

In structure A in Figure 11.5 we note that the entire marketing function in the organization reports to a single individual, the vice-president for marketing. This individual would be responsible for coordinating the marketing effort for *all products* in *all regions*. It would be likely that the budget for this officer would include individuals with very specialized marketing skills whose costs could be spread over a wide variety of products. Since the vice-president of marketing is responsible for the marketing effort of all of the firm's products, both the costs and the benefits of these specialized skills could be distributed across these products. Such is not the case in structure B. In this structure each region and product maintains its own marketing staff with an independent budget. Since each marketing group operates independently, it might be that no one group would be able to afford the costs associated with very specialized marketing personnel.

We note, however, that structure A, which utilizes a centralized approach to the marketing effort, might not be able to provide the individual attention and flexibility needed to market certain products in specific geographical regions. This limitation does not exist in structure B, where each product and region would have its own specialized marketing staff; thus, structure B would allow for increased flexibility or marketing effort, with specific attention to the needs and conditions of certain products or regions. This potential for flexibility could be offset by some duplication of the more basic marketing functions across divisions within the organization since each marketing group would most likely conduct its own research and information analysis. Some of the data might have application in other divisions of the organization. However, as a result of the type of structure employed, in which the functional departments are positioned at the second level of the organization, it is sometimes extremely difficult for one division to maintain close communication with other divisions which perform similar functional activities (in marketing, finance, production).

Management Development

The extent to which an organization involves itself in the development and training of its young managers is obviously a function of many variables other than simply the type of departmentalization utilized. We do note, however, that in structure B of Figure 11.5 managers at the product level are able to involve themselves in all

Exhibit 11.1. *Summary of Some Advantages and Disadvantages of Various Types of Departmentalization*

Centralization	*Functional* structure allows more centralization of authority and decision making than do *product* or *geographical* structure.
Flexibility	*Product* and *geographical* structure allow for greater attention to specific needs and conditions with respect to geographical areas or specific products.
Duplication	*Product* and *geographical* structure will normally entail more duplication of effort than will *functional* structure.
Specialization	*Functional* structure may allow for more specialization of talent spread over a larger number of products.
Management Training	As a result of the greater ability to decentralize, *product* and *geographical* structures may provide a better training ground for developing managers.

aspects of the marketing, production, and financing of a given product. Within structure A, on the other hand, individuals at the same organizational level would be restricted to a *single functional area*. Thus, if it is the goal of top management to provide young managers with an opportunity to understand the complex interrelationship among the various business functions (marketing, production, finance), structure B would appear to be more suited as a training ground for developing executives. This structure tends to allow managers to become involved in all aspects of a given product. As a manager moves to higher levels, these same principles can be applied to other products in other regions. In structure A we note that a manager can reach the level of vice-president and still not become involved in all of the functional areas of the organization. His or her responsibility would include all products and all regions but would be limited to a single functional area. This environment might present a more limited background against which to understand the complexity of the organization's operations.

Exhibit 11.1 presents a *general* summary of what is likely to be the case. Obviously, each organization must be evaluated independently to determine if indeed it displays these characteristics.

Span of Control: Tall and Flat Structures

Another important factor in corporate structure is the *span of control* at each level in the organization. *Span of control* simply refers to the number of subordinates that report directly to the same superior. Top management's policy regarding span of control at each organizational level will directly impact a great number of organizational functions. It usually provides a clue to the philosophy and attitudes of top management and also some indication of the nature of the particular industry in which the company functions. The impact of management's decision about span of control can best be illustrated by two simple organization structures, one having a span of control of three, the other a span of control of two (see Figure 11.6).

In structure A of Figure 11.6 we see an example of an organiza-

Figure 11.6. *Tall and Flat Structures*

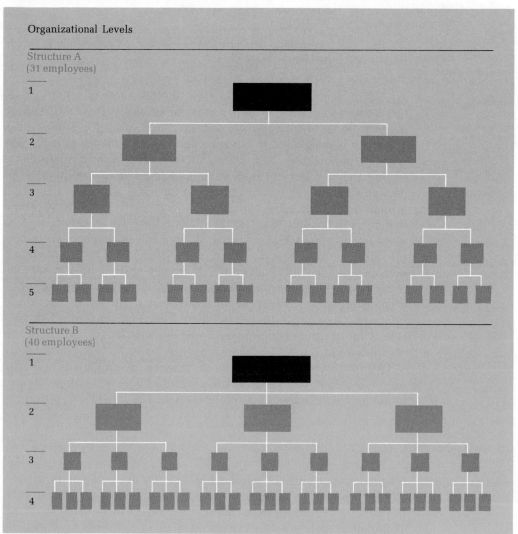

tional structure having a span of control of two. This means that at each organizational level there are two subordinates reporting to a single supervisor. Structure B represents an organization with a span of control of three, in which three subordinates report to a single supervisor. We note that structure A has a total of 5 organizational levels and 31 employees whereas in structure B there are a total of 40 employees in only 4 organizational levels. We can readily see that as the span of control for a given organization increases (more subordinates reporting to a given supervisor), the fewer the number of organizational levels there will be. The span of control as well as the number of organizational levels within an organization will have a significant effect on the overall operation of that corporation. Let us look at some of the possible implications of decisions regarding span of control.

Centralization and Decentralization

In structure A of Figure 11.6 we observe that each supervisor has two immediate subordinates. This situation will normally allow the supervisor in structure A to maintain a closer level of control over each subordinate than would be the case for the supervisor in structure B—for the simple reason that the manager in structure A has one less subordinate to be concerned with. As the number of subordinates directly reporting to a given supervisor *increases,* the ability of that supervisor to maintain tight control over each of these subordinates *decreases.* From our previous discussion of centralization and decentralization of operations, it becomes clear that as the number of subordinates (span of control) increases, the more decentralized the organization will *tend* to become. This is true because each subordinate will generally be more free to act independently; the supervisor does not have as much time to spend providing direction. Certainly, this rule cannot be applied in all cases. Many corporations with wide spans of control have policy statements so rigid that subordinates' behavior is dictated in almost every situation. In this way control and decision making within the organization remain highly centralized even though a large number of subordinates report to the same supervisor. What can be stated, however, is that as the span of control increases it creates an organizational environment in which increasing decision-making authority tends to flow to subordinates. *Wide spans of control tend to be organizationally consistent with decentralized operations.*

Organizational Hierarchy and Information Flow

We observe the following from Figure 11.6: given the same approximate number of corporate employees, the smaller the span of control the larger the total number of organizational levels. Thus, the smaller the span of control within an organization (other things being equal), the more *hierarchical* will be the organizational structure. This simply means there will be more organizational levels between the president and the operating employees. As the number of levels within the organization increases, information will normally take longer to move from the operating level up through the organization to top management, and vice versa. This can often result in increased information distortion within the organization; more individuals must receive and transmit this information as it moves up or down through the hierarchy. As the number of individuals increases, the likelihood of inaccurate reception and transmission of information likewise increases.

Management Development

The larger the span of control, the more difficult it is to maintain close supervision over subordinates. In these situations subordinates are generally given more freedom to act independently. As these employees become involved in a wider range of activities, they become more aware of the workings of the organization as a whole, and this experience is usually helpful in their development as managers. In organizations with a narrow span of control, operations tend to be highly centralized. This centralization rarely allows an individual the opportunity to take initiative and gain broad experience. The result is that subordinates functioning in a highly centralized structure are less likely to be aware of how the organization operates outside of their own defined job responsibility. This tends to limit their development as managers; it is more difficult for them to recognize the interrelationships of activities and the importance of these activities to overall corporate goals.

It should be noted, however, that in an organization with an extremely narrow span of control the large number of organizational levels does foster individual advancement; however, the route to the top is usually lengthy. The extreme hierarchical structure of such organizations means that many levels must be passed through.

Management Control

So far we have tended to point out what may appear to be advantages of wider spans of control in organizational structures. We must recognize, however, that there is a limit to the absolute number of individuals that any one manager can supervise. This absolute number will of course vary with the situation and will depend on a wide variety of organizational factors. The fact does remain that as the number of subordinates reporting to a single manager increases, the control that the manager has over those individuals and their resulting activities decreases. It stands to reason that no matter how well corporate policies and control procedures have been defined, at some point the manager will no longer be able to function effectively in supervising these subordinates.

Top management's policy regarding the appropriate span of control must strike a balance between the organizational chaos that may result from too wide a span and the highly bureaucratic and inflexible structure that can result from too narrow a span of control. It is obvious that there is no one precise number of subordinates that can be effectively directed by a single supervisor. In determining an appropriate span of control each organization must evaluate its own situation independently. What may be appropriate for one supervisor in one situation may be inappropriate for another in a different situation.

Analyzing the Span of Control

There have been many attempts to provide information that would aid management in determining the appropriate span of control for a particular organization. Perhaps the first attempt was made in 1933 by a French management consultant named V. A. Graicunas.[1] His approach was to analyze the possible number of relationships that could result from a given span of control. He theorized that at some given number of subordinates, the possible number of superior-subordinate relationships would become difficult for the manager to handle. Graicunas developed an equation giving the following approximation (see Figure 11.7):

$$R = N \left(\frac{2^N}{2} + N - 1 \right)$$

Graicunas found that the curve showing the number of possible relationships tends to turn upward rather sharply if one goes much beyond five subordinates. As a result of this analysis many classical management theorists advocated that the span of control for a given manager be limited to between five and eight subordinates. Clearly, this would represent a simplistic view of the span of control question since it deals with only one variable, namely the possible number of relationships that exist between superior and subordinates. This approach does not consider factors such as the skill and abilities of superior and subordinates, the frequency of the interaction or its importance, and the type of work being performed. It does, however, represent a first pass at gaining some insight into the question of span of control. Several other research studies have added to the work of Graicunas in shedding light on the question of span of control within organizations.

Although not specifically concerned with span of control, a paper published by A. Hare concluded that group size has a signifi-

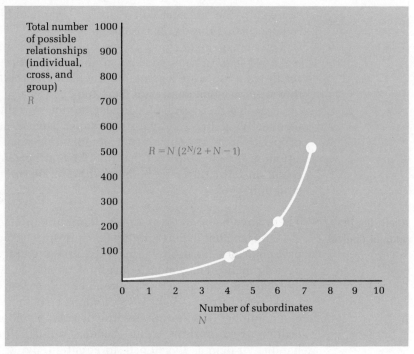

Total number of possible relationships (individual, cross, and group)
R

$$R = N (2^N/2 + N - 1)$$

Number of subordinates
N

Figure 11.7. *Graicunas' Analysis of Span of Control*

Source: Adapted from R. C. Davis, *The Fundamentals of Top Management* (New York: Harper & Row, 1951), p. 278.

cant effect on factors such as cohesiveness, participation, and satisfaction of individuals.[2] Hare stated that groups with memberships of more than five to seven individuals tended to break into subgroups with a corresponding disruptive effect on group cohesiveness. In addition, as group size increases there is less opportunity for individual participation and involvement. This tends to reduce satisfaction of group members since their satisfaction is normally a function of the opportunity for individual participation as well as the extent to which each member can grasp and identify with group goals. Hare's study points up the importance of psychological and sociological factors within the group and the extent to which group size may have an influence on performance.

A study by G. A. Miller investigated the limits of an individual's ability to process information.[3] Miller focused on the ability of an individual to act as a channel of communication, receiving information and then transmitting this information accurately. Miller measured individuals' ability to transmit information accurately as the input information was progressively increased. His experiments showed that an individual's span of immediate memory as well as the span of absolute judgment were both seven items while the span of attention could include up to six objects. The results of Miller's investigation provide some insight as to the absolute limits of the psychological capabilities of individuals to process and transmit information.

These studies and many subsequent ones have focused on the behavioral implications of group size. They have dealt with the psychological and sociological implications of an individual's participation in group effort. It seems clear that behavioral considerations play an important part in determining the appropriate size of the work group and the consequent span of control that will be most effective.

A Span of Control Model: Lockheed

Let us examine some of the organizational factors that must be considered in an evaluation of work group size and span of control.

Lockheed Missile and Space Company is a firm that has devoted attention to the span of control question. Lockheed developed a model that made use of seven variables to be considered in making decisions regarding span of control. These variables included:

1. *Similarity of function* performed by subordinates
2. *Geographical proximity* of subordinates
3. *Complexity of functions* performed by subordinates
4. *Direction and control* required by subordinates
5. *Coordination* required by subordinates
6. *Planning* activity required by the job
7. *Managerial support* received from staff assistance.[4]

Each of these factors was weighted in importance and a supervisory index was obtained for each managerial job. This index number was provided a guideline for the effective number of subordinates that could be supervised by a given manager.

In applying the model, the organization would evaluate each managerial job in terms of the seven variables mentioned. Given the requirements of the job, a specific point allocation could be made for each of the seven factors. For example, if a job involved working with subordinates who were all in the same building but not necessarily in the same area, then that job would receive two points for geographical continuity. Once all the factors were evaluated, the points associated with that job could be totaled and a reference could then be made to a table (see page 279) that supplies the suggested number of subordinates (span of control) for each range of points.

Factor	Range of values				
Similarity of function	Identical	Essentially alike	Similar	Inherently different	Funda-mentally distinct
	1	2	3	4	5
Geographical continuity	All together	All in one building	Separate building One plant location	Separate location One geo-graphical area	Dispersed geographical area
	1	2	3	4	5
Complexity of function	Simple Repetitive	Routine	Some complexity	Complex Varied	Highly complex Varied
	2	4	6	8	10
Direction and control	Minimum supervision and training	Limited supervision	Moderate periodic supervision	Frequent continuing supervision	Constant close supervision
	3	6	9	12	15
Coordination	Minimum relation-ships with others	Relationships limited to defined areas	Moderate relationship easily controlled	Considerable close rela-tionships	Extensive Mutual
	2	4	6	8	10
Planning	Minimum scope and complexity	Limited scope and complexity	Moderate scope and complexity	Considerable effort required Guided only by broad policies	Extensive effort required Area and pol-icies not defined
	2	4	6	8	10

Figure 11.8. *The Lockheed Model: Evaluation of Span of Control*

Source: Harold Stieglitz, "Optimizing Span of Control," *Management Record*, September 1962, p. 28.

The Lockheed model chart (see Figure 11.8) assigns points to only six of the seven key variables. The question of managerial support was treated somewhat differently. It was assumed that the availability of such assistance would serve to *increase* the span of control capabilities of a given manager, and so a percentage figure was used to modify the supervisory index number arrived at through the use of the chart. For example, the availability of a direct line assistant had a 70 percent figure associated with it. Thus, if the supervisory index for a given manager was calculated to be 40 by use of the chart but this same position had a direct line assistant assigned to the job, the index would be modified downward as follows:

$$40 \times .70 = 28$$

As a result, the recommended span of control for the particular managerial position would increase from a recommended 4 or 5 subordinates to 6 or 9 subordinates. (That is, the point total of 40 is revised downward to 28.)

Supervisory index	Suggested span of control
40–42	4–5
37–39	4–6
34–36	4–7
30–33	5–8
28–30	6–9
25–27	7–10
22–24	8–11

When the Lockheed model was applied to several units within the organization, increase or decrease in the span of control resulted, depending on the index number determined for each job. According to Lockheed, the model brought about substantial reduction in managerial personnel and supervisory payroll: "One application extended the average span from 3.8 people to 4.2 and reduced supervisory levels from five to four; another broadened the average span of middle managers from 3.0 to 4.2 and cut levels from six to five ...; the reductions in managerial personnel and supervisory payroll were 'substantial'."[5]

Factors Influencing Span of Control

Deciding the appropriate span of control for a given organization must clearly take into account the particular situation and environment in which that organization finds itself. Management must consider a wide variety of factors, both behavioral and organizational, in order to determine what would be the most effective span of control for a given situation. Using the Lockheed model as a basis for our discussion, let us examine in detail some of those factors covered in the table on page 279.

Skill and Ability Level of Superior and Subordinates. Perhaps the most important factor influencing span of control is the skill and abilities of the individuals involved. To the extent that a manager is capable of establishing clear policies to provide guidelines for subordinates' behavior and control procedures which give feedback on performance, the span of control may be quite large. If a manager is able to develop effective policy statements and operational procedures to guide the efforts of each member of the work group, less time will be required with each subordinate. This would normally allow the manager to supervise a greater number of employees (wider span of control). Moreover, a manager who is experienced and confident will usually provide a little more freedom to subordinates, and this lack of close supervision will allow a wider span of control. Subordinates who are capable and experienced in the work they are performing and willing to assume responsibility for their own activities permit a wide span of control.

If, on the other hand, the manager does not have great administrative ability or is new and perhaps insecure in the managerial position, the size of the span would tend to be reduced. A smaller span would also be necessary if the subordinates required a great deal of attention and direction, either because of lack of ability or because of unwillingness to take responsibility for their own performance. With respect to the subordinates, the overall level of maturity and dedication of each will play a large part in determining the size of an appropriate span of control. Thus, the appropriate span of control for a particular department would be a function of the behavioral characteristics of both superior and subordinate as well as the skills and abilities that each will bring to the work situation.

Interaction and Coordination of Work. In addition to the behavioral considerations that influence span of control, certain organizational characteristics must also be taken into account. Perhaps the most significant of these is the degree to which the work itself requires coordination and interaction. As the necessity for coordination and interaction increases, the manager will need to become more involved in the supervisory function. He or she will be required to spend more time with both individuals and groups of subordinates in order to insure that activities are being coordinated. This managerial requirement will necessarily limit the number of subordinates a supervisor can effectively handle. Conversely, if subordinates are able to carry on a series of well-defined activities in a relatively independent manner then the time required by the manager to supervise these activities would be substantially less. The manager could deal with a larger number of subordinates, thus permitting an increase in the overall span of control.

An example of such a distinction might be found in a "job shop" assembly department as compared with an "assembly line" department. In the job shop operation each individual is normally responsible for the complete assembly of a given component or product unit. The employee works independently and perfoms the same task over and over again with very little interaction or involvement with other workers in the department. In departments such as this the number of subordinates may often exceed twenty. This is possible because the manager is not required to spend much time interacting and coordinating the efforts of each worker. In the assembly line operation, however, each individual's *output* serves as *input* for the next worker on the assembly line. In these situations the manager must spend more time interacting with subordinates to insure coordination of work effort and high performance. In assembly line departments the span of control will rarely exceed 10 or 12 employees. This difference in the span of control of assembly line departments as compared with job shop departments is due primarily to the need for the manager to coordinate interaction within the department.

Change or Stability of the Work Environment. Another variable that will impact the size of the span of control within a department is the extent to which the environment of that department is subjected to change. Frequent modification of product design, new technologies, and variations in strategy, policy, and procedures are but a few of the changes to which a department may be subjected. As change occurs and new problems and situations must be faced, management must spend more of its time and effort dealing with these problems. The uniqueness of the problem situation may require extensive management involvement. This involvement will necessarily limit the number of individuals that can be supervised; here again, the manager will be required to spend significant amounts of time interacting with subordinates in order to insure effectiveness of operations. As the environment of the department becomes more stable and predictable the manager will not be required to interact as often with subordinates in solving new problems. The result will be that the span of control may therefore increase without loss of effectiveness.

Location of Work Group. Another factor influencing the span of control will be the specific geographical location of all of the members of the work group. As the locations of group members become more dispersed, it becomes more difficult to supervise their activities effectively. As the dispersion of work group members increases the manager will find it more difficult and time-consuming to interact with individual members of the department. Time will be lost in simply moving from one location to another, and the distances involved may force the manager to resort to other, possibly less effective, means of communication, such as phone calls, memos, or letters. The result of geographical dispersion will be to effectively reduce the number of subordinates that can be supervised by a single manager.

Line and Staff: Checks and Balances within the Organization

The final topic in our discussion of the anatomy of organizations is that of *line* versus *staff functions*. In any large organization individuals will occupy positions that may be designated as line or staff in nature. It is not always possible to determine from the organization chart exactly which positions fall into line or staff categories. We will point out the particular functional differences between line and staff areas and examine how these differing functions lead to the development of a system of "checks and balances" that may serve to promote organizational effectiveness and efficiency. At the same time, we recognize that this same system can often create areas of conflict between line and staff members of the organization. Conflicts of this type are not uncommon, and they are not necessarily unhealthy for the organization as a whole. The key to managerial success is to understand the underlying nature of these conflicts and to manage them in such a way that they serve to keep all members of the organization on their toes rather than bringing about a deterioration of work effort.

Defining Line and Staff Functions

The most common distinction between line and staff functions might be the following:

Line: Individuals and activities contributing directly to the accomplishment of the organization's primary objective.

Staff: Individuals and activities supporting or facilitating the organization's primary objective. (Staff personnel may have a variety of specialized skills; their functions may include investigation, research, and data analysis activities.)

When the terms are defined in this way, it is not possible to generalize that certain activities or business functions are line and others staff. Before line and staff activities in a given organization can be distinguished, a determination must be made as to the mission or primary objective of that organization. The primary objective may be simply defined as those products or services that are vital to the organization's existence. Once the primary objective has been determined, then a judgment may be made as to the importance of each function or activity in achieving this primary objective. Functions and activities judged to be critical are classified as line activities while those that support and facilitate these activities are referred to as "staff." It is through the line organization that major *decision and policy-making functions* take place. Staff activities are usually provided as informational or supportive to these functions. Staff activities often take the form of recommendations made to line management. In general, we associate the basic business functions of production, marketing, and finance as line, with other areas such as accounting, legal, personnel, and engineering being designated as staff. This distinction does not always hold. For example, in an organization heavily involved in technology or technical services, a department such as engineering may well assume a line function.

Let us examine a typical organizational structure in order to make some preliminary comments regarding the nature and types of line and staff departments that may exist in an organization. In Figure 11.9 we see a typical line-staff structure that might exist for a medium-sized manufacturing organization. The departments of accounting, personnel, legal, and research and development would be designated as *corporate level staff* since each reports directly to the president. These departments would represent *specialized staff,* since each is responsible for a specific function. The position of Assistant to the president also reports directly to the president but is normally designated as *general staff* since no specific function or area of expertise is associated with it. As we move down through the organization we find the traditional *line* areas of marketing, production, and finance. These departments also report directly to the president. We note that the span of control for the president of this organization consists of eight individuals:

Assistant to the president (general staff)
The heads of industrial engineering, personnel, legal, and research and development (specialized staff)
Directors of marketing, production, and finance (line officers).

We can see that each of the various staff departments shown in Figure 11.9 has as its primary function the support or facilitation of one or more of the major line functions (marketing, production, fi-

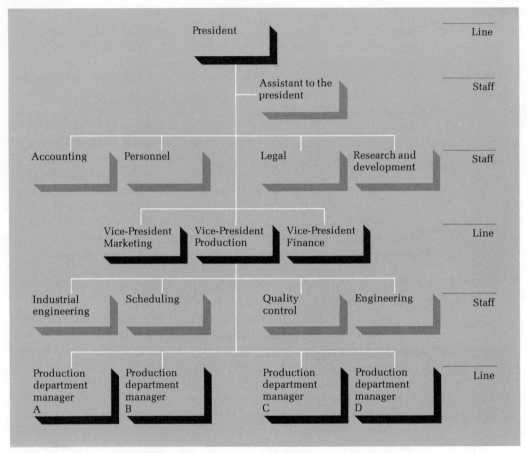

Figure 11.9. *Line-Staff Structure*

nance). At the corporate level, for example, the research and development group might provide information and recommendations to the production area regarding new technology or processes. The legal department would provide recommendations and information to any department requiring legal expertise. Within the production division itself, staff departments such as industrial engineering and scheduling might provide input to production department managers relating to the operation of their departments. Aids such as production schedules, methods analysis, and time standards would be provided by the various staff departments to the production department manager in the operation of that department. The assistant to the president would be engaged in information gathering or analysis to aid the president in decision making. In most cases, it is the function of the staff departments to provide specialized information or recommendations to members of the line organization. This information is based upon the staff's area of expertise and is designed to aid the line departments in performing their function more effectively.

Our discussion suggests quite strongly that the interaction of line and staff departments provides a potential for conflict within the organization. This conflict may be due to many factors; perhaps the most significant is the authority relationship between various line and staff departments.

Authority Relationship between Line and Staff

One of the principal sources of conflict between members of line and staff departments is the amount of authority each has to make decisions. Members of the line organization generally feel that they are involved in the primary functions of the organization, and that as line officers they are responsible for the successful operation of these functions. Therefore, they believe that they should have the authority to make all decisions in these areas. Staff officers, on the other hand, often believe that their specialized training and expertise qualify them to make decisions relating to their specific area or function. These differing points of view often bring the two groups into conflict. Each organization must choose how to deal with this conflict; the key to success, however, is that both line and staff groups have clearly defined for them the exact extent of their authority with respect to each situation. If the extent of authority has been clearly defined, line-staff conflict will be minimized, with each group generally accepting its role in meeting organizational needs. It is usually only when there is either a real overlap or gap in the authority relationship that heated line-staff conflict results, with both line and staff groups seeking to assert themselves in the area in question. Conflicts of this type must be avoided; they may bring about a deterioration of organizational effectiveness.

In order to define clearly the role relationship existing between line and staff departments, management may utilize as many as five possible authority structures. These structures, giving increasing degrees of authority to staff, appear in Figure 11.10.

Staff may be called in for advice. In some organizations staff groups are simply available to provide information or advice *if requested* by line personnel. This means that the staff personnel act primarily as a resource upon which the line officers may draw *if they so desire.* This philosophy provides a great deal of freedom to the line officers, but it can result in serious underutilization of staff personnel. Line officers may not feel it necessary to call upon a staff

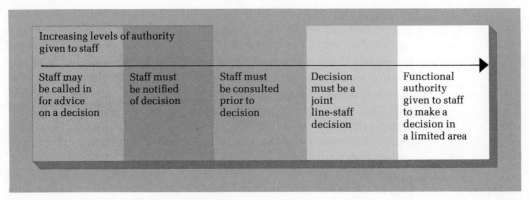

Increasing levels of authority
given to staff

| Staff may be called in for advice on a decision | Staff must be notified of decision | Staff must be consulted prior to decision | Decision must be a joint line-staff decision | Functional authority given to staff to make a decision in a limited area |

Figure 11.10. *Levels of Staff Authority*

specialist before making a decision. This may be true for a number of reasons:

The line officer may feel he or she is more qualified to evaluate the situation than is a member of the staff organization

The line officer may feel threatened in having to consult a member of the staff for advice prior to making a decision

The line officer may not really be aware of the skills or expertise that are available from staff personnel.

In situations such as these many decisions may be made by line officers not only without input from staff but without even letting staff know that a decision has been made. This environment can cause a great deal of unrest between line and staff, particularly among staff groups who feel they are being ignored by line decision makers. In such cases staff may go out of its way to "prove" that a line decision was wrong and must be changed or modified.

Staff must be notified of line decisions. Some organizations specify that *staff must be notified* of all line decisions that may impact the staff area. Clearly, this does not necessarily correct the problem of staff underutilization, but at least it does keep staff members informed so that they are better able to modify or adjust their own activities to meet possible new situations. We still have an environment in which staff personnel are normally notified only after the decision has already been made. Staff personnel argue that by that time it is often too late to correct the situation if indeed the decision proves to be in error. Staff argue that if they are consulted prior to a decision, they can provide useful input to line officers that will result in better decision making.

Staff must be consulted prior to decision. In order to obtain more timely input from staff specialists some corporations require that staff *be consulted* by line officers *prior to making a decision.* In this environment the staff specialist still does not have real authority over line officers, but at least staff advice and recommendations must be heard. This situation can also become frustrating to staff personnel if it is clear that their advice is constantly ignored by line officers. Staff may even perceive that members of the line organization never had any intention of utilizing their input—they may be called in simply to conform to organizational policy. If this perception does exist in the minds of the staff the ill will created may bring about a worse situation than that of not being asked for input at all.

Joint line-staff decision making takes place. In this relationship staff personnel actually take on some authority for making decisions. This condition exists in organizations that have a policy of *joint line-staff decision making;* line and staff personnel must reach a mutual agreement on decisions in certain specified areas. Full use is made of staff information, and both line and staff personnel collaborate on a decision. This arrangement can also create problems, however, since it may be impossible for line and staff individuals to reach a mutually acceptable decision. This may lead to a compromise agreement that satisfies neither group and in fact may not be in the best interests of the organization. When no mutually agreeable decision can be reached, the issue may have to be resolved by someone at a higher organizational level to whom both the line and staff groups report. This may also create a great deal of ill will, particularly on the part of the individual or department overruled on the issue.

Staff has functional authority. When *functional authority* is given to staff departments, actual authority over line is being given in a very limited or specific area. The key point is that the authority exists only in this limited and well-defined area. In almost all cases the functional authority is given to a staff specialist whose skills or knowledge can provide input that is critical to the organization. An example of the use of functional authority might be the case where an industrial engineer, whose responsibility includes plant safety, has the authority to stop the operation of a machine that does not meet safety standards. In this situation it is not necessary for the industrial engineer to have the approval of the line manager in order to shut down the machine. Rather, the engineer could use his functional authority in this area of safety and make the decision.

Other areas in which functional authority might be given to staff departments include quality control standards, accounting procedures, affirmative action policies, production schedules, and time standards. It is in this area of functional authority, in which staff personnel are actually given line authority to make decisions, that the most serious line-staff conflict takes place. For it is in these situations that there may be a direct confrontation over the location of decision-making authority with respect to a particular issue or area of responsibility.

Organizational Checks and Balances

As we have mentioned, one of the results of having both line and staff functions within an organization is to set up a system of checks and balances between line and staff departments. This system normally derives from the specific set of responsibilities given to each group. To understand the nature of this system let us examine how it might function in a small manufacturing organization.

Figure 11.11 provides a partial organization chart showing a series of line and staff departments often found in a manufacturing operation. Before discussing the checks and balances concept let us briefly mention the duties and responsibilities traditionally associated with the staff departments shown.

Industrial Engineering. Develops time and motion studies for each job in the production operation. These studies result in a determination of the layout of facilities, the exact method to be followed in performing the jobs, and the time standard to be applied to each job.

Quality Control. Develops sampling plans or other techniques to be used to determine if quality standards are being met in a given production department.

Production Scheduling. Develops production schedules defining both quantity and type of product to be produced in a specified period of time.

These descriptions represent the activities generally performed by staff departments shown in Figure 11.10. Let us now look at the responsibilities normally associated with the job of a line department manager in this same manufacturing facility.

Department Manager (Line). The manager of a production department is usually responsible for turning out a certain required number of units (determined by the production scheduling staff) with an acceptable level of quality (as evaluated by quality control) at a cost that is within budget (within the time standard determined by industrial engineering). This description somewhat oversimplifies the case; however, the point is that the overall performance of the line manager in the production department is determined by her or his ability to meet schedules, maintain quality, and produce to time standards—all established by staff departments. This situation

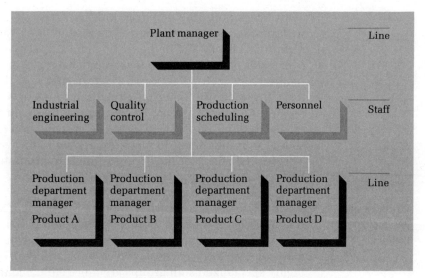

Figure 11.11. *Line and Staff in a Manufacturing Firm*

often brings the department manager and the staff departments into conflict. To understand the nature of this conflict let us examine in detail—as an illustration—the relation between the industrial engineering department and the production department line manager.

The industrial engineer is usually responsible for reviewing jobs in the production department. After determining both the method and layout to be utilized, the engineer will set a time standard for each job, which defines the length of time it should take an operator to perform the job. Clearly, the performance of the line manager will in large part be judged by his or her ability to induce workers to perform well against this time standard, and it is to the manager's advantage to have the time standards set "as loose" as possible (provide as much time as possible to perform the job). This would result in a higher efficiency rating for the department since workers' performance would be judged against a relaxed time standard.

In most manufacturing operations the line manager is quick to challenge any time standard that seems not to allow workers adequate time by requesting an audit of the time standard, in which instance its accuracy as applied to the given job will be judged. By requesting an audit the manager is publicly suggesting that the standard is in error. The result of the audit will generally mean a loss of face for either the manager, if the standard is accurate, or for the industrial engineer, if the standard is in error. The possibility of the audit keeps both line manager and industrial engineer on their toes with respect to time standards. This is but one example of the organizational checks and balances line and staff departments may exert over each other. Similar checks and balances may be seen in the relation between sales forecasting groups and the sales force. In these instances the accuracy of the sales forecasts and the effectiveness of the sales force are the issues. At this point we might ask the reader to think of other areas in the organization in which line and staff groups may serve to maintain a system of checks and balances. The desired effect for the organization is to promote the efficiency of both groups.

Attitudes and Personality Conflict

We have now seen two areas of potential line-staff conflict: authority relationships and organizational checks and balances. In some organizations the extent of conflict may be aggravated by educational and cultural differences between line and staff personnel. Often highly specialized staff groups are more educated than the line managers. These specialists may tend to look down on the less educated line officers who have worked their way up through the organization. The line officers, on the other hand, may regard the staff personnel as living in an ivory tower without awareness of the actual job environment or its requirements. The higher educational level of the staff personnel may also mean that these individuals entered the organization at a high level. This can result in significant age differentials between older line managers and younger staff personnel, with resulting difficulties as they try to bridge the generation gap. Staff personnel, in addition, usually tend to identify with the particular discipline or professional area in which they are involved, whereas line managers usually associate themselves with the corporation or company. This difference in orientation can often serve to increase tension between the two groups. Finally, staff personnel generally tend to be more mobile, moving from one organization to another, whereas line managers usually work their way up through the ranks. This can tend to reinforce the opinion of line managers that staff personnel are not knowledgeable about the way their specific organization conducts its business and therefore are in no position to offer constructive advice.

In summary, staff departments generally provide specialized services to facilitate line operations. These services can be invaluable in improving the efficiency and performance of the organization. In performing these services, however, the staff organization often comes into conflict with line departments. This conflict can be beneficial if the result is an effective system of checks and balances within the organization. If the nature of the conflict intensifies to the point where overall organizational efficiency is diminished, measures must be taken to improve the relationship between line and staff organizations.

Several organizations have experimented with rotating individuals between line and staff positions. Each is to gain perspective on the other's point of view. In other instances, management has attempted to bring both line and staff personnel into interaction situations that are perceived by each group as nonthreatening. They might serve together on committee assignments or take part in classroom training sessions. Here the purpose is to provide an interaction environment in which both groups are faced with problems and situations that are not directly related to their specific areas of responsibility. The hope is that in working together to solve these problems, each group will gain respect for the other and that this respect will carry over into the working environment.

Such a program was carried on at IBM Corporation's Poughkeepsie plant. Both production managers (line) and industrial engineers (staff) were assigned to classes whose objective was to teach the new method of standard data to be utilized in setting time standards for manufacturing operations. Although the subject matter of these classes did relate to the specific area of responsibility of the individuals involved, management found that in working together in the classroom both managers and industrial engineers found a great deal of common ground as well as many similar personal interests. These formed the basis for a new attitude in working relationships and greatly reduced conflicts between members of the line and staff departments.

Let us conclude our discussion of organizational structures by examining a typical industrial structure (Figure 11.12). The reader should study this structure in order to determine: (1) the type of *departmentalization* there is at each level and (2) the *span of control* for each managerial position. *Line* and *staff* departments within the organization should be differentiated.

Discussion Questions

1. Why is there no one single form of departmentalization that is most efficient for all organizations?
2. Apply the Lockheed model to some organization of which you are a member. How closely does the actual span of control conform to that determined by the Lockheed model?
3. Discuss the most common reasons for conflict between members of line and staff departments in an organization.
4. Discuss those elements of the organi-

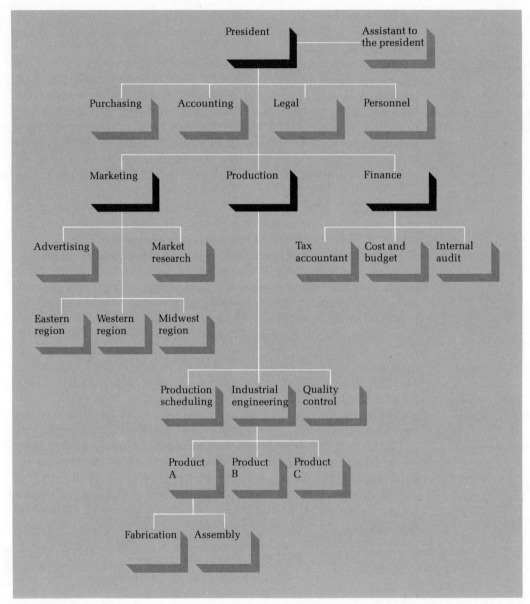

Figure 11.12. *Organization of a Typical Industrial Firm*

zational structure that may serve to increase frustration among employees.

5. How might a manager use span of control and departmentalization concepts to

implement a policy of decentralization within the organization.

6. Select an organizational chart from a company's annual report and analyze its

structure with respect to the following:
  a. Type of departmentalization at each level
  b. Span of control
  c. Line and staff departments within the organization.
7. What impact will changes in job design be likely to have on the future structure of organizations?
8. Discuss the concept of functional authority and its contribution to line-staff conflicts.
9. How might you determine which are the line and staff departments in an organizational structure?
10. Given the fact that the span of control may be different at each level in an organization, would you expect to find wider spans of control at the top or bottom levels? Explain.

Case for Discussion

Steve Horton, manager of market research for a small survey research firm based in Chicago, called a new employee, Dave Ripley, into his office. Ripley was given his first assignment, a project that involved phone contact and follow-up interviews with approximately 5000 residents of the small community of Harperville, forty-five miles northeast of Chicago.

The project required that each resident be contacted by phone (if there was no answer a follow-up phone call was to be made) and those residents who were willing would be interviewed about a current political issue. Based on experience, Steve Horton said he believed that each phone call would require about five minutes and each personal interview would take approximately fifteen minutes.

The town of Harperville, according to a detail map in Steve Horton's office, covered approximately ten square blocks within the town proper and also included several square miles of rural residents.

Steve Horton asked Dave to develop a proposal showing the following:

1. The size of the staff needed to complete the project.
2. The time that would be required to complete the project.
3. The type of personnel needed.
4. The organizational structure that Dave would set up to complete the project.

In addition, Steve asked that Dave discuss with him the methodology that would be used in order to insure that each resident was contacted. Dave then left Steve Horton's office to develop a complete proposal.

Selected References

Argyris, C. *Personality and Organization.* New York: Harper & Row, 1957.

Barnard, Chester. *The Functions of the Executive.* Cambridge, Mass.: Harvard University Press, 1938.

Blau, P., and Scott, W. *Formal Organizations.* New York: Chandler, 1962.

Davis, R. C. *The Fundamentals of Top Management.* New York: Harper & Row, 1951.

Drucker, Peter. *The Practice of Management.* New York: Harper & Row, 1954.

Filley A. and House, R. *Managerial Process and Organizational Behavior.* Glenview, Ill.: Scott, Foresman and Co., 1969.

Graicunas, V. A. "Relationship in

Organization." In *Papers on the Science of Administration,* L. Gulich and L. Urwich, eds. New York: Institute of Public Administration, 1937.

Homans, G. C. *The Human Group.* New York: Harcourt Brace and World, 1950.

Koontz, H., and O'Donnell, C. *Principles of Management.* New York: McGraw-Hill, 1968.

Lawrence, S. and Lorch, J. *Organization and Environment.* Homewood, Ill.: Richard D. Irwin, 1969.

Likert, R. *New Patterns of Management.* New York: McGraw-Hill, 1961.

March, J. G., and Simon, H. *Organizations.* New York: John Wiley & Sons, 1958.

McGregor, D. *The Human Side of Enterprise.* New York: McGraw-Hill, 1960.

Richards, M. and Greenlaw, P. *Management Decision-Making.* Homewood, Ill.: Richard D. Irwin, 1966.

Rue, L. W. and Byars, L. *Management: Theory and Application.* Homewood, Ill.: Richard D. Irwin, 1977.

Scott, William. *Organization Theory.* Homewood, Ill.: Richard D. Irwin, 1967.

Stieglitz, H. "Optimization of Span of Control." In *Management Record,* September 1962.

Thompson, V. A. *Modern Organization.* New York: Alfred A. Knopf, 1961.

Webber, Ross. *Management.* Homewood, Ill.: Richard D. Irwin, 1975.

Woodward, J. *Industrial Organization: Theory and Practice.* New York: Oxford University Press, 1965.

Understanding Organizations: The Linear Responsibility Chart

12

Esmark Spawns a Thousand Profit Centers

"In the past, we had an unwieldy business," says Robert W. Reneker, the 61-year-old chairman of Esmark, Inc., the holding company created in 1973 by Swift & Co., the nation's biggest meatpacker. "The only way we could develop a coordinated effort was to divide it into bite-sized bits."

So Esmark has been carved into 1,000 bite-sized bits, each of them a profit center with considerable operating authority, in a management restructuring that has taken six years to carry out. Each of these profit centers reports up through an operating company to one of the four major subsidiaries of Esmark, and the net effect of doling out authority to these units is to lift routine decision-making from Reneker's shoulders. Decentralization is evident everywhere but in Esmark's financial controls. In the old days, it lacked controls adequate for a company that rang up $4-billion in sales last year. Today, tight financial controls run from the top down to operating units.

The holding-company approach was necessary because Esmark has been trying to limit its dependence on the low-margin, highly cyclical meat business by accelerating its moves into a variety of nonfood businesses ranging from oil to insurance. Food still provided 90% of 1973 sales. The goal of a five-year plan launched last year, though, was to derive 40% of Esmark's sales from nonfood areas by 1978—a goal that will be temporarily reached this year because of soaring oil and fertilizer prices.

Reprinted from the August 3, 1974 issue of *Business Week* by special permission. Copyright © 1974 by McGraw-Hill Publishing, Inc., New York, N. Y. 10020. All rights reserved.

Years of Upheaval

Reneker, a 40-year Swift veteran, began reorganizing as soon as he became chief executive officer in 1967, and his moves have rocked the company—the only meatpacking giant that has not been taken over by someone else (Armour & Co. now belongs to Greyhound Corp., for instance, and Wilson & Co. to LTV Corp.). The shakeup has involved, among other things, the closing of 300 plants and offices and the firing or retirement of some 18,000 workers. It took all that, in Reneker's view, to turn what was a sick enterprise—burdened by a slipshod management structure and antiquated facilities as well as the vagaries of the meat business—into a well-managed, profitable company.

Esmark is making a lot of money these days—for a change. It earned $34-million in 1953 but then had to wait 18 years before it could top that figure. The U.S. economy was booming, but Swift lost money in 1961 and earned only $4-million in 1966. A $129-million write-off meant a $42-million loss in 1968, a year after Reneker took over.

But profits again reached $34-million in 1971, jumped to $37-million in 1972, and jumped once more to $49-million in 1973. In the first half of fiscal 1974, ended last Apr. 30, net soared from $19.6-million to $32.7-million on a 28% increase in sales. The five-year plan, launched last year, projects sales topping $5-billion by 1978, with profits up from last year's $3.86 a share to $7.

The new holding company structure shows how much Esmark has diversified under Reneker. There are now 20 operating groups under the four "subholding" companies:

Swift & Co. (food), with an estimated 60% of fiscal 1974 sales.

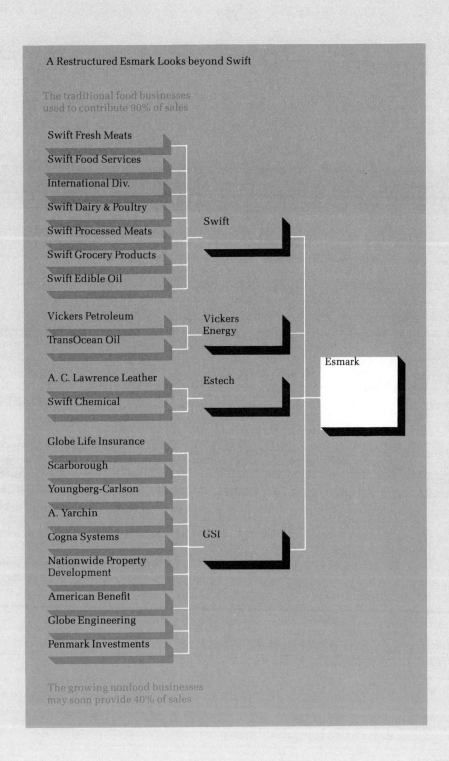

A Restructured Esmark Looks beyond Swift

The traditional food businesses used to contribute 90% of sales

- Swift Fresh Meats
- Swift Food Services
- International Div.
- Swift Dairy & Poultry
- Swift Processed Meats
- Swift Grocery Products
- Swift Edible Oil

Swift

- Vickers Petroleum
- TransOcean Oil

Vickers Energy

- A. C. Lawrence Leather
- Swift Chemical

Estech

- Globe Life Insurance
- Scarborough
- Youngberg-Carlson
- A. Yarchin
- Cogna Systems
- Nationwide Property Development
- American Benefit
- Globe Engineering
- Penmark Investments

GSI

Esmark

The growing nonfood businesses may soon provide 40% of sales

Vickers Energy Corp. (exploration, refining and marketing), with an estimated 15% of 1974 sales.

Estech, Inc. (chemicals), with an estimated 15% of 1974 sales.

GSI, Inc. (insurance and business services), with an estimated 10% of 1974 sales.

But decentralization was well along even before Swift became Esmark. By 1970, every one of Swift's line managers had been given profit responsibility for his operation and, for the first time, had been made accountable for his decisions. A typical case involves Joe Young, general manager of the plant that makes Brown 'N Serve sausages for Swift. Before restructuring, all decisions involving the plant were made at the corporate level. Today, Young sets his own production goals, determines the retail prices for his products, and can even go outside Esmark for marketing help. His performance is monitored weekly at meetings with the president of the Fresh Meat Co., a division of Swift.

Free to Think

By placing a management layer between himself and his operating chiefs, Reneker has removed himself from routine decision-making so he can spend more time looking at the long-range plans for diversification. "When I took over this job six years ago, there were 19 vice-presidents reporting to me directly," he says. "I was involved in everything because there was no one with the authority to make decisions." Now only a handful of Esmark staff executives and the presidents of the four subholding companies report directly to Reneker on a regular basis.

That Reneker, an alumnus of Swift's food business, was able to write off large chunks of the company startled both company executives and outsiders. He became chief executive officer after spending his entire career at Swift, where he first worked in the purchasing department for 10 years. He was assigned to the vice-president's office in 1944 and the president's staff in 1950. In 1955 he

was named vice-president and in 1964 president and chief operating officer. Having been an inside man when he took over, there was no indication in his track record of the major overhaul to come.

But Reneker says he really had no choice. Sitting in his expansive, contemporary office overlooking the Chicago Yacht Club harbor, he says: "My predecessor, Porter Jarvis, knew every aspect of our business and enjoyed digging into daily decisions. I didn't have that kind of expertise and needed a management system that could handle daily decisions."

Sloughing Off

Reneker also needed time to develop a new strategy for Swift. He assigned Donald P. Kelly—now Esmark's president but then controller—to head a committee to scrutinize all of Swift's businesses and recommend closing or divestiture where warranted. Profits were up in 1967, but Swift's return on investment was still less than in 1953.

Kelly started looking at what the company could get rid of. He discovered that much of its meat business could be saved, provided the company did something about its mostly out-of-date facilities and procedures. Most of its plants were older structures, six or seven floors tall, each trying to process beef, pork, and poultry. Productivity was abysmal because simple moving of carcasses from one step to another along the line often involved waiting for elevators. There was little automated equipment. By closing old facilities and building one-floor, single-species plants, Esmark estimates it has doubled productivity.

Even more troublesome were the confused lines of command. For example, the general manager of the Sioux City packing house reported to one Swift vice-president, but the plant's beef, pork, and poultry supervisors reported to three other vice-presidents. When problems arose, nobody knew to whom to go for help.

"The way the company was set up, men

were participating in decisions where their background did not give them sufficient expertise," Kelly says. "Not only did that lead to bad decisions; it also meant we couldn't pin down responsibility."

The Holding Company

Kelly's group recommended the holding-company approach. The various Swift units would function as independent operating entities while the parent company would ultimately provide only financial and planning assistance. This is exactly what is happening. The corporate staff now numbers only about 125, down from several thousand in 1967.

"Our various businesses had to become autonomous," says Kelly. "We had simply grown too large for Reneker and the cluster of men around him to be making all of the decisions."

To make certain that the line managers really assumed authority, Reneker gave the compensation program a new slant: Salaries and bonuses for every manager in the corporation were determined by how close they came to projections and by their over-all bottom-line performance.

Paradoxically, the new system pulled financial control to the top at the same time it was dispensing operating authority. When Roger T. Briggs became financial vice-president in 1971, he tripled the size of the financial staff to about 75.

While the four subholding company presidents are free to establish their own management procedures, they now all follow a unified reporting system. Esmark's standardized set of numbers can now calculate return-on-investment figures for each operating unit. It never could do so before, meaning the company could never pin down any operation's profitability.

The Right Information

Briggs insisted on biweekly financial summaries from the subholding companies, as well as the status of accounts receivable. He also set up a procedure for clearing purchases larger than $50,000 through his office. Purchases of more than $100,000 go to Kelly, Reneker, or the board.

The reporting system also means that Esmark executives can give the four presidents wide latitude in running their businesses. "If things are going well, I don't hear from Kelly all that often," says Joseph P. Sullivan, president of Estech, Inc. "There is a jawboning relationship as opposed to a boss-employee one," adds Richard J. Boushka, Vickers president.

Reneker insists that the biggest plus of the reorganization for him is the time it allows him for strategy planning: "I'm freed for the first time to look ahead five years and see where this company should be heading."

Further to reduce Esmark's dependence on meat processing, Reneker is pushing major expansion in Vickers, which plans $27.8-million in plant and equipment spending this year. And he wants to make at least one acquisition for Estech. GSI, Inc., is searching for a life insurance company to acquire and is expanding its business services.

Esmark is still producing most of the capital for expansion, but Reneker is hoping that the subholding companies can begin to handle some of their own financing, perhaps partly through the sale of stock in the subholding companies. TransOcean Oil Co., of which Esmark owns 51% through Vickers, recently negotiated a $24-million loan on its own for oil exploration.

Briggs is also launching a major program to examine the cost of capital against return on investment for each of the profit centers. "Any business whose return is less than the money costs stands in danger of being chopped off," says one Esmark executive, which means there may be additional shaking-out yet to come.

THIS CHAPTER presents a working model integrating a variety of organizational components. The model will be an aid in understanding the operation of modern organizations. From our discussion in Chapter 11 we developed an understanding of the use of organizational charts to represent the specific structure of an organization. For example, the organization chart provides information on

1. *Division of labor*
2. Type of *departmentalization* utilized
3. *Span of control* at each level
4. Guidelines as to *line and staff* activities
5. Approximate *size* of the organization
6. Position of various *functions* within the hierarchy
7. *Types of activities* in which the organization is engaged.

Figure 12.1. *Model of Organizational Structure*

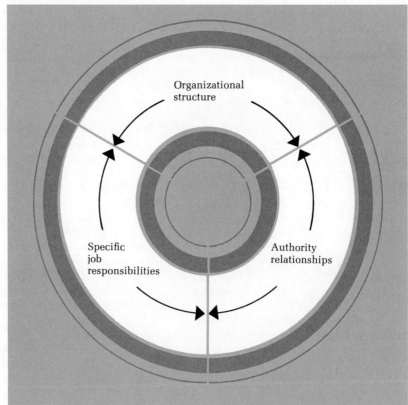

In most cases, however, the organization chart provides little or no insight into such vital information as *specific job responsibilities* of individuals within the organization or *authority relationships* between various positions. Without this information it is not possible to understand the inner workings of a particular organization fully. It will be the purpose of this chapter to develop a model that analyzes a company's *organizational structure* in terms of specific *job responsibilities* and *authority relationships* (see Figure 12.1). This model, known as the *linear responsibility chart,* provides a picture of the way a given organization carries on its activities. Included in the model is the relationship between various *positions* within the organization and the specific *jobs* or *tasks* to be accomplished. This relationship is defined in terms of the *authority* and *responsibility* of each position with respect to each job or task performed. By understanding the linear responsibility chart the reader should greatly broaden his or her insight into the inner workings of modern organizations.

Developing the Linear Responsibility Chart

The Linear Responsibility Chart (LRC) was developed in the early 1950s by the Serge A. Birn Co. of Louisville, Kentucky.[1] The purpose of the chart is to detail on paper the exact nature of the relationships within a given organization. The chart is in the form of a simple matrix in which each cell defines the relationship between a given individual and a specific job or task. In developing such a chart a manager is forced to consider the tasks for which his or her department or area is responsible. The manager must then determine the exact role or relationship of each subordinate to each of these tasks. When such a chart is completed it will define the responsibility of each member of the organization and specify how individuals are to interrelate in carrying out tasks. A linear responsibility chart can be set up for any size organization or department; if it is to be developed for a large organization it should be done in stages so that adequate attention can be given to each unit or department.

A complete linear responsibility chart is shown in Figure 12.7. The chart makes use of eight basic relationships that may define the responsibility of an individual within the organization. These relationships define not only specific job responsibility but also the exact nature of an individual's interaction with other members of the organization. The eight relationships are shown in Figure 12.2.

With these eight relationships forming the basis for any interaction related to any job performed in the organization, it remains for

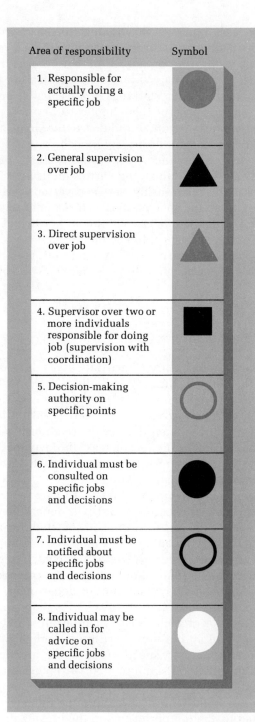

Figure 12.2

Areas of Responsibility

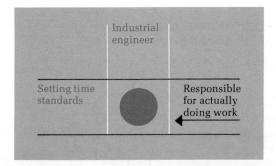

Figure 12.3

managers to define the relationships between jobs and organization members. Each relationship can be described by one of the eight symbols shown. Let us assume, for example, that an industrial engineer within a manager's department is responsible for setting time standards in the product areas. The LRC symbol would appear as shown in the matrix in Figure 12.3.

If this same industrial engineer were responsible for supervising a technician who performed all layout design work the chart would now look like Figure 12.4. The chart would expand until all jobs and all individuals were included.

In order to develop a linear responsibility chart (LRC) for a department or organization, a manager should begin by listing in a column all the jobs and responsibilities that exist in the department.

Figure 12.4

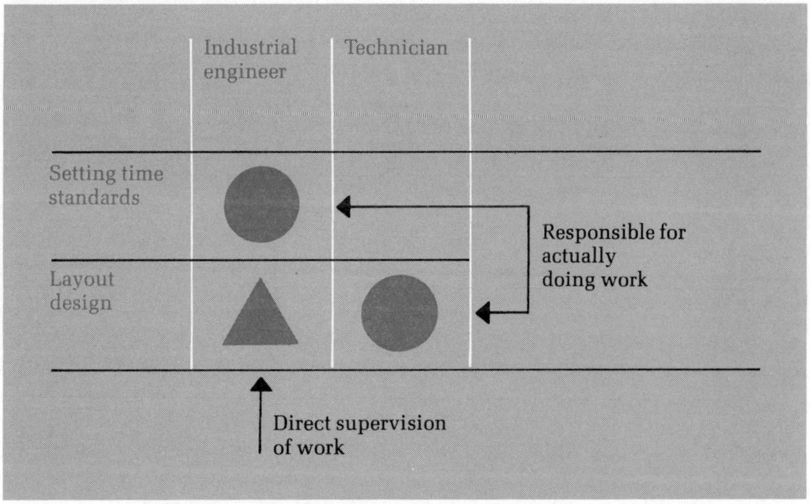

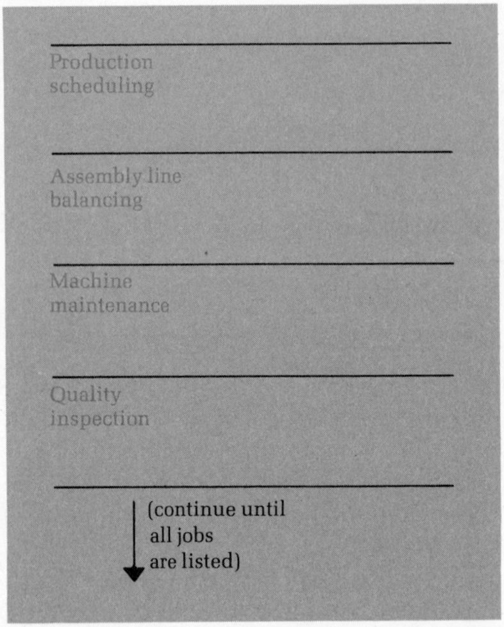

Production
scheduling

Assembly line
balancing

Machine
maintenance

Quality
inspection

(continue until
all jobs
are listed)

Figure 12.5

Figure 12.6

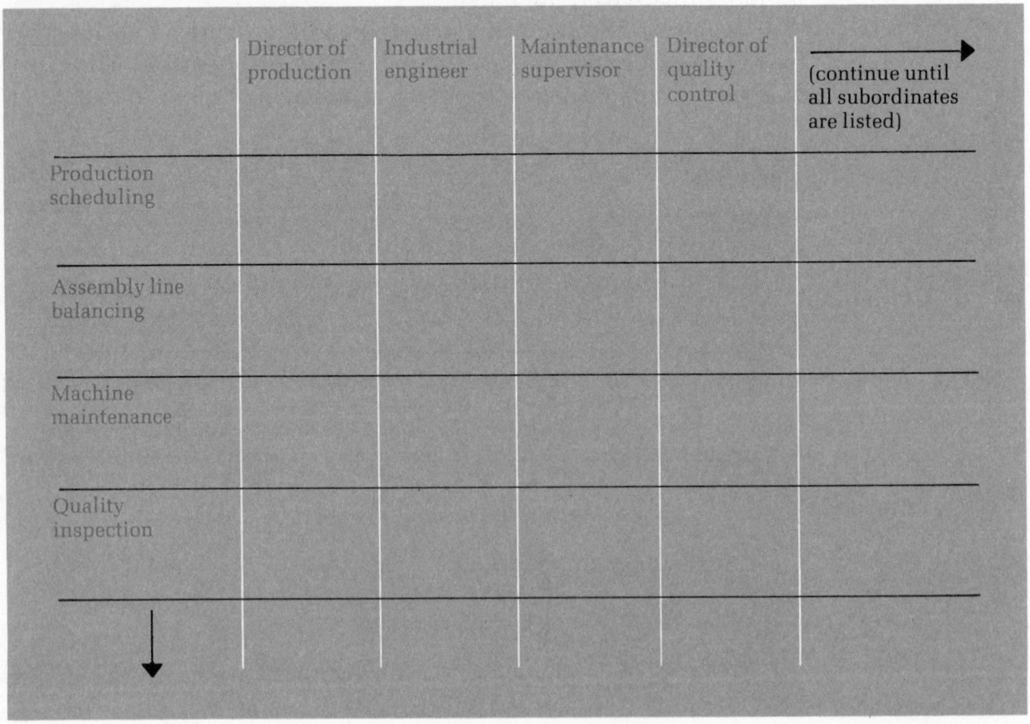

	Director of production	Industrial engineer	Maintenance supervisor	Director of quality control	(continue until all subordinates are listed)
Production scheduling					
Assembly line balancing					
Machine maintenance					
Quality inspection					

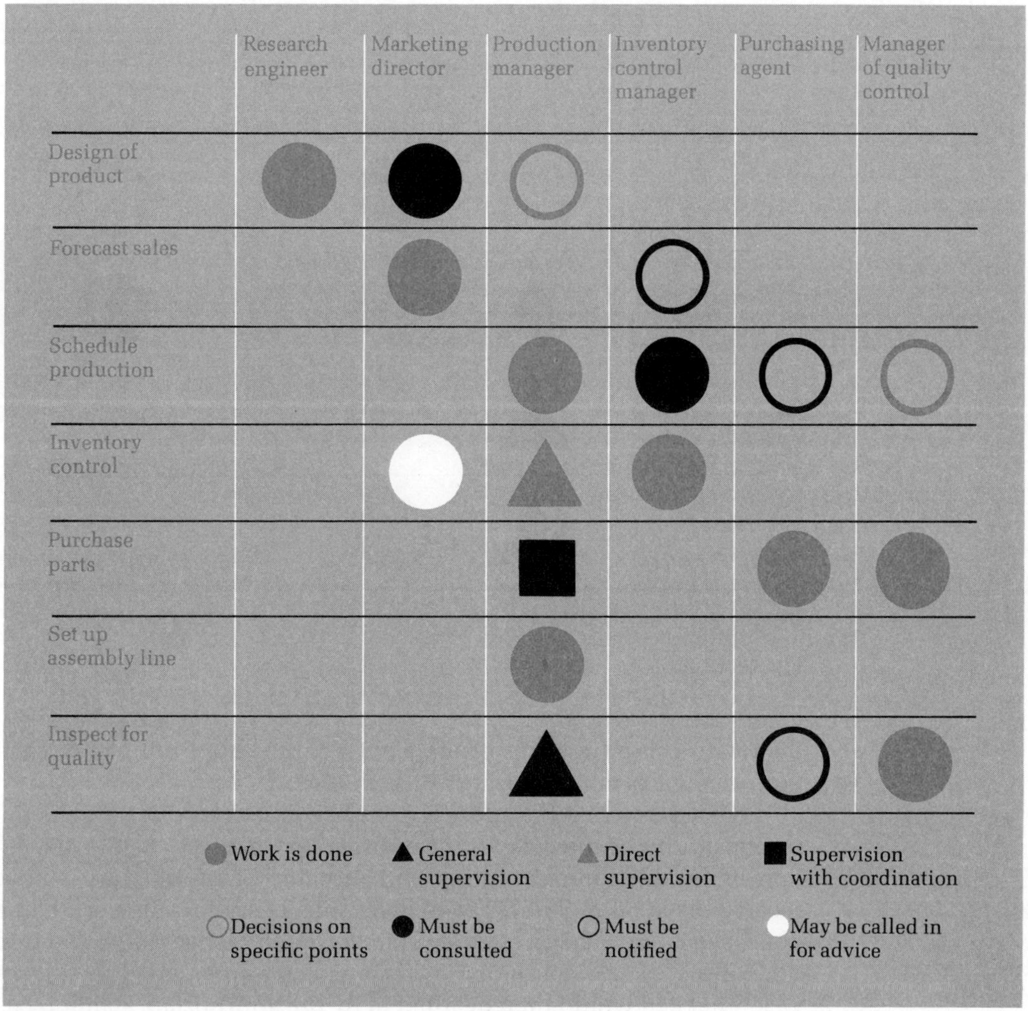

	Research engineer	Marketing director	Production manager	Inventory control manager	Purchasing agent	Manager of quality control
Design of product	●	⬤	○			
Forecast sales	●			○		
Schedule production			●	⬤	○	○
Inventory control	○	▲		●		
Purchase parts			■		●	●
Set up assembly line			●			
Inspect for quality			▲		○	●

● Work is done	▲ General supervision	▲ Direct supervision	■ Supervision with coordination
○ Decisions on specific points	⬤ Must be consulted	○ Must be notified	○ May be called in for advice

Figure 12.7

Let us assume that in a given production facility a manager starts off by listing the jobs in Figure 12.5. If the department is large, then the LRC should be developed in sections to insure that all jobs have been included. Once all the jobs and responsibilities have been included in a column down the page the manager should list all the individuals (by title) within the department or organization across the top of the page, in matrix fashion, as in Figure 12.6.

When the jobs have been listed in a column and the individual employees listed across the page it remains for the manager to define

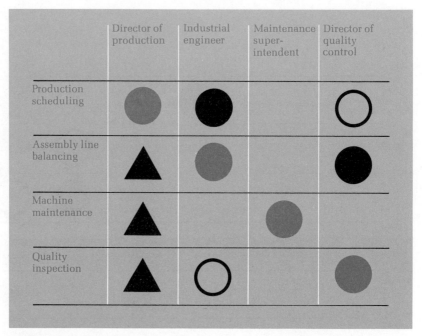

Figure 12.8

the relationship (in terms of the eight relationship symbols) of each person to each job (Figure 12.7, page 305).

If we assume that the specific job of production scheduling is the responsibility of the director of production, then that cell (intersection of production scheduling and director of production) would receive the symbol that represents responsibility for the work being done (see Figure 12.8). Let us assume that with respect to production scheduling issues, the industrial engineer *may* be called in for advice. That cell would then be filled in by the appropriate symbol, i.e., the intersection of production scheduling and industrial engineer would receive ◖. Finally, let us assume that the director of quality control must be *notified* of the final production schedule in order to plan the quality control program. The symbol ○ would therefore appear at the intersection of production scheduling and director of quality control. This same procedure is used for each job or area of responsibility until the chart is completed. If, with respect to a certain task or job, a given individual has no responsibility—i.e., no one of the eight symbols is appropriate—then that cell is left blank. A blank or empty cell indicates that the particular individual has no direct or indirect involvement in the task appearing on the left-hand side of the matrix.

Once the chart is completed a much clearer picture of the organization will emerge than can be seen in the simple organization chart. The linear responsibility chart both describes in detail the exact nature of the relationship that exists for each position with respect to each job and defines each position relative to every other position with respect to that same job. Such detailed information cannot be determined from the traditional organizational chart. Using the LRC, one is able to obtain a clear picture of the workings of an organization and in this way understand its structure and its communication and decision-making patterns.

The LRC and Job Descriptions

If we look at the chart in *column* fashion—select a given title or position and go down the column under that heading, we have in effect defined the job description for that particular position. In our example (Figure 12.8), the industrial engineer may be called in by the director of production on issues related to production scheduling; the industrial engineer is directly responsible for assembly line balancing and reports directly to the director of production in this area; finally, the industrial engineer must be notified by the director of quality control on issues related to product inspection. In this rather limited example we note that the responsibility of the industrial engineer has been totally defined by the LRC. In addition, the relationship of the industrial engineer to other members of the organization has also been defined. Thus, the columns of the chart show the detailed job description of each individual listed.

The LRC and Specific Job Responsibility

If, on the other hand, we look at the *rows* of the chart—by selecting a specific job or task and looking across to learn who relates to it, we see in detail which individuals are involved in that job or area of responsibility and also the specific nature of their involvement. Thus, if a problem arises with respect to a given job or if a change in procedure for a given job is anticipated, the manager knows all the individuals involved and in exactly what capacity they are involved. With respect to the balancing of the assembly line, for example, it is apparent from the chart (Figure 12.8) that the director of production has direct supervision over the task, that the industrial engineer is responsible for actually doing the line balancing, and that the director of quality control must be consulted with respect to line-balancing activities. Thus, all the individuals involved in the activity have been isolated and the exact nature of their involvement defined. If a change were anticipated in assembly-line balancing, a manager would thus be aware of each individual who would be impacted.

The linear responsibility chart has the benefit of requiring a manager to think through carefully the exact nature of the relationship between each job and job title (individual) in his or her area of responsibility. It is generally a simple matter to determine if *gaps* or *overlaps* exist that could cause confusion or conflict. In addition, by using the chart it is easy to pinpoint areas of specific responsibility when problems arise. Finally, the chart can prove an effective tool for making changes in assignment and detailing the new set of relationships that will exist after the change. Confusion and ambiguity can be reduced, and each new job or position can be clearly defined in terms of the rest of the organization.

Difficulties in Using the LRC

Perhaps the most common difficulty in utilizing the LRC is the time and effort required to develop such a chart. The amount of detail involved in preparing the chart necessitates a great deal of managerial time. Some managers feel, too, that the completed chart, with its variety of symbols representing organizational relationships, may be more confusing than helpful in illuminating the workings of the organization.

Many managers wish, furthermore, to provide more freedom to subordinates than the LRC dictates. They wish employees to be able to act when they see a need for communication or decisions. These managers argue also that each situation is somewhat unique and therefore does not lend itself to complete and exact classification. Responsibility and involvement of individuals must answer to needs as they arise. Managers may well depend more upon the ability and perceptions of subordinates in doing what needs to be done than on a strict adherence to the relationships defined by the LRC.

This looser type of environment relates to the "organic" structure discussed in Chapter 5. If the technology or environment of the organization is characterized by constant or rapid change, the effectiveness of the organization may be a function of a rather free-flowing authority and decision-making structure rather than the well-defined and specific structure found in the LRC. This does not mean that a LRC is applicable only to well-defined (mechanistic) organizational types; it simply indicates that to the extent that the environment of the organization is characterized by rapid or constant change, the LRC may be less applicable in defining desired organizational relationships.

Finally, the chart may do the disservice of crystalizing authority relationships in the organization that run contrary to the informal status of organizational members. In such cases, the chart may be the cause of conflict that might not have otherwise occurred if these relationships had not been so clearly spelled out. One engineering firm aware of this potential problem will not make available its organizational chart because it would identify one engineering department as being "higher" in the organizational structure than another. Members of these two departments perceive themselves to be at equal levels. Top management is concerned that if the "real" relationship were made clear the close working relationship that now exists between the two departments might be damaged.

Discussion Questions

1. What is the specific purpose of the linear responsibility chart?
2. How is it possible to develop a complete LRC of a large organization?
3. Define the use of the LRC when viewed (1) horizontally and (2) vertically.
4. Discuss some disadvantages of the LRC.
5. Discuss the use of the LRC in both "organic" and "mechanistic" organizations.

Selected References

Larke, Alfred. "Linear Responsibility Chart—New Tool for Executive Control." In Dun's Review and Modern Industry, 1954.

Stieglitz, Harold. "What's Not on the Organization Chart." In The Conference Board Record, September 1964.

New Approaches to Organizational Structure

13

Business Says It Can Handle Bigness

"In practically all of our activities, we seem to suffer from the inertia resulting from our great size. It seems to be hard for us to get action . . . there are so many people involved."

That introspective analysis of grappling with bigness was made by Alfred P. Sloan, Jr., in 1925. It reflected his concern as president of General Motors Corp., when the company's employment roll was little more than a shadow of today's figure of 794,000 and sales by what is now the world's biggest manufacturer were only a fraction of last year's total of $24-billion.

Concern with managing bigness obviously extends beyond GM today, into the other multibillion-dollar corporations that have proliferated across the industrial scene. There are worries that these giants will become frozen into institutionalized bureaucracies that lack the dynamism to compete effectively. The advent of the trillion-dollar economy, with its expanding markets and labor force, finds more than one chief executive officer pondering whether the single most limiting factor on his company's fortunes is simply being able to manage it.

Early Stage

Alternatives to existing management structures are still in the embryonic stage, and they fly in the face of the rigid traditional way of running a company. Temporary management teams, created for specific projects and with members plucked from throughout companies if their talents mesh with the need, portend the kind of fluid management that many executives find

Reprinted from the October 17, 1970 issue of *Business Week* by special permission. Copyright © 1970 by McGraw-Hill Publishing Inc., New York, N. Y. 10020. All rights reserved.

unpalatable. Such a group approach, in which the leadership often rotates to the man with the most experience on a given aspect of the problem, exposes the shibboleth of the hard-driving man in command whose business acumen can see him through any circumstance.

GM's approach to the bigness problem, of course, was decentralization coupled with a large dose of coordinated control. It worked well enough to be copied by numerous companies wrestling with problems of size. But despite its immensity, GM is primarily in one business—making cars and trucks. For most companies, a big chunk of their growth has come with diversification. And trying to manage a burgeoning multiproduct, multimarket company such as a General Electric or a Textron, which is simultaneously expanding internationally and trying to keep pace with waves of new technology, puts management to a severe test.

Yet, it is the rare executive who will concede that growth is not a permanent part of his strategy. The "more-is-better" thesis, though more loudly challenged by business critics today than ever before, remains intact. "Business is hypnotized by size," says Peter F. Drucker, author, educator, and consultant. "The $5-billion company is still seen as a good in itself in both the public and private sector. To me, it is an affliction." Too often, says the Conference Board's Wilbur McFeely, "a large organization really lives on momentum rather than vitality."

Professional managers contend that it is simply a matter of keeping things in perspective and using the right techniques to obtain optimum results. Reflecting on his years with Royal Dutch/Shell, Monroe E. Spaght says he came to the view that there is no limit to the size at which a company can be managed efficiently. "It's rather a matter of dividing it into bite-sized chunks with clear-cut lines of authority to the top," says Spaght, who retired in June as a managing director of the international oil giant.

Consultant Richard Neuschel, a McKinsey & Co. director, asserts that there "is no real significance to bigness *per se*." He says: "There may be a limit to complexity. If a company becomes too heterogeneous, the threat of unmanageability becomes greater."

"What we really need is for a company to see that one of its undermanaged, under-exploited activities is really big enough to run itself, and then spin it off as an independent business," contends Drucker. "I could name 75 places where a business with volume ranging from $50-million to $300-million could be created if the big companies could divest and get out," Drucker says. "I'm convinced that we'll have to come to that."

The problems of managing increased diversity, says Ernest Dale, consultant and academician, may lead corporations to follow the route taken by many individual executives who have become specialists in order to cope with bigness and complexity. The multiproduct company would winnow out unrelated activities and concentrate on a more homogeneous and manageable mix.

Local Control

But for the present, decentralization will remain the primary device. And it is not limited to the biggest corporations. General Cable Corp., with 1969 sales of $366-million, is an example of a smaller company that took the step. President Donald Frey divided the company, which makes items ranging from household scouring pads to huge underground transmission cable, into five divisions when he arrived there two years ago.

Though his new environment at General Cable was dwarfed by his previous one—he had been vice-president of product devel-

opment at Ford Motor Co.—Frey found decentralization was indeed applicable. While Ford's market is enormous, it does not have General Cable's variety of distribution outlets, which range from supermarket suppliers to electrical wholesalers. And in the markets it serves, General Cable is often the biggest. Decentralizing, says Frey, allows "you to match your small competitors' attention to customers. Then you apply economies of scale to research and product development. But you have to be fluid. The only constant part of this company is my desk—with me, hopefully, behind it."

Effective control of a diversified and decentralized enterprise requires a constant information flow between headquarters and operating units. And at about the time the information flow started to clog, computer technology was applied. If it has not been the panacea its proponents predicted, it has spread throughout industry to a point that not having a "management information system" tied to a computer puts a company in the bush league.

When the system works, says John Diebold, considered by many to be the high priest in the field, "the man half a world away can be more cognizant of what is happening in an operating unit than the man on the scene." From the initial applications of computers to payroll, billing, and accounting, Diebold and his associates see the computer becoming a routine tool in corporate decision making.

Accompanying the numbers and equations will be an "overlay of the qualitative factors" behind the formulas, to be used as another tool for operating in a volatile environment, says Cleburn E. Best of Cresap, McCormick & Paget. The consulting firm is already working with its clients on "an early-warning system for top management to see what is going into decisions rather than seeing results on financial reports at a point when it may be too late for correction," says Best.

And there is no dearth of more esoteric

techniques—such as linear programming, risk analysis, or decision trees—waiting in the wings.

The majority of today's top managers are struggling to grasp the jargon used by younger managers who are attempting to apply the new techniques in their companies. In many instances, a "fear-and-sneer" syndrome arises, says the Conference Board's McFeely. But just as size and complexity will not diminish, neither will the number of young managers coversant with these techniques. As they ascend to top decision-making positions where the penalty for poor performance matches the stakes, they will call on new tools to help.

Testing Solutions

When, for example, a development group comes up with ideas for three new products, company executives may choose to use risk analysis—combining computer simulation with crap-shooting odds—to pick the one most likely to produce the best return. Once that decision is made, the product group may use venture analysis to ride herd on the product until it reaches the marketplace.

If a new plant has to be built, managers may call on a complex mathematical tool called linear programming (LP) to help determine the best geographic location, optimum plant size and product mix, the most efficient means of distribution, and the most economic inventory size. If a company project is extremely big, complex, expensive, and involves the coordination of large numbers of skilled people, executives may want to call on PERT/CPM (program evaluation and review technique/critical path management) to determine the fastest, most efficient ways of getting the job done.

Paralleling the ventures with new techniques will be more experimentation in organizational structure. More sharing of the chief executive's responsibilities by committees of senior executives—concepts such as the office of president or corporate executive office—will logically evolve. While the concept of a high powered team at the top is well entrenched at companies such as Du Pont and Jersey Standard, it picked up momentum in the late 1960s.

Project teams and task forces will become more common in tackling complexity, contend behavioral science advocates such as John Paul Jones, senior vice-president for personnel and organization development at Federated Department Stores, Inc. A team of executives from various departments, formed to cut costs throughout a company, is not unusual. But normally the practice is limited to staff functions.

Expertise

The cutting edge of what has been tabbed "matrix management" is operating in high-technology fields such as the aerospace industry. There, the group leadership role flows to the member most qualified when the task of developing a piece of hardware reaches a point that calls for his expertise. Once this particular hurdle is out of the way and another pops up calling for a different skill, leadership moves to another team member.

Matrix management will force companies to search out talent earlier. This will mean substantial upgrading of management development efforts. More companies will use computers to create employee "skills inventory" data banks to rapidly assign people with the right capabilities to a project. The resulting mobility may turn the corporate recruiting promise so often proffered—that the work will be challenging—into a reality.

Spencer Stuart, chairman of Spencer Stuart & Associates, an executive recruiting firm, sees the technique penetrating the inner circles of top management. "There will be more of what some people call 'temporary management systems' or 'project manage-ment systems,' where the men who are needed to contribute to the solution meet, make their contributions, and perhaps never become a permanent member of any fixed and permanent management group."

But top management's job will remain one of managing the totality of the enterprise and trying to identify the strategic moves to make in a changing and growing business environment. Seeking new management "secret weapons" at the expense of existing techniques, warns McKinsey's Neuschel, could make the task unnecessarily complicated. "The real job for managers," he says, "is to apply the fundamentals they already know about. Few companies are as well organized and as well managed as they could be if they were doing this."

IN CHAPTER 11 we discussed some of the more traditional approaches in the design of organizational structures. In recent years, however, many organizations have departed from the more traditional approach in order to accomplish specific objectives. We will discuss some of these structural modifications as well as hypothesize about some of the changes in organizations that may take place in the years to come.

Project Management

The concept of project management had its genesis in the aerospace industry and has since found application in a wide variety of industrial settings. Corporations that employ the project management concept are usually involved in the production of large-scale products or in projects that require the coordination of many disciplines over an extensive period of time. The nature of such projects does not warrant a "product-type" of organizational structure because the projects usually last for only a relatively short period of time. Within the aerospace industry, for example, many projects may involve a concentrated effort of many disciplines for a period of months, at the end of which the project is completed and all activities terminate. For projects involving activity for a period of only months or even one to two years, it is not feasible for a company to adopt a new product structure with each new series of projects. Companies involved in these situations have found that other organizational structures, such as functional or geographical, did not provide the capability for exercising the proper amount of coordination among all departments to insure efficient operation. This deficiency resulted from the fact that there was not available an organizational mechanism whereby a single individual was directly responsible for overall product or project coordination. Conflicts and problems with respect to a particular project would usually result in significant delays while the conflict was being resolved at some higher organizational level.

In Figure 13.1 it is clear that within the functional organization structure problems having to do with the coordination of activities for product A would necessarily move up through the organization to the presidential level for resolution. In most cases, a procedural problem like this can be resolved by restructuring the organization to a product-type structure in which all functions related to a single product or product group are included in one division. As we have mentioned, however, many companies are involved in products or

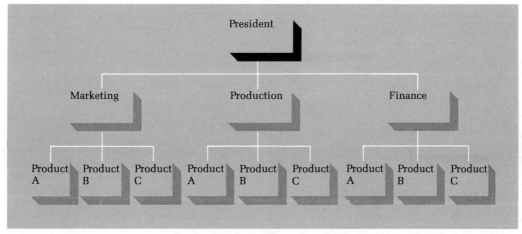

Figure 13.1. *Product-Oriented Structure*

services whose limited market life does not justify reorganization to a product structure.

Organizations finding themselves in this situation have found that greater coordination can be achieved if a single individual is placed in charge of the project and held responsible for all activities associated with it. This job involves the coordination of all activities throughout the entire life of the project. Such a position is usually designated that of project manager. For a manufacturing operation this might include all activities from research and development through design, engineering, production, test, and follow-up (Figure 13.2).

The project manager would have the chief responsibility of coordinating all activities in each of these functional areas for the spe-

Figure 13.2. *Project Management*

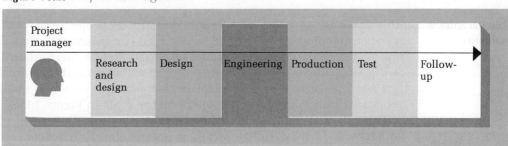

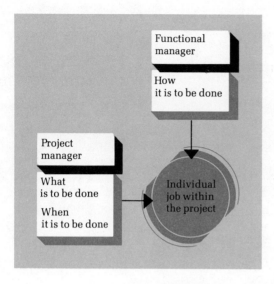

Figure 13.3.
Project and Functional Managers

cific project. This coordination would take place *across* a number of functional departments within the traditional organizational structures. Since a project manager has access to the *total* planning schedule for the project, he or she is usually in a position to make decisions on *what* is to be done and *when* it is to be done. The question as to *how* the various jobs are to be performed remains with the functional areas involved (Figure 13.3).

It is apparent that in addition to the obvious advantage of coordination which the project management concept provides, a very real problem area is also created. This problem results from the violation of one of the so-called principles of management, that of *unity of command*. For example, from Figure 13.4 we can see that the personnel in the engineering, production, and marketing departments who are assigned to project A will come under the possible influence of two superiors, their own functional manager and the project manager.

The Question of Authority

This potential problem area is inherent in the project manager's place in the organization. It can be resolved—or minimized—only if top management takes great pains to clearly define the *authority relationship* that is to exist between project managers and functional line managers. The authority of the project manager for a particular project will normally fall somewhere on the scale in Figure 13.5.

This scale is not meant to be representative of all degrees of authority and responsibility within an organization, but it does rep-

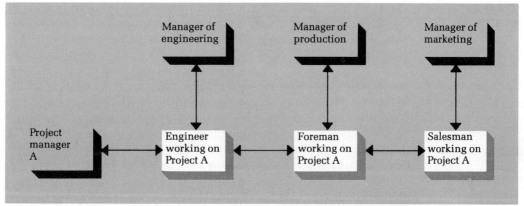

Figure 13.4. *Project Manager Relationships to Other Departments*

resent typical areas of potentially overlapping responsibility that must be resolved if project management is to work effectively. The scale presents the two extremes of authority that may be given to a project manager. Most project managers function at some point in the middle of the scale, and it is this point that must be clearly defined and mutually understood by both project managers and line officers if the project management concept is to work.

With respect to the degree of authority and responsibility given to project managers there is no clear-cut definition of what is appropriate. What is important, however, is that each project manager and each functional manager know exactly where his or her authority and responsibility begin and end.

Figure 13.5. *Project Manager's Authority*

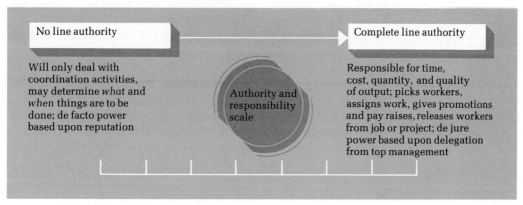

The Determination of Authority Thus in each organization in which project management is utilized, top management must define carefully the authority of both project managers and functional line managers with respect to four key questions.

Who Selects and Assigns Personnel to the Project? Is this question left up to the functional line manager, or can the individual project manager handpick employees? A case can be made for each side of the question. Functional managers would argue that they are aware of all of the demands each project is making and know when each job must be completed and are therefore in a better position than a particular project manager to assign personnel to a given project. On the other hand, the project manager who is responsible for meeting time or cost schedules would argue the need to be allowed to pick project workers. In most corporations utilizing project management, the assignment of workers to a project usually rests with the functional manager involved. Project managers are, however, usually given the opportunity to provide input to the functional manager before a decision is made.

Who Evaluates Employees for Promotions and Pay Raises? Will the project manager or the functional manager have the ultimate decision with respect to pay raises and promotions for an individual who is working on a given project? In almost every company both managers provide input with respect to these decisions. In fact, many companies consider this to be an area of joint decision. The fact remains, however, that one or the other manager is going to have a stronger voice in this decision. If the company does not state specifically who is primarily responsible (project manager or functional manager), then the major input will usually be provided by the manager who possesses a stronger personality. In these situations each employee working on a project will have to make a judgment as to which of the two managers will be the more influential in making the decision regarding pay and promotions.

Who Determines How Employees Charge Their Time? A project manager who is being held responsible for meeting a cost schedule on a given project will be very concerned about the extent to which he or she can control employees' charging time against the project.* If a particular project is overrunning its budget, it is sometimes permissible

---

* "Charging time" means the department that will pay for the time of the employee (the department whose budget will be charged).

for an employee working on that project to charge time against a project which still has funds available. This is commonly done even though the employee is not actually working on the project charged. This practice is acceptable, providing that top management and the project manager both know this is being done and know how much time is being charged. If these records are kept, budgets can be adjusted and the project manager can then still be judged for effectiveness in meeting project goals. If, however, the project manager is not aware of the time being charged against a project, the entire cost control mechanism within the organization becomes ineffective, because it becomes impossible to determine exactly what costs are actually associated with each project. Clearly, control of time charged is very important to project managers.

Who Terminates Workers? This question bears directly upon the question of assigning personnel since it dictates how long employees will be working on a given project. The same arguments hold true for this decision as well. Here again top management must determine where the specific authority will rest for this decision, and this must be made clear to both project managers and functional line managers.

In most corporations in which project management is utilized, the authority of the project manager tends to be minimal (toward the left in Figure 13.5). This means that most project managers depend heavily on de facto power, that is, power based simply on their own ability to persuade and explain the reasons behind a given request. In addition, their own personal status or position within the organization may provide them with some degree of influence in their dealings with others.

The project management concept, in which the project manager determines *what* and *when* specific tasks are to be performed while the functional line manager determines *how* they are to be performed, places the line manager in a unique position. From our previous discussion of line and staff functions it seems clear that the role of the functional line manager corresponds closely to what is normally considered to be a staff role. As we recall, it is staff that are usually the experts in the specialized fields and as such are responsible for determining *how* something is to be done. The fact that within the project management organization functional line managers perform a staff function can be a source of problems. Many line managers, not used to this unique relationship, perceive this as a potential, if not real, loss of authority. Consequently, they often find it difficult to deal with this role relationship when interacting with project managers.

With respect to the project managers, two problems may arise in addition to the ones already discussed. These come into focus after the project manager has completed the project assignment. If there is no new project available, the project manager will usually be assigned back to the functional area from which he or she was selected. In many cases the new job in a functional department will be dull and routine compared with the former activities as project manager. A loss of motivation may result, which may even lead to resignation from the company. Another problem in returning to a functional line department is that the former manager must now report to a line manager—perhaps even one with whom there may have been conflict. Such a situation may prove difficult for a project manager now the target of hostility or discrimination by the functional line managers.

Figure 13.6. *Matrix Structure*

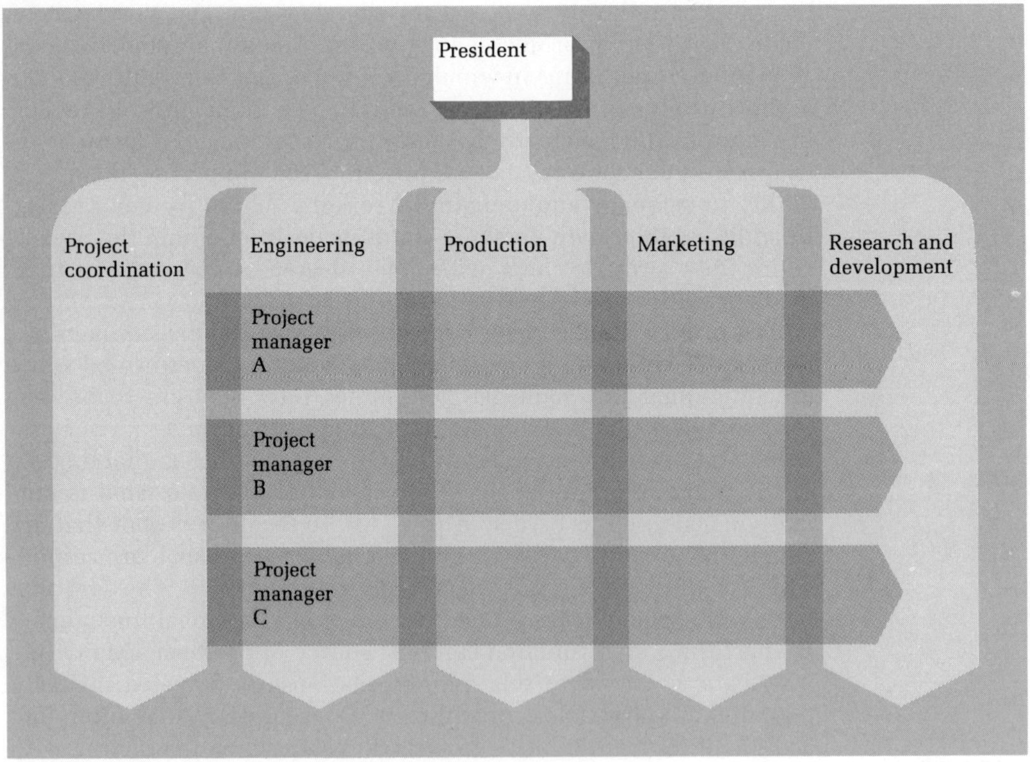

Matrix Organizations

The concept of matrix organizations, which has received much attention in recent years, is simply an extension of the project management concept. In the matrix structure, project managers are assigned to a variety of projects—rather than a single one—whose activities cut across traditional functional departments. Within the larger structure at any given time a series of project managers direct the activities of a number of projects, while functional line managers allocate their resources in order to meet the needs of these various projects. Figure 13.6 presents a typical matrix structure of this type.

The structure appearing in Figure 13.6 is a two-dimensional grid, hence the name "matrix organization." In this type of organization, the authority of the project manager is usually greater than that given under the more traditional project management concept. There is usually a more equal division of authority between project managers and functional line managers, which sets up a true "matrix" within which the organization must function. The issues, questions, and problems inherent in project management apply equally to the matrix structure. Each of these must be addressed and defined by top management if the matrix organization is to prove effective.

Organizations of the Future: An Application of the "Organic" Structure

As corporations find that they must deal with rapidly changing social, economic, and technical environments, new philosophies are finding their way into the traditional organization structure. These have as their purpose the creation of a more flexible and adaptive structure to meet the needs of both the corporation and the individual employee. These structures, and the policies and procedures that govern their operation, would not be suitable for all corporations in all industries, but their evolution serves to fill a gap in the ever-increasing spectrum of organizational structures and philosophies designed to meet a wide variety of conditions.

Rather than discussing each of these possible structural and operating changes independently let us create a hypothetical organization and examine in detail how it might utilize some of these innovative concepts. In approaching the discussion in this way we will leave many loose ends, but our main purpose is to stimulate the reader to think about how such an organization might function. In addition, our discussion should serve to highlight some of the organizational problems that might result from these new philosophies. Much of the discussion to follow is based on the ideas of R. Johnson, F. Kast, and J. Rosenzweig as well as J. Forrester.[1]

The organization we will consider will follow the basic matrix design discussed in the section on project management. Figure 13.7 provides a chart of this organization. This chart gives an approximation of how such an organization might be structured. The top management group might consist of eight individuals, including the president, the heads of marketing research, research and development, legal, and accounting and financial analysis; also included would be the vice-president for projects (to whom all project managers report) and the vice-president for personnel and information systems (this function will be discussed in greater detail later in the chapter). The departments listed are not meant to be all-inclusive but rather typical. The exact number of departments and function of each would vary with the organization and the situation.

Top Management Overall direction and control of the organization would be the responsibility of a top management committee. The exact nature and make-up of this committee would vary from company to company. It would be the responsibility of this group to define the direction and organizational philosophy of the corporation. This direction and philosophy would be the basis for decisions regarding products and services offered. To make these decisions, the top management group would receive input on market conditions and future market needs, legal and financial recommendations, and technical input and research and development data.

Information of this type is not an unusual part of the long-range planning of many modern firms. Where our representative organization might appear unusual is less in how it carries on its planning function and more in the way it attempts to implement its planning in a constantly changing environment—an environment that includes a rapidly progressing technology, changes in market conditions, a significant increase in the education and awareness of the work force, and increasing corporate concern for the natural environment and for issues of social responsibility. Our responsive, flexible organization might be described as an "organic" structure.

Figure 13.7. *Model of an Organization of the Future*

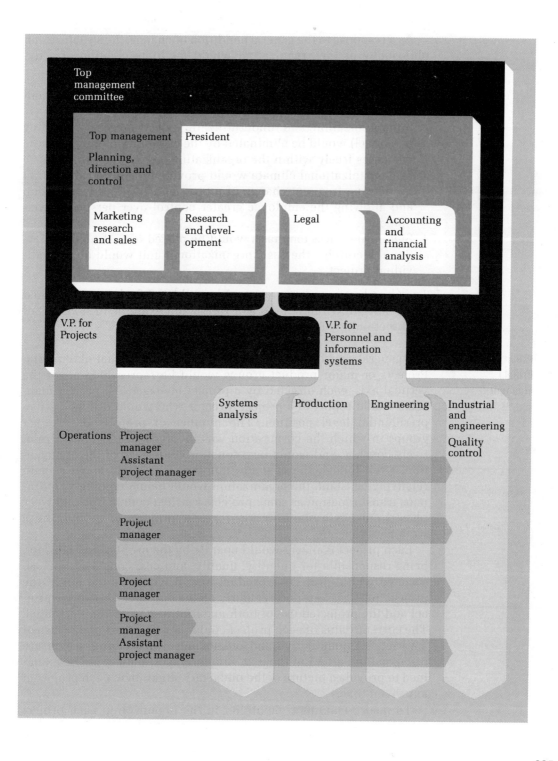

Top management committee

Top management

Planning, direction and control

President

Marketing research and sales

Research and development

Legal

Accounting and financial analysis

V.P. for Projects

V.P. for Personnel and information systems

Systems analysis

Production

Engineering

Industrial and engineering

Operations

Project manager
Assistant project manager

Quality control

Project manager

Project manager

Project manager
Assistant project manager

As a response to the general condition of change, the structure and philosophy of the organization would facilitate creation of a dynamic working environment:

1. The organization could adapt rapidly to changes in external conditions.
2. Suboptimization and underutilization of resources (including personnel) would be eliminated by the capability of moving these resources freely within the organization.
3. The organizational climate would provide high need satisfaction by offering frequent change of job assignments and work group and allowing the employee greater control over personal development.
4. Significantly less emphasis would be placed on a strict organizational hierarchy; the basic organizational unit would be the individual project.

To gain a better understanding of how this might be accomplished let us move down into the organization and examine in some detail the functioning of individual project units.

Projects and Project Managers

The general structure of the organization would be that of a matrix. Projects or major product groups would be represented along the vertical axis, each directed by a project manager. All project managers would report to a project director who would occupy a vice-presidential level position. The number of projects or product groups in which the corporation was involved would remain relatively constant and would be a function of the size of the organization. Even though the absolute number of projects might remain relatively constant, the organization would be undergoing a continuous transformation as some projects reached completion and were phased out while opportunities for new projects or product lines were being sought.

Each project manager would operate by the *profit center* concept, being responsible for quantity, quality, and cost considerations associated with a project or product line. It would be the job of the project manager to report regularly on the current status of the project and the projected use of both material resources and personnel. The current status of each project could then be monitored by use of a variety of quantitative and other control procedures which are discussed in Part VI of the text. Similarly, cost data could be examined to provide a picture of the budgetary situation of each project at any given time.

To insure maximum flexibility in the organization each project manager would provide projections of personnel needs over some specified period of time. These projections would be developed from subjective and objective estimates and would represent the project manager's forecast of the number of hours, days or weeks that specific skills or areas of expertise would be required on the particular project. The project manager's forecasts would represent the "flow" of skills into and out of the project over some period of time. These "skills" can also be thought of as the individual employees who would be assigned to projects as they are needed and then moved on to new projects when their skills are required by another project manager.

It is clear that the key to success for such an approach would be the organization's ability to *forecast needs* and *locate and transfer* personnel resources throughout the organization. Project managers would be required to plan activities in sufficient detail to determine the needs of a given project at a given point in time. These needs would then be translated into particular employee skills and forecasts of *when* and for *how long* these skills would be required. For example, a project manager might determine a need for an industrial engineer with a background in methods analysis and standard data time study techniques. The project manager might wish also for the industrial engineer to be experienced in small-component assembly operations. According to the project schedule, the project manager might estimate needing the industrial engineer on the project from the 23rd to the 31st week, a total of two months of the industrial engineer's time. This requirement could be represented as in Figure 13.8, which shows the forecasting of needs within a project. In order to function effectively the corporation must also have the capability of "searching out" the particular skill needed and making a determination as to whether that skill would be available at the time required by the project. This would represent the "location and transfer" phase of the operation. In order to understand how this would be done, let us discuss the key role that would be played by the *personnel and information systems group.*

Personnel and Information Systems Group

The function of the personnel and information systems group would be to maintain an accurate and up-to-date professional profile on each employee. This profile would contain information on such items as skills, background, experience, and test scores. In addition, it would include past performance evaluations by supervisors and peer groups that an employee might have received. Finally, each employee would be asked his or her personal desires with respect to career and professional development. Included might be particular

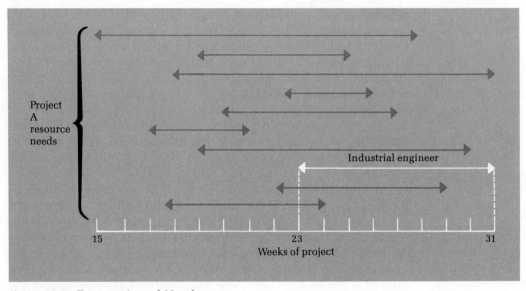

Figure 13.8. *Forecasting of Needs*

jobs, assignments, or projects of interest to the employee (see Exhibit 13.1).

The objective of the professional profile would be to have an accurate inventory of one of the most valuable of resources, namely, the employees within the organization. This inventory would combine not only the skills and experiences of the employee but also—and perhaps more importantly—the desires, interests, and perceptions of each regarding professional development and career path expectations. The employee profile could be utilized by the organization to match project assignments not only with the skills of the employee but also with his or her interests and orientation. The philosophy behind the profile would not be to maintain a "big brother" record system but rather to provide information for both individual and corporate benefit. If properly utilized, the profile would allow for individual employees to be assigned to projects in which they had expressed an interest. To the extent possible, jobs would be matched with employees for maximum need satisfaction. Corporate policies might be established giving the individual employee the right to refuse job assignments—perhaps one out of every three—if the employee perceived them as not enhancing his or her professional development. Such a policy would enable the employee to maintain some control over his or her destiny in the organization and in this way serve to reduce the sense of helplessness that many employees feel currently.

Exhibit 13.1. *Employee Profile*

Education	Degrees held, special training, etc.
Experience	Previous work experience
Test score data	IQ, dexterity, personality, emotional make-up, mathematical ability, etc.
Performance evaluation	Supervisor ratings, peer group ratings
Employee career interest	Project interests, specific jobs desired, long-range career orientation

Job assignment is not without problems. The organization is busy with an ever-changing grouping of projects. Employees may find it necessary to leave one job environment and move to another as one project is completed and another begun. Even though the new job assignments would attempt to incorporate employee needs and desires, it is clear that not everyone would find such a changing environment compatible with their needs and psychological make-up. For an employee who required a stable job situation with work group familiarity as well as the security of knowing that his or her job would not change significantly in the foreseeable future, this environment would be most unattractive. On the other hand, an employee who thrived on a constantly changing and challenging work environment with new problems and new personal interaction, this environment might prove extremely rewarding.

In discussing the compatibility of individual needs and the environment that might exist within this type of organization, it becomes apparent that the initial hiring process for the organization is critical. Care should be taken to insure that employees brought into an organization find a situation that would, in general, be satisfying to them and that they would choose to remain in. Let us examine what this hiring process might be like.

Hiring Procedures

The role of the personnel and information systems group would be critical in the initial hiring process. For maximum flexibility, this group would have to maintain an accurate and up-to-date file on each potential employee, including a professional profile. Information would have to be obtained on the personality as well as the needs and desires of employee candidates. This information would help a company make an initial determination of the suitability of a potential employee for a changing organizational environment. During the initial hiring process, moreover, the flow of information would not be entirely one way. Both the organization and the individual must devote time and effort to evaluating each other's desirability.

In order to perform this mutual evaluation, the initial hiring process may extend over several days of intensive interaction. During this period both individual and organization will get to know each other in order to determine the extent to which each is capable of meeting the other's needs. This process will involve the normal interview procedures but may also include small trial projects, presentations, and T-group interactions, all designed to promote familiarity. The purpose of the interaction is certainly not to probe and analyze the candidate like a machine but to explore the mutual compatibility of the candidate and the company.

As we have mentioned, organizations are becoming much more varied, in both structure and operation, as research provides guidelines for responding to industrial, social, and technical conditions. In addition, higher levels of education, affluence, and social awareness have made individuals far more complex in their striving to satisfy higher-level needs. The combination of these two factors has created a situation in which an ever-smaller portion of the work force is compatible with a given organization and its method of operation. Effort on the part of both individuals and organizations is needed to evaluate each other in terms of need satisfaction. The concept of "recruiting" will be modified so as to reduce its present "win-lose" implications and be replaced by a less ego-threatening process in which both parties may come to a realization that continued interaction would not prove beneficial. Such an environment can only come about as society becomes more receptive to a broader definition of personal achievement and success. This definition will allow for a wider range of behavior, in which each employee will seek a work environment compatible with his or her own needs. Such an environment may not exist in all organizations, and it may not be compatible with upward movement through the organizational hierarchy.

In conjunction with the initial employment process, many organizations might undertake a placement function designed to find alternative employment opportunities for individuals who find that they do not have the psychological make-up necessary to find satisfaction in a particular organizational environment. Here again, this would require a change in current thinking regarding the movement of individuals from one organization to another. There must be a greater recognition and acceptance of the fact that certain employees may choose to leave a particular environment because it is not satisfying to them and not necessarily because they have some deficiency in skill or ability.

At the conclusion of the hiring process, if both individual and organization find each other mutually acceptable, the individual employee profile would be retained by the personnel and information systems group and the employee would be ready for his or her first assignment.

**Resource
Transfer**

We have discussed briefly the role of the project manager with respect to the forecast of individual skills needed by the project over time. In addition, we discussed the function of the personnel and information systems group with respect to the maintenance of up-to-date employee profiles. We will now consider the organization's ability to transfer individual resources throughout the various projects as skills are needed. The personnel and information systems group will maintain the employee profiles and will utilize input from project managers that will allow the personnel group to keep track of the current assignment of each employee as well as the length of time each is expected to remain on a given project.

In Figure 13.8 we noted that a project manager forecast the need for an industrial engineer with a particular background between the 23rd and 31st week of the project. This need would be forwarded to the personnel and information systems group. The information could be used to "advertise" skills that will no longer be required on a given project. For example, at the end of the 31st week the industrial engineer will no longer be required on project A and would be available for reassignment (Figure 13.9). It would be the function of the personnel and information systems group to keep track of the status of all individuals and recommend matching up between employees and particular job assignments. Matching would be a function of employee availability, interests, and skills in conjunction with requests from project managers regarding project requirements.

Figure 13.9 represents a cross section of the status of several projects at a point in time. As we remember from Figure 13.8, the manager of project A projected a need for an industrial engineer from week 23 through week 31. The personnel and information systems group would search current employee profiles to determine: (1) if the organization employs an industrial engineer with the skills requested; (2) what the current job assignments are for such industrial engineers in the company; and (3) when each of these engineers would no longer be needed on his or her current project and would therefore be available for a new assignment. In Figure 13.9, accord-

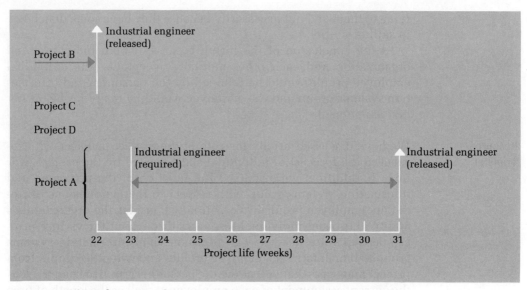

Figure 13.9. *Matching Employees and Project Needs*

ing to forecasts from the manager on project B, an industrial engineer would be released from that assignment at the 22nd week. This would theoretically make this engineer eligible for reassignment to project A at that time.

Of course, every project request will not necessarily match up with the release of a desired skill from some other project. It may be necessary for the organization to maintain some slack within the system with surplus skills in critical areas—or it may be necessary to hire new employees to fill project needs.

What we have attempted to demonstrate is the flow of personnel that would take place as individual skills became available in one project and required in another. The key to the success of this organizational arrangement would be the ability of project managers to forecast needed skills as well as the ability of the personnel and information systems group to maintain up-to-date records on employees. In general terms, the model we have been discussing is illustrated in Figure 13.10.

When information from the various project managers flows to the personnel and information systems group to be analyzed, recommendations based on this analysis can be made for the reassignment of organizational employees.

Free flow of personnel resources enables an organization to take full advantage of all of the individual skills and talents at its disposal. This approach minimizes the underutilization of personnel so often found in many large firms. The resource flow concept also serves to prevent "empire building," since individuals move to new projects on a regular basis. Each project must be charged the salaries of all individuals working on that project. This discourages project managers from requesting to keep an individual whose skills are no longer required.

If the personnel and information system group had been functioning properly, it would have anticipated the availability of this

Figure 13.10. *Project-Personnel Relationships*

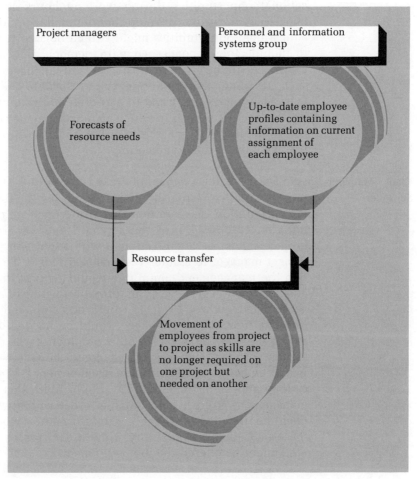

Project managers

Personnel and information systems group

Forecasts of resource needs

Up-to-date employee profiles containing information on current assignment of each employee

Resource transfer

Movement of employees from project to project as skills are no longer required on one project but needed on another individual and would have analyzed the requests of current project managers in order to recommend a new job assignment. After completing each assignment, each individual would be evaluated by his project manager as well as the peer group with whom he worked. These evaluations would then become a part of the employee profile.

To provide some relief from the demands of the constantly changing job environment, as well as to provide an opportunity to sharpen professional skills, corporate policy might allow some type of sabbatical leave for employees after many years of service. This leave would be similar to the sabbatical given in the educational environment and would be part of the employee's development program.

In conjunction with this idea the corporation might provide educational opportunities during working hours so that employees might seek to further develop individual skills and abilities. These educational opportunities might extend beyond work-related fields to include topics concerned with personal development as well. Courses could be given in music, art, and languages, as well as areas such as sailing or scuba diving. With respect to courses of this type, there is an increasing trend in corporate philosophy toward the belief that there is no area in which an individual may develop that will not, in the long run, make him or her a more desirable and productive member of the organization.

Project Manager Selection

Let us go back for a moment to take a closer look at the top management committee responsible for determining the future direction of the corporation. Assume that this group makes a decision to enter into a new product line or new service. If the new area is to become a project within the organization, it will be necessary to select a new project manager to assume responsibility for it. To make this selection the management committee would request that the personnel and information systems group provide a listing of any current project managers whose projects would be completed on or about the time the new project manager would be needed. In addition, any assistant project managers or other employees who might be ready to assume project manager status could be evaluated. Evaluation would be based on the individual's experience, skills, and interests as they appear in the employee profile. With this information the management group would be able to determine which individuals might be qualified for the job. The information would also indicate these individuals' availability. Now a decision can be made as to who might be offered the job assignment.

The employee offered the assignment could choose to reject it if the person believed that the assignment was not consistent with his or her perceptions and values concerning career development. Rejection of a new job opportunity without fear requires an organizational philosophy that does not attach any negative connotations to such a rejection. This would require significant change from the prevailing attitudes in industry today. Present attitudes still place a high value on upward mobility and often question the philosophy, loyalty, or values of those who may not view job advancement as their only career goal.

The newly selected project manager meets with various management personnel to get acquainted with the nature and scope of the new project. This information enables the project manager to make an initial determination of personnel and resource needs over a period of time. Then, with access to the information systems group for data about individuals available who have skills needed by the project, the project manager makes an initial selection of personnel for the project. If the project manager requests an individual not available to work on the new project (or one who *prefers* not to work on it), a number of alternatives might be available:

1. The top management committee might assign a priority number to each project based upon its relative importance to the organization. Projects having the highest priority might be given the opportunity to select some number of personnel from projects having lower priorities.
2. Each project could be assigned a certain number of points, again based upon its overall importance to the organization. Each project manager might then be allowed to bid for choice personnel within the total number of points allocated. An employee would then be given the opportunity to work for the project manager who had bid the highest for his or her services.
3. A more traditional approach to the problem would be to arrange a negotiating session to see if some mutually agreeable solution might be worked out. For example, one new project manager might require a particular engineer for some limited time period. If during that time the engineer would not be required on a full-time basis on her current project, the engineer might work as a consultant on the new project, charging her time accordingly. This would allow the engineer to remain on her current project but would also enable her to provide the new project manager with her expertise.

It is obvious that not all industries have the characteristics necessary for the continuous change of product orientation sketched in this chapter. Industries which exhibit a more stable product life would not be suited to all the concepts discussed. For example, if it became apparent that significant numbers of employees were in effect sitting and waiting for job assignment, serious questions would be raised regarding the overall efficiency of such an organization. Clearly, this philosophy would be inappropriate for the environment in which the corporation was functioning. On the other hand, this situation might indicate not an inappropriate philosophy but an improperly staffed organization. Some of the employees who are consistently ignored by project managers in the staffing of new projects might lack ability or appropriate skills. Another possibility is that the company is simply overstaffed.

The point is that we have focused on a series of possible ways in which a hypothetical organization might function in order to create an adaptable and satisfying work environment. Each concept presented may or may not have application to a particular organization within a given industry. Only by carefully examining each situation can top management determine if any or all of these concepts would serve to improve the effectiveness of the company. In applying some of these concepts management must also anticipate some new organizational problems, which could create difficulties and possibly lead to a reduction in the overall effectiveness of the organization. In order to deal with some of these problems there will be a need for clear-cut policies and procedures to deal with the following issues:

1. Possible adverse union reaction to a job environment which may require a frequent change in work assignments.
2. The fact that, even with careful hiring procedures, certain employees may not be comfortable in the rapidly changing work environment.
3. The need to define in great detail exact procedures to be followed in the transfer of personnel from one project to another. These procedures would specify the way priorities would be assigned to specific projects and spell out procedures to be followed if more than one project manager requests the services of a particular employee.
4. Organizational mechanisms to provide short-term staff services to particular projects. These short-term services would be designed to cover gaps that could occur in the normal transfer process.
5. Establishing procedures to provide an equitable arrangement for employee evaluation with respect to merit pay raise consideration.

6. Policies to insure that records and files contained in the personnel and information systems group would not be utilized for inappropriate purposes.
7. Procedures for resolving conflicts over employee assignment to specific projects.

Discussion Questions

1. Discuss the advantages and disadvantages of project management as an organizational concept.
2. How does the role of the project manager differ from that of the functional line manager?
3. Discuss the issue of authority as it relates to the project manager concept.
4. Define what is meant by the term *matrix organization.*
5. What is an "organic" organizational structure?
6. What are the key concepts involved in a successful implementation of an "organic" organization?

7. "Not all employees will find the organic structure a satisfying work environment." Discuss.
8. What information might be in an employee profile?
9. Describe how hiring procedures may be modified in organizations of the future.
10. Discuss the role of the personnel and information systems group in the representation organization discussed in this chapter.
11. Discuss some of the problems (both human and organizational) that might be encountered in the "organic" organization.

Case for Discussion

Dennis Harrison, manager of an air frame production department for a large aerospace firm on the east coast, was responsible for meeting the production schedule for a new air foil to be used in weather satellites that were to be launched in six months. Dennis was having trouble meeting the schedule; the assembly process in his department was experiencing great difficulty in completing assembly within specifications. Those units that were completed within specifications failed under test conditions and had to be rejected.

Dennis spent much time with his superiors to determine if the assembly problem resulted from his department's personnel or equipment. He was repeatedly assured, however, that the skill and ability of his

assemblers as well as the capabilities of his equipment were more than adequate to complete assembly operations within specifications. Because final assembly took place in Dennis' department, the division manager, Dennis' superior, looked to Dennis for an answer to the problem. Because he had ruled out his own department as the source of the problem, Dennis believed he had to look elsewhere. To gain some insight into the complexity of the problem, Dennis called a meeting with the following individuals:

Manager of design engineering (designer of the air-foil)
Manager of component assembly department A (department where components were

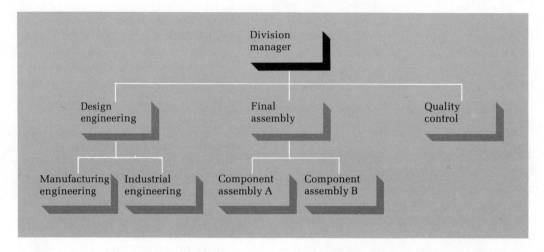

assembled prior to final assembly)
Manager of manufacturing engineering
(where parts were machined and
processed)
Manager of quality control (where parts were
tested)
Manager of industrial engineering (where
manufacturing methods were determined)

A partial diagram of the organizational
structure for the firm appears as shown.

Once the managers were gathered, Dennis
reviewed the problem and expressed his
concern as to whether the division would be
able to meet its production schedule
commitment. Each manager acknowledged
Dennis' concern, but indicated that they were
performing their tasks to the best of their
ability. At the end of their discussion the
manager of industrial engineering looked at
Dennis and asked, "Are we a task force on
this problem or what?"

Selected References

Blumenthal, S. *Management Information
Systems.* Englewood Cliffs, N.J.:
Prentice-Hall, 1969.

Cleland, D. and King, W. *Systems,
Organizations, Analysis, Management: A
Book of Readings.* New York:
McGraw-Hill, 1969.

———. *Management: A Systems Approach.*
New York: McGraw-Hill, 1972.

Forrester, J. "A New Corporate Design." In
Industrial Management Review, Fall 1965.

Johnson, R., Kast, F., and Rosenzweig, J. *The*

Theory and Management of Systems. New
York: McGraw-Hill, 1963.

Murdick, R. and Ross, J. *Information
Systems for Modern Management.*
Englewood Cliffs, N.J.: Prentice-Hall, 1971.

Ross, J. *Management by Information System.*
Englewood Cliffs, N.J.: Prentice-Hall, 1970.

Schoderbek, P. *Management Systems.* New
York: John Wiley & Sons, 1967.

Young, S. *Management: A System Analysis.*
Glenview, Ill.: Scott, Foresman and Co.,
1966.

THE INDIVIDUAL IN THE ORGANIZATION

Part V

Introduction

The following three chapters build on the foundation provided earlier and seek to tie together some of the concepts previously discussed. Three major concepts are presented, each dealing with some aspect of modern management. The first is the idea of integrating the individual and the organization through the method of participation. The second concept probes the area of management training and development and how some of these programs are conducted. The final concept is contingency theory, a dominant force in current management thought; we will give particular emphasis to how this concept can be applied to organizational development.

Major Themes

Integrating the Individual and
the Organization:
Participative management

Management Development:
Approaches and techniques

Contingency Theory:
An analysis of its application to
organizational development

The Individual and the Organization

14

GM's Test of Participation

The Inland Div. of General Motors Corp., with sales estimated at more than $275 million a year, ranks as a big operation in its own right. But within GM, which Inland supplies with such equipment as steering wheels and padded dashboards, its size is hardly more than a speck on a windshield.

So, for nearly 10 years, Thomas O. Mathues, Inland's general manager, has been running a participatory management system intended to keep the division's 600 line managers from getting lost in the corporate shuffle. Mathues insists—and most of his managers agree—that the system allows the division to respond more quickly to the dictates of annual model changes. More important, the division's managers get broader, more varied experience, and more opportunity to make key decisions than do executives at most companies.

Mathues' brand of team management includes these innovations:

Teams of 25 to 75 members operate internally as individual companies and are responsible for one or more of Inland's product lines, which range from foam seats to ball joints.

Rotating team chiefs, who are specialists in manufacturing, product engineering, or production engineering, serve as boss for four months each year when the product cycle is especially demanding of their talents.

A nine-member division staff acts as a "board of directors" for each of the teams, reviewing progress at quarterly "board" meetings at which up to a dozen members of a single team may discuss problems such as quality control and manufacturing performance.

Reprinted from the February 23, 1976 issue of *Business Week* by special permission. Copyright © 1976 by McGraw-Hill Publishing, Inc., New York, N.Y. 10020. All rights reserved.

Mathues began deemphasizing the traditional vertical line-management organization at Dayton-based Inland and replacing it with his team concept almost as soon as he took over as general manager in 1966. "We were a sluggish giant," says Mathues, 53, a General Motors Institute graduate who began testing brake linings at Inland in 1947 and has spent his entire career there. "We had to improve response time. And the way to do this was to get decision making and the over-all direction of the division down to lower levels. It gives people a sense of proprietorship."

Before Mathues took over, manufacture of all of the division's products was supervised by the division staff, and at times there was little cooperation or coordination among the engineering, manufacturing, sales, and other personnel.

In forming the teams, the first step was to bring together managers involved in engineering and manufacturing. Later the teams became more autonomous as salaried employees were added for such functions as purchasing, finance, and sales. Recently the teams have been trying, with mixed results, to bring hourly workers into the team effort as well.

No Empires

The whole idea of the teams has been to tear down the little empires that develop within large organizations and that often work at cross-purposes. "Before the teams, a guy would say, 'I'm the quality control inspector and I don't give a damn about your production problems,'" says George Francis, manufacturing manager for hose assemblies who has worked under three general managers at Inland. "Now all of us are working on common problems." Adds Mathues: "If something isn't working right, they're all in the same boat."

The teams have wide latitude in operating so long as they get the job done. Some form sub-teams, for example. The instrument-panel pad team has six sub-teams, while the brake hose team has two sub-teams—all of which meet on their own.

All team members have access to information necessary for general management of the team, such as selling price, competitive position in the marketplace, and materials costs for their product. Based on the data, each team makes up its own annual operating budget, giving up—on paper—50% of its profits for taxes and 70% of its after-tax earnings to GM as "dividends." Whatever is left, plus depreciation, the teams may use for capital investment. Any remaining profit is "loaned" to the division at 9% interest. But, if the team's capital needs are unusually high, it can "borrow" from the division at the same rate of interest. Last year, for example, a bumper rub-strip team had to take out a substantial loan to buy a new $500,000 rubber mixing machine to replace one carried on the books at only $250,000.

Inland will not release sales or earning figures, but Mathues says there is clear evidence the system works. Since he began phasing the teams in, he says, sales in constant dollars (eliminating the effects of inflation) have increased 45% per employee, 35% per salaried employee, and 20% per square foot of plant space.

Having a Say

Most managers at Inland think the system works smoothly because everyone has his say, and even newcomers feel they have visibility. At the "board" meetings, says Mathues, who acts as "chairman," "a young engineer two years out of college, will be shoved on stage to make a technical presentation on cost savings because the older engineers may not be able to explain it as well as this kid. The team approach allows a young person to show his talent earlier."

Daniel P. Sullivan, 30, a production engineering superintendent, agrees. "I hadn't been here a year the first time I stood up before the general manager and told him our problems and what we were doing about them," he says. "In all the eight years I worked at Frigidaire [another Dayton-based GM division] I only saw the general manager once."

Team managers say the Inland organization allows materials to be altered and engineering innovations to be made quickly to chip away at costs. During a vinyl shortage a year or so ago, a production engineer suggested ways to reduce the amount of vinyl in steering wheels. "Actually, he was infringing on product design's responsibility," says Sidney G. Dunford, a staff engineer in product design and current chief of the steering wheel team. "But we told him, 'If you guys want to take the time, we'll sure look at it.' The result was a 10% saving in vinyl."

The bumper rub-strip team persuaded the division's rubber compounders to change their formulas, enabling Inland to reduce the number of different carbon blacks it inventories from 13 to 6. The change resulted in annual savings of $30,000 and freed considerable storage space.

Emphasizing We

Mathues believes a major advantage of teams is the increased mobility it offers young salaried employees. He claims there has been 10 times as much movement between various types of jobs as there was before.

The system has its problems, however. One is that the team emphasis on "we" instead of "I" leaves some ambitious managers disgruntled about their lack of personal recognition. Mathues counters that the system actually pushes stars to the front. Another problem is all the time spent communicating—supposedly one of the system's strengths, but at times a drawback. "If you're not careful you can have too many people in too many meetings," admits Sullivan. One manufacturing manager is more blunt: "We can't do anything without team action. Nine times out of ten it will turn out O.K., and you could have started two weeks earlier without the team."

The teams have yet to make much headway involving hourly workers either. A few hourly workers have joined the brake hose team and the instrument panel team but this is only a handful of Inland's 5,500 hourly personnel. "The question," says Mathues, "is how to make it intelligible that our well-being and theirs is tied together. We have yet to find an entirely appropriate way."

THIS CHAPTER will describe a series of programs that may be utilized to increase involvement and participation by organizational members. The purpose of these programs is to create an environment in which each individual becomes more aware of his or her role in the organization and achieves greater involvement in its planning and decision-making processes. It is hoped that this increased awareness and involvement will enable individuals to have a greater degree of understanding of, and control over, their job environment and as a result to find the job more challenging and satisfying.

Employee Participation

In recent years organizations have focused on the development of programs having the objective of creating a more satisfying and stimulating work environment. These programs have come about as more and more research results are indicating that certain elements of the work environment may significantly contribute to employee frustration and dissatisfaction. There is reason to believe that frustration and dissatisfaction lead to increased employee turnover, low levels of performance, and a generally negative attitude toward the work environment. This problem has become more critical as more highly educated workers enter the job market.

As we stated in Chapter 6 many workers today are seeking satisfactions quite different from those sought by prior generations. To better satisfy today's needs, many organizations are attempting to develop new methods and techniques to provide greater challenge and satisfaction for employees. In many cases these programs attempt to solicit active *participation* of work group members in a wide variety of organizational and managerial processes. The philosophy behind these programs is essentially that employee motivation and performance will be a function of the involvement and participation of the employee in setting goals. A great deal of research indicates that individuals who feel they have participated in the goal-setting process will be more highly motivated in working toward the successful achievement of these goals. Figure 14.1 on page 346 represents two types of organizational situations. In (A) the individual and the organization do not interact in goal setting and decision making, whereas in (B) there is joint participation.

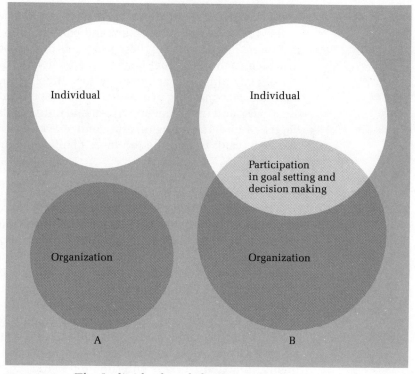

Individual

Individual

Participation
in goal setting and
decision making

Organization

Organization

A

B

Figure 14.1. *The Individual and the Organization*

Harwood Manufacturing

In one of the classic studies of employee participation in the goal-setting process, Lester Coch and John French examined the impact of changes in job design on employee performance in a manufacturing plant in Marion, Virginia (Harwood Manufacturing Corporation).[1] The company had been experiencing difficulty in bringing workers back up to a desired level of performance after a change had occurred in the method or procedure by which a job was to be performed. An analysis of several hundred employees whose performance was rated as acceptable prior to a job change showed that "38 percent of the changed operators recovered to the standard ... level of performance whereas 62 percent either became chronically substandard or quit during the relearning period."[2] What is even more interesting is that experienced workers took longer to learn the new job than did less experienced workers. During the relearning period company records indicated high levels of employee turnover and absenteeism. Finally, interviews with operators revealed that high levels of employee frustration and attitude of failure were common in the work force. It seemed clear that a change necessitating that the employee "learn" a new method or procedure had significant impact on factors such as absenteeism, turnover, and frustration levels.

To study this phenomenon Coch and French utilized three experimental groups, each of which was subjected to a change in work methods. The way the change was introduced, however, differed in each of the three groups.

In the first group the employees were called together and told that competitive pressures required a change in method; the employees were then told about the specific change, questions were answered, and the meeting was concluded.

In the second group the need for the change in method was dramatized by the display of two identical garments (products produced by Harwood); the one produced in 1947 cost 100 percent more than the one produced in 1946. The employees were asked to examine each garment and identify the cheaper one. After inspection it became clear that the employees could not identify the less costly garment. In this way the employees recognized and accepted the need for a company cost reduction program. Recommendations from employees were made as to ways costs could be reduced, and a series of special operators were selected to be trained in these new methods. These special operators then developed specific methods to be used in the job.

In the third group, the need for the cost reduction was dramatized as it was for Group 2; however, smaller groups were utilized for discussion, allowing *all* operators to take part in the design of the new jobs (as opposed to the special operators selected in Group 2). In summary, the groups were divided as follows:

Group 1 (control group): Change instituted as usual; no employee participation.

Group 2: Need for the change dramatized to employees so as to create group acceptance; employee participation by representation (special operators).

Group 3: Need for change dramatized; accepted by employees; total group participation in the development of new methods.

After the changes were introduced, Group 1 experienced an initial decline in performance and never again achieved performance equal to that prior to the change. In addition, there was a 17 percent turnover rate in the group in the first 40 days after the change. Group 2 was able to reach a slightly improved level of performance only 14 days after the change was introduced. Within this group there was no turnover and morale remained high. Group 3 improved its performance even more quickly than did Group 2, and performance eventually reached a level 14 percent higher than it was prior to the introduction of the change. This group too had no turnover during the period immediately following the change.

The Harwood results and other research in the field have shown that employee participation in the goal-setting and decision-making processes seems to have a significant impact on employee morale and performance. This concept of employee participation is consistent with the philosophy of job enrichment discussed in our chapter on job design (Chapter 10). It appears that the employees' participation in establishing goals and objectives that they are to achieve creates a greater degree of internalization of these goals and leads to higher levels of commitment and motivation.

Management by Objective

This desire to create an environment in which employees are encouraged to participate in goal setting and decision making has led many corporations to establish programs designed to increase employee involvement in the management process. "Suggestion awards," job simplification programs, and job enrichment all have as one of their prime objectives the increased involvement and participation of employees.

Perhaps the most widely utilized program concept designed to involve employees more actively in the goal-setting process is "management by objective." The concept was first discussed by Peter Drucker in *The Practice of Management*.[3] Drucker's program is usually oriented toward managers at all levels, but the concept applies to employees at any job or position. Drucker attaches a great deal of importance to a manager's need to participate in goal setting. He suggests that a meeting of minds within the management unit can be achieved "only when each of the contributing managers is expected to think through what the unit objectives are, is he to participate actively and responsibly in the work of defining them."[4]

The underlying philosophy behind this participation is that a manager who has had an opportunity to provide input to superiors in establishing objectives regarding his or her own performance will be more likely to better *understand* and *accept* these objectives as they relate to his or her own work effort, identify more closely with these objectives and therefore be more likely to regard them as valid, and by this identification and acceptance will have a greater degree of *commitment* and *motivation* in seeking to achieve the stated objectives. A program of management by objective (MBO) is designed to incorporate each of these points into the superior-subordinate relationship in order to make for a more committed and motivated subordinate. Let us now examine the specific steps that might be taken to implement a program of management by objective.

Establishing Goals

The first step in implementing an MBO program is the establishment of *clear* and *concise* goals of performance which are *accepted* and *understood* by both superior and subordinate. This may seem an obvious point. However, one of the most common mistakes a manager can make is to assume that subordinates know exactly what *is* expected of them. Many managers, for a variety of reasons, fail to take the time to sit down with subordinates and discuss in detail a specific set of performance goals. These managers may feel they have other more important duties to perform, or they may not have thought through themselves what exactly is expected from each subordinate. In addition, it is often difficult for a manager to sit down with a subordinate to discuss the latter's performance, particularly if the subordinate has not been performing up to expectations. In establishing clearly defined and meaningful goals the manager must be as specific as possible.

If the subordinate's area of responsibility lends itself to tangible measurement, the establishment of clearly defined goals can usually be determined straightforwardly. Goals might be defined in terms of a specific increase in dollar sales volume, production output, or quality improvement. In areas such as these measures exist to spell out performance levels at any point in time. With respect to manufacturing and production, for example, most organizations have time standards which measure employee performance quantitatively against an established standard. These performance measures are usually reported to the employee's superior on a weekly basis. Measures such as these might form the basis for a performance goal for a particular manufacturing employee. For example, if a particular worker was performing at an 85 percent level as compared with the time standard for a given job (this would mean the worker took more time to complete the task than was considered normal), the manager might establish a goal of improving the worker's performance to a new level of 95 percent. This goal would be reached over some period of time agreed to by supervisor and worker. In areas where quantitative measure is available, the establishing of these goals is not as difficult as in areas where no measures exist.

In the case of many white-collar jobs the specific performance measurements are often vague. In jobs such as these goals must be established with respect to the less tangible aspects of performance. Here, managers may be able to focus their attention on three major areas of skill development: human relations skills, technical skills, and administrative skills. With respect to each of these skill areas, some areas for consideration in approaching goal definition and measurement are discussed below.

Human relations skill improvement. This would focus on the ability of the subordinate to function effectively in his or her relationships with others. How successful is the individual in working with others in accomplishing a goal or objective? Output in this area might be measured by interaction in work groups, evaluation by coworkers, effectiveness on committees, or performance on joint projects.

Technical skill improvement. This relates to the acquisition or improvement of specific skills needed for success in the current job; e.g., computer programming ability, financial analysis techniques, quantitative methods. Specific handicaps to performance could be discussed with the subordinate.

Administrative skill improvement. Here the manager may wish the subordinate to acquire knowledge and skills that would lead to assuming more responsibility. Administrative skill may relate to the two areas discussed above but may also include leadership training, decision making, and problem solving, as well as training in planning and control procedures.

A manager should evaluate the performance of each subordinate with respect to each of the three major skill areas. Such an evaluation enables the manager to define more specifically the strengths and weaknesses of each worker and thereby to define areas in which improved performance is desirable.

It has been previously mentioned that the established goals should be mutually understood and agreed upon. This objective is often difficult to achieve unless the subordinate has some input in the goal-setting process. It is at this point that the concept of participation enters into the MBO program. Some managers find this concept difficult to accept since they perceive participation by subordinates in establishing goals as an undermining of their own authority. It is felt, too, that allowing subordinates to provide input in goal setting may take more of the manager's time and require more interaction with the subordinate. It should be emphasized, however, that it is precisely this interaction that can bring about the motivation needed for the subordinate's attainment of goals.

There are two simple techniques for the establishment of clear and mutually agreed-upon goals. First, a manager may ask the subordinate to prepare a list of specific goals the subordinate believes he or she can achieve in some specified time period. Second, the manager and subordinate may independently prepare a list of goals and then compare their lists as a basis for discussion.

With the first approach, prior to the subordinate's preparing this list the manager would normally provide the subordinate with guidelines on specific areas of desired goal improvement. The manager may wish to start the conversation with a discussion of the long-range career plans of the subordinate. It may then be possible to narrow down areas in which specific skills will be required for the employee to reach these long-term objectives. If these skills are consistent with the manager's perception of the employee's needs, the employee may then be asked to prepare a list of specific goals and the time frame needed for achievement. The manager could then review and perhaps modify the goals of the subordinate and then discuss these modified goals. When goal modification does take place, the manager should take care not to simply reject the subordinate's goals and substitute his or her own perception of what the subordinate should accomplish. To ignore the concept of mutual agreement in this way will usually cause a great deal of resentment on the part of the subordinate. If this happens, the subordinate is almost sure to lose confidence in the "participation" process and perhaps even reduce performance. If the concept of participation in goal setting is to be effective, then each manager must be prepared to engage in some true give and take with the subordinate. It is up to the manager to determine at what point give and take might be degenerating into an abdication of the manager's leadership role. The key to success is the ability to walk the fine line, allowing input from subordinates and yet still providing managerial leadership and direction.

With the second approach, once lists were developed by both manager and subordinate the two could sit down and compare their lists in order to develop one, mutually agreed upon set of subordinate goals. Manager and subordinate both have an opportunity to see where variations in perception may occur with respect to individual strengths and weaknesses of a subordinate. This process can provide insight to each party regarding the other's expectations and perceptions with respect to subordinate performance.

Perhaps the single most important factor in determining the success of the *mutual* goal-setting process lies in the ability and willingness of the manager to allow true participation by the subordinate. The manager must be willing to take the time necessary to think through his or her expectations regarding this subordinate and must be willing to modify these goals somewhat after interaction with the subordinate. If these two conditions can be met, the manager has gone a long way to attainment of the first step in the implementation of an MBO program.

Specific Plan for Goal Attainment

The next step in the effective implementation of an MBO program is the setting up of a specific plan of action by which the subordinate will seek to achieve the agreed-upon goals or objectives. This plan of action will set out in detail exactly how the subordinate will proceed, what steps will be taken, and what activities will be engaged in as the subordinate progresses. The specific action plan may be developed by both manager and subordinate or by the subordinate alone within a short time after the goals or objectives have been agreed upon.

The manager must again be willing to sit down with each subordinate and review the plan of action once it has been developed. The plan should contain, if possible, certain checkpoints that can be isolated and identified so that periodic review of progress can be made. The plan of action will also detail the specific amount and type of support that will be required by the subordinate in order to achieve the stated objectives. It becomes a planning and control tool from which both the manager and the subordinate can chart progress over time. For the time period in question (the time covered by the plan of action) the plan becomes an integral part of the job description for the subordinate, detailing the exact nature of activities with respect to the goals the subordinate seeks to achieve.

Reward System

We have been discussing the process by which mutually agreed-upon goals may be established, as well as the development of a specific plan of action that can be utilized to chart progress toward these goals. One other condition that must be present in an effective MBO program is a clear definition of the *rewards* the subordinate will derive as a result of achievement. This simply means that in order to truly motivate a subordinate toward the achievement of certain goals, the subordinate must see how the reward system within the organization will tie into these goals.

Some managers may feel somewhat uneasy in this situation, since they may not be used in discussing rewards for performance not yet achieved. Other managers may feel threatened at the prospect of entering into a bargaining process with subordinates—negotiating rewards for goal achievement. Still other managers may not feel they have sufficient control over the reward system, especially in the area of promotion, to be able to promise specific rewards in advance. The degree to which specific rewards need be spelled out will be a function of the degree of trust a subordinate has in the manager. The greater this degree of trust, the less specific the rewards may need to be.

It is absolutely imperative to the continued success of an MBO program that a manager make every effort to carry through on the rewards initially discussed. The rewards associated with goal achievement will usually be pay raises, promotion, additional authority, or increased staff. In addition, job title, office space, or vacations may be explored as possible rewards. The specific rewards desired will be a function of the needs and wishes of each individual subordinate.

Review Process

Thus far, the implementation of the MBO program has consisted of setting up *clear* and *concise* goals that have been *mutually agreed upon,* establishing a *plan of action* to detail how goals are to be achieved, and integrating specific rewards with goal achievement. The next step is the *periodic review process* necessary to monitor progress toward goal achievement. This is a critical component of the MBO program because it indicates to the subordinate the manager's continued interest in achievement. It is in this area that most managers fail to take the time necessary to insure the effective operation of the MBO program. If the subordinate appears to be progressing satisfactorily it is easy for the manager to postpone the review process. If the subordinate does not appear to be progressing, the manager may find it difficult to sit down and discuss the lack of progress. If the discussion does take place, too often it takes the form of criticism of the subordinate rather than a constructive attempt to isolate the causes of lack of progress and the setting up of specific performance improvement objectives for the immediate future.

The manager should regard the review sessions as mutual planning sessions in which both manager and subordinate can discuss progress or problems. In conducting these review sessions the manager must be careful not to create an environment that is hostile or threatening. If the subordinate's progress has been less than expected it is extremely likely that the subordinate will come to the meeting exhibiting a great deal of tension—the extent of this tension will be a function of the results of past interactions with the manager. In this situation the attitude and behavior of the manager should be designed to *help* the subordinate. The manager's comments should help the subordinate perceive the manager as trying to help rather than *criticizing* his or her failure to make sufficient progress. Reasons for lack of progress should be discussed and specific steps detailed as to how to proceed in the future. If genuine disagreements do come to light, they should be carefully spelled out so that both manager and subordinate know the position of the other and how this position is likely to influence future goals and rewards. The review session should be closed with a summary of the discussion as well as an agenda to be discussed at the next review session. Every effort should be made to end the session on a positive note so that the subordinate does not leave the meeting with a sense of failure or lack of accomplishment.

Figure 14.2. *Managers and Subordinates in an MBO Program*

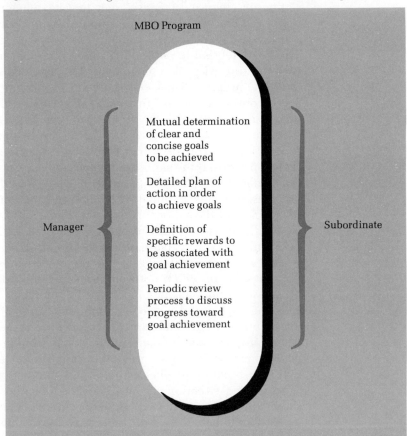

Summary of MBO

In essence, implementation of the MBO program is made up of four essential steps:

1. Establish *clear, mutually understood,* and *agreed-upon goals.*
2. Establish a *plan of action* detailing *how* goals are to be achieved.
3. Set up specific *rewards* to be associated with achievement.
4. Set up and conduct periodic *reviews* designed to discuss progress toward goal achievement.

If these steps are carried out effectively, the manager can usually expect improved motivation in subordinates. An effective MBO program can reduce uncertainty in the mind of the subordinate as to what the superior expects. This reduction in ambiguity creates an environment in which subordinates are more confident and motivated. In addition, defining the relationship between performance and rewards enables both manager and subordinate to deal more effectively with the eventual merit and performance appraisal review related to promotions and pay raises.

Decentralization

There has been a growing trend recently among large corporations to decentralize operations. The reasons for the trend to decentralization are varied. The rapid growth of business as well as the rapidly changing economic and social environment with its corresponding need for quick decisions have placed many top level managers in a situation of information overload. Many managers are faced with an environment in which they can no longer handle all the information necessary to use in the decision-making process. The situation is compounded by the fact that the time available to make many of these decisions is contracting, not expanding. As a result, many top managements have had to turn to a greater degree of decentralization in order to maintain an effective and adaptable organization. *Decentralization* essentially means to move the overall decision-making responsibility further down into the organization. This movement gives added responsibility to managers at all levels below the top. Such a program is in fact consistent with the concept of job enrichment discussed in Chapter 10. Decentralization need not have anything to do with the geographical location of operations nor with the type or number of products offered. It is primarily an organizational change that shifts areas of authority and responsibility as they related to each manager in the company.

A program of decentralization instituted properly can increase the flexibility of the organization in dealing with the constantly changing business and economic environment. An effective decentralization program will enable each manager to make a greater number of decisions with respect to meeting competition or coping with new situations. Since overall decision-making authority has been moved to lower organizational levels, information need no longer travel all the way up through the organizational hierarchy before certain decisions can be made. This capability allows more rapid decision making as well as an increase in the overall flexibility of the organization with respect to market needs. The decision can now be made by the individual closest to the situation rather than by someone higher up who may not be as familiar with the details of the problem. It is apparent that a vital part of any decentralization program is a clear definition of the exact areas in which each manager will have decision-making authority.

Another reason for the trend toward decentralization has to do with the desire on the part of top management to provide a more challenging and satisfying work environment for subordinates. Employees who seek a work environment in which they can test and develop their skills and abilities find that the highly centralized organization, in which most decisions are made at the top, can prove very frustrating. As decision-making responsibility is moved further down, many of these individuals become more involved in the management process and find their jobs more satisfying and rewarding. The decentralization program makes it possible for many talented young employees to assume more responsibility. This requires the use of skills and techniques acquired through either past experience or education. In these situations the individual is given the opportunity to apply his or her knowledge to a specific problem or area of responsibility and to make the decision on how to proceed. These same individuals, having made the decision themselves, are often much more motivated to see their decisions work effectively than they might be if the decision were made higher up and simply passed down to them for implementation. An environment in which greater control is given to lower-level managers is particularly appealing and motivating to many of today's young workers, especially professionals who often seek challenging and responsible opportunities. If management is not responsive to the needs of these employees, the organization will find itself losing many of its most highly qualified and competent young managers.

The fact that decentralization may offer an organization the opportunity to adapt more readily to a changing environment and may provide lower and middle management with a more challenging

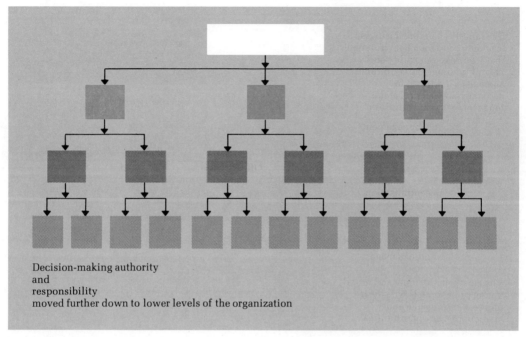

Decision-making authority
and
responsibility
moved further down to lower levels of the organization

Figure 14.3. *Decentralization*

work environment are two of the main reasons for recent trends toward decentralization within many organizations (Figure 14.3). Top management should keep in mind, however, that a shift toward decentralization, if it does represent a significant change in corporate policy, should be undertaken only after careful consideration has been given to a number of variables. Many corporations have found to their regret that the advantages of decentralization may be more than offset by the problems it can create if management does not adequately prepare for its implementation. Some corporations have in fact realized that certain conditions within their own organization make decentralization a *nondesirable* alternative as a means of building a more effective operation. Let us at this point discuss some of the areas that need to be examined prior to embarking on a decentralization program (Figure 14.4).

Philosophy and Orientation of Top Management

In any program of decentralization it will be necessary for the top levels of management to revise the way they carry on their functions. Many of these managers will have to give up some of their authority, which will, in most cases, move to a lower level of the organization

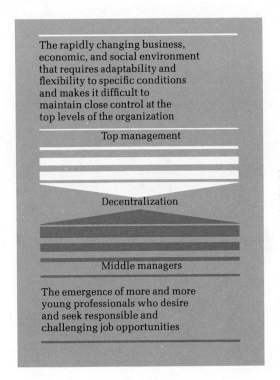

Figure 14.4.

Pressures toward Decentralization

and increase the decision-making responsibility at these lower organizational levels. If this movement of authority is to be successfully implemented, the higher levels of management must be truly willing to allow subordinates more freedom and latitude. The eventual success of any program of decentralization lies in the attitudes and philosophy of top management itself. Will certain managers feel that giving up this authority represents a sign of weakness or failure? If attitudes such as these do prevail and are not dealt with prior to the implementation of a program of decentralization, there is a strong possibility that some of these managers will do everything in their power to *hinder* the program so that it does not succeed. Needless to say, if these people occupy the top levels of the organization they can be quite effective in making the program fail. Top management should therefore seriously review and discuss the proposed changes to insure full agreement and cooperation within this group as to the desirability of such a program. Attitudes and feelings must be aired openly so that the program is not viewed as a threat. This spirit of open communication is not always easily achieved, for rarely will an individual be candid enough to admit he or she may feel threatened by some proposed change in a given situation. In cases such as these, inferences must be drawn from individual as well as group discussions on the topic of decentralization. Care should be taken to recognize what might be considered excessively negative comments as well as emotional rather than rationally based arguments against such a program. If it appears that a significant number of upper-level management personnel are opposed to such a program, serious consideration must be given to whether the program could be successfully implemented.

Attitudes and Skill Levels of Middle Management

If it is concluded that top management is willing to accept a move toward decentralization then attention must be given to an evaluation of the willingness and competence of subordinates who will be asked to assume this additional responsibility. The *willingness* of the subordinates to take on additional responsibility is not generally an issue. Most employees will generally desire a change that enables them to make better use of their abilities. This is particularly true of younger, well-educated workers. Management should never simply assume, however, that this is the case. Some employees continue to be motivated by security and physiological needs, and they might well perceive the additional responsibility not as a challenge but as a threat.

The more serious potential problem with respect to middle management will be the ability of these managers to handle the additional responsibility. This problem may exist for several reasons: (1) the existing centralized top management may have been influential in recruiting subordinates who were not especially strong managers; the selection process may have concentrated on individuals who were very willing to accept direction and decisions from higher up; (2) since not a great deal of responsibility was attached to many of the middle management positions, the salary level may have been lower and as a result the more capable employees may have left for better paying jobs; (3) the competent and enterprising individual employed in such a centralized environment may well have left after a short time to seek a job offering greater challenge and opportunity.

The point is that before a decentralization program can be instituted, a judgment must be made as to the capabilities of the individuals who will have to assume the decision-making responsibility. If they are not equipped to handle the additional responsibility, management must decide whether to replace these individuals or to develop suitable training programs to equip them with necessary skills. A training program would normally focus on the development of leadership and decision-making skills, which are critical under a program of decentralization. Such programs may be provided in house by the corporation or they may be developed in conjunction with a local college or university executive program.

**Corporate
Policies**

One area that must be included in the preparation and training prior to implementation of a decentralization program would be a complete analysis and evaluation of existing corporate policies. Many centralized corporations have never found it necessary to take adequate time to set down in writing the policies that guide their decision making. In highly centralized organizations very often this is not necessary because one or a very few top managers make all major decisions. For a small group, formally written policy statements may not be needed.

A program of decentralization, however, requires managers scattered throughout the organization to make decisions regarding their own areas of responsibility. To provide guidelines to these middle managers it is necessary to have precise, clearly written policy statements that will define the attitudes, philosophy, and direction of the corporation. Without these policies there would be no assurance that the decisions made by even the most competent middle managers would be *consistent* throughout the organization nor that they would lead the organization in the desired direction. Thus, policy statements must provide the guidelines to insure that even though many members of middle management are now making decisions which affect the total organization, the overall result will move the company in some consistent direction toward a desired set of goals. Divisions and departments must not work at cross purposes. The specific areas for which policies must be defined will of course vary with the particular company. In general, policy statements should cover those situations that top management feels are critical to the effectiveness, image, or goals of the organization as a whole. Policies may define the corporate position on issues such as product quality, pricing, credit, advertising, personnel, and hiring practices.

As many corporate managers have discovered, the writing of effective policy statements is not easy. One reason is simply that many managers have not had much experience in formal policy formulation. A second, more critical, reason lies in the fact that while the purpose of any policy statement is to serve as a guide to decision making it must still allow enough flexibility for each decision maker to handle his or her circumstances or situation. If the policy statement is so rigidly worded that no flexibility is permitted, then decision-making authority has not truly been passed downward. On the other hand, a policy statement that is too vaguely worded may not provide a sufficient guideline for consistent decision making throughout the organization. The key to success is therefore the ability to develop policy statements that provide guidelines for decision making yet allow for flexibility in their application.

Control Procedures

Another area to be considered when instituting a program of decentralization is the system of *control procedures* to be used in monitoring decision making. A well-defined system of control procedures is necessary in order to enable top management to determine the effectiveness of decisions made by subordinates. Without some method of control, top management would have difficulty evaluating the performance of middle managers and would therefore find it hard to determine the extent to which corporate goals were being met. It should be noted that the essential difference between *policies* and *control procedures* is that policies seek to guide decision making *before* the fact, while control procedures seek to determine the effectiveness of decisions *after* the fact. By far, the most common control procedures utilized by decentralized organizations are *financial*. The budget is one very common example of a control procedure. By use of budget comparisons such as projected expenses versus actual data over some period of time a manager is able to evaluate the effectiveness of subordinates' decision making. In some cases budgeted versus actual results can provide information on areas in which a given manager may be performing unsatisfactorily. Although the budget is an effective control procedure it can only present one aspect of subordinate performance. It does not provide the manager with information on the less tangible aspects of what is going on: Did a subordinate jeopardize the long-run good of a corporation by reducing R and D or advertising expenditures in order to meet short-term budget projections? It is this type of information that requires a manager to evaluate each situation somewhat subjectively. The budget figures alone do not give a true picture of the overall effectiveness of an employee.

One problem area that has caused legitimate concern among middle managers who are involved in a decentralization program is that in many cases they are not in complete control over all of the factors for which they may be held responsible; a given manager might be responsible for manufacturing costs but may not have control of the purchase of raw materials which made up a significant portion of these costs. This problem has led many corporations to turn to a profit center concept of decentralization. Under the profit center concept, a corporate department or division is considered as an individual entity and all concerns pertaining to that entity are placed under the responsibility of a single manager. In this situation a manager can be held responsible for meeting return on investment or profit projection in the area over which he or she has control. This approach allows top management to evaluate the overall decision-making ability of a given manager more meaningfully. In addition, the profit center concept allows young managers to gain valuable experience in decision-making areas that involve a wide variety of situations and variables; it provides them with an effective training ground for future growth and development.

Organizational Structure

The extent to which a corporation can move toward decentralizing operations will to some degree be influenced by the type of organizational structure the corporation has. We indicated earlier that some organizational structures lend themselves more readily to decentralization than others. We will again consider three basic structural types: functional, product, and geographical. (For a review of these structural types refer to Chapter 11.) In the *functional structure,* the basic business functions form the individual units of the organization. The *product structure* divides the organization

Figure 14.5. *Product Structure*

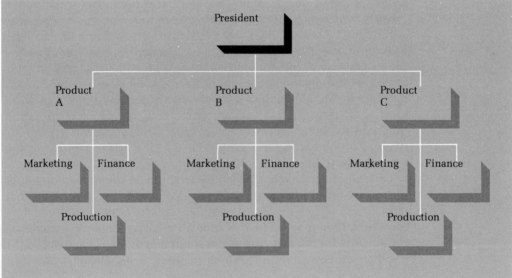

according to the various products or groupings of products the organization produces. The *geographical structure* divides the organization according to the geographical markets or regions served.

We note that in the *functional* type of structure a decision affecting a given product can be made only at the top level of the organization (see Figure 11.1). In this structure it is necessary that the decision be made by the president—the only one who is directly responsible for all aspects of that product. On the other hand, with respect to either the *product* or *geographical* structure, a decision affecting a given product can be made at the next lower level within the organization, the vice-presidential level. We may conclude that these latter structures (product, geographical) lend themselves a little more readily to a program of decentralization and particularly to the profit-center concept, since they tend to allow division into more distinct and easily divided units (see Figures 14.5 and 14.6).

In addition to the type of departmental grouping just discussed, another element of the structure that will have an impact on a program of decentralization is the overall span of control at each level within the organization. The *span of control,* as you will recall from Chapter 11, refers to the number of subordinates reporting to a single manager. As the span of control for an individual manager becomes wider, that is, the number of subordinates supervised increases, it becomes more and more difficult for the manager to maintain close

Figure 14.6. *Geographical Structure*

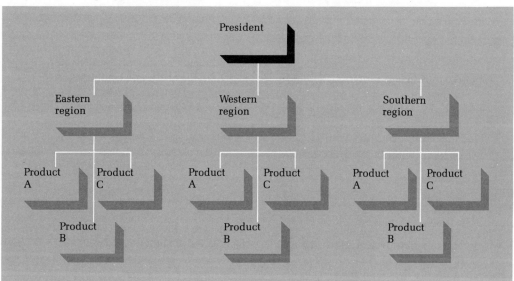

supervision over each subordinate. This being the case, managers who have wide spans of control (large numbers of subordinates reporting to them) often find it necessary to give up some decision-making authority to their immediate subordinates, if for no other reason than that they simply lack time. It would thus appear to be the case that, in general, wide spans of control tend to be consistent with decentralization of decision-making authority. These wider spans of control will normally create an environment in which subordinates are able to exercise a greater degree of judgment and latitude in the carrying out of their day-to-day activities.

In summary, a program of decentralization should not be initiated until the following points have been adequately settled:

1. *Top management:* is willing to give up authority for decision making.
2. *Middle management:* is capable and is willing to accept new responsibility.
3. *Policies:* are adequate to guide decision making but are not unduly restrictive.
4. *Control:* system exists to evaluate effectiveness of middle management decisions.
5. *Existing structure:* must lend itself to, or can be modified to, facilitate decentralized operations.

Discussion Questions

1. With your knowledge of individual behavior, explain the results of the Coch and French study at the Harwood Manufacturing Plant.
2. Define what is meant by *management by objective* (MBO).
3. Discuss the steps necessary to implement an MBO program.
4. What is meant by decentralization?
5. What factors should be considered before an organization undertakes a program of decentralization?
6. Discuss how MBO and decentralization can create a more challenging and satisfying work environment for organizational employees.
7. Discuss some advantages and disadvantages of providing greater opportunity for employee participation within an organization.

Case for Discussion

John Walker, director of the data processing division of a large midwestern computer corporation, decided the time had come to reorganize the divisional structure to take better advantage of some of the recently installed automated equipment.

To allow participation of each of his departmental managers, he called a meeting to discuss ways in which the reorganization might take place. The current divisional organization was comprised of three departments—data preparation, operations, and programming—each under a department manager.

Mr. Walker began by stating his reasons for wanting a reorganization and then asked each manager for input as to how the reorganization might take place. After each manager had spoken, it was clear that there was disagreement among them. Mr. Walker adjourned the meeting, announcing he would consider all ideas and make his decision the following day.

The next afternoon, Mr. Walker sent a memo to each manager presenting in detail his decisions on the new organizational structure. The new structure incorporated the basic ideas of the manager of the data preparation, rather than the suggestions of the other two managers. After reading the memo, the managers of operations and programming came to Mr. Walker's office and indicated their dissatisfaction with the decision, saying that they had had no "input" into the final decision.

Seeing that two of his department managers were upset with his decision and not wanting to destroy the spirit of participation that he had tried to foster, Mr. Walker called his managers together once again and asked them to meet without him to reach a new agreement regarding the reorganization.

After a week of meetings, the three managers submitted a set of recommendations for the proposed reorganization. After reading these recommendations, it was clear to Mr. Walker that the proposal contained features that were completely unacceptable.

Selected References

Carroll, S. and Tosi, Henry. *Management by Objectives.* New York: Macmillan Co., 1973.

Coch, Lester and French, John. "Overcoming Resistance to Change." *Human Relations 1* (1948).

Davis, K. *Human Behavior at Work.* 4th ed. New York: McGraw-Hill, 1972.

Drucker, Peter. *The Practice of Management.* New York: Harper & Row, 1954.

———. *Managing for Results.* New York: Harper & Row, 1964.

French, J., Ross, I. C., Kirby, S., Nelson, J. R., and Smyth, P. "Employee Participation in a Program of Industrial Change." In *Personnel* 35, No. 3 (1958).

Homans, G. *The Human Group.* New York: Harcourt Brace & World, 1950.

Humble, John, ed. *Management by Objectives in Action.* London: McGraw-Hill, 1970.

Katz, D. and Kahn, R. *The Social Psychology of Organizations,* 2nd ed. New York: John Wiley & Sons, 1978.

Likert, R. *The Human Organization.* New York: McGraw-Hill, 1977.

Luthans, Fred. *Organizational Behavior.* New York: McGraw-Hill, 1977.

McGregor, Douglas. *The Human Side of Enterprise.* New York: McGraw-Hill, 1960.

Olmsted, M. *The Small Group.* New York: Random House, 1959.

Porter, D., Applewhite, P., and Misshauk, M. *Studies in Organizational Behavior and Management,* 2nd ed. Scranton, Pa.: Intext, 1971.

Richards, M. and Greenlaw, P. *Management Decision-Making.* Homewood, Ill.: Richard D. Irwin, 1966.

Scott, W. *Organization Theory.* Homewood, Ill.: Richard D. Irwin, 1967.

Webber, Ross. *Management.* Homewood, Ill.: Richard D. Irwin, 1975.

Management Training and Executive Development

15

The Big Business of Teaching Managers

Managing a company may be more complex than ever, but executives who want help in the form of in-house training, at-home courses, outside seminars, and how-to books do not have far to look these days. Training and information services for management make up a booming business, not only for such old-line organizations as the American Management Assns. and the Conference Board, but for a host of competitors that includes consultants, universities, magazine publishers, trade associations, and business school professors turned entrepreneurs.

"The services fill a void for very practical training," says Jay Jacobs, director of human resources at Black & Decker Mfg. Co. "It's a void that is missed by formal academic education, and most companies are too small to afford development and training departments of their own to do this kind of work." Even those companies that can afford to develop their own training programs usually cannot do it all.

Beefing Up

As a result of this void, many training and management organizations are growing rapidly, helped along by the upward curve of the business cycle. AMA membership rose to 59,300 from 52,538 in the last 18 months. Its Center for Management Development now stages 2,000 meetings a year for 47,000 participants. Revenues jumped to an estimated $50 million in the fiscal year that ended last month, from $39.5 million in fiscal 1976. And the AMA is beefing up its sales force to capitalize further on what it sees as a growing market. In the past year it has increased its regional sales force by one-third, to 24, and the AMA's senior

Reprinted from the July 25, 1977 issue of *Business Week* by special permission. Copyright © 1977 by McGraw-Hill Publishing, Inc., New York, N.Y. 10020. All rights reserved.

vice-president for operations, John Budlong, expects the sales force to be several times larger within three years.

The Conference Board, which has 4,000 "supporters" and which had revenues of $13.1 million in the fiscal year that ended in May, expects to open a West European operation in Brussels this fall. It will be similar to the one the organization already has in Canada.

Some of the smaller, newer service firms are doing even better. The Sterling Institute, which was turned into a full-time business four years ago by former Harvard Business School Professor J. Sterling Livingston, claims to be doing some $4 million worth of business this year, a 40% increase over 1976. Among companies that have bought "master licenses" for Sterling's video cassette programs at prices ranging from $100,000 to $375,000 are Scott Paper, Coca-Cola, and Abbott Laboratories.

Inside Jobs

The universities are cashing in, too. The University of Michigan, which is currently staging a program for public utility executives, offers 51 different seminars for managers. "The market is expanding faster than our collective ability to fill it," says Albert W. Schrader, director of Michigan's division of management education. "We are turning people away. Many of our programs are full months in advance."

Among the most effective competitors of the management services companies are corporations' own in-house training units. Crown Zellerbach, which has a $300,000 training budget, hired a former consultant a year ago to bring new ideas into its management training program. Although some managers will still go to outside courses, Crown Zellerbach's training director,

Robert Wall, says the company's own staff is more effective.

Fluor Corp., the Irvine (Calif.) construction company, also makes limited use of outsiders, depending more on an internal training staff. John M. Blackmore, Fluor's director of training, claims he can stage a three-day seminar in-house at $40 per person, while outside organizations would charge at least $350 per person for the same course. Last year Fluor trained 2,700 of its own supervisors, and next year it expects the number to reach 3,500.

More than cost is involved, of course. Some of the training directors do not like much of what is offered by outsiders. Many of the training organizations, including the AMA, "are moving away from functional areas of management—marketing, law, finance," complains Blackmore, "and into fad or human-relations areas, such as transactional analysis, transcendental meditation, assertiveness training, and the quality of working conditions." Blackmore labels such seminars "scope programs," and he says they can be performed better by such TV programs as 60 Minutes.

Custom-Made

To combat the companies' do-it-yourself trend, many professional trainers are increasingly tailoring their product to the specific needs of potential customers. Sun Co., for example, trains 1,500 to 2,000 personnel a year, but the AMA provides many of the materials and trains Sun's trainers.

"More and more, the smart groups will tailor their programs to a company, with front-end analysis to find out what gaps are there, and then plug in whatever training is necessary," says Daniel Lobash, training manager at United Bank of Denver.

Filling in gaps is the name of the training game. The U.S. Chamber of Commerce offers executives a week-long, $750 crash course in becoming Washington-wise. The Columbus Div. of Battelle Memorial Institute, capi-

The Wide Diversity of Services for Management: A Sampling of Organizations Offering Services to Train and Inform Managers

Organization	Services
American Management Associations	Management courses, books, audio cassettes, in-house training, Presidents' Assn., Extension Institute, Planning Center
Battelle Memorial Institute	Technical Inputs to Planning, a subscription program designed to bridge management-technology gap
Conference Board	Conferences, seminars, publications, custom research, chief executive lunches
Institutional Investor	Financially oriented seminars, Institutional Investor Institute by annual subscription for corporate executives
Mantread Inc.	Clearing house for management training programs and seminars, and for evaluation of training
Sterling Institute	Standard courses and custom-tailored management development training conducted in-house
Strategic Planning Institute	Data bank based on information from 150 companies, analysis of data for corporate members
University of Pittsburgh	Executive MBA program, middle-management program, two-day conferences, training programs tailored for specific companies

talizing on its technological expertise, is launching a new management service this fall, "Technical Inputs to Planning." For a $4,500 subscription fee, it allows a company's managers to attend conferences, have a Battelle expert at their company for a day, and receive reports—all intended to bridge the gap between technology and management.

Mantread Inc., a company that acts as a clearinghouse for member companies facing the array of training programs and outside seminars, estimates that there are more than 1,000 suppliers of such services and well over 3,000 programs. But a trend in the direction of mass training, especially in the booming management-development courses, may begin to concentrate most of the business in a few large firms.

All Levels

"Instead of sending people off to programs in groups of 1 to 25, companies are sending managers through all at once," says Sterling's Livingston. "We have several clients who have put 500 to 1,000 managers through our video programs this year. Some plan to put 5,000 through in the next several years." New trainees are coming from all levels of management. The AMA has its Presidents Assn., an exclusive group of some 1,900 presidents and chief executives, whose membership is up from 1,400 just four years ago. And the Conference Board offers its CEO luncheons and conferences. Conference Board President Kenneth A. Randall has spoken at 20 of the luncheons so far this year.

But it is the upsurge in the training of middle- and lower-level managers, along with an increased desire on the part of the companies to "develop" such talent, that is at the heart of the training boom. "We're sending more middle managers to outside training services now because we're interested in developing the management of the future," says John Stapleton, vice-president for organization and personnel at

International Minerals & Chemical Corp. IMC's use of outside training services has risen about 25% in the last five years.

Consumer Complaints

When companies begin training so many managers, either in-house or outside, evaluating the alternative programs—and the results—becomes increasingly difficult. That is why some 70 corporations now subscribe to Mantread's services, which include evaluations of programs by managers in its subscribing companies. "Companies are getting more and more concerned because so many have been burned," says Mantread Vice-President John R. Savage.

Complaints are indeed common. One of the most frequent is that the quality of even the same program can vary widely, depending on the instructor. "The fact is that a lot of the AMA's seminar programs just aren't any good because they really don't control the quality or content of the instruction," says one organization vice-president. "Some of the people they bring back year after year aren't that good."

The AMA's Budlong contends that registrants' own ratings of the association's meetings have been rising steadily for the past five years. But he says that the AMA, which has been using two volunteer instructors for each one that is paid, is now tending to use paid trainers because volunteer executives are harder to find—particularly for programs held in several cities. "The quality generally is not as high in sessions where volunteers predominate," Budlong admits.

Taking Stock

The final test, of course, is whether the training helps the manager perform better. Many training firms, as well as their client companies, now ask not only participants for an evaluation but also query their bosses on whether the training improved the participants' performance. Peter Janetos, second vice-president at John Hancock Mutual

Life Insurance Co., says that his staff debriefs all those who have attended outside training programs. If he gets two or three bad reports in a row, he says, "we may drop a specific program for two or three years before we try it again."

Meanwhile, some companies have even called a halt to training until they can better evaluate what it is accomplishing. "Training is a mishmash in most companies—and in Saga," says William J. Crockett, Saga Corp.'s human resources vice-president. Saga's $10,000 training budget has been suspended until the company can decide what its training needs are. "This is one area where companies can blow a lot of money," cautions Crockett. "It's hard to measure the results. It's a mystique. We want a better answer for ourselves."

THIS CHAPTER will focus on individual development within the organization, with particular emphasis on programs designed to develop executive potential. Most employees involved in these programs are college educated. We will seek to analyze the conditions, situations, and behavioral changes marking the development of people as they progress through the organizational structure.

Education and Jobs

One of the most cherished ideas in America is that the most certain way to guarantee success in our society is to obtain a good education in particular, a college degree. In recent years, however, the correlation between a college education and job security has been eroded to the point that the college degree no longer guarantees its holder a secure job. Our country has been experiencing a surplus of college graduates in some fields, such as education, a lack of job opportunities in other fields, such as the liberal arts and social sciences, and the cancellation of government contracts, which has eliminated many jobs in engineering and hard sciences. Consequently, part of the glamor of the college degree has faded dramatically in recent years. When these facts are combined with the salary and fringe benefit advances that have been made by organized labor, Americans no longer believe that a college degree guarantees superior financial rewards.

College education is no longer regarded as the American dream. Indeed, the status of a college education has reached a point where fewer and fewer of our college-age children choose to attend college. It is even thought that "for the first time in our history the next generation may be less well educated than the last one."[1]

Along with a change in attitude regarding the desirability of a college education, there has also been a change in the philosophy and orientation of our youth in the last ten years. Emphasis on the more aesthetic and cultural values has shifted toward a desire for practical and salable skills. Enrollments in colleges and universities have undergone a trend from the liberal arts and social sciences toward the more technical and professional fields. This shift has resulted from the fact that it is mainly in the professional and technical areas that one is now likely to find jobs. Contrary to what the corporate president might say to the commencement class, the corporation is not overly interested in the well-educated generalist who is able to communicate effectively. The college recruiter for that same company almost invariably is seeking individuals with specific skills—often technical—that can be readily and immediately applied within the business organization. As a result of this situation more and more college curricula are being modified to provide skills that are marketable.

More and more colleges and universities are involving the business community in their efforts to design a curriculum to meet the needs and desires of the corporation and thus result in greater job opportunities for graduates. Colleges such as Northeastern University in Boston, which alternates full-time classroom and full-time work experience for students, or the University of Southern California, whose internship program requires each full-time (day) student in the MBA to spend a semester working in a corporation on a job-related problem, are examples of universities that are attempting to provide the student with real-world skills and experiences.

The College Graduate and Jobs

As we have mentioned earlier, the young worker today comes to the job market with different values and expectations than did workers in previous generations. The following factors have been listed as "very important" and "important" to the new college graduate in evaluating job opportunities:

Very important

Opportunity for advancement.
Social status and prestige—the feeling of doing something important and the recognition of this by others.
Responsibility.
Opportunities to use special aptitudes and educational background.
Challenge and adventure.
Opportunity to be creative and original.
High salary.

Important, but less so

A stable and secure future.
A chance to exercise leadership.
Opportunity to work with people rather than things.
Freedom from supervision.
Opportunity to be helpful to others.[2]

With these factors in mind, newly recruited college graduates may perceive their first job experience to be frustrating and lacking in opportunity for creative expression. Indeed, many recruiters believe that most graduates are really not aware of what the real world of work is like and as a result come to the job experience with unrealistic expectations. It is often in the first full job experience that these somewhat unrealistic expectations may collide with the realities of the job situation. If the impact results in a high level of frustration, the young employee may leave the organization and seek new challenges in another work environment. This situation is recognized by most corporations. There is a general feeling among corporate executives that everything evens out. Some new employees that leave after training are replaced by young people that have been trained elsewhere. In some cases the young graduate continues to move from job to job until he or she finds a job with the desired level of opportunity or else his or her expectations are reduced until they *are* "satisfied" in a job with less opportunity and challenge.

Job Challenges and Responsibility

In an effort to provide more challenging opportunities for young college graduates, more and more companies are making efforts to put them in jobs with more responsibility. This approach, sometimes referred to as "sink or swim," is typified by a program developed at Michigan Bell in the mid-1960s.[3] In this program newly hired MBA graduates were given complete responsibility for the administration of an entire department. Technical aid and assistance were provided, but decision-making authority and financial responsibility rested with the young manager. At the end of one year the new manager's performance in all areas was evaluated. This evaluation meant either that the manager left the company or was given additional responsibility. This program, enabling the new graduate to demonstrate his or her skills immediately, eliminated years of frustration and waiting around in the corporate structure. The price for participating in this type of program may of course be great for those who fail to perform effectively. Failure could result in permanent scars, which could have a long-term effect on both the confidence and employment record of the unsuccessful individual in other organizations.

Training programs such as this one and others that will be discussed later in the chapter are designed to enable the newly hired college graduate to translate theoretical concepts and techniques into real-world applications in the business environment. The ability to do this is imperative if the college graduate is to succeed in positions of responsibility in any organization.

But even though programs of this type may seem to answer the needs of young people, the fact remains that they are not appropriate for everyone. Many students who graduate from college are not psychologically prepared to assume the level of responsibility demanded in the Michigan Bell program. Even though most students would indicate that they would find such a program desirable and challenging, experience has shown that some of these students, when given the opportunity to perform, prove themselves unable to handle the situation. This was demonstrated in the Entrepreneurship Program at the University of Southern California. This program confers a master's degree in business, and its curriculum is designed to develop the entrepreneurial abilities of participating students. Pursuant to this objective, the students are given a great deal of freedom to do things like develop venture proposals during the course of their program. Experience has shown that many of these students, although *intellectually capable* of handling the work, are not emotionally and psychologically prepared to handle the freedom and lack of specific direction provided by the curriculum. This inability runs contrary to one of the most necessary characteristics of the entrepreneur, namely, the ability to work on one's own in carrying out a project.

With this thought in mind, we may soon see testing, evaluation, and counseling programs in both academic and business environments that will help individuals determine whether or not they possess not only the intellectual ability but also the emotional and psychological maturity to perform well in a given job environment. Such an evaluation program would not deny anyone access to any field, but it would communicate to individuals the extent to which they might find it satisfying or frustrating.

Obsolescence and the Job

Within the constantly changing environment in which we find ourselves, effective job performance in our early years of employment no longer provides a guarantee of future advancement in the organizational structure. As the technological, legal, and sociological environment of our society becomes more and more complex, it is no longer possible for the skills acquired in college to last an individual through retirement. As one executive recently stated, "I'm in a race between obsolescence and retirement, and I'm afraid obsolescence is winning." This situation is becoming more and more common among middle-aged employees in our corporations. As one survey demon-

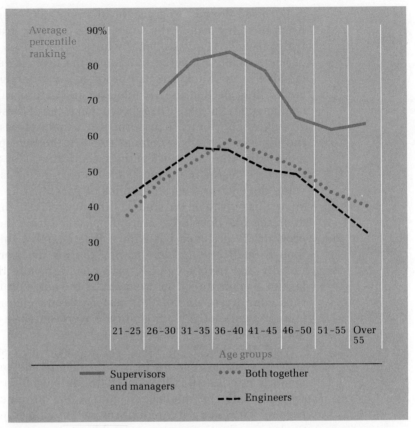

Figure 15.1. *Comparison of Age and Performance Rankings of Managers and Engineers*

Source: G. Dalton and P. Thompson, "Accelerating Obsolescence of Older Engineers," *Harvard Business Review,* September–October 1971, p. 111. Copyright © 1971 by the President and Fellows of Harvard College; all rights reserved.

strated, there is a general tendency for performance—as perceived by management—of both supervisors and engineers to deteriorate at about age 40 (Figure 15.1).[4]

Technical obsolescence is not the only reason for deteriorating job performance. There are often many other factors that contribute to lower performance as one reaches middle age. The fact remains, however, that our rapidly changing society makes it more and more difficult for the average professional to keep up with changes and developments that are taking place within his or her field.

In an effort to combat this increasing likelihood of employee obsolescence, more and more universities and private corporations are designing and developing programs of *continuing education* whose purpose is to provide individuals with updated old skills and the acquisition of new skills within a particular field. For such programs to be effective, however, employees must establish an attitude that enables them to adapt to a constantly changing environment. The burden falls on the individual employee to recognize and accept the fact that he or she must constantly grow and develop professionally to remain effective in the modern organization. This requires the individual to be eager to maintain up-to-date skills to be applied within the job environment.[5]

With this kind of approach an individual looks beyond his or her current job to anticipate possible job opportunities or advancement in the future. The individual should take the time and effort to plan a career path designed to foster advancement and growth over time. Within many organizations there is often a clearcut path or ladder of jobs, one building on the other, which describes the standard development of an individual within that organization. New employees should attempt to identify such jobs within their organization and then chart their progress with respect to new job opportunities they may be offered. Care should be taken by the individual that he or she does not "plateau-out" (move into a job with limited or no growth or advancement opportunities) within the organization and as a result limit future development potential.

A second aspect of this approach involves the recognition and acceptance that our society is indeed in a state of constant change. Such change is evidenced by the simple statistic that approximately 20 percent of our nation's work force changes address each year. In addition, General Electric Corporation estimates that 30 percent of its revenue comes from products which were nonexistent twenty years ago. Facts such as these attest to the rapid changes taking place in our society with respect to both technological advancement and increase in the mobility of our labor force.

It has always been a characteristic of youth to anticipate, accept, and even seek to bring out change. As one advances in age, however, one has a tendency to become more complacent and even reluctant to accept changes. This reluctance can often prevent an individual from viewing change with an open mind and thereby recognizing the value that may result from a modification of current policy or procedure.

A third element of career planning requires each individual to recognize and develop the *applicability* of the skills and techniques he or she already has learned. An important value of the educational process is for the individual to *apply* knowledge to some problem, situation, or condition. More and more business organizations, as well as society in general, have learned to recognize the difference between "textbook knowledge" and "street wisdom." The former represents an awareness of facts and a general understanding of ideas, the latter representing the ability to use data and experience in dealing with the problems of the real world.

Finally, every individual should seek to learn, grow, and develop in areas which are likely prospects for future career development. In a society characterized by an information explosion, in which the number of texts, journals, articles, and other sources of information far exceeds any individual's ability to keep up with what is going on in the world, each individual must be selective in order to focus those areas in which he or she may expect a career to develop. Granted that many corporate executives have found themselves in jobs which they could not have anticipated early in their career, the fact remains that each of us should prepare as well as possible for likely job requirements in the future.

In summary, the following would represent an approach that might be utilized to strive for maximum professional growth and development.

Look beyond the current job in order to develop a career path.
Anticipate change and be willing to accept it.
Learn to apply new techniques and skills to real-world situations.
Be selective in learning, developing those skills that are most likely to be required in a desired career.

Management Training

There are few modern corporations of any size that do not engage in some form of training for their supervisors and managers. The fact that most organizations have such training programs does not necessarily indicate that they are effective in developing the talents and skills of their young managers. In this section we will discuss some approaches that might be utilized in developing training programs that succeed in their objectives.

Objectives of the Program

Perhaps one of the most important—yet most often neglected—aspects in the development of a management training program is the need to define exactly what objectives are to be achieved. Too often a corporation institutes a training program without considering carefully the needs of the employees who will participate. The corporation often seems to be motivated by a desire to "have a program" rather than by a true desire to develop its young managers. With this situation in mind, let us examine three of the most fundamental objectives that should serve as the basis for the initiation of a management training program.

Developing an Awareness of Corporate Policy and Procedure. The most basic objective of a management training program is to develop in new managers an awareness of how the company behaves and why. A program with this aim usually focuses on newly hired or newly appointed managers. It is designed to familiarize these individuals with corporate operations. Newly hired college graduates are usually required to participate in a program of this type, and in many cases it may be their first opportunity to make a transition between theoretical and conceptual knowledge and every-day corporate policy and decision making. The theme of many such programs might be, "We don't know what you were told when you were being recruited, but this is the way it really is."

Programs of this type make the participant aware of the way things work within the organization. Attention focuses on such areas as policies, procedures, channels of communication, decision making, and chain of command. The objective of such a program is to provide the newly hired manager with an understanding of how to function effectively within that organization. Rather than training managers for advancement within the organization, the purpose is to aid them to do a better job in the position they now occupy. Programs of this type are usually of relatively short duration (perhaps 1–3 weeks) and are normally begun as soon as possible after the manager begins his or her employment.

Developing Improved Skill Levels. A second objective of management training may be to develop skills that will enable the manager to perform his or her current job with increased effectiveness or to prepare the individual for future advancement. Skill-oriented training programs usually focus on such areas as communication (speaking, writing), financial analysis (accounting, financial statements), or technical expertise (computer programming, quantitative techniques). They are usually of relatively short duration, some perhaps only 3 or 4 hours in length, and may be offered periodically during a manager's career. More and more often corporations are looking outside their own walls in order to provide such skill development courses. Local high school, college, and university programs are often utilized in order to provide training in these skill development areas.

Executive Development. A third objective of management training would be at the heart of programs designed to develop skills and talents perceived as necessary for the advancement of managers to more responsible positions. Programs of this type (about which more will be said later) are usually more broad-based than either procedural or skill level training. They usually include training in leadership development, behavioral concepts, administrative skills such as planning and control techniques, and the structure and design of organizations. Programs of this type may run from a few weeks to several months, with participation usually limited to managers who have been earmarked for advancement. In almost all cases programs of this type are provided and administered by colleges and universities that specialize in such programs.

The Objectives of the Program and the Needs of the Corporation

Once aware of what may be achieved through management training, the corporation must analyze its own situation in order to determine which type of program or programs would be best suited to meet its own needs at a given point in time. In order to make such a determination the organization will normally examine two components of its current operation, the nature of the management positions currently utilized by the company (position analysis) and the capabilities of the specific individuals occupying these positions (manpower analysis).

Position Analysis. The purpose of position analysis is to determine the exact nature of the jobs being performed in the organization. The analysis should focus on the skills, talents, and abilities that may be required by managerial positions within the organization. The key question is, "What does it take to perform this job effectively?" Care should be taken to isolate and identify specific areas that are necessary components of each job and that may lend themselves to development through training.

For lower-level managerial positions identifying likely areas for management training is fairly straightforward. Such areas usually identify *themselves* by the very nature of the position. For example, the position of manager of quality control would most certainly require a knowledge of the latest quantitative techniques for making statistical applications to problems of inspection and sampling.

It is at the upper levels of management that position analysis becomes most difficult. Once we begin to examine the positions of vice-president or director, an exact analysis of specific job requirements is far more difficult. With these positions there is a tendency for training programs to shift from an orientation of developing specific skills and talents toward the development of broader abilities.

Manpower Analysis. Manpower analysis is a necessary complement to position analysis. The purpose of the manpower analysis is to assess the skills, abilities, and performance of current management personnel as compared with the skills and abilities required by their jobs. Such a comparison will enable top management to determine those areas most in need of development through training. The manpower analysis would seek to identify those areas in which specific managers may need improvement, either for their current position or for possible advancement. In addition, the likelihood of the effectiveness of the training program may be assessed. It may be perceived by top management that because of certain individuals' past experience, education, or attitude, these managers may not be capable of developing needed skills through training. In such situations alternatives may need to be explored in order for managerial effectiveness to be maintained. When managerial performance indicates that specific skills may be lacking in the manager's background but there is a likelihood that, through effective training, these skills may be acquired, then appropriate training programs may be developed. For example, as a result of MBO (management by objective) programs utilized by many organizations, individual managers are learning which skills and abilities they need to develop in order to improve performance or prepare for advancement.

Types of Training Activity

Let us now examine some of the more common types of training methods included in most corporate management training programs.

On-the-Job-Training (OJT). Perhaps the most common as well as the most basic method of training would be through skills, knowledge, and abilities acquired in actual work experience. This training method can be highly effective because the skills and abilities learned obviously have *direct* application to the job experience. In addition, the cost to the company is minimal since the utilization of OJT does not require development and administration of a formal training program.

Although OJT may often form part of the overall training program, rarely can the corporation rely on OJT as its only method of management development. OJT often has limitations which prevent this method of training from meeting the total needs of the corporation. The pressure of the job itself may often interfere with the learning process of the new manager. In such situations, the individual may be so caught up in the daily situation that he or she may fail to recognize and learn the lesson of the job experience. Another limitation is that the job experience may provide only for the development of skills needed to perform the current job; it may not provide any opportunity to acquire new skills for job advancement. Thus the manager who has performed the same job for five years may have acquired one year of experience five times over, rather than five years experience.

Job Rotation. Somewhat related to OJT, a job rotation training program moves the trainee from one job to another over some period of time. The purpose of this rotation is to familiarize the individual with the skills and abilities that may be required by other jobs as well as to make the individual aware of the interrelationships that exist between one job and another. This rotation process provides the individual with a broader overview of corporate operation. In addition, as the individual becomes more aware of the nature of different jobs, new skills and abilities are developed which may allow the manager greater latitude in future advancement.

Job rotation programs have also been utilized in blue collar work areas as a way of reducing the level of frustration and monotony that may often result from repetitive job requirements. Within these programs, individual workers are given the opportunity to work on different jobs over a period of time and thus are provided with some degree of variety.

Lectures. Another basic and often used method of training is the classic classroom lecture. This method is both simple and inexpensive and has proven to be relatively effective in communicating certain types of information and knowledge. Its greatest advantage is when the information to be communicated is factual in nature and not subject to misunderstanding. In this case the lecture method can provide a great deal of information to a large number of people in a relatively short period of time.

The difficulty with the lecture method lies in its inability to deal on a one-on-one basis with individuals. Lack of individual participation can greatly hinder the learning process, particularly when the individuals involved are full-time working managers who may find it difficult to maintain close attention throughout a lengthy lecture session.

Case Discussions. A variation of the lecture method is case discussion. Utilizing this methodology, each participant is provided with a body of information drawn from real-world experience. The "case" presents facts, comments, and other material which may or may not be relevant to the particular points or objectives to be covered in the discussion. Each participant is asked to examine and analyze the material provided and present and discuss his or her views of what is of significance in the case material. Within the discussion itself, there is no attempt to identify right or wrong opinions or perceptions but rather to extract each individual's thoughts regarding the material and expose each to the perception of others regarding the same material.

The advantage of the case discussion, as opposed to the lecture, method lies in the individual participation and personal involvement that can be obtained through the use of the case discussion methodology. Through the use of extensive case analysis, the individual should learn to recognize underlying concepts and principles that have application to a wide variety of actual situations.

Programmed Instruction. Another method of training that is receiving more and more widespread use in industry is programmed instruction. This method provides specific point-by-point information to the learner along with periodic inquiries to determine if the information is being properly assimilated. According to the response by the individual to the inquiry, the program may refer the individual to the next step in the learning process or to some previous step which may need review. There is no need for an instructor for the material because the instruction is provided by the programmed textbook or, as is more often the case, by a computer terminal which interacts directly with the learner on an individual basis. Companies such as General Precision Corporation, Bell Telephone, and IBM have found programmed instruction to be effective in imparting certain types of information to individuals. As with the lecture method, the type of information that lends itself most readily to programmed instruction is generally of a factual nature. For example, computer programming, language, mathematics, electronics, and accounting have been areas in which programmed learning modules have been developed and utilized for training purposes. Exhibit 15.1 on page 384 provides a simple example of a typical programmed instruction learning sequence.

Based upon the selection of the respondent, the program would direct the individual either back to *FRAME 1* to review the TE

Exhibit 15.1. *Programmed Instruction Learning Sequence*

FRAME 1: In order to obtain the estimated time of completion (TE) for a PERT network, the equation to be utilized is

$$TE = \frac{a + 4m + b}{6}$$

where a = optimistic time of completion
m = most likely time of completion
b = pessimistic time of completion

FRAME 2: If

$$a = 2$$
$$b = 4$$
$$m = 3$$

the TE for the PERT network would equal

Select from the following

[2]　　[3]　　[5]

Source: Frederick C. Weston, "Operations Research Techniques Relevant to Corporate Planning Function Practices: An Investigative Look," *Academy of Management Journal,* September 1973, p. 510.

equation or on to *FRAME 3* to continue the learning process. This type of instruction places maximum responsibility on the learner and allows for development at a pace each individual establishes.

Management Games. One method of training that has proved effective in recent years is the technique known as *gaming* or *simulation.* Simulation and games have been developed in a wide variety of areas including education, business, and government. The value of simulation is that it presents a realistic picture of an environment in which the participant is required to interact in some way. This interaction normally requires the individual to make some set of decisions based upon the environment as he or she perceives it. In most simulations, other participants are required to make similar decisions, based on their own perceptions of the same environment. The gaming or simulation process then provides feedback to the decision makers on the effectiveness of their decisions. A new set of decisions can then be made based on the feedback, which should enable participants to improve their performance within the simulation.

The main value of the gaming methodology is that it attempts to present a series of conditions that represents a particular environment (corporation, hospital, city government). The participant is then able to interact in a *dynamic* fashion with this environment and through this interaction is able to recognize relationships and concepts which can be applied to the real world.

Role Playing. Another method which seeks to make use of individual participation and involvement in the training process is role playing. *Role playing* is somewhat similar to simulation and gaming in that it attempts to set up a situation which represents some aspect of the real world. This situation might be a negotiation between a union representative and a member of management regarding a wage settlement. Utilizing role playing as a training device, one manager participating in the training program might be asked to play the role of management and another, the role of the union representative. Each might be given certain cost data as well as economic information and then be asked to represent "his" position with respect to the wage settlement. The manager who was playing the part of the union representative would be required to present as strong a case as possible for the union position. Each of the two participants would then interact (negotiate) in order to reach an agreement on an acceptable wage settlement.

Through the process of role playing it is hoped that various individuals will become more open-minded and more willing to recognize and accept another's point of view. For instance, in our example, the manager who was representing the position of the union might leave the role playing situation much more aware of and sensitive to the needs and orientation of the union position. This sensitivity might well make this manager more effective in dealing with union representatives in the future. Exhibit 15.2 on page 386 presents a simplified role playing situation that might be utilized in a management training program.

Sensitivity Training. One additional method of training that requires the involvement and participation of those taking part is *sensitivity training*. This method of training focuses most deeply on the emotions and attitudes of participants in the sessions. Its objective is to bring about an increased awareness of feelings, values, and attitudes and to explore the sources of such attitudes as well as the ways in which the attitudes may influence behavior patterns.

This methodology requires the most sophisticated and professional administration and direction if it is to be effective. Since we are dealing with individual behavior, emotions, and attitudes, care must be taken to conduct the sessions so as to bring about an atmo-

Exhibit 15.2. *Role Playing Situation*

Assume you are a resident of a major metropolitan city on the east coast. The city has a population of five million residents with an average income of $9,000/resident. The city has an unemployment rate of 12 percent and one out of ten residents is currently receiving welfare benefits.

The city has an opportunity to bid for the 1984 summer Olympic Games which would require a commitment of $100 million to be allocated to new facilities without any guarantee of a dollar return on this investment.

Role 1: Mayor of this city who believes that the Olympics would bring new revenue and industry to the city.

Role 2: Tax-paying resident who is concerned about the effect on taxes as a result of the possibility of acquiring the Olympics.

Role 3: An unemployed family man on welfare who believes that the money could be spent more effectively in order to provide jobs within the city.

sphere of personal growth and development and not create an environment which may be perceived by individuals as threatening or dangerous. For a more thorough discussion of sensitivity training see Chapter 16.

Exhibit 15.3 summarizes an approach for the development of a management training program within an organization. If we examine the objectives to be achieved through management training and compare these with the methodologies and approaches normally utilized in training programs, we find that certain techniques lend

Exhibit 15.3. *Plan for Management Training Program*

Position analysis + manpower analysis
Individual and corporate needs

Objectives of program
  Procedure and policies
  Skill development
  Executive development

Selection of specific type of program
  On-the-Job training
  Job rotation
  Lecture
  Case analysis
  Programmed learning
  Role playing
  Gaming and simulation
  Sensitivity training

Methodology	Objectives		
	Policy, procedures, operations, knowledge	Skill development	Executive development
On-the-job training	X		
Job rotation	X		X
Lecture	X		
Case analysis		X	X
Programmed learning	X	X	
Gaming and simulation		X	X
Role playing		X	X
Sensitivity training		X	X

Figure 15.2. *Training Methodology and Skill Development*

themselves more readily than others to the achievement of specific objectives. Figure 15.2 provides a guideline that may be utilized in the selection of appropriate training programs in corporations.

Executive Development Programs

Thus far our discussion of management training has touched only briefly on the concept of *executive development,* though we have listed it as one of the objectives of a training program. In recent years, however, the topic of executive development training programs has become a more and more important part of both corporate and university activities. When considered most broadly, executive development programs would include all formal training and educational programs whose objective is to prepare managers to perform more effectively in the future. This being the case we might also include under this general heading degree-oriented academic programs whose admissions policies and curriculum orientation are directed toward employed managerial personnel. One extreme example is Adelphi University on Long Island, which has over 200 individuals working toward MBA degrees through classes held on commuter trains entering and leaving New York City.[6] Columbia University, the University of Pennsylvania, and Michigan State Uni-

Exhibit 15.4. *Executive Development Programs: Where to Go for More Schooling*

	Description	Who attends
Degree programs		
MBA (general)	Covers basic business management skills, with specialization in such areas as accounting, management, marketing, etc.	Newly hired to lower middle management level; ages mostly 22 to 35, but sometimes to 50.
MBA (executive)	Same as general MBA but with less specialization and more focus on management.	Middle to upper management, usually with company sponsorship. Ages mostly 35 to 45, with an average 10 years' work experience.
MS in business	Some basic management training, but emphasis is on specialty training: accounting, computer science, quantitative methods.	Newly hired to junior executives, sometimes company sponsored. Ages mostly 22 to 30.
PhD in business	Advanced education in various specialties: accounting, computer applications, finance, economics.	Usually corporate staff rather than line managers, often with company sponsorship. Ages mostly 25 to 40.
Nondegree programs		
Advanced management courses	Covers contemporary management techniques, with emphasis on senior-level policymaking and problem-solving.	Senior managers plus highly promotable middle managers, with corporate sponsorship required. Ages mostly 35 to 50; salary range mostly $25,000 to $50,000.
Middle management courses	Same as advanced management, but the emphasis is on problem-solving at the department or division level.	Junior to middle managers, usually with corporate sponsorship, with some top managers of smaller companies. Ages mostly 25 to 40.
Certificate programs	One course or group of courses to teach a specific skill: computer use, taxation, portfolio management, etc.	Mostly newly hired to junior executives seeking a necessary qualification for advancement.
Evening college	Continuing education courses in everything from business skills and public speaking to arts and sciences.	Newly hired to middle management, but programs are open to everyone.

Source: Reprinted from the March 8, 1976 issue of *Business Week* by special permission. Copyright © 1976 by McGraw-Hill

Cost	Time	Best Schools
$4,000 to $8,000 at private colleges; 40% less at public colleges.	Usually 60 semester hours spread over three to four years part-time. Figure on a minimum of two classes per week.	Boston U., California (Berkeley), Chicago, Cincinnati, Denver, Emory, Indiana, Miami (Fla.), Michigan, NYU, Northwestern (starts in fall, 1976), Rutgers, San Diego State, San Francisco State, Syracuse, Texas, Tulane, Washington U. (St. Louis).
$5,000 to $10,000.	Usually 45 semester hours, over two calendar years. Course usually involves one full day a week.	Columbia (MS degree), Chicago, Denver, Illinois, Michigan State, Penn, Pittsburgh, Rochester, SMU.
$2,000 to $4,000 at private colleges; 40% less at public.	Usually 30 semester hours, one to two evenings a week for 12 to 18 months.	Brigham Young, Colorado, Florida State, Georgia Tech, Massachusetts, NYU, Northwestern, Ohio State, San Diego State, Syracuse, USC.
$8,000 to $12,000 at private colleges; $4,000 to $6,000 at public colleges.	Usually five to eight years, with eight-year limit; minimum of two nights per week, plus thesis.	Cincinnati, Georgia, Michigan State, Michigan, NYU, Northwestern, Ohio State, Temple.
$2,500 to $7,500.	Three weeks to three months, full-time; live on campus or at study center. Four to five hours of daily classes, plus discussion groups and reading assignments.	California (Berkeley), Carnegie-Mellon, Chicago, Columbia, Cornell, Dartmouth, Harvard, Illinois, Indiana, MIT, Northwestern, Stanford, USC, Virginia, Western Ontario (London, Ont.).
$2,500 to $6,000.	Same as advanced management program.	Chicago, Cornell, Harvard, Houston, Michigan, North Carolina, Penn State, Pittsburgh. (Virginia senior program admits some junior managers.)
$500 to $1,500.	Usually 12 to 18 months, studying one night a week.	Offered by evening colleges in most cities. (NYU has a unique post-MBA certificate program that should spread.)
$75 to $150 per course.	Usually one or two two-hour classes a week.	Widely available throughout U.S.

Publishing, Inc., New York, N.Y. 10002. All rights reserved.

versity offer more conventional executive MBA programs oriented exclusively to those individuals with managerial experience.

Most formal executive development programs carried on within colleges and universities, however, are nondegree programs; most offer a certificate of completion for individuals who take part. Within recent years more and more corporations are taking advantage of executive development programs that are being offered by a wide variety of colleges and universities. Reasons for this increasing corporate interest are varied, but two seem prominent:

Keeping Managers Up-to-Date. As the pace and complexity of the legal, economic, technological, and sociological aspects of our society continue to change rapidly, it becomes more and more necessary to update skills and abilities of managers. New techniques in organization and control, as well as advances in financial analysis, planning processes, and computer utilization, require that today's manager continue his or her educational process long after the formal college education is over. It is the purpose of many executive development programs not so much to provide managers with a detailed knowledge of each of these advances as to provide an awareness that these new techniques exist and may have application to their current job or position.

Building Behavioral Skills. Perhaps the most important reason for the increase in the utilization of executive development programs is the realization on the part of many corporations that many highly talented managers and executives are often lacking in one key area of development, an awareness and understanding of the behavioral aspects of job performance. Too often managers are moved up within an organization solely on the basis of some demonstrated competence in a technical or professional area. These individuals are now required to shift their orientation from technical to managerial or administrative ability, and the corporation often finds that the manager does not possess the basic behavioral skills necessary to perform in the new capacity. Some of these behavioral skills are communicating, leading, delegating, and motivating. It is precisely in the development of these skills that many executive programs place their greatest emphasis. The objective is to teach the manager to change his or her role from one who has been accustomed to performing a job to one who now must effectively motivate and supervise others to perform their jobs. Methods such as case analysis, role playing, gaming and simulation, and sensitivity training give individual managers training and development in these human relations skills.

These programs often require participants to leave the work environment and return to the college or university classroom. This itself can be somewhat of a traumatic experience for an executive who believes that it would be simply impossible to leave corporate responsibilities for even a short period of time. In addition, the return to the classroom can itself be a difficult experience for the executive who may be 20 or 25 years out of college. The adjustment to the learning environment of the executive programs often requires some change in the participant's orientation.

Factors such as these often cause the chance to participate in an executive development program to be viewed with mixed emotions. The importance of such training and development in the eyes of corporate management, however, is evidenced by the statement that "turning down a chance to attend Harvard's thirteen-week Advanced Management Program . . . is like refusing a company transfer. You don't do it if you expect to get ahead."[7] Exhibit 15.4 (pages 388–389) presents a summary of programs available in 1978 in the area of executive development.

Discussion Questions

1. Discuss the present relationship between formal education and job opportunities.
2. What is meant by the term *salable skills*?
3. Discuss job obsolescence. Is this condition becoming more or less significant with respect to current job opportunities? Explain.
4. List and discuss some guidelines that may help employees avoid becoming "obsolete" prior to retirement.
5. Discuss some of the objectives of management training programs.
6. Define *position analysis* and *manpower analysis*. How do these two concepts relate to management training?
7. List and discuss some of the advantages of five typical methodologies used in management training programs.
8. What are the main reasons for the increased popularity of executive development programs in industry?
9. Discuss the role of colleges and universities in executive development training.
10. What changes and directions do you see executive development programs taking in the next ten years?

Case for Discussion

Larry Bradley was the director of training and development for Apex Products, a large midwestern manufacturing corporation. Apex had been engaged in an attempt to upgrade the skill and training of its personnel at all levels. In addition, Apex had recently instituted an affirmative action program designed to recruit unskilled minority workers from the immediate community. Based on the positive attitude of corporate management toward upgrading and training personnel, Larry believed that the time was right for his office to develop a proposal for an extensive corporate training program. Because he had just completed his MBA degree at a local college, Larry believed he was familiar with the latest research in training and development techniques.

Larry then prepared an outline of a training program that might be used at Apex. After several days, Larry had outlined the programs he believed would improve the skill and ability of all Apex workers. Each program required two days of training, as follows:

I. *Training Program for Managerial Personnel*
   Included in this group were foremen, managers, and top executives of the corporation.
   A. *Research results in management:* three hours of presentation on the latest research in management theory
   B. *Lecture on management techniques:* three hours of presentation by one of Larry's professors during his MBA program
   C. *Role playing:* five hours of role playing, using foremen, managers, and executives to act out typical management situations within an organization and then to discuss the results of the role play
   D. *Discussion:* three hours of open discussion among foremen, managers, executives about the current state of Apex management and possible improvements in its overall effectiveness

II. *Training Program for Nonmanagerial Personnel*
   Included in this group were all operative employees including the recently hired affirmative action personnel.
   A. *Management training:* five hours of training in the development of planning, organizing, and controlling techniques that would develop the management ability of operative employees
   B. *Current research in management:* similar to Program I (A), in which recent research results would be presented to the operative group
   C. *Communiation and interaction:* five hours of gaming and role playing designed to improve the communication skills of operative employees
   D. *Leadership and group behavior:* three hours of lecture by an Apex executive on the development of leadership skills and the behavior of individuals within the work environment

Larry Bradley then went to get a reaction to these programs from his immediate superior, the director of personnel for Apex.

Selected References

Bass, B. and Vaughan, J. *Training in Industry: The Management of Learning.* Belmont, Calif.: Wadsworth Publishers, 1966.

Bienvenu, B. *New Priorities in Training.* New York: American Management Associations, 1969.

Bower, C. "Let's Put Realism into Management Development." In *Harvard Business Review,* July-August 1973.

Carlson, J. and Misshauk, M. *Management Decision Simulations.* New York: John Wiley & Sons, 1971.

Desatnick, R. *A Concise Guide to Management Development.* New York: American Management Associations, 1970.

Dill, W., Crowston, W., and Elton, E. "Strategies for Self-Education." In *Harvard Business Review,* November-December 1965.

"A Guide to Executive Education." In *Business Week,* 8 March 1976.

Gummings, L. and Schwab, D. *Performance in Organizations.* Glenview, Ill.: Scott, Foresman and Co., 1973.

Guzzardi, W., Jr. "The Uncertain Passage from College to Job." In *Fortune.*

"How IBM Avoids Layoffs through Retraining." In *Business Week,* 10 November 1975.

Rogers, Madeline. "Outplacement Specialists." In *MBA,* July-August 1977.

Schein, Edgar. "How to Break in the College Graduate." In *Harvard Business Review,* November-December 1964.

_____. "The Individual, the Organization and the Career: A Conceptual Scheme." In *Organizational Psychology,* D. Kolb, I. Rubin, and J. McIntyre, eds. Englewood Cliffs, N.J.: Prentice-Hall, 1974.

Tosi, Henry and Carroll, S. "Management by Objectives." In *Personnel Administration,* July-August 1970.

Tracey, W. *Designing Training and Development Systems.* New York: American Management Associations, 1971.

Contingency Theory and Organizational Development

16

Business Tries Out 'Transactional Analysis'

Hundreds of thousands of amateur psychologists, armed with such books as Eric Berne's *Games People Play* and Thomas Harris' *I'm OK—You're OK*, have been using a behavioral technique called "transactional analysis" since the mid-1960s to unravel snarled communication lines with family and friends. Now the concept is taking hold in business. It has been used mainly to teach employees who deal with the public how to relate better to the customer, but managers also are beginning to experiment with TA to try to smooth out communication within a company itself.

Dozens of companies, including American Airlines, Bank of America, United Gas, Inc., Westinghouse Electric Corp., and Questor Corp., already have run executives, ranging from marketing managers to engineers, through TA courses. And some of TA's leading practitioners—Harris, Dorothy Jongeward, and Jut Meininger—are moving the TA crusade into the executive suite. In the past two months alone, the American Management Assn. has offered three-day seminars on TA in four cities.

Many executives who have been exposed to TA training swear by it. Others dismiss it as just another fad. Unfortunately, results are almost impossible to evaluate objectively. And while most bosses have been more than willing to prescribe TA training for line employees, relatively few show much enthusiasm for applying the insights of TA theory to themselves.

A Simpler Language

Transactional analysis, developed by the Canadian-born Berne, is basically a simplified approach to psychological therapy. Impatient with the technical jargon, exclusiveness, high fees, and prolonged treatment that characterize Freudian analysis, Berne devised a new and simple behavioral vocabulary that is probably TA's fundamental strength. "TA is essentially a language," says Dr. Donald Bower of the University of Pittsburgh's Graduate Business School. "It translates past psychological ideas into easily understood concepts which even lay people can handle."

Berne said that three primary "ego states"—parent, child, and adult—exist in all of us. In each social situation, or "transaction," one of the ego states predominates. The parent acts as he was taught to, the child as he feels at the moment, the adult after independent thought. When a person assumes the ego state, or role, that the other person expects of him, communication takes place. Otherwise it is blocked.

The "transaction" that gives TA its name is, to Berne's way of thinking, the basic unit of social intercourse. It involves a stimulus ("Good morning") from one person and a response ("Hello there") from another. By studying transactions, Berne said, a person can determine which ego states he and those around him are operating in and respond accordingly. This may require his reacting as an adult, parent, or child—to fit the role in which the other person places him and to achieve "a parallel transaction." Otherwise there will be a "crossed transaction," and communication will end altogether.

Communication that works brings positive "strokes," a TA concept that establishes love and good feelings. This helps avoid the psychological "games" people play that make themselves and others feel bad.

Reprinted from the January 12, 1974 issue of *Business Week* by special permission. Copyright © 1974 by McGraw-Hill Publishing Inc., New York, N.Y. 10020. All rights reserved.

Skepticism

The vocabulary and the concept leave some managers cold. "Business and industry were burned by the sensitivity training phenomena," acknowledges Dr. Hedges Capers, director of the San Diego Institute of Transactional Analysis, a center for retreats and therapy sessions. "But managers have learned that TA will make them money. TA training teaches respect for others, and that cultivates customers."

Lyman Randall, director of passenger services training at American Airlines' flight academy in Dallas, was one of the first to push for the use of TA in industry, and he admits, "It was a little difficult to sell to top management." The American program, which still is oriented to customer-contact personnel, not managers, has been the model for similar projects in banks, hospitals, hotels, and utilities. Some 15,000 employees at American have had TA training, and its program has been used to train 30,000 employees in other companies.

But the lower-level TA programs often spark an interest in the ranks of management. At Bank of America, for example, where consultant Dorothy Jongeward has been conducting TA programs for four years, 50 executives last year attended day-and-a-half TA conferences on affirmative action programs for women. Says William Bessey, the bank's vice-president of management development: "Many of the people were tough old bankers who had some pretty firm ideas about women. But these bankers have been touched by the course. TA made affirmative action programs much easier to implement."

No one gave the program a bad review, says Bessey, and one executive, Walter W. Minger, group vice-president of the bank's national division, was so turned on by the workshops that he suggested that his entire department of some 150 persons enroll in a TA course. "I started with partial apprehension and some disbelief about TA, but I found it has changed my personal life as well as my interactions with people at the bank," says Minger. "I find I take more care in my relationships with people."

From the Top Down

Getting management involved also helps alleviate fears of other employees that the company is trying to tamper with their personalities. "I ran into this fear at American Airlines," says Thomas Harris, whose book triggered the first use of TA in companies. "Some of the employees were afraid of being manipulated."

To avoid such feelings, United Gas is putting two corporate executives and 15 key division executives through an experimental TA seminar before offering a TA course to the 600 employees of its Houston division. "There is always the danger that management could try to play church or psychologist or Big Brother," explains Vice-President Roger D. Armstrong.

United Gas's seminars for executives are being conducted by Oklahoma City management consultant Jut Meininger, author of *Success Through Transactional Analysis,* a book that has sold 20,000 copies. While insisting that his corporate clients introduce TA into the company through top management, Meininger learned that there are many companies where TA "just doesn't seem to fit." That discovery led him to a study of executive and company "scripts."

Life Dramas

Berne had promulgated the concept that most individuals live out scripts, or life dramas, usually based on fairy tales— Sleeping Beauty, Red Riding Hood, Cinderella, or whatever—that were heard repeatedly during childhood. "But executives don't have fairy-tale scripts," Meininger says. "They have adventure-story scripts—Batman, Robin Hood, Buck Rogers, Tarzan, the Lone Ranger and Tonto."

The type of company that tends to reject TA is the one with strongly "parented" people at the top, who believe in tough, dictatorial management, several TA consultants contend. Says Meininger: "Let the market change and they often are in deep trouble. They aren't interested in TA because they can't see that giving people autonomy is productive."

Jongeward agrees. Corporations that play the parent role "may be locked into this autocratic pattern, spending their energies maintaining the old script rather than keeping up with the times," she says.

In fact, part of the attraction of TA to businessmen lies in the fact that it can lay bare the psyche of corporations as well as of individual executives. Not surprisingly, company scripts are largely determined by the scripts of key executives, past and present, says Chicago psychologist and corporate consultant Julian S. Frank, who has worked with such companies as Sears, Roebuck, Bell & Howell, and Zenith. "If I had the life scripts of top executives of all major firms, I would know which stocks to buy and which to sell," Frank contends. "People are programmed from an early age into success or failure patterns."

Changing the Script

But the script can be altered. TA's value lies in making people think about their relationships with others and giving them some kind of framework to evaluate and improve them. At Bank of New York, which has sent some vice-presidents as well as lower-level supervisory personnel through TA courses, management-training staff man Thomas C. Lincoln says: "One fellow who was strongly parental had never realized how parental his posture was. He went from recognizing it and laughing about it to doing something about it."

Most companies lump TA training with other behavioral studies. "TA is no panacea," says Lincoln. "Everyone won't be comfortable with it. For some, it will seem too psychological, and for others, it won't be deep enough. But clearly it can be valuable for all levels of management."

Today's young business recruits seem more receptive to TA than some of their predecessors. "The trend to conceptual

schemes like transactional analysis is there," says Raghu Nath, director of the management training laboratory at the University of Pittsburgh's Graduate Business School, which uses TA in training executives and MBA students.

The Beauty of TA

That view seems to be shared by many in business itself. All of the 68 middle managers at Bank of America who went through TA seminars believed that their adult ego states had been strengthened, 86% felt that they were better able to handle difficult interpersonal problems, and 79% found the concept useful at home as well as on the job.

"That's the beauty of TA," says Peter J. Burton of the Mountain States Employers Council in Denver. "It's taken home by people. Spouses get together and use it on their kids. It works on a five-year-old as well as on a fellow executive."

That is why so many executives exposed to TA refer to it as "the great equalizer." With TA, the manager strives for adult-to-adult transactions whether he is dealing with a superior or a subordinate. "More than anything else," says a Sears executive, "TA has shown people here that no one is any better as a person than anyone else. We have opened up some tolerance for ideas from guys down below us."

The tolerance can work horizontally too. At Questor, a company that uses TA extensively, a severe conflict arose in a Canadian operation between the manufacturing and finance groups. "It was about to cost us money," says Malcolm Warren, Questor's director of planning and development. "TA did a lot to solve the problem and keep the division in the black."

To consultant Julian Frank, all the TA activity in business signifies the beginning of what he calls a quiet revolution. "People are adopting a transactional way of life," he says. "They want to know how to live with themselves and others. They want to learn what's going on inside their own heads."

THIS CHAPTER will review the research that has led to the development of *contingency theory* as it applies to business organizations. The evolution of this theory was discussed in Chapter 5 and simply refers to the idea that the most appropriate type and style of management will vary with the situation. Application of this theory has made it necessary for many organizations to make changes in their ideas about their own nature and operation. In bringing about such changes, many corporations have instituted programs of *organizational development*. We will examine the nature of these programs and how they may aid organizations in dealing with certain types of environmental conditions.

Contingency Theory: A Review of the Research

A number of studies have tended to reinforce the concept that no one type of organizational structure and philosophy is necessarily appropriate for all industries and market conditions.[1] In one study (the Woodward study), in which firms were classified according to complexity of technology, the author found that significant differences existed in the way successful organizations carried on their operations.[2] These differences correlated quite closely with the type of technology in which the firms were involved. The complexity of the technological process had significant impact on areas such as emphasis placed on job descriptions, organization of work groups, leadership style, and the delegation of authority. For purposes of the study, the firms were divided into three basic levels of technological complexity: 1) unit and short run production; 2) mass production, high quantity runs; 3) continuous process production (as for liquids and chemicals). The results indicated that successful firms utilizing unit and short run production or continuous process production differed in their method of operation from successful firms utilizing mass production technology. Exhibit 16.1 summarizes some of the findings of this research. This study shows that the type of technology in which a firm is engaged plays a significant role in the way that firm is organized and how it carries on its management activities.

The study by Lawrence and Lorsch examined industries having differing rates of technological *change*.[3] Here results indicated that the rate of technological change in a given industry brought about significant difference in the orientation of various organizational members with respect to goals, time, and interpersonal behavior. These differences tended to affect the way an organization was structured, the relationship of individuals within the organization,

Exhibit 16.1. *Organizational Characteristics of Successful Firms*

Unit/short run production firms; Continuous process production firms	Mass production firms
Less importance attached to written job description	More importance given to written job description
More of a tendency to delegate authority	Less delegation of authority
More flexible leadership style	More rigid leadership style
Less attention given to classical principles of organization	Organized along classical lines
Less emphasis on written forms of communication and control procedures	Greater emphasis on written communication and control procedures
Less closely organized work group	More closely organized work group

and the way the organization dealt with its environment. Lawrence and Lorsch examined firms in the plastics industry (high rate of technological change), food industry (lesser rate of technological change), and the container industry (least rate of technological change). The results are essentially consistent with those of the Woodward study and serve to reinforce the notion that successful firms organize and carry on their activities not necessarily according to a single set of organizational principles but rather according to the nature of their technology and their environment.

The results of these studies as well as research carried on by Worthy, Udy, and others have brought about a recognition that the principles of organization as defined in the classical sense may not necessarily apply to all organizations in all market conditions.[4] This recognition has led to the evolution of a *contingency theory* of organizations. This theory, simply stated, recognizes that certain structures and methods of operation may be appropriate in some situations and inappropriate in others. The result is that each situation must be considered independently: proper attention must be given to such variables as technology, environmental change, type of industry, and nature of competition. Only after an analysis of these variables has been made can a conclusion be drawn as to the most appropriate type of structure and operating philosophy for the organization.

Perhaps one of the first attempts to recognize the need for a more flexible view of this sort can be found in the differentiation between mechanistic and organic organizations made by T. Burns and G. M. Stalker.[5] The terms *mechanistic* and *organic* refer to the basic philosophy, structure, and orientation of an organization. The terms are not intended to represent a dichotomy but rather are used to define the extreme points on our organizational continuum. The mechanistic-organic continuum allows for a classification of each organization according to the degree to which it meets certain specific criteria.

Mechanistic organizations
1. Strong emphasis on methods to be followed, specialization and job definition.
2. Emphasis on hierarchical structure to handle coordination, communication, and control within the organization.
3. High value placed on organizational loyalty.
4. Interaction tending to follow hierarchical patterns in superior-subordinate rather than peer group.

This sampling of the characteristics of a mechanistic organization shows that such an organization would closely resemble the classical "bureaucratic" structure defined by Max Weber. In these organizations there exists a clearly defined hierarchy with communication, coordination, and control following the lines defined by this hierarchy. Jobs are well defined and highly specialized, and the organization is governed by exacting rules, policies, and procedures.

Organic organizations
1. Coordination, control, and communication based upon expertise rather than strictly along hierarchical lines. Responsibility for these functions varying from situation to situation, depending on the skills required.
2. Recognition of the changing nature of job assignments, with each individual contributing particular skills in a given situation.
3. A more open flow of communication, which flows both upward and across the organizational structure.
4. A high value placed on commitment to organizational goals and objectives.

When viewed as a continuum, movement from a mechanistic to an organic structure should therefore result in the following:

1. Less emphasis on the hierarchical structure of the organization and more emphasis on the individual value and contribution of the worker.
2. More open communication in all directions with less concern for strict lines of communication as defined by the organizational structure.

3. Authority and leadership more related to individual expertise in a given situation and less concerned with organizational hierarchy.
4. Less well defined operating procedures and more emphasis on a free-flowing approach to organizational problems.

From our analysis thus far we must be careful not to draw the conclusion that the organic structure is necessarily the more desirable and effective. We have previously discussed the fact that factors such as the capability of individual workers and possible need for a secure and predictable environment may create a situation in which a highly structured and well-defined organization is appropriate. The mechanistic organization is most appropriate when dealing with a stable environment, while the organic structure is most suited to an environment experiencing rapid change. The work of Burns and Stalker serves to reinforce the concept that no single organization type or method of operation is appropriate for all environments and market conditions. The key to understanding and managing organizations thus becomes not so much a matter of learning how to apply organizational principles but rather of being able to determine which principles, if any, would have application to a particular environment. In other words, (1) the tasks to be performed and the technology to be utilized (Woodward) and (2) the stability of the environment (Lawrence and Lorsch, Burns and Stalker) determine what is most appropriate in the following areas:

1. Organizational structure
2. Method of coordination and control
3. Communication patterns
4. Leadership style
5. Utilization of policy and procedures.

It is clear that each organization must analyze its own situation and make a determination as to the most appropriate format in which to conduct its operations. Each organization is unique and must be considered as an independent entity.

Some Assumptions Regarding Human Behavior

In examining this contingency approach to organizational design one immediately becomes aware of the fact that along the continuum from mechanistic to organic organization there is a decreasing emphasis on the organizational structure and formal hierarchy and a corresponding increase in emphasis on the independence, value, and contribution of the individual within the organization. It is apparent that within the organic structure the behavior of the individual is governed and directed not so much by a rigid set of rules and regulations imposed by the organization as by a set of values internal to the individual. The fact that research has indicated that, under the proper conditions of technology and environment, organizations can function most effectively in this organic mode leads us to examine some basic assumptions about the nature of behavior in the work environment. As we have stated, within the organic structure, individual behavior is not so much regulated by organizational guidelines and methods as by a desire and willingness on the part of the individual to contribute to organizational goals. This philosophy represents a significant change from that which was prevalent in classical organization theory. It correlates more closely with the writings and research of the *behavioral school of management thought* as found in the works of Argyris, Maslow, Likert, and, perhaps most clearly, Douglas McGregor.[6]

In his classic work, *The Human Side of Enterprise,* McGregor questions some of the classical theory assumptions regarding basic human behavior. These classical assumptions characterize the individual as having an inherent dislike for work, a basic desire to avoid responsibility, and little ambition. It is therefore the duty of management to direct the efforts of individuals by means of persuasion, reward, punishment, coercion, and threat so as to modify individual behavior to fit the needs of the organization. This view of individual behavior and management's response to it is characterized by McGregor as *Theory X.* McGregor questioned the validity of this theory and postulated a different approach, which he referred to as *Theory Y.* This new theory rested upon a totally different set of assumptions regarding human behavior, in total contradiction to those made by Theory X. In Theory Y, people are assumed to be basically dependable, trustworthy, willing to take initiative, and act in an essentially responsible manner.

The point to be made in discussing McGregor's Theory X and Theory Y is that as an organization moves along the continuum from mechanistic to organic it must of necessity also move from Theory X to Theory Y assumptions about individual behavior. The fact that organic organizations do exist, and indeed, may be highly successful in certain environments, indicates that some changes are taking place within our society in general, and within organizations in particular, regarding the nature of individual behavior:

1. An increasing recognition that individuals often have far more to contribute than is required by the particular job they are performing. This situation may result in employee frustration and often

prevents the organization from making full use of the talents and skills available to it. Recognition of this untapped talent has resulted in programs designed to make better use of employee skills and ability. Job enlargement, job enrichment, and work simplification programs are typical of such attempts.

2. A recognition that the individual is not a static being but must constantly grow and develop. Abraham Maslow recognized that once an individual is able to achieve satisfaction to one need, a new need assumes priority. The constant attempt to achieve need satisfaction may lead the individual in different directions at different times, creating a search for new outlets for energy and achievement. Society is experiencing an increase in the number of individuals who seek midcareer job changes, some of these changes involving new fields totally unrelated to previous work experience. Programs of continuing education are becoming more and more a part of the fringe benefit package offered by various organizations. Some of these programs provide instruction in areas that are not job-related, so as to provide a wider variety of need satisfactions.

3. A recognition that individuals are responsible enough to take an active role in their own career development. More and more organizations are initiating programs to increase the individual involvement in the work environment. *Participative management* and *management by objectives* are but two programs that allow subordinates to interact with superiors in the planning and organizing of work activities. Programs such as these provide individuals with the opportunity to exercise greater control over their own destiny and provide an increased feeling of importance in the contribution they make toward the goals of the organization.

4. There is an increasing effort to bring individual feelings, attitudes, and emotions out into the open where they can be examined and discussed. This effort seeks to improve channels of communication so that individuals can deal more openly with their own feelings and attitudes as well as become more aware of the feelings and attitudes of others. It is believed that in this way an organizational environment will be created such that individuals will become more willing to cooperate and collaborate in seeking solutions to problems. Corporations utilizing techniques such as T group, encounter group, and role-playing sessions represent tangible evidence of such organizational efforts.

5. Greater recognition and acceptance of the notion that leadership and direction may come from anywhere within the organization and should not necessarily be restricted to the upper levels in the hierarchy has evolved. This decreasing emphasis on adherence to

the strict hierarchical structure has led to the development of both *project management* and *matrix organizational structure*. In addition, the inherent characteristics of these new organizational structures emphasize a rather free-flowing nature of environment. These structures are designed to meet specific organizational needs even though in so doing they often violate classical organizational principles.

6. There is an increase in the attitude that human beings are basically "good" and will respond positively if given the chance. This attitude represented one of the central themes of Jimmy Carter's campaign for the Presidency. Mr. Carter constantly appealed to the underlying strength and goodness inherent in the American people. The results indicate that this appeal was able to more than offset what many experts felt was perhaps a lack of clarity on the issues. There is a growing indication that this positive attitude toward individuals is finding its way into the organizational philosophy of many of today's corporations.

7. There is a clear desire on the part of many individuals to return to more fundamental values and to seek more meaningful experiences within their lives. More and more, it is becoming apparent that the high level of affluence achieved by American society has not always brought about a correspondingly high level of personal satisfaction. On the contrary; perhaps more than ever society is plagued by a variety of social ills that seem to grow worse as greater economic growth is achieved. More and more individuals are seeking expanded self-awareness through a wide variety of psychological, religious, and other involvements.[7]

In our discussion thus far we note the emergence of two key concepts that have had significant impact on organizations and the individuals within them. The first concept represents the evolution of a theory of organization that departs from the total acceptance of classical principles as being applicable in all situations and environments. The new theory represents a much broader and more flexible approach to organizations in which each situation is considered independently and evaluated on its own merits. This *contingency approach* allows for a wide variety of organizational designs and operating philosophies. This variety would fill the continuum between the mechanistic and organic organizational poles previously discussed. Organizations are now becoming much more aware of their environment and recognizing that this environment will have a significant impact on the way they carry on their operations. Increasing flexibility provides management with a new series of tools for meeting organizational objectives; at the same time it also means that management must use care in selecting the mode of behavior that will best meet the needs of the organization in particular situations.

The second concept which has emerged deals with attitudes toward individuals within organizations. As we have mentioned, the new attitudes regarding individual behavior not only permit, but indeed encourage, a more expanded and diversified role for each member of the organization. As these attitudes become a part of the modern organization they have a significant impact on such things as leadership styles, communication patterns, work group behavior, organizational structure, and decision-making processes. As changes take place in these areas, the individual is provided with a much wider variety of activities in which to become involved. The results of this involvement are expected to bring about greater individual need satisfaction as well as improved organizational performance. Figure 16.1 might serve to illustrate the impact of these two emerging concepts.

In the classical approach to the design and understanding of organizations, the structure and operation of the organization were governed by a series of principles believed to have application to all organizational situations. This approach, which closely approximates the mechanistic form previously discussed, provided little opportunity for flexibility in individual behavior. The individual functioned in a highly prescribed manner, and there existed limited opportunity for creative and innovative behavior. Such creative and innovative behavior normally found its outlet only through the "informal organization."

In summary, we might state that in the mechanistic structure both the individual and the organization are limited in the types of behavior they may exhibit. Here again, we do not mean to imply that such an organizational framework is necessarily undesirable or ineffective. On the contrary, research results indicate that under certain conditions (stable environments, mass production technology), this approach may prove highly effective. Changes that have taken place in our society, however, have diminished the number of organizations that can function effectively with such an approach. We have discussed the rapid changes taking place in technology, social values, and economic conditions, and these have tended to create an environment in which significant and rapid change is to be considered more the rule than the exception. As these changes become more frequent, organizations must find ways of anticipating and adapting to a constantly changing environment.

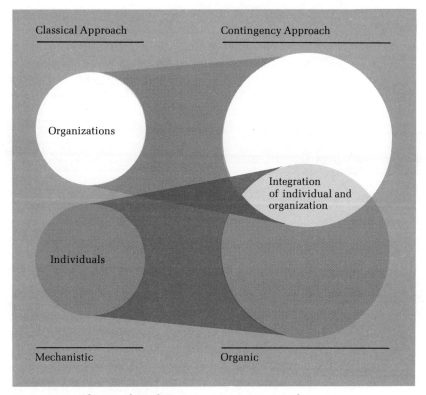

Figure 16.1. *Classical and Contingency Approaches to Organization*

In addition to the rapid changes within the environment, the emerging social values we have discussed have also brought about a change in the way we view the role of the individual within the organization. Organizations are now more willing to recognize and accept the fact that individuals may behave in a wide variety of ways to achieve higher-level need satisfactions.

The above factors have created a change in the way many of today's organizations function. The change represents a significant shift from a more mechanistic to a more organic organizational framework. This movement has had as its objective the creation of an environment in which both the organization and the individual are better able to respond to particular situations and environments. This creates a much more free flowing and spontaneous organization, one whose behavior is governed not by a series of rules but rather by the needs of the environment, of technology, and of the individual. As the behavior of both organization and individual becomes more flexible and varied, these behaviors have greater impact on each other. Efforts by organizations to better understand this mutual impact, and in doing so, to bring about an environment in which both organizational goals and individual needs may be achieved, have been referred to as programs of *organizational development.*

Organizational Development

As top management has become more aware of the complexity of the interactive process between the individual and the organization, it has also begun to recognize that many of the problems faced go far beyond those that can be corrected by conventional management techniques. Many of these problems are not so much a function of organizational structure or operating policies but rather are related to the attitudes, ideas, and values of the individuals making up the organization. This being the case, many corporations have sought outside help, not necessarily from the conventional consulting firms but rather from the ranks of the behavioral scientists, many of whom had been attempting to deal with these types of problems. Professionals like Douglas McGregor, Robert Blake, and Chris Argyris were perhaps some of the first to become involved in the development of programs designed to aid the organization in dealing with these complex problems.

What Is Organizational Development?

Organizational development is essentially a series of programs that have as their objective the facilitation of change within the organizational environment. "Organizational development refers to a long-range effort to improve an organization's problem-solving capabilities and its ability to cope with changes in its external environment...."[8] As can be seen quite clearly from the preceding definition, the term "organizational development" is generic. There are a large number of techniques, methodologies, and specific interventions that can be subsumed under this term. The objectives are all quite similar, however.

Some of the specific objectives of a program of organizational development might include

1. Improved level of trust and support within the organization
2. Increased willingness to confront and deal with problems in an open and free manner
3. Bringing about an environment in which authority and decision

making are based upon knowledge and skill and not upon organizational position

4. Providing an atmosphere in which free and open communication will take place at all levels
5. Improving overall levels of satisfaction within the organizational environment.[9]

Achieving Change in People (The Lewin Model)

Kurt Lewin has developed a model of individual or organizational change which includes the following phases.[10] In order to bring about change within an individual or organization, a series of steps should take place:

Desire for Change. Before change can take place, there must exist a recognition that the current state or situation is not totally acceptable and therefore must be changed. Essentially, this means that individuals to be changed must recognize that either (1) the current situation is unacceptable or (2) that there is some better alternative to the situation currently in effect.

Unfreezing. Once the need for change has been recognized, it becomes necessary to break down or eliminate those values, ideas, or philosophies that have been instrumental in bringing about and maintaining the current state of affairs. In most cases, this "unfreezing" will require modification of ideas that may form a basic part of the individual or the organization. This process of unfreezing old ideas is necessary before new ways of interpreting and reacting to the organizational environment can be accepted.

Conversion. The process of conversion refers to the way in which the organizational development program seeks to instill new ideas or philosophies. It represents the transformation from one frame of reference to another as the individual adopts new ideas. It is this process of conversion that forms an essential part of an organizational development program.

Refreezing. Once the conversion process has taken place, it is necessary to solidify the new values and philosophies so that these now represent the frame of reference the individual will utilize in future interaction situations. Care must be taken to establish a program that will constantly reinforce these newly acquired values so that behavior does not revert to old ways with the passage of time.

In summary, the change process would involve the following elements:

1. Desire for change: Acceptance of idea that current situation can be improved.

2. *Unfreezing:* Elimination of values, ideas, and philosophies that currently contribute to existing situation.
3. *Conversion:* Instilling new values, ideas, and philosophies that will bring about a change in the behavior of the individual and the organization.
4. *Refreezing:* Reinforcement of these newly acquired values, ideas, and philosophies so that they become internalized by the individual and form the basis for future behavior.

Summary of Organizational Development Objectives

Although organizational development efforts vary, most of these programs have as their objective the bringing about of change in the organizational climate. The climate of an organization can be thought of as the general perception of the participants of what it is like to be a functioning member of that organization. The main objective of this change is the establishment of a feeling of mutual trust. This feeling can then be utilized to bring about a more open pattern of communication as well as an improvement in the overall level of support organizational members provide to each other.

As this atmosphere of trust, support, and open communication becomes more a part of the organizational environment, individuals will tend to develop better working relationships with other members of the organization. In addition, these relationships will be based upon the need to solve organizational problems rather than on the established organizational hierarchy. Both individuals and groups tend to increase their overall level of satisfaction and also achieve greater success in solving organizational problems.

In order to accomplish such an ambitious objective, there must be a thorough examination of the organizational structure, as well as its operating policies and procedures, in order to determine the possible impact of such a program on both individual and group behavior. In addition, behavior normally associated with corporate politics, competition among line and staff departments, and organizational "game-playing" must be recognized and dealt with. Such a program, dealing as it does with individual attitudes and values, is likely to have a significant impact on many people and possibly bring about dramatic changes in organizational practice. For this reason it is clear that the program will require a great deal of soul-searching by top management. They must make a determination of their willingness to deal with these rather delicate issues in an honest, open, and straightforward manner. Because many of these issues have their roots in both the psychological and sociological background of organizational members, most corporations have found it necessary to call upon specially trained outside consultants to implement an organizational development program. These consultants have both the background and experience to work with people in bringing about a recognition of problem areas and to identify and deal with underlying causes. In addition, outside consultants bring with them a level of objectivity that can rarely be found within the organization itself.

The Role of the Consultant

The consultant who comes to an organization to help bring about a change in the existing climate brings along his or her own set of attitudes and values. In general, these may be summarized in terms of a basically positive attitude and philosophy regarding people. The consultant will tend—in McGregor's terms—toward a Theory Y orientation with respect to beliefs regarding individual behavior. The consultant needs this orientation since it is exactly this philosophy that is to be instilled and encouraged. With this orientation and with knowledge of behavioral research, the consultant views the organization as potentially able to improve its effectiveness through creation of a more open and supportive environment. It therefore becomes the task of the consultant to work with members of the organization, both individually and in groups, in order to bring about this environmental change.

Perhaps the first step in this task is to sit down with top management and gain insight into their perceptions of the existing organizational climate and operation. I addition, some initial determinations can be made as to possible problem areas. After these initial discussions, some preliminary problems may be isolated for investigation. In attempting to make an accurate diagnosis of organizational problems, the consultant will engage in a series of data-gathering activities. The techniques used would include an examination of the current organizational hierarchy, channels of communication, decision-making processes, and operating policies and procedures, as well as open-ended interviews with various individuals. In addition, the consultant might use questionnaires to obtain additional information and data from various organizational groups.

Using these and subsequent data-gathering efforts, the consultant will attempt to define and isolate specific problem areas. In some cases problems may be related to the inability of the organization to define its objectives adequately or to assess its external environment accurately. In other instances, the internal workings of the organization (communication, decision making, authority, structures) may impose barriers to effective organizational operation. In any event, once these problems have been defined, the consultant will work with management in developing a plan of action.

T Groups (Sensitivity Training)

In almost all cases the plan developed by the consultant to bring about desired change in the organizational climate will involve some type of laboratory training technique. Such techniques have become almost synonymous with programs of organizational development. *Sensitivity training* had its genesis in the late 1940s, largely as a result of work done by Kurt Lewin and Ronald Lippitt. This work, originally associated with the National Training Laboratory in Group Development, has led to a wide application of laboratory techniques in dealing with organizational problems.

Accoding to Argyris, the T group is "... a group experience designed to provide maximum possible opportunity for the individuals to expose their behavior, give and receive feedback, experiment with new behavior and develop an everlasting awareness and acceptance of self and others."[11] Within the group environment the focus is not placed on the solution to a particular problem but rather the group interaction itself. Argyris sees the T group as designed to enable individuals to:

Determine if they wish to modify their old values and develop new ones and

Develop awareness of how groups can inhibit as well as facilitate human growth and decision making.

T-group training is most beneficial for individuals who have:

A relatively strong ego that is not overwhelmed by internal conflicts

Defenses which are sufficiently low to allow the individual to hear what others say to him (accuratcly and with minimal threat to his self) without the aid of a professional scanning and filtering system (that is, the therapist or educator)

The ability to communicate thoughts and feelings with minimal distortion.

In other words, the operational criterion of minimal threat is that the individual does not tend to condemn others or himself.

The basic assumption underlying the use of the laboratory in training and development programs is that true learning and understanding will be more likely to take place if the individual has an opportunity to actually experience and participate in the learning process. The acceptance of this basic assumption is becoming more and more widespread as greater use is made of simulations, games, role playing, and other techniques to reinforce the learning process.

Such reinforcement is virtually impossible through the more usual forms of lecture presentation. Within the laboratory environment, the participant is able to actually experience the emotion and feelings associated with a given mode of behavior. These experiences, as the individual feels them internally or observes them in others, can serve to bring about an expanded awareness of personal ideas, values, and feelings, as well as a sensitivity to the ideas, values, and feelings of others. Awareness and sensitivity, if properly developed by the consultant (trainer), can bring about significant improvement in the individual's own self-understanding as well as the ability to understand and empathize with others. This understanding will generally lead to an improvement in communication skills and also make the individual far better able to deal effectively with interpersonal relationships. It is the improvement in these abilities that seems to bring about increased individual satisfaction as well as increased organizational effectiveness. Exhibit 16.2 on page 414 presents some of the changes in attitude that may take place as a result of T-group training.

The following represents an excerpt from a discussion about T-group training. A group of executives who had participated in a typical program are discussing their experiences.

No. 4: (after reporting that his superior, a member of the experimental group, had made a decision which should have been left to him): I was really fuming. I was angry as hell. I walked into his office and I said to myself, "No matter what the hell happens, I'm going to tell him that he cannot do that any more." Well, I told him so. I was quite emotional. You know it floored me. He looked at me and said, "You're right; I made a mistake, and I won't do that again." Well I just don't think he would have done that before.

No. 7: The most important factor in motivating people is not what you say or do; it's giving a person the opportunity to express his views and the feelings that one is seriously interested in his views. I do much less selling but it sure takes longer.

No. 2: I've had a problem. I now have a greater need for feedback than before, and I find it difficult to get. The discussion on internal commitment made much sense to me, and I try to see if I can create conditions for it.

The thing that bothers me is that I try to handle it correctly, but I don't get feedback or cues as to how well I'm doing, as I used to at the lab. The meeting is over, and you don't know whether you've scored or not. So after each

Exhibit 16.2. *Before and After Values of Eleven Executives Who Experienced Laboratory Education*

	In an administrative situation, whenever possible . . .	Before T-group	Six months after
1a.	The leader should translate interpersonal problems into rational intellective ones	100%	10%
1b.	The leader should deal with the interpersonal problems	0	81
2a.	The leader should stop emotional disagreement by redefining the rational purpose of the meeting	90	10
2b.	The leader should bring out emotional disagreements and help them to be understood and resolved	6	81
3a.	When strong emotions erupt, the leader should require himself and others to leave them alone and not deal with them	100	18
3b.	When strong emotions erupt, the leader should require himself and offer others the opportunity to deal with them	0	82
4a.	If it becomes necessary to deal with feelings, the leader should do it even if he feels he is not the best qualified	100	9
4b.	The leader should encourage the most competent members.	0	90
5a.	The leader is completely responsible for keeping the group "on the track" during a meeting	100	0
5b.	The group members as well as the leader are responsible for keeping the group "on the track"	0	100

Source: R. Morton and B. Bass, "The Organizational Training Laboratory," *Training Directors' Journal,* October 1964.

meeting I've got 10 question marks. The things that before were never questions are now question marks.

You don't get feedback. You ask for something and they respond, "I know what you're trying to do." They think I've something up my sleeve. All I want is to get feedback. It was obvious to me they were all waiting for me to make the decision. But I wanted them to make it. This was their baby, and I wanted them to make it. Two days later they made it.

Fine, in this case I got feedback. The point was that their decision was a severe reversal, and I realize it was difficult for them to make. But they made it. Before, I simply would have pointed out the facts, and they would have "agreed" with the reversal, but down deep inside they would have felt that they could have continued on. As it is now, it's their decision. I think they now have a greater sense of internal commitment. People are now freer to disagree.

No. 11: My list of decisions to be made is longer. I am hoping that they will make some decisions. I now know how much they wait for me.

No. 11 (after telling how he wrote a note which in effect damned No. 2 and maintained his own correctness, then reread it and realized how defensive he was): Before I wouldn't have seen this.

No. 2: One of our most difficult jobs will be to write our feelings and to write in such a way that others can express their feelings.

No. 3: I have some difficulties in evaluating this program. What have we gotten out of this? What are we able to verbalize about what we got out of this? Do others of you have difficulty in verbalizing it?

No. 2: I have the same difficulty. I have been totally ineffective describing the experience.

No. 8: Each time I try I give a different answer.

No. 1: I don't have too much difficulty. One thing that I am certain of is that I see people more as total human beings. I see aspects of them that I had never seen before.

No. 9: I'm frustrated because I now realize the importance of face-to-face communication. I'm so far from the general managers that it is not so hot. Has anyone tried to write memos that really get feelings brought out?

I find myself questioning much more than I ever did before. I have a more questioning attitude. I take into account more factors.

No. 4: We've been talking about things as if we've slowed down a bit. We haven't. For example, remember you (No. 1) and I had a problem? I'm sure Arden House was very helpful. If I hadn't been there, my reaction to you would have been different. I would have fought you for hours.

No. 1: I know we can talk to each other more clearly. It's not a conscious way. It's spontaneous.

No. 3: I have to agree we can make some decisions much faster. For example, with No. 2 I simply used to shut up. But now I can be more open. Before the laboratory, if I had an intuitive feeling that something was wrong, but I wasn't sure, I'd keep quiet until things got so bad that then I'd have a case to go to the boss. Now I feel freer to talk about it sooner and with No. 2.

I now feel that we are going to say exactly how we feel to anyone. You (the president), for example, don't have to worry, and, therefore, question, probe, and draw us out.

President: Yes, and today I found No. 1, who told me that he simply would not agree with me. And I said to myself, "God bless you. He really is open now."

No. 1: I agree. I would not have expressed this feeling before being in this group. It's obvious that one should but I didn't.

(No. 2 and No. 1 show real insight into how they are being manipulated by people outside and above the group. They are much more aware of the manipulative process. "This kind of manipulation is dynamite. It burns me up.")

No. 1: Yes, it's really horrible to see it and not be able to do anything about it.

No. 7: In this case it seems to me you've got to really hit hard, because you're dealing with an untrained man (laughter). . . . I think I now have a new understanding of decision making. I am now more keenly aware of the importance of getting a consensus so that the *implementation* is effective. I am not trying to say that I do this in every meeting. But I do strive more to give opportunity for consensus.

No. 1: One of the problems that I feel is that the "initiated" get confused so they don't play the game correctly. Sometimes I feel walked upon, so I get sore. This is difficult. (Many others expressed agreement.)

No. 6: Does it help to say, "I trust you"? I think it does.

No. 11: For example, No. 2; you went to a meeting where you admitted you had made a mistake. Boy, you should have heard the reaction. Boy, Mr. —— admitted a mistake. Well, wonderful; it helped to get these guys to really feel motivated to get the job done.

No. 9: Yes, I heard that many took on a deeper feeling of responsibility to get the program on the right track.

No. 7: I'd like to come back to what No. 6 said. I used to say to people that I trusted them, that I was honest, and so on. But now I wonder if people really believe me, or if they don't begin to think if I'm not covering that I'm not honest.

No. 3: Another example which I am now aware of is the typical way we write memos. We start off: "I have confidence in your judgment to handle this question," and so on. Few more paragraphs. Then fifth paragraph reads: "Please confirm by return mail exactly what you have done and what controls have been set up."

No. 2: I agree. We do an awful lot to control people, although I think that we're trying.

(No. 7 gave examples of how he stopped making a few phone calls to exert pressure. Others agreed.)

The Researcher: Aren't there negative comments?

No. 11: We have one man who has chosen not to be here. I wonder why?

No. 3: Well, really, to me that is a sign of health in the group. He feels he would still be accepted even if he didn't come. It certainly would be easy for him to come and just sit here.

No. 1: Yes, he wouldn't go to the trouble of avoiding a meeting that you didn't think was important.

No. 3: The only negative that I can think is: "What can you tell me that actually increases effectiveness?" I am not sure, but I must agree that there is a whale of a different climate.

No. 7: Well, I'd like to develop a list of things that we feel we have gotten out of this program so far. How do others of you feel? (All agreed, "Let's try.")

(All Group Members reporting they reached the following conclusions):

(a) All of us begin to see ourselves as others see us . . . a real plus.
(b) A degree of greater confidence in oneself in meetings and in interviews. Beginning to be more comfortable with self.
(c) Greater confidence in associates. We feel more secure that you're telling what you think. . . . Greater feeling of freedom of expression to say what you really think.

(d) Individuals have a greater understanding and appreciation of viewpoint of associates.

(e) Greater appreciation of the opposite viewpoint.

(f) An awareness of what we do and others do that inhibits discussion.

(g) More effective use of our resources . . . getting more from them, and they feel this . . . patient to listen more.

(h) Meetings do not take longer and implementation is more effective. Internal commitment is greater.

(i) We have had a great realization that being only task-oriented, we will not get the best results. We must not forget worrying about the organization and the people.

(j) We get more irritated to infringements of our jobs and unique contributions.

(k) Fewer homemade crises.

No. 6: One of the difficult things about the list is that when you look at it, you wake up to the fact that you haven't really been using these principles. When you tell someone who doesn't realize the gap between knowing something and actually doing it, he doesn't realize.

No. 7: But I think I really did learn and do care. Now when I think what I used to do, because that was the way. Today I realize that I could have had three times as much if I had known what I know now.[12]

Organizational Training

Another development of note is the Organizational Training Laboratory created by Robert Morton for the purpose of improving organizational performance and developing executive ability. The orientation of OTL is toward developing the effectiveness of teams in dealing with job-related problems.

According to Morton, "the Organizational Training Laboratory attempts to change not only the individual but the organizational climate in which the individual must continue to live."[13] With this technique the focus is the team, not the individual, and emphasis is placed on developing an ability to utilize available resources in decision-making and problem-solving situations within the organization itself. The technique is based on the belief that the team approach to work-related problems will have a significant impact in developing the employee's ability to work with other members of the organization in reaching solutions to on-the-job problems.

Whatever the technique utilized, the overriding objective of these approaches is to change the behavior of individuals so as to improve their level of personal satisfaction and also increase the overall effectiveness of organizations. Perhaps the most important key to achieving these results lies in the *ongoing* commitment of management to maintain the atmosphere of trust and support that is hoped to result from the initial organizational development program. Even though the relationship between consultant and organization may be temporary, the objectives of the organizational development program must remain an integral part of the organization's operating philosophy. Ongoing management commitment should be reflected in changes in the evaluation, counseling, and training procedures within the organization as well as in the system utilized by the organization in determining promotion, pay raises, and other rewards.

In summary, programs of organizational development focus on the *individual,* seeking to provide him or her with an awareness of self and environment as well as developing a set of skills that can be brought to bear in the solution of organizational problems. Once these skills have been developed, the emphasis shifts to one of *team building,* such that members of the organization can more readily work together in an atmosphere of trust and support. This focus and approach differ somewhat from the approach normally taken by the more traditional management consultant, whose orientation and analysis are generally more concerned with the organization itself. Exhibit 16.3 on page 420 lists some typical distinctions between conventional consulting activities and the organizational development approach to the consulting process.

Summary of Organizational Development Philosophy and Objectives

In summary, the following would represent the major philosophies and objectives of a program of organizational development:

1. *Planned change:* Designed to anticipate and bring about a formal change process within the organization. This process may be intended to meet rapidly changing market, technological, or economic conditions.
2. *Total organizational change:* Programs in organizational development usually have as their objective the achievement of change within the total organizational framework. Because of the very nature of these programs, it is difficult to bring about the desired change in small or limited scope.
3. *Work group behavior:* The tools and techniques utilized by organizational development have as their focus the work group within

Exhibit 16.3. *Comparison of Management and Organizational Development Consultants*

Feature compared	Management consultant	Organizational development
Objective	Improve organizational effectiveness	Improve organizational effectiveness Increase individual personal satisfaction
Focus	Organization	Individuals within the organization (and groups)
Variables analyzed	Structure, policies, procedures, communication, decision making, authority relationships	Structure, policies, procedures, communication, decision making, authority relationships Individual values, attitudes, ideas, perceptions
Approach	1. Limited primarily to organizational modifications designed to improve structure and operating policies of the organization	1. Team building and laboratory training designed to change the attitudes and behavior of individuals within the organization 2. Organizational modifications designed to facilitate these changes

the organization. Heavy emphasis is placed upon the "group" environment in dealing with organizational change.

4. *Long-range change:* Since organizational development is dealing with changes in the values and ideas of individuals, it is recognized that in most cases change will take place gradually over a long period of time.

5. *Use of a consultant:* Most organizational development programs make use of an outside consultant (change agent) whose function is to interact directly within the organizational environment in order to bring about or facilitate the desired change.

Discussion Questions

1. Define *contingency theory* as it is now applied to modern organizations.
2. Discuss assumptions about human behavior that are the basis of classical organizational theory.
3. Give examples of some of the emerging philosophies now being applied to individuals within the work environment.
4. What is meant by *organizational development?*

5. Discuss some of the objectives that programs of organizational development are designed to bring about.
6. What steps are necessary in order to bring about a change in people?
7. Discuss the role of the consultant in the implementation of an organizational development program.
8. Compare the traditional role of the management consultant with the role of the consultant in an organizational development program.
9. What is a T group?
10. What function does the T group play in programs of organizational development?

Case for Discussion

Bill Harman was the president of a medium-sized manufacturing firm. Since Bill started Harman Manufacturing six years earlier, he and a small group of executives had run the company through an executive committee responsible for establishing policy and making all operational decisions. As a result, middle management at Harman had little experience in either day-to-day or long-range decision making.

As the company grew in size and complexity, Bill decided it was time to decentralize operational decision making to take some of the burden from the executive committee. This decentralization was designed to transfer much of the day-to-day decision process to middle management.

To accomplish this objective Bill contacted a local university and contracted with a Professor Abbott for a three-day executive development program focused on the decentralization with particular emphasis on training middle managers to assume the responsibility for operational decision-making.

The first day was spent in a discussion of how the decentralization process might impact Harman manufacturing. Participants in the first day program included Professor Abbott (who had designed the program), Bill Harman, the two other members of the executive committee, and the seven middle managers who would be assuming new responsibility as a result of the

decentralization. The seating arrangement for the first session appeared as shown.

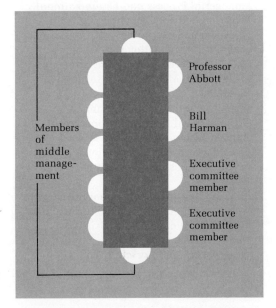

Professor Abbott opened the meeting by asking Bill Harman how effective he thought the Harman Manufacturing decision-making process had been up to that point. Bill answered that he believed that the executive committee had done very well in guiding the company through its early years. With that Professor Abbott looked toward the members of middle management and asked, "Does anybody agree with that?"

Selected References

Argyris, C. "T-Groups for Organizational Effectiveness." In *Harvard Business Review,* March-April 1964.

Bennis, W. *Changing Organizations.* New York: McGraw-Hill, 1966.

————. "A New Role for the Behavioral Sciences Effecting Organizational Change." In *Administrative Science Quarterly,* September 1963.

Davis, S. "An Organic Problem Solving Method of Organizational Change." In *Journal of Applied Behavioral Science 3,* No. 1 (1967).

Filley, A., Hourse, R., and Kerr, S. *Managerial Process and Organizational Behavior.* 2nd ed. Glenview, Ill.: Scott, Foresman and Co., 1976.

French, W. "Organizational Development: Objectives, Assumptions, and Strategies." In *California Management Review 12,* No. 2 (1969).

Greiner, L. "Antecedents of Planned Organizational Change." In *Journal of Applied Behavioral Science 3,* No. 1 (1967).

————. "Patterns of Organizational Change." In *Harvard Business Review,* May-June 1967.

Hall, R. H. "Intra Organizational Structural Variation: Application of the Bureaucratic Model." In *Administrative Science Quarterly,* December 1962.

Lawrence, P. R. and Lorsch, J. W. *Organization and Environment: Managing Differentiation and Integration.* Homewood, Ill.: Richard D. Irwin, 1969.

Leavitt, H. "Applied Organizational Change in Industry: Structural Technological and Humanistic Approaches." In *Handbook of Organizations.* J. March, ed. Skokie, Ill.: Rand McNally, 1965.

Lewin, K. "Group Decision and Social Change." In *Readings in Social Psychology,* T. M. Newcomb and E. L. Hartley, eds. New York: Holt, Rinehart and Winston, 1958.

Luthans, F. *Organizational Behavior.* New York: McGraw-Hill, 1977.

Margules, N., and Raia, A. *Organizational Development: Values, Process, and Technology.* New York: McGraw-Hill, 1972.

McGregor, D. *The Human Side of Enterprise.* New York: McGraw-Hill, 1960.

Schein, E. and Bennis, W. *Personal and Organizational Change Through Group Methods.* New York: John Wiley & Sons, 1966.

Tannenbaum, R. and Davis, S. "Values, Man and Organizations." In *Industrial Management Review,* Winter 1969.

Woodward, J. *Industrial Organization: Theory and Practice.* New York: Oxford Press, 1965.

Worthy, J. "Organizational Structure and Employee Morale." In *American Sociological Review 15* (1950).

QUANTITATIVE TECHNIQUES

Part VI

Introduction

The purpose of these next two chapters will be to present a cross section of techniques utilized to improve planning, decision making, and controlling in a manager's job. The field of management has received significant contributions from the mathematical sciences, contributions which play a significant role in the methods, techniques, and approaches managers use in performing their administrative function.

Major Themes

Predicting the Future:
Forecasting and estimating techniques

Improving Decision Making:
Techniques and applications

Quantitative Techniques in Planning and Controlling

17

Olin's Shift to Strategy Planning

A few years ago, Olin Corp. was awash in aggressive marketing plans for goosedown sleeping bags, propane stoves, tents, and other camping products. At the same time, Olin was pushing industrial mainstays such as polyester film and polyvinyl chloride. But profits were still lackluster at best. Today, however, the $1.5 billion Stamford (Conn.) conglomerate has jettisoned all these products and is putting its capital into such areas as brass sheeting and hydrazine chemicals—products that fit in much better with its established corporate expertise. Reason: Olin has turned to a planning method that stresses overall corporate goals above individual product potentials.

The concept, known variously as strategy planning or strategy management, enables a company to spot—and capitalize on—its strengths in certain markets, and to sacrifice those market areas where growth is marginal. Although its cutthroat nature can make individual product managers unhappy at times, "it shows you how to drop your dogs and pick up stars," explains one veteran corporate planner.

The Strategic Moves

The concept is by no means unique to Olin, a company that this year is struggling just to match its record 1977 profits. In fact, most management consultants—many of whom are pushing a form of strategy planning to their clients—credit General Electric Co. with pioneering the rudiments of the concept more than a decade ago. And today any number of companies, still reeling from the recession of 1974–75, are using variations of the theme in hopes of surviving in a continuing climate of

Reprinted from the March 27, 1978 issue of *Business Week* by special permission. Copyright © 1978 by McGraw-Hill Publishing, Inc., New York, N.Y. 10020. All rights reserved.

declining capital resources and heightened foreign competition.

But Olin, which introduces fresh thinking to its units' strategy planning sessions by having an "outsider" sit in, claims the system, among other things, has helped it weed out such ailing businesses as a polyester film plant in Greenville, S.C., sold in 1974 for $22 million, followed by the sale of its Statesville (N.C.) tent business to National Canvas Products Corp. of Toledo, its Seattle Quilt Co. to Raven Industries Inc. in Sioux Falls, S.D., and its Turner Co. (propane camping appliances) to Cleanweld Co. in Los Angeles—all for a total of $9 million.

At the same time, the system has helped pinpoint the need for investments: more than $100 million to build a chlorine-caustic soda plant in McIntosh, Ala., which will boost the line's production 60%; $75 million to $80 million to expand its polyols, hydrazine, and swimming-pool chemical operations; and $80 million to boost growth in its copper-based alloy markets.

"Enlightened Objectivity"

The key to Olin's system is the process in which plans are formulated. In a traditional planning approach, managers of a business unit would sit down by themselves once a year to hammer out a five-year plan. But at Olin, managers from each of 30-odd strategic planning units (components for which the company can define specific goals) meet with two or three managers from other areas of the company who generally know very little about that unit's operation. Such outside managers are called profilers, and it is their job to lend perspective and to help the planning unit's managers communicate better. "We act as a catalyst to stimulate discussion," explains Joseph R. Rindler, a profiler whose main job is director of financial analysis. "We're there to offer planning unit managers enlightened objectivity."

Profilers, who number about 35 to 40, come from both staff and line jobs that range from personnel executive to product manager. But because they are not professional planners—they spend only 3% to 5% of their time in the profiler role—each must go through a brief training program to prepare for the annual planning sessions, which last one or two days. The planning sessions focus on reaching a consensus on the business unit's optimum strategy. The resulting profile is outlined in a standard two-page format and, in turn, is passed up the line to top management.

From this profile, management prepares a yearly "action document" for each of Olin's five groups—a kind of nonfinancial budget of actions that should be taken to meet long-range goals. Actions prescribed involve moving into new geographic markets or phasing out of existing ones, seeking acquisitions, or unloading properties. "Recent decisions have mostly been to improve our position in existing markets," notes James F. Towey, Olin's chairman and chief executive officer. "We think there are enough opportunities in the businesses we're now in."

"Olinizing"

Although Olin's corporate staff has two full-time planners and the five operating groups have one each, the meat of the planning analysis is done in the profiler sessions. The benefits, according to Olin executives, are that each unit is forced to think through its ideas carefully; the profilers gain knowledge of the unit's activities, which helps them work with or serve the unit better in their primary jobs; the process is a good management development tool; and top management gets a clear picture of where each unit stands and where it should be headed. For example, Rindler says a recent shift in marketing of Olin's pool chemicals,

HTH and Pace, came directly from a profiling session. Under profiler questioning, unit managers discovered that one product made from an inorganic compound was more effective in certain densities of sunlight than another product made from an organic compound. Thus, the company decided to concentrate domestic sales of one product in the Sunbelt region and the other product elsewhere.

The profiler concept originated at Arthur D. Little Inc., the Boston-based consulting firm that helped Olin get its system off the ground in 1972. At that time, ADL staffers assumed the role of profilers. Since then, however, Olin has used its own personnel. "We 'Olinized' the ADL system," says James M. Sheridan, manager of corporate planning analysis. Adds Gilbert C. Mott, vice-president of planning: "It's been considerably [changed] since. And it has the side benefit of improving communications throughout the company.

The Pitfalls

Still, company officials agree, the system is far from perfect. "We have to introduce some new questions and new reviews each year to make sure that people rethink their situations," observes Mott. "We are constantly alert to ensure that the process, by repetition, doesn't become too mechanical." Mott also cautions that there are other dangers built into strategy planning, such as a temptation to "develop a lot of sophisticated concepts like futurology," an attempt to project trends 10 years into the future and beyond. "But we try to keep ours on a practical level," Mott adds. Moreover, friction occasionally occurs between profilers and unit planners who feel the profilers are meddling or spying. "But this is a natural part of constructive dialogue," explains Sheridan.

Nonetheless, says William L. Wallace, who was one of the prime movers in setting up Olin's system before he left the company in 1974, the system has brought a beneficial

Making the Concept Fit a Company's Needs

Olin Corp. is just one of an estimated 100 U.S. companies that have taken strategy planning concepts and modified them to suit their existing markets and management style. Here are some ways they try to make the systems work:

Mead Corp., the Dayton papermaker, credits its six-year-old system with lifting return on total capital to 12% in 1977 from 5% in 1972, and jumping its industrywide rank among forest-product companies to No. 2 of 15 (tied with three others) from No. 12 in 1972. Mead's method: rejuggle 24 former profit centers into that number of strategic business units, and move 24 top executives into new slots so that their expertise matches the businesses they would run. "If you have a business you want a lot of cash out of instead of growth, you don't put a high-powered marketing man in charge, and if you want growth, don't put a conservative accountant in charge," explains William W. Wommack, Mead's vice-chairman. Mead also is allocating money differently. Instead of funding projects with "fair share" allocations, it now funds strategies, a method that lets the company weed out "dog" products, milk its mature cash producers, and concentrate investment on potential growth lines.

Gulf Oil Corp. has one of the weightiest systems around, with 35 planners at corporate headquarters and 73 planners at seven strategy centers. The system has helped Gulf steer clear of the solar energy field, for instance, an area that an energy company might have felt compelled to enter, but one in which Gulf found it would not have competed profitably. Nonetheless, chief planner Juergen Ladendorf says the system, now in its fourth cycle, may take six years to improve bottom-line results.

Daylin Inc., a $300 million Los Angeles retailer that was in deep financial trouble two years ago, asks each product-area manager to draw up a five-year plan to assess his unit's competitive position and spell out a set of actions to enhance it. William M. Duke, planning director, credits the two-year-old system with substantially boosting profits at Daylin's Handy Dan Home Improvement Centers, for one, and with bolstering Daylin's fortunes as a whole. Success has come at a price, however. At the

change in outlook. In the past, he says, "we never asked ourselves how we could win." Though Olin started five-year planning as early as 1963, it was not until 1971, after the company experienced four consecutive years of falling profits, and a drop in return on equity to 4.1% from 12.5% in 1966, that the company decided to rethink its controls on its diverse operations. This led management to ADL and its system of strategy planning. "We needed somebody to give us structure from which to start," says Towey. Since then, Olin's net income has fluctuated on rising sales, but net income from continuing operations has tripled, to $78.1 million in 1977.

No one at Olin credits all of the company's major moves to strategy planning. For example, the spinoffs of its aluminum business to Consolidated Aluminum Corp. for $126 million in 1974 and its Olinkraft subsidiary to Olin shareholders as a separate company in 1974 were in progress before the system was instituted. Nonetheless, says Wallace, "the thing the planning process did was keep us from reneging [on the aluminum business sale] when the market turned up."

Despite an expected profit decline in the first quarter, resulting from rising costs, work stoppages, and bad weather, and despite uncertain prospects for the remainder of 1978, Olin executives think the system has proven itself. The acid test, according to former Olin planner Wallace, was what happened to strategy planning at Olinkraft. "We weren't sure if the new venture would continue using the system, because the former president had only accepted it grudgingly," he recalls. "Once they got spun off that would have been a perfect time to ditch it, but they didn't."

company's Diana Fashion Stores division—a group of about 150 women's specialty shops—Daylin President Sanford C. Sigoloff called for an assessment of lifestyle changes to determine a proper merchandise mix over the next five years. "We wanted to gear store openings accordingly," Duke notes, but the division's managers were reluctant to comply. He says Sigoloff had to recruit "a whole new [management] team that was responsive" to the idea.

Fairchild Camera & Instrument Corp., faced with accelerating changes in technology and reversals in key markets, jumped into strategy planning just last fall by realigning top management and naming Vice-Chairman C. Lester Hogan director of strategy planning. Hogan concedes that Fairchild planning has not always

been successful. For example, the company was badly burned by last year's price war in the digital watch industry. So the company has now augmented its product planning staff with a corporate team of six planning specialists to map out orderly entries into new markets. For example, industry processing techniques may make it possible to put as many as 10 million transistors on a single chip of silicon in 1985, says Hogan, adding: "You don't sell [high-technology] components the way you sell simple diodes."

Eaton Corp., a $2.1 billion automotive and industrial parts maker, began its form of strategy planning four years ago by creating 400 "product market segments" within its 26 divisions. Eaton's system identifies two primary factors that affect strategy planning—"push" and "pull." The pull factors, which

are largely uncontrollable, include inflation, exchange rates, and the growth rate of one business as compared with others. All operating divisions monitor the impact of such factors on their businesses, then contribute data on them to a 10-year benchmark report. The push factors are actions the company can take to control operations: increase R&D, build a new plant, or aggressively pursue market share growth. To influence the push factors, explains corporate development chief Robert C. Brown, each division and market segment unit creates a five-year plan, as does the corporation. To date, Eaton attributes rapid growth in its automatic cruise control product line to the planning system.

The Role of Quantitative Techniques

Regardless of how undesirable or difficult the study of mathematics may be to some (for many years student enrollment in schools of business was made up primarily of those who could not succeed at the more mathematically oriented "hard sciences"), the fact remains that the business manager today must deal with quantitative concepts in order to run a complex operation effectively. One study reports that an impressive variety of techniques are being utilized by corporations in carrying out their planning functions (Table 17.1).

The increasing use of these quantitative techniques has enabled managers to make more intelligent use of the vast amounts of data now available to the business organization. As a result of the use of the many available quantitative techniques, this data can be processed to provide information valuable to the manager in carrying out planning, decision-making, and/or controlling functions.

In simple terms, facility with the "language" of mathematics has become one of the necessary skills that a manager must acquire to function effectively within today's organizations. Managers who do not acquire this skill will find themselves at a distinct disadvantage in carrying out their managerial responsibilities.

This need to understand the language of the mathematical sciences does not mean that tomorrow's manager must become an expert in mathematics. What it does mean, however, is that each

Table 17.1. *Planning Techniques*

Technique	Number of corporations using	Percent of total corporations responding
Linear programming	43	21
Nonlinear programming	16	8
Dynamic programming	8	4
Integer programming	7	3
Queuing theory	7	3
Inventory theory	24	12
Network analysis (PERT or CPM)	28	14
Simulation	60	29
Other	12	6
Total	205	100

Source: Frederick C. Weston, "Operations Research Techniques Relevant to Corporate Planning Function Practices: An Investigative Look," *Academy of Management Journal* (16: 3), September 1973, p. 510.

corporate manager should be aware of useful available quantitative techniques. In addition, the manager should be familiar with the particular types of business problems that may lend themselves to solution through these quantitative techniques. Finally, the manager should be able to interpret the results of a quantitative analysis using the data provided to more effectively carry out the management function.

In making use of the wide variety of quantitative techniques, the manager should always keep in mind that the results of these techniques provide information to the manager; they do not make decisions for the manager. This simply means that the ultimate responsibility for the decision rests with the manager, not with the results of the quantitative analysis. The manager must, therefore, learn to use quantitative data as a tool or aid in the decision-making process and not become so dependent on the numbers as to exclude judgment, experience, and nonquantitative factors.

The specific techniques we will discuss *do not,* in general, require the reader to know a great deal of mathematics or to have a high level of mathematical ability.

Forecasting

Forecasting Assumptions

In most business situations it is necessary to make some assumptions about future conditions prior to making decisions. These assumptions reflect the decision maker's *forecast* or prediction about some future state or condition and, based upon this forecast or prediction, the decision maker is then able to select the most appropriate course of action. Perhaps the most fundamental prediction or forecast that must be made in the typical corporate environment is that of projecting future sales. Let us therefore use future sales projection as the basis for gaining some insight into forecasting tools and techniques.

Most forecasting methods base future projection on some knowledge of historical data. Suppose a corporation believed that its sales for any given time period were closely related to some economic indicator; for example, the sales of automobile tires in a given year might be related to new automobile sales for some previous year, or the sale of lumber might well be related to the number of new homes under construction. In situations such as these, it is possible to plot the relationship between the indicator and the volume of sales over a period of time. For example, assume that Table 17.2 represents the relationship between a particular indicator and sales. This relationship may be plotted in a graph (Figure 17.1). The plot of the relation-

Table 17.2

Indicator	Sales (millions of dollars)
10	5
20	7
29	14
42	17
50	25

ship between sales and the indicator seems to indicate a high degree of relationship between the two factors (sales and indicator). The relationship is such that if it is possible to obtain the value of the indicator for some future time period, one would be able to estimate the corresponding value for sales in that same time period. In order to obtain (forecast) the sales figure, given the value of the indicator, it is first necessary to identify the *exact* nature of the relationship between sales and the indicator. This is accomplished by "fitting" a straight line to the points such that the line represents "the best fit" in terms of the available data (see Figure 17.2). The question then is, how does one go about determining this line of "best fit"?

Method of Least Squares

The *method of least squares* makes use of the general equation for a straight line,

$$Y = a + bX,$$

where Y = the value to be determined (sales) (a dependent variable), a = Y intercept of the line of best fit, b = slope of the line of best fit

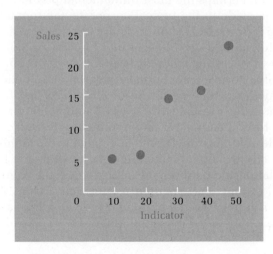

Figure 17.1

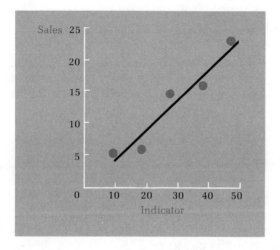

Figure 17.2

(the slope indicates the relationship of the change in one factor for a given change in the other), X = the value of the factor which is known (indicator, an independent variable; Figure 17.3).

In order to utilize the least squares approach the following equations are needed:

$$\Sigma Y = na + b\Sigma X$$
$$\Sigma XY = a\Sigma X + b\Sigma X^2$$

Figure 17.3

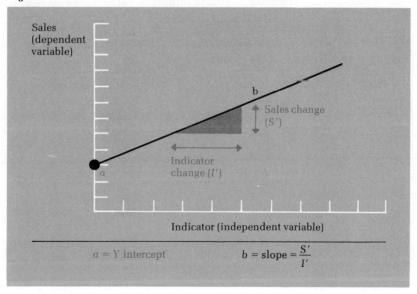

where Σ = summation of all values, X = values of independent variable (indicator), Y = values of dependent variable (sales), n = number of pair values which are to be utilized. Since the solution to the line of best fit requires that we know the Y intercept (a), and the slope of the line (b), it is necessary to solve the above equations for both a and b. This solution would provide the following:

$$a = \frac{\Sigma Y - b\Sigma X}{n}$$

$$b = \frac{n\Sigma XY - (\Sigma X)(\Sigma Y)}{n\Sigma X^2 - (\Sigma X)^2}$$

Given these two equations it is now possible to solve for the Y intercept *(a)* and the slope *(b)*. Let us examine the data in Table 17.3. Since we now know all of the values needed to solve for b (slope), we substitute in the equation

$$b = \frac{5(2560) - (151)(68)}{5(5605) - (151)^2}$$

$$= 0.4846$$

and then solve for a:

$$a = \frac{68 - .4846(151)}{5}$$

$$= -1.0375$$

We now have the equation for the line of best fit as follows; which now allows us to forecast sales for some future quarter (Y').

$$Y' = -1.0375 + 0.4846\ X$$

| *Sales value to be forecast* | | *Known value of indicator* |

Table 17.3

n	(X) Indicator	(Y) Sales (in millions of $)	XY	X²	Y²
1	10	5	50	100	25
2	20	7	140	400	49
3	29	14	406	841	196
4	42	17	714	1764	289
5	50	25	1250	2500	625
	151	68	2560	5605	1184

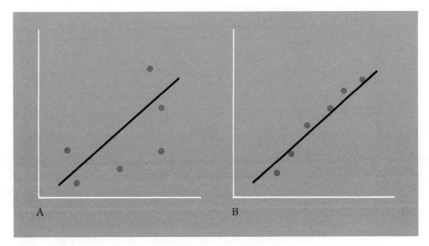

Figure 17.4

In order to use this line of best fit, to forecast some future sales value, we need only obtain the value for the appropriate indicator. For example, let us assume that the value of the indicator for next year was determined to be 65. By inserting this value into our equation we obtain the following:

$$Y' = -1.0375 + 0.4846 (65)$$
$$= 30.46 = \text{sales forecast of } \$30,460,000$$

When the least squares method of forecasting is used, the accuracy of the forecast will be a function of the closeness of the relationship between the dependent and independent variables. Figure 17.4 shows graphs of two sets of data points in which a "least squares" line has been determined for each. It is clear that the relationship between the dependent and independent variable in graph B is much greater than in graph A. This being the case, the accuracy of the forecast obtained utilizing a relationship similar to that found in graph B should be much higher than could be expected if the relationship between the independent and dependent variables were similar to that in graph A. A measure of the closeness of the relationship between the independent variable and the dependent variable is referred to as the *coefficient of correlation*. The higher the value of this correlation coefficient, the greater the strength of the relationship between the dependent and independent variables. That is, the correlation between two variables can provide an indi-

Table 17.4

Year	Sales (millions of dollars)
1	3
2	4
3	6
4	7
5	10

cation of the degree of confidence that one may have in the value of the forecast variable).

This same method of least squares analysis can be applied to data in which the independent variable may be simply past sales history over time, as given in Table 17.4. Applying the least squares method to such data is referred to as *time series analysis*.

If the company wished to forecast sales in year 6, it would simply utilize the following equations:

$$a = \frac{\Sigma Y - 6\Sigma X}{n}$$

$$b = \frac{n\Sigma XY - (\Sigma X)(\Sigma Y)}{n\Sigma X^2 - (\Sigma X)^2}$$

For example, if Table 17.5 represented sales figures (Y) over time (X), then to obtain a sales forecast for year 6 we would proceed as follows. Substituting in our equations would yield

$$b = \frac{5(107) - (15)(30)}{5(55) - 225} = 1.7$$

$$a = \frac{30 - 1.7(15)}{5} = 0.9$$

giving

$$Y = 0.9 + 1.7(X)$$

Table 17.5

n	Year (X)	Sales (Y)	XY	X²	Y²
1	1	3	3	1	9
2	2	4	8	4	16
3	3	6	18	9	36
4	4	7	28	16	49
5	5	10	50	25	100
	15	30	107	55	210

In our example, X would equal year 6 or

$$Y = 0.9 + 1.7\ (6) = 11.1$$

Therefore, forecast sales for year 6 would equal $11.1 million.

The sales forecast model can be extremely useful to managers in providing information regarding possible future demand. This information will allow decision makers to anticipate future needs and plan in advance of these needs. Models of this type are invaluable to the management *planning* function. Through the ability to forecast future demand, the decision maker is able to anticipate resource needs such as the manpower, inventory, and financial requirements necessary to meet forecast future sales.

Break-Even Analysis

Perhaps one of the most fundamental quantitative techniques available to managers is the *break-even analysis*. This is a graphic representation of the interrelationship between *revenues* and *costs* at various levels of output. The break-even point in the analysis is that point (level of output) at which *total revenues will equal total costs,* thus resulting in neither a profit nor a loss for the firm. The determination of break-even point is a vital piece of information for management, for it defines the sales volume that must be achieved in order to cover total costs of operation. It thus also indicates the point in sales volume at which *profits* will begin to accrue. Figure 17.5 on page 438 is an example of a break-even analysis graph.

In order to understand the break-even graph it is necessary to define some commonly used financial terms. In the formula

$$\underset{\text{Total cost}}{TC} = \underset{\text{Fixed costs}}{FC} + \underset{\text{Total variable costs}}{TVC}$$

fixed costs (FC) are costs that remain essentially *constant* regardless of level of output or sales volume. These costs are normally associated with factors such as machinery and equipment overhead. *Variable costs* (TVC) are costs that will *vary* depending upon the level of output of the firm. These costs are normally associated with factors such as wages and materials. Costs such as these are related to the level of output and will vary depending upon the number of units that are produced.

$$TVC = \underset{\substack{\text{Variable cost} \\ \text{per unit}}}{VC} \times \underset{\substack{\text{Number of} \\ \text{units produced}}}{X}$$

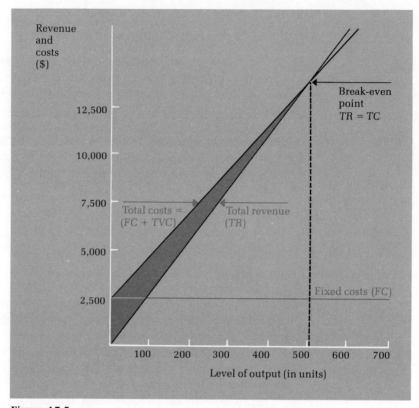

Figure 17.5

Therefore,

$$\underset{\textit{Total revenue}}{TR} = \underset{\substack{\textit{Number of} \\ \textit{units produced}}}{X} \times \underset{\textit{Price per unit}}{P}$$

Since we have defined the break-even point as the point at which total revenue equals total costs, we may write the following

$$TR = TC$$

at break-even point. Since

$$TR = X \times P \quad \text{and} \quad TC = FC + VC(X)$$

therefore at the break-even point

$$X \times P = FC + VC(X)$$

We can now solve the equation for X (the number of units at which we would break even):

$$X = \frac{FC}{P - VC}$$

To illustrate the break-even concept let us use the following example. Assume fixed costs = \$2,500.00, variable costs = \$1.00/unit, and price of product = \$6.00/unit. Calculate the sales volume needed to break even.

$$X = \frac{2,500}{6.00 - 1.00} = 500 \text{ units}$$

(This result is expressed graphically in Figure 17.5.)

The information provided by a break-even analysis can aid management in making decisions such as the pricing of a product (impact of some increase or decrease in price per unit) or determining the sales volume needed to achieve some desired profit goal. In addition, decisions regarding the purchase of new equipment, which would have an impact upon both fixed and variable costs, could be evaluated by means of a break-even analysis. In summary, the break-even analysis provides management with a simple quantitative technique that illustrates the relationship between revenue and costs at various levels of output. The knowledge of this relationship allows management to determine profit potential at various sales levels and thus aids in developing a pricing and marketing strategy for the product.

Program Evaluation and Review Technique (PERT)

First developed by the consulting firm of Booz, Allen and Hamilton for the Department of the Navy in the late 1950s, PERT has become one of the most often used of management planning and control techniques. The primary value of PERT lies in its ability to provide information for use in the decision-making process. Properly utilized, PERT can provide vital information at both the *planning* and *control* stages of a given project. PERT is most effective on those projects where a highly complex series of jobs or components must be molded together in a critical sequence of activities resulting in a single product or project. An example of this is the Polaris Submarine Project for which PERT was originally developed. PERT has been utilized extensively since by the military, and it has also found wide acceptance in private industry in construction projects and airplane and shipbuilding.

PERT is a schematic model utilizing the network concept to show the sequencing of work activities. In the area of *planning*, it provides information regarding the total series of tasks that must be performed in order to complete a particular project. Perhaps more importantly, the PERT network also provides information regarding the sequencing and timing of these tasks. In order to set up the PERT network the manager must think through carefully all the tasks and activities involved in a given project and must give careful consideration to the sequencing of these tasks. In some larger projects the number of jobs or activities may reach the thousands; in such cases, the project is broken down into stages and individual PERT networks are developed for each stage. With respect to information utilized for *control* purposes, PERT provides the manager with data regarding the current status of a project at any given time and also provides a series of alternative courses of action for making up lost time or missed target dates.

What Is a PERT Network?

In setting up a PERT network it is first necessary to define the particular target or project that management is seeking to achieve; the project might be construction of a housing development or the complete assembly of an airplane. The *network* will then represent the series of activities and events (in proper sequence) which represent progress toward completion of the project. Let us define the terms *event* and *activity*.

An *event* is any recognizable or measurable plateau in the progression toward completion of the project. For instance, in the construction of a housing project, an event might represent the completion of the foundation for the building. In the setting up of an assembly line, an event might be the initial blue print of the layout. An event itself does not take time; it is a point in time at which a given set of activities has been completed.

An *activity*, on the other hand, represents work necessary to take a project from one event to another (Figure 17.6). An activity thus represents ongoing work over a period of time. In our housing project, for example, the construction of the building walls would be an activity. The point at which the walls were completed would be an

Figure 17.6

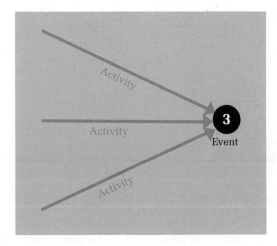

Figure 17.7

event (Figure 17.6). In most projects, an event will normally have more than one activity leading up to it (Figure 17.7).

Key Points in Constructing a PERT Network

In constructing a PERT network it is important that the manager keep in mind the following conditions:

1. Events represent recognizable check points in moving toward project completion and must be placed in their necessary order or sequence
2. Activities represent ongoing work as one moves from one event to another
3. No event can be reached until *all* of the activities leading up to it have been completed
4. No activities can be completed until the event preceding it has occurred.

Let us set up a hypothetical PERT network in order to demonstrate how the program would operate. Let us assume that the tasks listed in Table 17.6 are necessary for setting up and operating a machine in a manufacturing operation. A diagram of the above project would appear as in Figure 17.8 on page 442.

Notice from the activities reflected in the diagram in Figure 17.8 that certain tasks must be done in sequence (i.e., machine cannot be purchased until supplier is selected) while others can be accomplished simultaneously, i.e., job description for operator can be written at same time as the design of the space layout (see Table 17.5).

It is clear that in diagraming the PERT network the manager is

Table 17.6

Task description	Activity	
	Event	Event
1. Select machine design	1 ⟶ 2	
2. Select supplier of machine	2 ⟶ 3	
3. Design space layout	2 ⟶ 4	
4. Write job description for operator	2 ⟶ 5	
5. Purchase machine	3 ⟶ 6	
6. Set up layout	4 ⟶ 6	
7. Install machine	6 ⟶ 7	
8. Recruit machine operator	5 ⟶ 7	

forced to think through all of the activities that will be necessary in order to complete the project. In addition, consideration must be given to activities that can be done simultaneously as opposed to those that must be sequenced. The completed PERT network thus represents the flow of work to be done on the project over some specified time period.

Once the network is completed in diagrammatical form it is necessary for the manager to obtain time estimates for each activity in the network. At this point, let us introduce the abbreviation *te*. This represents the expected time or *time estimate* to complete an activity or task. To begin an analysis of the PERT network it is necessary that a manager obtain a time estimate (*TE*) for each activity within the network. In order to obtain *TE* values for each activity, the manager

Figure 17.8

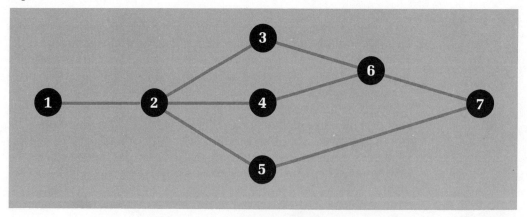

should communicate with the individuals responsible for actually doing the particular tasks; with respect to machine design, the individual working on the design should be consulted. The designer should be asked to provide three different time estimates:

a: optimistic time to complete task (assuming all goes extremely well)
m: most likely time to complete task
b: pessimistic time to complete task (assume significant problems along the way).

With these three time estimates, the manager can determine a TE value for each activity. The equation used to determine the TE value follows the beta distribution:

$$TE = \frac{a + 4m + b}{6}$$

Some users of the PERT network have abandoned the optimistic and pessimistic time estimates and utilize only a single most likely estimate in their calculations. The decision to do this is often based on the difficulty of actually determining optimistic and pessimistic time estimates.

Let us assume that the estimates in Table 17.7 have been provided by those involved in the various activities. Based upon the values of a, m, and b, TE estimates are developed by use of the TE equation above. Using these estimates for TE, the PERT network diagram in Figure 17.9 (page 444) will be obtained.

With the data we have available it is possible to calculate the expected time of completion of each *event*. The expected time of completion of a given event will be represented by TE. In order to calculate the TE for each event *(expected time of completion)*, we simply go through the network, working from left to right, calculat-

Table 17.7

Activity	a (weeks)	m (weeks)	b (weeks)	TE (weeks)
1 ——→ 2	2	3	6	3.3
2 ——→ 3	1	4	5	3.6
2 ——→ 4	4	6	8	6
2 ——→ 5	1	2	3	2
3 ——→ 6	3	5	7	5
4 ——→ 6	4	5	7	5.1
6 ——→ 7	1	3	6	3.1
5 ——→ 7	3	4	5	4

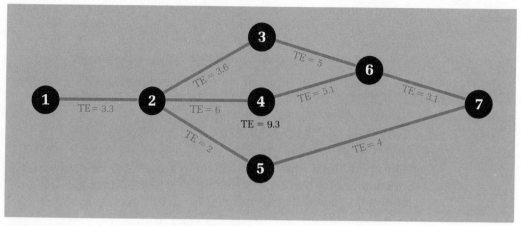

Figure 17.9

ing the longest time it can take to reach the completion of a given event. This is done to comply with the rule that no event can be completed until all activities leading up to it have been completed. The results of this analysis appear in Figure 17.10.

For example, the *TE* for Event 2 would equal 3.3 weeks: only one activity need takes place prior to Event 2 and this activity will take 3.3 weeks. The *TE* for Event 3 would be the *TE* for Event 2 plus the time it takes to go from Event 2 to Event 3, or 3.3 + 3.6 = 6.9 weeks. Keeping in mind our previous statement that no event may be completed until *all* activities leading up to it have been completed, we

Figure 17.10

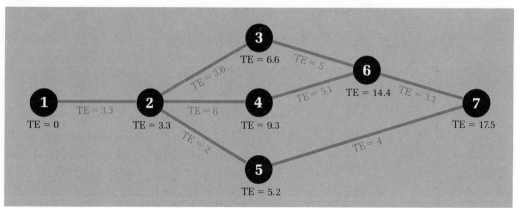

may state as a general rule that the *TE* for any event is the sum of the *TE*'s on the *longest* path leading up to the given event. Following this rule, the *TE* for each event is shown. An illustration of this "largest sum" rule is demonstrated in Event 6. We note that there are two possible paths leading to Event 6: 1–2–3–6 and 1–2–4–6. Since Event 6 cannot be reached until *both* paths have been completed, the time required to reach Event 6 will be a function of the *longest* path, which happens to be 1–2–4–6. This path takes 14.4 weeks, and thus *TE* for Event 6 is 14.4 weeks.

Once we have completed the *TE* value for each event we note that *TE* for Event 7 (the last event, or project completion) is 17.5 weeks. This represents the expected time to complete the project. The path taken to complete the project in 17.5 weeks is 1–4–6–7. This is the most time-consuming path through the network and is referred to as the *critical path*. It is called critical because any delay in time along this path will necessarily delay the completion of the project beyond the 17.5-week expected completion time. (Delays in other paths along the network may or may not delay the completion time of the project.)

In order to determine the impact of delays within the network we will make use of the concept of *slack*. *Slack* simply refers to the amount of time a given event within the network is ahead of or behind schedule. In order to provide management with information for use in the planning, control, and decision-making processes, an analysis must be made with respect to slack at various points in the network.

A *slack analysis* begins with the calculation of a *TL* for each event. *TL* represents the *latest time* a given event can be completed and still not delay the project beyond its *scheduled* completion date. Note that the key word is *scheduled*—not *expected* completion date (*TE*). The scheduled completion date is a function of the time that management can allow for completion of the project. This completion time may be related to a contract commitment or may be simply based on management's own scheduling requirements. The *scheduled completion date* for the final event in the network is represented by the abbreviation *TS*, and *TS* = *TL*.

Let us assume that the *TS* for the project diagramed in Figure 17.11 (page 446) is 15 weeks. This means that management (for whatever reason) wishes to complete the project in a 15-week time period. But it is obvious from a comparison of the scheduled completion time (*TS* = 15 weeks) and the expected completion time (*TE* = 17.5 weeks) that the project will be behind schedule; management wishes to know how bad the situation is and whether anything can be done

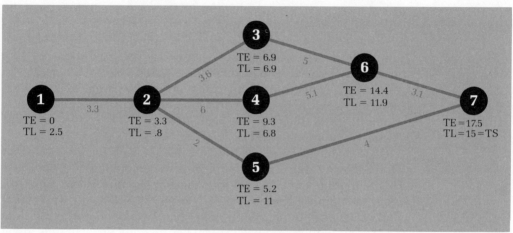

Figure 17.11

about it without incurring across-the-board cost increases. A slack analysis will provide this information.

We proceed with the slack analysis by calculating a *TL* for each event, just as we did a *TE* for each event. The *TL*s, however, are calculated by starting at the *last* event and working from right to left (backward) through the network. As we have mentioned, the *TL for the last event is the scheduled or desired completion time, TS*. Thus from our example, *TL* for Event 7 would equal 15 weeks. *TL* for the last event will always equal *TS*. Proceeding from left to right across the network we see that for Event 6 the latest time that this event could be completed and not delay the project beyond its scheduled completion date would be 11.9 weeks. This is the case since once Event 6 has been reached it will still take 3.1 weeks to complete the project.

Having established *TL* for Event 6 at 11.9 weeks we now proceed to determine the *TL* for Event 3. If Event 6 must be completed by 11.9 weeks (*TL*) and it takes 5 weeks of work to proceed from Event 3 to Event 6, then Event 3 must be completed by 6.9 weeks.

By the same logic we can determine the *TL* for Event 4. Since it will take 5.1 weeks of work to proceed from Event 4 to Event 6, and since Event 6 must be completed by 11.9 weeks (*TL*), then Event 4 must be completed by 6.8 weeks (*TL* = 6.8).

To determine the *TL* for Event 2, we must examine the time necessary to proceed from Event 2 to both Event 3 and Event 4. We find that the latest time Event 2 can be completed and not delay Event 3 is 3.3 weeks (3.3 + 3.6 = 6.9). In similar fashion, the latest time that

Table 17.8. *Slack Analysis Table*

Event	TE	TL	Slack
1	0	− 2.5	−2.5
2	3.3	.8	−2.5
3	6.9	6.9	0
4	9.3	6.8	−2.5
5	5.2	11	5.8
6	14.4	11.9	−2.5
7	17.5	15	−2.5

Event 2 can be completed and not delay Event 4 is .8 weeks (.8 + 6 = 6.8). This being the case, the most critical time in order not to delay the project would be .8 weeks and thus *TL* for Event 2 would equal .8. The *TL*s for each event are shown in Figure 17.11.

Slack Analysis   The slack is now obtained from the equation

$$\text{Slack} = TL - TE$$

Based upon an inspection of *TL* and *TE* values we note that slack can be positive, negative, or zero. *Positive slack* means that the project is ahead of schedule at this point. *Negative slack* indicates that the project is behind schedule. *Zero slack* indicates that the project is right on schedule. The larger the number—either positive or negative—the more the project is ahead of or behind schedule.

An inspection of the slack analysis table shows that this project is behind schedule by 2.5 weeks along path 1-2-4-6-7 (the critical path). We note however that Event 5 shows a certain amount of positive slack, equal to 5.8 weeks. The presence of positive slack indicates that this event is actually ahead of schedule. Management may wish to consider the possibility of shifting resources from an event with positive slack to events along the critical path in order to bring the project up to schedule. This is possible if the equipment or labor skills are at all interchangeable. The possibility of shifting resources from one path, having positive slack, to another with negative slack (critical path) would allow management to reduce the total time needed to complete the project without adding any additional costs. In shifting resources from one path to another, however, management must be careful to measure the resources taken from one path so as to be able to determine at what point this path may become part of the critical path. It is possible that the transfer of resources will cause one job to take a longer time and thus reduce the positive slack in that path. At some point all positive slack will be depleted, and this path will then become part of the critical path within the network. For example, in Event 3 the slack analysis shows 0, which means that there is no slack in the system and any delay would also cause that path to fall behind schedule.

It is not always possible to shift resources within a network in order to reduce the time along the critical path. In many jobs the types of skills and equipment needed for one job are not interchangeable for other jobs in the project. Management may wish to bring in outside resources or schedule overtime in order to make up the needed time (2.5 weeks). The slack analysis table (Table 17.7) indicates where the overtime or new resource should be allocated in order to most effective. Based upon this table, it is clear that only on those jobs along the critical path will there be any advantage to the scheduling of overtime or the allocation of new resources. This is the case since it is these jobs that now determine the amount of time needed to complete the project.

Variance and Probability of Success

The last concept to be introduced in the PERT analysis deals with an analysis of the uncertainty associated with the original TE estimates. This uncertainty is a function of the relative spread (range) between the optimistic and pessimistic times provided by those from whom the estimates were obtained. From this data it is possible to calculate both a standard deviation and a variance. Following the beta distribution, the standard deviation is arbitrarily established as 1/6 of the range, or

$$\sigma = \frac{b - a}{6}$$

From our example (Table 17.7), we may now calculate the values for each of the TE's within our network.

Once we have calculated the standard deviation and the variance for each of the activities within the network, it is possible to determine the probability of meeting the scheduled completion time, TS, given the time estimates utilized. We recognize that even though the expected time of completion (TE) may exceed the scheduled time (TS) there is still some likelihood of meeting the target; this is the case since some or all of our optimistic time estimates may actually occur.

Without going into the theoretical background, we may calculate the probability of success by summing up the variances along the critical path, taking the square root of the sum of those variances and dividing it into (TS − TE). The resultant number is referred to as the Z *factor* and can be converted into a probability by referring to a

Table 17.9

Activity	a	m	b	TE	Standard deviation σ	Variance* σ^2
1	2	2	3	6	3.3	.66	.43*
2	3	1	4	5	3.6	.66	.43
2	4	4	6	8	6	.66	.43*
2	5	1	2	3	2	.33	.11
3	6	3	5	7	5	.66	.43
4	6	4	5	7	5.1	.50	.25*
6	7	1	3	6	3.1	.83	.69*
5	7	3	4	5	4	.33	.11

* The variance is simply equal to the square of the standard deviation.

table of standard normal deviations. Thus for our example the variances in question would be along path 1-2-4-6-7 or, from Table 17.9, the values for the variances would equal substituting these values in the following equation:

$$Z = \frac{TS - TE}{\sqrt{\sigma^2}}$$

$$= \frac{15 - 17.5}{\sqrt{.43 + .43 + .25 + .69}}$$

$$= \frac{-2.5}{\sqrt{1.80}} = \frac{-2.5}{1.34} = 1.86$$

From our normal distribution tables we see that the project, given the time estimates, has a probability of success of 3 percent. If management wishes to improve on this probability, then additional resources must be allocated to the project along the critical path. If management does choose to improve its probability of successfully meeting the completion time (TS) it should examine those activities along the critical path that have the widest spread (range) between optimistic and pessimistic times. Allocation of resources to these activities in order to approach the optimistic time estimate would probably have the greatest impact upon the reduction of overall project time. This allocation of resources will obviously increase the costs associated with the project but will also improve its probability of meeting the target completion date. Thus, management must reach a point where it is satisfied with the trade-offs between the costs of the project and its relative probability of successful completion.

In summary, the PERT network is one of the most powerful *planning* and *control* techniques available to management. This technique requires that management think through a project in terms of its logical sequence and then enables management to control and measure progress toward completion over time.

Discussion Questions

1. Discuss the role of quantitative techniques in the managerial decision-making process.
2. For each quantitative technique discussed in Chapter 17 indicate the following:
   a. Type of problem that can be solved.
   b. Information required for the technique to be used.
   c. Possible limitations of the technique.
3. If a firm produces a product for which it charges a price of $10.00/unit, and the firm has fixed costs of $3,000 and estimates its variable costs to be $5.00/unit,
   a. Calculate break-even point in terms of number of units.
   b. How many units would have to be sold to make $5,000 profit?

4. A company recorded·its sales over the last 7 years. The figures appear as follows:

Year	Sales (millions of units)
1970	9.0
1971	8.5
1972	9.5
1973	9.6
1974	10.7
1975	10.5
1976	11.3
1977	12.0

Using the above data, forecast sales in units for 1978.

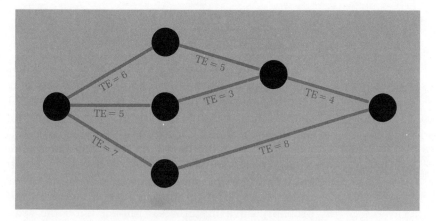

5. For the PERT network shown: (a) calculate TE for each event; (b) calculate TL for each event (assume scheduled time of completion TS = 14 weeks): (c) perform a slack analysis and interpret the results.

6. Would you consider PERT to be a *planning* or a *control* tool with respect to the management function?

Quantitative Techniques in Decision Making

18

The Decision-Making Powers of Management Information Systems

Despite their shortcomings, management information systems provide more benefits to large and small firms than are possible without MIS.

by Joseph Sass

What constitutes an MIS system? Any firm, large or small, that uses a formalized approach or EDP system for its daily business has the foundation for an MIS. In simpler terms, an MIS has two functional parts: 1) the data collection subsystem, and 2) the analysis and reporting subsystem. If these two parts are organized, an MIS base has been established. In general, the larger the company and the more formal its approach to data collection, the more likely the MIS system can be used by top management to establish company policies and plans, monitor company performance and adapt company strategies in response to changing situations.

Conversely, the smaller the company, the less likely the tasks just mentioned can be achieved. How, then, if this is true, can small firms have an MIS system? Because, although top management in the small company may not be obtaining pertinent data for its needs, the more mundane, functional aspects of the business can be concluded with the aid of data supplied through the system. The difference is that there is a much lower level of sophistication. This idea can be illustrated clearly by referring to the flowchart (figure opposite). Large and small companies alike can process the requirements on the first three levels.

From Joseph Sass, "Management Information Systems: The Decision-Making Powers of MIS," *Infosystems*, September 1976. Reprinted by permission.

The gap, however, appears at the bottom level. Only in the highly technical, sophisticated system does the simulation and projection capability appear. This is the area of MIS where real payoffs can occur. Unquestionably, whether the payoffs do or do not occur determines the success or failure of MIS systems in management's eyes. More often than not, at present, the payoffs do not occur.

Does this imply that MIS has been less than successful for businesses? Not necessarily. It is clearly a differentiation between low-level and high-level MIS systems. Sometimes, only on-line, fancy terminals and real time responses are thought of as constituting an MIS. This is not true.

According to a recent column by Arnold Kneitel in *Infosystems*, "What should a manager/user expect from a management information system?—if you believe that an MIS must be: 1) totally integrated, 2) complete with sophisticated models, 3) capable of issuing alternative courses of action ranked by probability of success, 4) able to handle unstructured and judgmental data, or 5) on-line ... then be prepared to join the 'MIS Is Dead' alumni."

In general, it is accepted that there are four levels of sophistication. At the lowest level, the functions include data collection of information such as year-to-date sales by customer, by state, etc. and making this information available to the manager. This is a base point in forming an MIS system, with both large and small firms having the capability to perform this operation.

In the next level, the capability to draw inferences or evaluate policy alternatives is inherent in the system. Model building, simulation, and operations research

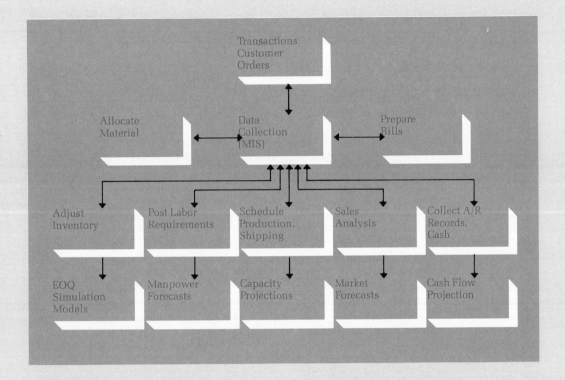

techniques are incorporated in the system. Here, the small firm has not, to any degree, implemented these operations as well as the larger firms have.

The second highest level involves the ability to evaluate alternative policy choices—a more sophisticated extension of the modeling capability mentioned previously. Usually implied in this level is the use of on-line terminals and up-to-date data manipulation.

Even fewer firms can claim success at the highest level of sophistication. In this state, alternative policy choices are *determined by the system*, not the manager.

So in essence, there are varying levels in the implementation of MIS systems. The majority of MIS systems are performing at the lowest level. How good is a particular MIS? How is one rated? There are a number of factors.

The discussion thus far has centered on conceptual MIS systems. But in relating MIS to small businesses, what needs are peculiar to them? What questions are to be answered by their MIS system? More than likely, they are looking for functional decisions; those that are of help in the day-to-day operation of the company. But are computer capabilities available to the small business? And, how small is small? How can a computer with its associated costs be justified? An examination of several small firms with computers includes those with sales of as little as $1 million up to $10 mi.

There are several characteristics of these small firms, all centering about the theme—limited resources, including: 1) limited technical skills—the firm does not have computer personnel nor do they generally hire a specialist in today's market, 2) limited money—how much can or will they spend? Usually the figure of $1,000/month or less is the norm, 3) as a direct result of the above, limited computing power is available to them. Considering these limitations, what alternatives are open?

Two hardware modes are available: commercial timesharing and small computers.[1] For example, timesharing has been very useful to firms that are required to collect personnel data, government statistics and other types of data that are essentially independent files. These specialized, segregated data files can be manipulated to provide MIS-type answers for these firms.

The second approach involves the lease, rental or purchase of a small computer. With the dramatic decreases in cost and similar increases in capability, these systems are very powerful in comparison to what was available just a few years ago.

Now assuming that the small business has acquired such a computer, how is it programmed and by whom? Recall that these firms have limited resources from which to draw. The computer manufacturers are

aware of these restrictions and have given the companies three alternatives: 1) the company can buy a package(s) from the computer manufacturer that will do most of the common accounting procedures for the firm, like payroll, accounts receivable and payable and sales analysis, 2) a software firm or third-party programmer can be hired to perform the software development on a one-time cost basis (This need arises when the package programs do not fit the particular installation), 3) the computer manufacturer will supply the programming support necessary.

The IBM System/32 which has made significant inroads in the small business market, fits the criteria of supplying MIS-type information well. With this machine comes a number of software packages and an MIS information retrieval capability. The capability is supplied through an on-line CRT that permits interruption of normal processing and allows interrogation of data files in effect, on a real-time basis.

With this and other similar machines, the small company with limited resources and skills, has the opportunity of implementing and capitalizing on the fruition of an MIS.

[1] Excluded from this discussion are service bureaus and accounting machines.

The EOQ Equation

One fundamental quantitative technique that forms the basis for inventory analysis and decision making is the Economic Order Quantity *(EOQ)* equation. The purpose of inventory in sales and manufacturing is to offset uncertainties regarding future sales or manufacturing processes. In effect, inventory provides a buffer or measure of safety against unexpectedly high sales volumes or irregularities in manufacturing which might otherwise result in sales delays. This measure of safety is not without cost, however, for by maintaining a certain level of inventory the manager incurs various real costs that must be absorbed by the firm.

The purpose of our discussion is to focus on a single component of the complex inventory problem and attempt to determine a decision rule that can be utilized to aid the manager in making the most appropriate decision. Let us assume that a manager anticipates requiring 6000 units of a particular component over the next year. This component is purchased from another supplier and is utilized in a product that is produced by the manager's firm. The manager must decide how best to order the 6000 units. Let us examine two possible alternatives (Figure 18.1).

Alternative 1 would represent a case in which the manager ordered all 6000 units at one time. In this situation the manager would

Figure 18.1

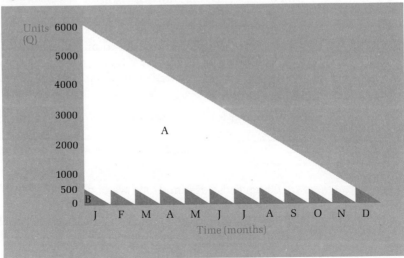

place only one order with the supplier and would then utilize the units, as needed, over the entire year. Area A (the large light triangle) would describe such a situation.

On the other hand, *Alternative 2* would represent a situation in which the manager might choose to order 500 units a month each month over the year in order to meet the firm's annual needs of 6000. Area B (the total of the dark triangles) would graphically present this situation. In this case, the manager would be required to place 12 orders each year rather than a single order.

In order to evaluate these two alternatives, it is necessary to understand something of the costs associated with the ordering of inventory. For purposes of our discussion we will focus upon only two areas of cost.

Inventory carrying costs. These are the costs associated with carrying or holding units of inventory. These costs increase as the number of *units (Q)* of inventory increases. Examples of these costs include taxes, depreciation, insurance, obsolescence, and storage space.

Inventory ordering costs: These are the costs associated with placing orders for units (inventory) from supplier. Since these costs are associated with ordering inventory, they will increase as the total number of *orders* increases.

In Figure 18.1 we note that under Alternative 1 we would only place a single order, receiving all 6000 units at one time, thus minimizing *ordering* costs; but we would maintain a high level of inventory *(Q)*, thus maximizing overall inventory *carrying* costs. The reverse would be true under Alternative 2. The question for the manager thus becomes how to determine how many units (lot size) to order from a supplier in order to minimize the total of both carrying and ordering costs for inventory.

In order to assess this situation it is necessary to make the following assumptions:

1. Demand for the component is constant and is known by the manager.
2. The time between the placement of an order and its arrival (lead time) is known by the manager.

Given these assumptions we can now examine Figure 18.2, which represents what is called a "sawtooth" inventory model. This model shows the arrival of Q units of inventory in stock, along with their gradual depletion over time until time t, at which the original order of Q units is totally depleted and a new order arrives. In this situation the *average* level of inventory would equal $Q/2$.

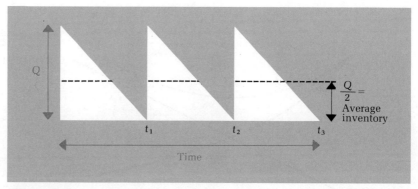

Figure 18.2

If we allow inventory carrying costs to equal C, then the total cost of carrying the inventory would equal carrying costs (C) times average inventory level ($Q/2$):

$$\text{Total carrying cost} = C \times \frac{Q}{2}$$

On the other hand, the total inventory ordering costs would equal the cost of placing each order (S) times the number of orders that must be placed. If R is the total annual requirement and Q is the number of units that are ordered each time an order is placed (lot size), then the number of orders placed per year would equal R/Q and, therefore, total inventory ordering cost would be

$$\text{Total ordering cost} = \frac{R}{Q} \times S$$

Since the variable which the manager controls is the lot size (Q), the impact of both ordering costs and carrying costs can be seen in Figure 18.3. The objective for the manager is to select that value of Q (lot size) which will *minimize* the total costs associated with ordering and carrying inventory.

From a knowledge of algebra, we can determine that the minimum total costs will occur at the intersection of the carrying cost and ordering costs curves.* Thus, we set the curves equal to each other (point of intersection) and solve for the value of Q.

* The magnitude of the slope of the hyperbola is negatively as great as the positive magnitude of the carrying costs line at the point of intersection. Thus, the sum of the two slopes is zero. Since the slope-of-total-cost curve is equal to the sum of these two slopes for any value of Q, its value is zero for the value of Q at which the hyperbola and the line intersect. The slope on the total cost curve at which the slope equals Q represents a minimum point. (Richards and Greenlaw, *Management Decision Making* [Homewood, Ill.: Richard D. Irwin, 1966], p. 473.)

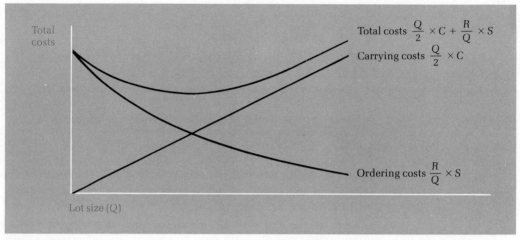

Figure 18.3

$$\frac{Q}{2} \times C = \frac{R}{Q} \times S$$

$$QC = \frac{2RS}{Q}$$

$$Q^2C = 2RS$$

$$Q^2 = \frac{2RS}{C}$$

$$Q = \sqrt{\frac{2RS}{C}}$$

This value of Q represents the lot size to be ordered that will minimize total costs of carrying and ordering inventory (EOQ).

For example, if we require 6000 units (R) annually, and the cost of carrying inventory is $2.00 unit/yr (C), and the cost of ordering is $10.00 an order, the *Economic Order Quantity* will equal:

$$Q = \sqrt{\frac{2RS}{C}} = \sqrt{\frac{2 \times 6000 \times 10}{2}} = \sqrt{\frac{120,000}{2}}$$

$$= \sqrt{60,000} = 245.$$

With the value of EOQ being 245, the following cost would result over the year:

$$\text{Cost} = \left(\frac{Q}{2} \times C\right) + \left(\frac{R}{Q} \times S\right)$$

$$= \left(\frac{245}{2} \times \$2.00 \right) + \left(\frac{6000}{245} \times \$10.00 \right)$$

$$= \$245 + \$244.89$$

$$= \$489.89$$

This indicates that the manager would meet his or her annual requirements of 6000 units by placing orders (lot size) of 245 units each. Such a policy would require that a total of roughly 25 orders would be placed during the course of the year and would result in a total carrying and ordering cost of $489.89. This value of cost would represent the minimum total cost that could be obtained in this situation (see Figure 18.4).

Payoff Matrix: Decision Making under Risk and Uncertainty

Perhaps the most important function of any manager is making decisions. The ultimate evaluation of any manager will scrutinize the effectiveness of his or her decisions over some period of time. It is necessary, therefore, for each manager to take whatever steps possible to develop the ability to make sound business decisions. What is of prime importance in the decision-making process is that some well-defined, rational approach be taken. Alternatives should be

Figure 18.4

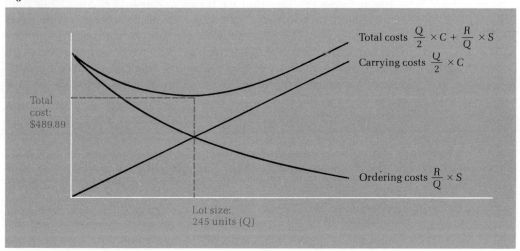

Total costs $\frac{Q}{2} \times C + \frac{R}{Q} \times S$

Carrying costs $\frac{Q}{2} \times C$

Total cost: $489.89

Ordering costs $\frac{R}{Q} \times S$

Lot size: 245 units (Q)

evaluated according to predetermined criteria. By this means, a single alternative can be selected to maximize the probability of achieving an objective. The following discussion will present a series of such "rational" approaches to the decision-making process.

In most of the decision-making situations faced by managers, a series of alternatives is available, each of which will have some consequence depending on the occurrence or nonoccurrence of some future variable or condition. These future variables or conditions (states of nature) may have to do with the action of a competitor, the state of the economy, or a technological advance. It is up to the manager to assess the probability of occurrence of each variable or condition and to select one of the alternatives based upon this assessment. If the manager knew with certainty what would occur, the choice among alternatives would be a simple one. In reality, the manager does *not* know what variables or conditions will in fact occur. It is therefore necessary to determine some way of approaching the decision-making process with a guideline that will help in making "rational" decisions in the face of a series of alternative choices.

This concept of "rationality" is not easily defined. Different decision makers may look at the same situation, make similar assumptions about the future, and still choose different alternative strategies. Each individual may be operating under a different set of criteria upon which to base his or her decision. These criteria may have to do with varying degrees of *optimism* or *pessimism* about the future or with a given individual's *ability* or *willingness* to risk losses, and they tend to be "subjective" rather than "rational."

Recognizing the fact that each individual brings his or her own unique set of values, orientations, and attitudes to the decision-making process, we will present several different ways in which one may examine a particular set of alternatives. The decision selected in each case may differ according to the differing criteria used for evaluation. A manager should review each approach to determine which one most closely represents his or her own typical orientation in such situations.

Expected Value: Decision Making under Conditions of Risk

In order to understand the various approaches to the decision-making process, it is necessary to introduce the concept of *expected value. The expected value of a given decision is the conditional value (what the event is worth) times the probability of the event's actually occurring:*

$$\text{Expected value} = \underset{\text{of event}}{\text{Conditional value}} \times \underset{\text{occurring}}{\text{Probability of event's}}$$

Table 18.1

Conditional value	| X | Probability	Expected value
Property A with hotel: $100,000	0.25	$25,000
Property B with apartment: $60,000	0.50	$30,000

Suppose, for example, that a manager had a chance to invest $10,000 in one of two pieces of property. On one piece of property (Property A) there was a 25 percent chance that a new hotel would be built that would return $100,000 to the manager. On the other piece of property (Property B), there was a 50 percent chance that an apartment building would be built that would return $60,000 to the manager. In order to determine the *expected value* from each alternative, we simply multiply the *conditional value* of each property by the *probability of occurrence* (see Table 18.1).

If we look at the two alternatives and consider the expected value associated with each, the rational decision maker would select Property B with its expected return of $30,000 rather than Property A with an expected return of only $25,000. Note that in no case will the manager *actually* receive either $25,000 or $30,000. The philosophy behind the expected value theory is that *over the long run the decision maker will "do better" to select the alternative with the highest expected value.* It is this concept of a theoretical expected value that forms the basis for the development of a *payoff matrix* that can be utilized to evaluate decision alternatives. Let us now set up a payoff matrix in order in order to examine a series of alternatives.

Assume that a manager has two different levels of inventory she may carry for the coming season (inventory A or inventory B). Because of production scheduling demands, once a given level of inventory is selected it may not be changed. The amount of profit derived from each of the two levels of inventory will be a function of the demand experienced during the season. Let us imagine that three possible levels of demand may occur:

> Demand 1 (D1) with a 20% chance of occurring
> Demand 2 (D2) with a 40% chance of occurring
> Demand 3 (D3) with a 40% chance of occurring

If demand D1 occurs, the manager will make a profit of $20,000 by selecting inventory level A; she will make $50,000 by having selected inventory level B. Note that demand D1 has a 20 percent chance of occurring. Table 18.2 on page 462 represents the payoff to the manager under each of the other demand possibilities.

D1, D2, and D3 represent differing demand levels along with their

Table 18.2. *Conditional Values*

	If D1 = 0.20	If D2 = 0.40	If D3 = 0.40
Inventory A	$20,000	$25,000	$40,000
Inventory B	$50,000	$20,000	$10,000

probability of occurrence. The expected value (expected value = conditional value times probability) for each level of demand would be as shown in Table 18.3. The *total expected value* resulting from each of the two possible inventory levels can be obtained by simply summing up the expected value associated with each possible level of demand.

From the above payoff matrix it is clear that inventory A has a higher overall expected value than inventory B. In the above situation the manager would select inventory level A.

The obvious problem associated with expected value matrices and decision making under risk is the manager's inability to determine the probabilities of occurrence of a given condition—in the above problem, the probability of each level of demand. Nevertheless, the manager may gain considerable insight into the probabilities associated with different conditions through a variety of approaches.

Past history. In many cases it is often possible to look at historical data in order to gain some indication of future conditions. This approach has application in the analysis of historical sales information as well as various areas of the production process in which learning curves have application. It must be recognized, however, that historical data are exactly that—historical—and do not necessarily serve as a true prediction of future conditions.

Expert opinion. With respect to certain areas such as the state of the economy or technological advances, it is often possible to obtain opinions from individuals considered to be knowledgeable. This approach forms the basis for the Delphi Technique used in long-

Table 18.3. *Expected Values*

	D1 = 0.20	D2 = 0.40	D3 = 0.40	Total expected value
Inventory A	$ 4,000	$10,000	$16,000	$30,000
Inventory B	$10,000	$ 8,000	$ 4,000	$22,000

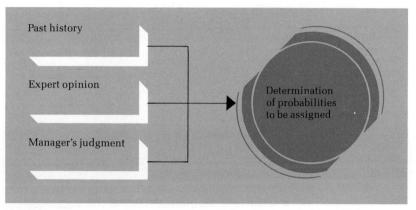

Figure 18.5

range forecasting. Such opinions are often published, available on request. It is unlikely that all experts will agree on any given issue, but an analysis of a cross section of opinions may provide a good indication of a set of probabilities.

Manager's own judgment. In many cases a manager will simply have some "gut feeling" about possible future conditions. In these situations the manager can often set down a set of probabilities, based upon past experiences or simply this gut awareness.

In making a final determination of the probability distribution to be assigned to each condition in the payoff matrix, it is often best to make use of some combination of the three approaches mentioned (Figure 18.5).

Decision Making under Conditions of Uncertainty

Thus far we have discussed rational decision making under conditions in which the manager can assign (however subjective) a probability to each of the possible conditions likely to be encountered. There do exist, however, many decision-making situations in which the manager will find it impossible to set up even subjective probability distributions. In these situations, in which decisions must be made under *conditions of uncertainty,* there is nevertheless also a series of "rational" approaches to the decision-making process.

Let us assume that a manager of a manufacturing facility must decide whether to simply maintain his current plant, to modify the plant to accommodate some technical advances, or to build an entirely new plant. Let us further assume that there are three possible states that could exist in the near future: (1) current technology will continue, (2) new advances will be made in technology, (3) substitute

Table 18.4

| | "States of nature" (possible situations) | | |
Decision strategies	Value assuming current technology	Value assuming new technology	Value assuming substitute products
I. Build new plant	$1,000,000	$500,000	− $1,500,000
II. Modify current plant	$ 400,000	$500,000	− $ 300,000
III. Maintain current plant	$ 250,000	0	0

products will be developed making current products obsolete. As in decision making under risk, it is necessary for the manager to assign conditional values to each of these possible situations, as shown in the matrix (Table 18.4).

In the above matrix, the manager has determined a conditional value for each decision alternative and its corresponding state of nature; i.e., if he builds a new plant and a new technology is developed, the manager will make $500,000. On the other hand, if he modifies his current plant and a substitute product comes along he will lose $300,000.

We will now consider a series of rational alternative approaches to this decision-making process:

Maximin: Criterion of Pessimism. With this approach the manager assumes that the *worst* will happen and selects a strategy accordingly. An inspection of our matrix (Table 18.4) reveals that under strategy I (building a new plant) the worst that could happen would be the development of a substitute product which would cost the manager $1,500,000. Under strategy II the manager could lose $300,000 if a substitute product were developed. Under strategy III the worst the manager could do would be to break even. Given the *maximin criterion* the manager would be wisest to select strategy III, since the worst that could happen in this case would be better financially than the worst possibilities in the two alternative cases.

It is clear that this criterion represents an ultra-conservative approach. In general, it would not be conducive to long-range profit making. Such a strategy could prevent a business person from taking advantage of profit opportunities simply because they have loss possibilities associated with them.

Maximax: Criterion of Optimism. The opposite of the pessimistic strategy is one of total optimism. Under this approach the manager makes decisions based upon complete optimism about the future. The manager assumes that the most favorable condition would occur and then makes a decision accordingly. In our example, we note that if our manager builds a new plant and current technology prevails the manager will make a $1,000,000 profit. This is far and away the most profitable alternative. Thus under a strategy of Maximax the manager will select strategy I and build a new plant.

It seems clear that in most cases a manager will be neither totally optimistic nor totally pessimistic about the future. This means that a manager may need to evaluate decision alternatives by means of some other "rational" criterion or criteria.

La Place: Criterion of Rationality. This approach represents a modified expected value criterion. It is used when the decision maker has no reason to believe that any one state of nature has any different probability of occurring than any other; that is, the decision maker considers each possible occurrence as equally likely and therefore assigns to each an equal probability of occurrence. In our example, because there are three possible events the decision maker would assign a probability of .33 to each event. In this situation equal probabilities are assigned to each state of nature (possible occurrence) and the corresponding expected value is determined. The strategy selected is then the one having the highest expected value.

Utilizing the La Place criterion, strategy II (to modify current plant) has the highest expected value ($198,000) and would be the one selected (Table 18.5).

Criterion of Regret. The last criterion to be considered is referred to as the *criterion of 'regret.'*[1] Under this strategy, the manager attempts to *minimize* the difference between the *maximum* payoff possible for a given state of nature and the payoff for *each* strategy within that state of nature. Consider the data in Table 18.4. We will show the corresponding "regret" associated with each strategy is found in Table 18.6.

Table 18.5

| Decision strategies | States of nature | | | |
	Value assuming current technology	Value assuming new technology	Value assuming substitute products	Expected value
I. Build new plant	$1,000,000 × (.33)	$500,000 × (.33)	− $1,500,000 × (.33)	$ 3,000
II. Modify current plant	$ 400,000 × (.33)	$500,000 × (.33)	− $ 300,000 × (.33)	$198,000
III. Maintain current plant	$ 250,000 × (.33)	$ 0 × (.33)	$ 0 × (.33)	$ 82,000

Table 18.6

Decision strategies	States of nature		
	"Regret," assuming current technology	"Regret," assuming new technology	"Regret," assuming substitute products
I. Build new plant	$ 0	$ 0	$1,500,000
II. Modify current plant	$ 600,000	$ 0	$ 300,000
III. Maintain current plant	$ 750,000	$ 500,000	$ 0

If the state of nature "current technology" occurs, the maximum the manager could make would be $1,000,000. Thus, if he builds a new plant his regret is 0 since he has made $1,000,000. If, however, he modifies his current plant, he would make only $400,000; *but he could have made $1,000,000:* therefore his regret is $600,000. Finally, if he maintains his current plant he will make $250,000. Again, he could have made $1,000,000, and therefore his regret is $750,000. If a substitute product is developed, the best the manager could do would be to break even. If, however, he builds a new plant, he would lose $1,500,000 as opposed to breaking even, and therefore his regret would be $1,500,000. The complete Table of Regret is represented in Table 18.6.

Under this approach the manager selects the strategy that would *minimize his maximum regret.* Inspection of our regret table indicates that maximum regret under strategy I is $1,500,000; under strategy II, $600,000; and under strategy III, $750,000. In this situation the manager would select strategy II and modify the current plant.

What has been presented in this section is a series of methods or approaches that can help a manager in making rational choices. It is recognized that each individual has different values and circumstances within which he or she must make decisions. Given these value differences and varying situations, a decision maker may modify any or all of the above approaches. However, this does not lessen their value, for they do form a sound foundation upon which a decision may be made.

"Monte Carlo" Simulation

We will now turn our attention to a technique which attempts to replicate important features of the "real world." "Monte Carlo" simulation derives its name from its probabilistic appoach to prob-

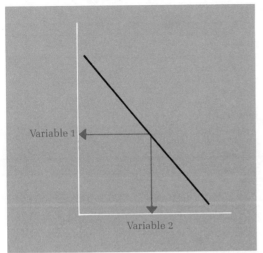

Variable 1

Variable 2

Figure 18.6

lem evaluation. This technique is often applied to problems of inventory control and maintenance analysis, in which various decision strategies are *simulated* over time so that their effectiveness can be assessed. The strategies are simulated by making use of probability distributions in order to determine the relationship between the variables involved in the analysis. In simulations, as well as the real world, the relationship between variables may be either *deterministic* or *probabilistic*. If a relationship between variables is deterministic, it can be represented by a graph or chart of some kind in which the definition of one variable *automatically* defines the value of the second variable, as represented in Figure 18.6. If on the other hand, the relationship between the variables is described by a probabilistic function, then at least one of the variables involved will have *multiple values*. As an illustration, let us look at a probabilistic relationship describing a hypothetical demand situation (Figure 18.7, page 468).

Figure 18.7 represents a probabilistic relationship that might exist between the demand (in units) and the probability that each of the demand values might actually occur. The distribution in the graph gives the following relationship:

> There is a .10 probability that demand will equal 10 units.
> There is a .20 probability that demand will equal 20 units.
> There is a .30 probability that demand will equal 30 units.
> There is a .25 probability that demand will equal 40 units.
> There is a .15 probability that demand will equal 50 units.

Simulation techniques are most effectively utilized when relationships among variables follow probabilistic lines. This is the

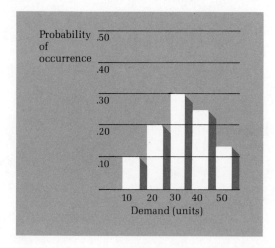

Figure 18.7

case because deterministic relationships often lend themselves most readily to some type of analytical approach whose solution is found by means of an equation or series of equations. Where the relationship between the variables is not deterministic and does not lend itself to one of the more common standard distributions (Normal, Poisson, etc.), simulation is often an effective method of seeking a solution to a given problem. As the number of variables or the complexity of the relationship among variables increases, it often becomes necessary to deal with simulation approaches by means of a computer analysis. The speed with which the computer can determine probability relations and calculate the results of a given decision provides the analyst with the capability of performing many iterations of the problem in order to obtain an optimum solution.

In order to understand how the Monte Carlo approach to simulation is utilized let us take an example from inventory control. Let us suppose, for example, that we wished to evaluate the implication of an inventory policy in which we would place an order for a new shipment of 70 units of stock to be delivered from our supplier whenever our current inventory level dropped to 40 units or below. Further let us assume that we start the simulation with 100 units of inventory in stock. At this point we have defined the *inventory policy* we want to evaluate—to place an order for 70 units of stock whenever current inventory levels reach 40 units or below. We have also defined the *beginning inventory* (100 units) at which we will start the simulation. We have not as yet however identified two key variables which would still be needed to simulate the problem. These two variables would be:

Table 18.7

Probability of occurrence	Demand (units/day)
.10	10
.20	20
.30	30
.25	40
.15	50
1.00 (= 100%)	

1. The daily *demand schedule* (how many units will be taken from inventory each day).
2. The *lead time* for reorder (once an order for a shipment of inventory is placed, how many days do we expect to wait before the shipment will arrive).

It is with respect to each of these two variables that the probabilistic relationships will take place. For example, in Figure 18.2 we set up a hypothetical distribution representing the relative probability of a given demand occurring on any particular day. The demand distribution from Table 18.7 is presented graphically in Figure 18.7.

To arrive at such a probability distribution representing the actual demand schedule a manager might make use of past sales data, or forecasts and projections from experienced sales personnel, or, as is often the case, some combination of these two approaches. Once the *demand* distribution has been determined it is necessary to develop a probability distribution representing the *lead time* associated with a given order.

Let us assume that information from the supplier and our own past history tell us that the following distribution would provide an accurate assessment of the lead time probabilities (Table 18.8). This distribution simply means that once an order is placed for new units to be delivered, there is a 20 percent chance that these units will arrive in 1 day, a 40 percent chance they will arrive in 2 days, a 30

Table 18.8

Lead time	Probability of occurrence
1 day	.20
2 days	.40
3 days	.30
4 days	.10

Table 18.9

Probability of occurrence	Demand (units)
.10	10
.20	20
.30	30
.25	40
.15	50
1.00 (= 100%)	

percent chance they will arrive in 3 days, and a 10 percent chance they will arrive in 4 days.

Now that the probability distributions for both *demand* and *lead time* have been determined, it becomes necessary to set up some method or technique by which actual demand and lead times can be simulated over time. The technique that is utilized depends on the generation of a series of random numbers. To understand how the procedure works, let us look again at the demand distribution shown in Table 18.9.

Interpreting this distribution, we have stated that there is a 10 percent chance that a demand of 10 units will occur. Since the total probability is 100 percent, we are actually saying there are 10 chances out of 100 that a demand of 10 will occur. This being the case, we could let the numbers from 1 to 10 represent the probability that a demand of 10 will actually occur. Looking at the next demand level (20 units) we note that there is a 20 percent chance that this demand will occur. Thus, we could let the numbers 11 to 30 represent a demand of 20 units. Utilizing this approach throughout we would arrive at Table 18.10.

Table 18.10

Probability of occurrence	Demand (units)	Random numbers
.10	10	1– 10*
.20	20	11– 30**
.30	30	31– 60
.25	40	61– 85
.15	50	86–100
1.00 (= 100%)		$\Sigma = 100$

* Ten numbers out of 100 is a 10 percent probability.
** Twenty numbers out of 100 = probability of 20 percent.

Table 18.11

Probability of occurrence	Lead time (days)	Random numbers
.20	1	1– 20
.40	2	21– 60
.30	3	61– 90
.10	4	91–100
1.00 (= 100%)		$\Sigma = 100$

By making use of a random number table utilizing numbers from 1 to 100 we can determine the exact demand for any given day in *the same proportion as the probability representing the demand relationships.* For example, let us assume that the random number 39 was drawn. This would represent a daily demand of 30 units. Since the numbers between 31 and 60 represent a total of 30 out of a possible 100, there is a 30 percent chance that one of these numbers would turn up on a random number table. This represents the same 30 percent chance that a demand of 30 units would occur on any given day. This same approach when utilized in determining *lead time* distribution would result in Table 18.11.

Now that the probability distributions for both *demand* and *lead time* have been determined we may proceed to evaluate the inventory policy under consideration. The final requirement is to make a determination as to how many days we wish to "run" the simulation; that is, over what period of time we wish to simulate the inventory policy. In this example let us assume we will run for a seven-day period.

We begin the simulation with 100 units of inventory in stock. Since we currently have 100 units on hand and have defined the reorder point which we are evaluating to be 40 units or less, it is not necessary to place an order at the beginning of the simulation. At this point we must make a determination as to the demand for units over the time period covered by the simulation. Let us assume that we generate, in order, the following seven random numbers: Day 1: 22; Day 2: 67; Day 3: 43; Day 4: 17; Day 5: 57; Day 6: 29; Day 7: 51. Looking at our demand schedule (Table 18.10), we now can determine the "actual" demand for each day that the simulation is to run. The first random number is 22. Because 22 falls between 11 and 30, the demand is 20. On the second day, the random number is 67. Because 67 falls between 61 and 85, the demand equals 40. This actual demand schedule appears in Table 18.12, page 472. By utilizing the above

Table 18.12

Day	Random number	Actual demand (units)
1	22	20
2	67	40
3	43	30
4	17	20
5	57	30
6	29	20
7	51	30

demand schedule let us now plot the daily inventory levels (Figure 18.8) in order to evaluate our inventory policy.

We note that demand for Day 1 is 20 units; thus at the end of day one, our inventory level will drop to 80 units (100 − 20). The second day's demand level is 40 units and thus at the end of the second day our inventory has dropped to 40 units (80 − 40). At this point, since our inventory level has reached 40 units (or less), our reorder rule would come into effect and we would now place an order for more stock. The order for an additional 70 units would be placed at the end of this second day of the simulation. It now becomes necessary for us to generate a random number which will determine how many days lead time will be required before the order will arrive. Let us assume that the random number generated is 27. This would represent a lead time of 2 days (see Table 18.11). We must therefore now wait two days before our order of 70 units will arrive. We proceed with the simulation of demand plotted in Figure 18.8.

Our third day's demand level is 30 units. This brings our inventory at the end of the third day down to 10 units (40 − 30). We still have one more day to wait before our order will arrive. Fourth-day demand is for 20 units; since we only have 10 units in stock, the company has, in effect, experienced a "stock out" of 10 units. This simply means that 10 units were demanded that the company could not supply. For purposes of our example let us assume that these are lost sales and cannot be recovered when new inventory does arrive. By the end of the fourth day, however, our new inventory has arrived and we now start the fifth day with an inventory level of 70 units in stock. Carrying out the simulation for the next three days we find that the fifth day's demand is for a total of 30 units, bringing our inventory at the end of the fifth day to 40 units (70 − 30). At this point, since our inventory has once again reached the 40-unit level we must generate a random number in order to determine lead time for our next reorder. In this second case let us assume the number generated

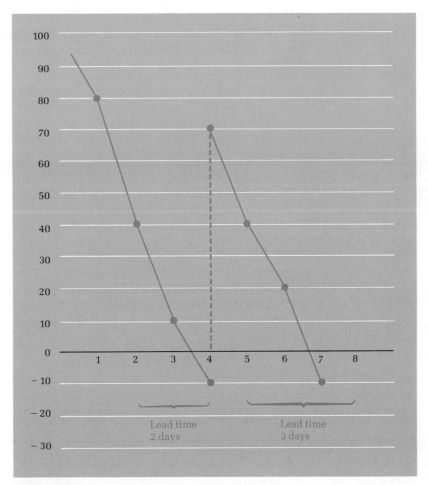

Figure 18.8

is 68; this would represent (Table 18.11) a lead time of three days. Demand for Day 6 is 20 units, and thus at the end of the sixth day our inventory stands at 20 units (40 − 20). (We now have two more days until our new order arrives.) The seventh and final day of our simulation generates a demand of 30 units, which would mean that we again have a stock-out situation of 10 units in lost sales. Were the simulation to continue we would still have one more day to wait until our new order arrived.

Let us now examine the cost implications of the inventory policy we have attempted to simulate.

To obtain accurate estimates of the various costs associated with a given inventory policy, management may make use of historical cost data, industry trends, and financial projections and forecasts. Let us assume management has used such information and determined the following:

Inventory carrying cost (insurance, theft, storage, spoilage, etc.) equals $.10/unit for each day the inventory is held.
Reorder cost (the cost of employee time and paperwork needed to place an order with our supplier) equals $10.00/order.
Lost sales cost (loss in profit and good will from not being able to supply a requested unit) equals $5.00/unit.

Based upon the above cost data, we can determine the costs associated with our current inventory policy.

Lost sales   = 20 units (total) × $5.00/unit = $100.00
Reorder cost = 2 orders placed × $10.00/order = $20.00

(Inventory carrying costs are calculated in Table 18.13.) Our total inventory carrying cost would therefore come to $27.50. The total cost of the inventory policy would thus become

Lost sales	$100.00
Ordering costs	20.00
Inventory carrying cost	27.50
	$147.50

It is clear from the simulation that, by far, the greatest cost associated with the inventory policy being evaluated lies in lost sales. Since this is the case, it appears that the company would be better off maintaining an inventory policy of having more inventory on hand.

Table 18.13. *Inventory Carrying Cost*

	Beginning inventory (units)	End inventory (units)	Average daily inventory* (units)	Inventory cost per unit per day	Inventory cost per day
Day 1	100	80	90	.10	$ 9.00
Day 2	80	40	60	.10	6.00
Day 3	40	10	25	.10	2.50
Day 4	10	0	5	.10	.50
Day 5	70	40	55	.10	5.50
Day 6	40	20	30	.10	3.00
Day 7	20	0	10	.10	1.00
Total inventory cost for 7 days					$27.50

*Average daily inventory = (beginning inventory + end inventory) ÷ 2.

Along these lines, the reader might wish to find out the total costs of an inventory policy in which orders were placed for *100 units* each time the inventory level dropped to *60 units* or below. By comparing the cost of such a policy with the one just evaluated the reader might be able to make a recommendation as to the more appropriate inventory policy for that particular corporation.

The use of simulation techniques enables management to determine and evaluate the probable costs associated with a variety of possible decision alternatives. Based upon the implications of the simulated condition, management is able to anticipate the results of a particular decision strategy.

Linear Programming: Graphic Method

The quantitative technique of linear programming is normally associated with problems involving *the allocation of limited resources* in maximizing profits or minimizing costs. Although linear programming techniques can become quite complicated if the problem is complicated, the essential element in the analysis is the solution of a series of equations as a means of finding some optimum allocation.

The *graphic method* of linear programming is perhaps the most fundamental of the linear programming techniques. The graphic method is limited in application to problems having a maximum of two decision variables (three variables if three-dimensional graph), but the technique does provide the reader with the conceptual framework upon which more complex problems may be solved through the use of *linear programming analysis*. As a way of studying the graphic method of linear programming, let us consider the following problem of optional allocation of supplies for profit.

A chemical company produces two products, Product X and Product Y. Each product is sold in one gallon containers. Each product is made up of chlorine and potassium in the following combinations.

	Chlorine	Potassium
Product X	60%	40%
Product Y	50%	50%

The *profit* derived from each product is $1.75/gallon for Product X, $2.00/gallon for Product Y. Industry supply conditions limit weekly availability of each chemical to 3,000 gal/week of chlorine

Table 18.14

Chemical	Required for:		Available supply (weekly)
	Product X	Product Y	
Chlorine	0.6 gallon	0.5 gallon	3,000 gallons
Potassium	0.4 gallon	0.5 gallon	2,500 gallons
Profit ($/gal)	1.75	2.00	

and 2,500 gal/week of potassium. Table 18.14 summarizes the data available to management.

The question confronting management is how best to allocate the available supplies of chlorine and potassium to each of the two products in order to maximize profit for the firm.

With respect to each of the two chemicals we see that management must make a decision within the following constraints:

1. *Chlorine* (0.6 gallons for product X plus 0.5 gallons for Product Y) cannot exceed 3,000 gallons.
2. *Potassium* (0.4 gallons for product X plus 0.5 gallons for Product Y) cannot exceed 2,500 gallons.

Expressing these constraints as inequalities we may write:

$$0.6X + 0.5Y \leq 3,000 \quad \text{(chlorine)}$$
$$0.4X + 0.5Y \leq 2,500 \quad \text{(potassium)}.$$

It is possible to plot these as shown in Figure 18.9 and describe how the plot for each was obtained.

Examining the availability of each of the two chemicals, we find that we could use chlorine to produce only Product X, in which case we could produce a maximum of 5,000 gallons of Product X; or we could use the available chlorine to produce only Product Y, in which case we could produce a maximum of 6,000 gallons of Product Y. In like manner, we could use the available potassium to produce only Product X, producing 6,250 gallons or only Product Y, producing 5,000 gallons (line b, Figure 18.9).

These relationships are shown in Figure 18.9. The shaded area under the curve represents the various combinations of Product X and Product Y that are technically feasible (that would be possible given the availability of chlorine and potassium). This shaded area is referred to as the *feasibility polygon*.

As has been stated, the objective of management is to maximize the total profit to the firm from the production of some feasible combination of the two products. Since the profit from product X is

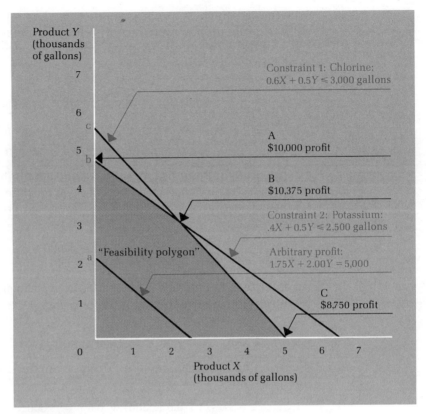

Figure 18.9

$1.75 and the profit from product Y is $2.00, the equation for maximized profit would be

$$\text{Maximum profit} = 1.75X + 2.00Y$$

In order to plot this line on the graph in Figure 18.9 it is necessary to select an arbitrary profit figure and determine where the line would cross the X and Y axes. For example, we can take

$$1.75X + 2.00Y = \$5,000 \text{ profit.}$$

In this equation, if X = 0, then Y = 2,500; if Y = 0, then X = 2,857, as plotted in Figure 18.9, line a.

It can be shown mathematically that the maximum profit, given the constraints, will always occur at the extreme point of the feasibility polygon. This point can be obtained by "moving" the profit line upward to the right until the most extreme point of the polygon is determined (highest profit). Another method of determining the highest profit point within the polygon is to evaluate mathematically each of the points of the polygon. These points would include A, B, and C in Figure 18.9.

The profit at Point A (0 units of X, 5,000 units of Y) is

$$\$1.75 \ (0) + \$2.00 \ (5,000) = \$10,000.$$

The profit at Point C (0 units of Y, 5,000 units of X) is

$$\$1.75 \ (5,000) + \$2.00 \ (0) = \$8,750.$$

The profit at Point B. To determine the amount of Product X and Product Y that are produced at point B we must find the intersection of the curves that form point B. These curves are represented by the equations

$$0.6X + 0.5Y = 3,000$$
$$0.4X + 0.5Y = 2,500.$$

In order to eliminate one of the variables we can subtract one equation from the other to obtain the following:

$$0.2X = 500$$
$$X = 2,500 \text{ gallons.}$$

Substituting X = 2,500 in either of the two equations we can solve for Y:

$$0.6 \ (2,500) + 0.5Y = 3,000$$
$$0.5Y = 1,500$$
$$Y = 3,000$$

Therefore, at point B

$$1.75 \ (2,500) + \$2.00 \ (3,000) = \$10,375 \text{ profit.}$$

The data in Table 18.15 indicate that maximum profit is obtained at point B, which results from producing 2,500 gallons of Product X and 3,000 gallons of Product Y.

Table 18.15

| Highest profit points | Product X | | Product Y | | |
	Quantity produced (gal)	Profit (at $1.75/gal)	Quantity produced (gal)	Profit (at $2.00/gal)	Total profits
A	0	$ 0	5,000	$10,000	$10,000
B	2,500	4,375	3,000	6,000	10,375
C	5,000	8,750	0	0	8,750

Linear Programming: Transportation Model

Quantitative textbooks offer a wide variety of fairly complex approaches to the optimization of allocation of resource problems. Most types of linear and dynamic programming techniques require a fairly sophisticated background in mathematics for the solution of the equations involved. One of the most well known of the techniques for determining the optimum solution for problems of allocation is the *transportation method*. The reason for its inclusion in this text is that the method provides a solution to certain types of allocation problems having application in industrial organizations, and the method requires only simple addition and subtraction for determining solutions.

Assumptions

The transportation problem covers situations in which there is a given number of sources of supply and a given number of destinations to be reached. Either the sources of supply or the destination may be a warehouse, factory, store, etc. The objective for which the method is used is to route shipments from sources of supply to destinations so as to minimize the total cost of the allocation process. To obtain the minimum cost solution, transportation costs from each source of supply to each destination must be known. In addition, it is assumed that per unit transportation cost remains constant and known regardless of the number of units shipped. Finally, the units must be substitutable, one for another; that is, a manager who decides not to transfer a certain number of units from one source must be able to transfer the same number of units from another source of supply.

Problem Definition

To solve the transportation problem the manager must develop an *initial* solution to the problem and then by a process of formalized search improve on the initial solution until an *optimum* solution is achieved. In order to understand the transportation approach let us set up a simple problem and work through to a solution.

Let us assume that a manager may obtain products from three different production plants and then allocate these products to three different warehouses as needed. The manager's problem is to transfer products from the plants to the warehouses in such a manner that overall transportation costs will be minimized. For purposes of illustration let us assume the following conditions:

Plant 1 production capacity = 100 units.
Plant 2 production capacity = 50 units.
Plant 3 production capacity = 150 units.

	Warehouse A	Warehouse B	Warehouse C	Capacity (units)
Plant 1	5	3	4	100
Plant 2	2	6	5	50
Plant 3	4	3	6	150
Total requirements (units)	75	125	100	

Figure 18.10

In addition:

Warehouse A requirement =   75 units.
Warehouse B requirement = 125 units.
Warehouse C requirement = 100 units.

A transportation matrix must be set up. The matrix would take the forms seen in Figure 18.10. The matrix indicates that Plant 1 has a production capacity of 100 units, Plant 2 a production capacity of 50 units, and Plant 3 a production capacity of 150 units. In addition, Warehouse A has a requirement of 75 units, Warehouse B, a requirement of 125 units, and Warehouse C, a requirement of 100 units (Figure 18.11). The numbers in the smaller boxes in the matrix indicate the cost associated with moving one unit from a given plant to a given warehouse. Thus, the cost per unit, to move one unit from Plant 1 to Warehouse A is $5.00. The cost, per unit, of moving one unit from Plant 3 to Warehouse C is $6.00, and so on.

Initial Solution

The next step in our approach is to make an initial allocation from the various plants to the various warehouses. It must be kept in mind that the production capacity of each plant cannot be exceeded nor can the requirement of any warehouse be exceeded. For purposes of the initial solution we will utilize what is referred to as the "northwest corner" approach. This simply means that the initial allocation of units from a plant to a warehouse will be made in the *upper left hand corner* of the matrix and proceed either down or across the matrix, depending upon whether the plant capacity or warehouse requirement is filled first. The cells (blocks of the matrix) are then

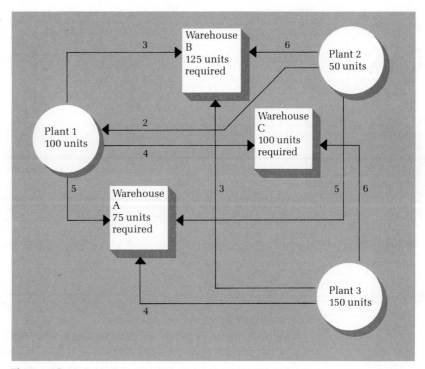

Figure 18.11

filled one at a time as one moves toward the "southeast" corner of the matrix. An illustration of this approach for our example appears in Figure 18.12 on page 482.

Utilizing the northwest corner approach, our first allocation will be made to cell 1A; we note that cell 1A is assigned the value of 75 units. We have now filled up Warehouse A, but Plant 1 is still left with 25 units capacity. These units are assigned to Warehouse B and the total capacity of Plant 1 (75 units to Warehouse A and 25 units to Warehouse B) are now utilized. Warehouse B, however, still requires 100 units. Fifty of these units can come from Plant 2, but this will reach the limit of Plant 2 capacity. Therefore, the additional 50 units to meet the needs of Warehouse B must come from Plant 3. Plant 3 will still have 100 units. These may go to Warehouse C, which will then be filled up. All units have now been assigned and all warehouses filled.

As a result of this initial allocation we observe that all of the *capacities* of each plant as well as the *requirements* of each ware-

	Warehouse A	Warehouse B	Warehouse C	Capacity (units)
Plant 1	75 5	25 3	4	100
Plant 2	2	50 6	5	50
Plant 3	4	50 3	100 6	150
Total requirements (units)	75	125	100	300

Figure 18.12

house have been met. This is referred to as satisfying the "rim" requirements of the problem (capacities of plants and requirements of warehouses cannot be exceeded).

Later in this section we will discuss how to proceed when the total capacity of all the plants *does not equal* the total requirements of the warehouses. In setting up the initial solution as we did above, one rule that must be observed is that the number of cells used *(to which an allocation has been made)* must equal the total number of plants plus the total number of warehouses minus 1. In our example we have three plants and three warehouses; therefore

$$(3 + 3) - 1 = 5.$$

The number of used cells in our initial allocation, (Figure 18.12) also equals 5: (cells 1A, 1B, 2B, 3B, 3C). Therefore we may proceed. If this condition is not met, however, a situation known as *degeneracy* will be said to exist. This will prevent an optimum allocation from being achieved. (The problem of degeneracy will be covered at a later point.)

Now that a satisfactory initial solution has been obtained, we must determine if another solution is possible—one that would yield a lower overall cost of transportation. Let us first calculate the cost of transportation for our example. Total cost of transportation is obtained by multiplying the number of units in a cell by the cost per unit of transportation for those units. The total cost of *transportation for our initial* solution is seen in Table 18.16.

Table 18.16

Units	$/unit	Cost
75	5	$ 375
25	3	75
50	6	300
50	3	150
100	6	600
		Total: $1,500

Evaluation of Initial Solution

The method we use to evaluate this solution is to determine the effect *of transferring one unit from any of the five used cells to each of the unused cells.* The purpose of this evaluation is to determine if some transfer of units from one cell to another would reduce the overall cost of transportation. In Figure 18.7 the unused cells are: 2A, 3A, 1C, 2C. In order that the rim requirements still be met, we note that the addition of one unit to an unused cell will require that modification be made throughout the matrix. In seeking to determine the effect of one unit on an unused cell we must take a path through the matrix that will leave all rim requirements the same (no plant capacities or warehouse requirements violated). An unused cell is *evaluated* by determining the impact of the one-unit transfer on total costs. Let us go through an example (Figure 18.13).

Let us consider the evaluation of unused cell 2A. If one unit is added to 2A, it will add $2.00 to the cost of transportation (the cost of

Figure 18.13

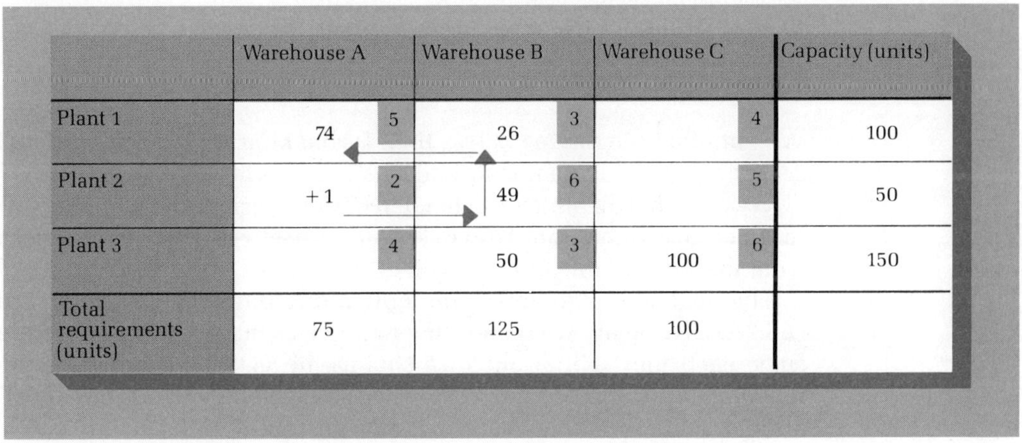

	Warehouse A	Warehouse B	Warehouse C	Capacity (units)
Plant 1	74　　5	26　　3	4	100
Plant 2	+1　　2	49　　6	5	50
Plant 3	4	50　　3	100　　6	150
Total requirements (units)	75	125	100	

483

moving a unit from Plant 2 to Warehouse A). However, in order to maintain rim requirements, we will reduce to 49 the number of units moved from Plant 2 to Warehouse B. This is necessary so that only 50 units will be shipped from Plant 2. The effect of the reduction to 49 will be to reduce this cost by $6.00 (the cost of shipping from Plant 2 to Warehouse B). However, we must now add one unit to cell 1B so that the needs of Warehouse B are met, and this will add $3.00 to the cost. Finally, we must now subtract 1 unit from cell 1A so that the capacity of Plant 1 is not exceeded. This will reduce costs by $5.00. The net effect of the movement of one unit to cell 2A is therefore

$$\$2.00 - \$6.00 + \$3.00 - \$5.00 = -\$6.00$$

This tells us that for every unit that can be moved into cell 2A there will be a net reduction of $6.00 in total transportation cost. Before proceeding to move units into cell 2A, however, we must first determine if there is an even more attractive alternative. In order to evaluate each of the other unused cells we proceed in the same manner as for cell 2A. In each case we must find a "path" through the matrix that does not violate rim requirements. Keep in mind that in subtracting units from a cell we cannot subtract units from a cell that has no units assigned to it.

To provide one more example, in evaluating cell 1C we would proceed as follows:

Change	Result
We add 1 unit to cell 1C	+ $4.00
We must subtract 1 unit from cell 3C	− $6.00
We must add 1 unit to cell 3B	+ $3.00
We must subtract 1 unit from cell 1B	− $3.00
Net change:	− $2.00

We note that our saving is less than for making an allocation to cell 2A. The process is demonstrated in Figure 18.14.

We note that an allocation to *each* of the unused cells would result in a net cost reduction. However, the *largest* reduction still comes from making an allocation to cell 2A (Table 18.17).

The next step is to determine *how many* units may be moved to cell 2A. Obviously, we would like to move as many units as possible since each unit will result in a savings of $6.00. We note that by moving units into cell 2A it will be necessary to move units out of cell 2B and also move units into cell 1B and out of cell 1A. Since it is

	Warehouse A	Warehouse B	Warehouse C	Capacity (units)
Plant 1	75 5	▲ 24 3	+1 4	100
Plant 2	2	50 6	5	50
Plant 3	4	51 3	▼ 99 6	150
Total requirements (units)	75	125	100	

Figure 18.14

impossible to have a negative number of units in a cell, the number of units that can be transferred to cell 2A will be dictated by the minimum number of units remaining in a cell from which we will be *subtracting*. Since we will transfer from cell 2B and 1A, and since 2B contains 50 units and 1A 75 units, the maximum that can be added to cell 2A will be 50 units. Following the transfer the new matrix will appear as in Figure 18.15, page 286.

The total cost of transportation for Solution II is seen in Table 18.18.

We now proceed as we did before to determine if a transfer to any unused cell would result in a reduction in the total transportation cost (Table 18.19).

We note that in two of the unused cells there is a possible reduction in the total cost of transportation. These two cells are 1C and 3A. The net reduction in 1C is $2.00/unit, and in 3A the reduction is $1.00/unit. This being the case, we would select cell 1C as the cell to receive additional units. By proceeding with the addition and sub-

Table 18.17. *Unused Cell Evaluation*

Unused cell	Cost changes (dollars)	Net result (dollars)
3A	+4 −3 +3 −5	$ −1
1C	+4 −6 +3 −3	$ −2
2C	+5 −6 −3 −6	$ −4
2A	+2 −6 +3 −5	$ −6

	Warehouse A	Warehouse B	Warehouse C	Capacity (units)
Plant 1	25 5	75 3	4	100
Plant 2	50 2	6	5	50
Plant 3	4	50 3	100 6	150
Total requirements (units)	75	125	100	

Figure 18.15

traction of units from other cells so that rim requirements may be maintained we find that cell 1B, with 75 units to be subtracted, is the most restricting cell and therefore only 75 units can be added to cell 1C. (If we add to 1C we must subtract 100 units from 3C, add 50 units to 3B, and subtract 75 units from 1B.) The total transportation costs

Table 18.18

Units	$/unit	Cost
25	5	$ 125
50	2	100
75	3	225
50	3	150
100	6	600
		Total: $1,200

Table 18.19. *Unused Cell Evaluation*

Unused cell	Net changes (dollars)	Net result (dollars)
3A	+4 −3 +3 −5	−1
2B	+6 −2 +5 −3	+6
1C	+4 −6 +3 −3	−2
2C*	+5 −6 +3 −3 +5 −2	+2

 * *Note:* In order to find a path to evaluate unused cell 2C it was necessary to go through each used cell.

	Warehouse A	Warehouse B	Warehouse C	Capacity (units)
Plant 1	25 5	3	75 4	100
Plant 2	50 2	6	5	50
Plant 3	4	125 3	25 6	150
Total requirements (units)	75	125	100	

Figure 18.16

for this solution are seen in Table 18.20. Our new matrix appears in Figure 18.16.

In order to determine if this is the optimum solution we must again evaluate each unused cell.

In Table 18.21 we note that in only one case, that of cell 3A (−$3) would there be any reduction in total costs resulting from a transfer of units. By evaluation we determine that the most units that could

Table 18.20

Units	$/unit	Cost
25	5	$ 125
50	2	100
125	3	375
75	4	300
25	6	150
		Total: $1,050

Table 18.21. *Unused Cell Evaluation*

Unused cell	Net changes (dollars)	Net result (dollars)
3A	+3 −6 +4 −5	−3
1B	+3 −3 +6 −4	+2
2B	+6 −3 +6 −4 +5 −2	+8
2C	+5 −2 +5 −4	+4

Table 18.22. *Unused Cell Evaluation*

Unused cell	Net changes (dollars)	Net result (dollars)
1A	+5 −4 +6 −4	+3
1B	+3 −3 +6 −4	+2
2B	+6 −2 +4 −3	+5
2C	+5 −6 +4 −2	+1

be added to cell 3A would be 25. By adding 25 units to cell 3A we would thus eliminate all units from both cell 1A and 3A and our new matrix would appear as in Figure 18.17.

We observe in Figure 18.17 that when the transfer is made we have eliminated all the units in two of the cells (1A and 3C). When this is done *we now no longer meet the criterion* that the number of used cells equals the number of plants and the number of warehouses minus one. This being the case, it will now no longer be possible to find a path through the matrix in order to evaluate each unused cell. This situation is normally referred to as *degeneracy* of the matrix. In order to deal with this problem of degeneracy we simply select one of the unused cells and treat it as a used cell with zero units assigned to it. For purposes of our example let us select cell 3C. By placing zero units in cell 3C our new matrix would appear as shown in Figure 18.18.

We may now proceed to evaluate each of the unused cells.

Figure 18.17

	Warehouse A	Warehouse B	Warehouse C	Capacity (units)
Plant 1	5	3	100 4	100
Plant 2	50 2	6	5	50
Plant 3	25 4	125 3	6	150
Total requirements (units)	75	125	100	

	Warehouse A	Warehouse B	Warehouse C	Capacity (units)
Plant 1	5	3	100 4	100
Plant 2	50 2	6	5	50
Plant 3	25 4	125 3	0 6	150
Total requirements (units)	75	125	100	

Figure 18.18

We observe that any transfer of units to any of the unused cells would result in a net *increase* in the total cost of transportation. This being the case, *we have arrived at the solution matrix which now represents the minimum total transportation cost that can be obtained* (Table 18.23). The minimum total cost of transportation is, therefore, the amount seen in Table 18.23.

The Slack Variable: When Supply and Demand Are Not Equal

It is often the case in industry that the supply and demand factors are not equal. In this situation there is a need to make a slight modification in the transportation matrix. This modification involves the introduction of what is referred to as a *slack* variable. Let us suppose for purposes of illustration that the capacity of Plant 1 was increased by 50 units. This would result in a total plant capacity of 350 units and total warehouse requirements of only 300 units. In order to solve this problem, a dummy warehouse (X) is introduced into the matrix, as in Figure 18.18. (In order to evaluate unused cells, assume that

Table 18.23

Units	$/unit	Cost
50	2	$100
25	4	100
125	3	375
100	4	400
		Total: $975

	Warehouse A	Warehouse B	Warehouse C	Dummy warehouse (slack) X*	Capacity (units)
Plant 1	5	3	100 4	50 0	100
Plant 2	50 2	6	5	0	50
Plant 3	25 4	125 3	6	0	150
Total requirements (units)	75	125	100	50	350

*In order to evaluate unused cells, assume that costs of transportation to the dummy warehouse are zero.

Figure 18.19

costs of transportation to the "dummy" warehouse are zero.) An initial solution is then determined and unused cells are evaluated as was done in our previous example. The solution to the problem involving the dummy warehouse is shown in Figure 18.19. The allocation of 50 units from Plant 1 to the dummy warehouse (X) simply means that Plant 1 will *not produce* 50 units of its total capacity. The remaining 100 units of Plant 1 capacity will be shipped to Warehouse C.

In summary, the transportation model is a powerful mathematical tool designed to aid managers in the decision-making process. The model can be easily adapted to problems of profit maximization by simply replacing costs with profit figures. As real-world problems become more complex—that is, as large numbers of warehouses or plants must be considered—the evaluaton of these matrices lends itself readily to computer programming solutions. For these reasons the transportation model of linear programming is perhaps one of the most commonly used quantitative techniques in both the classroom and the corporate environment.

Discussion Questions

1. A company estimates it will need a total of 12,000 component units to be supplied over the next year. Analysis of expenses indicates that the cost of carrying one unit is $2.50 per year. The cost of placing each order has been estimated to be $50.00.

Action/Outcome Matrix for Problem 2

	Outcome		
Action	Depression	Stable economy	Growth economy
Buy stocks	− $50,000	$ 0	+ $60,000
Buy home	− $ 5,000	+ $5,000	+ $20,000
Put money in a savings account	+ $ 5,000	+ $5,000	+ $ 5,000

Given this information, determine the number of units that should be ordered each time an order is placed. In addition, determine the total annual cost associated with ordering and carrying the firm's inventory of component units.

2. Evaluate the following information and make a decision based on the following criteria: (a) Maximin, (b) Maximax, (c) La Place.

An individual must decide what to do with a certain amount of money. He is considering three alternatives: (1) investing in stocks, (2) purchasing a home, or (3) putting money into a savings account. He believes there are three possible future states of the economy (see table). The dollar values in the table represent the individual's estimates of what would be gained (+) or lost (−) as a result of a given investment decision under the conditions of each possible state of the economy.

3. Simulate the following inventory policy over a seven-day period. The policy is to place an order for 100 units of new product whenever current inventory levels reach 60 units or below. Utilize cost data and demand and lead time probabilities given in the example in the text (Tables 18.7, 18.8, 18.13). Let the following random numbers represent demand and lead time:

Demand	32, 47, 21, 19, 53, 42
Lead time	23, 18, 52

4. In the matrix below
   a. Evaluate each unused cell.
   b. Where would you make the first new allocation?

	Warehouse A	Warehouse B	Warehouse C	Capacity (units)
Plant 1	40 · 4	10 · 5	6	50
Plant 2	3	40 · 2	10 · 5	50
Plant 3	3	2	50 · 1	50
Total requirements (units)	40	50	60	

Selected References

Buffa, E. *Modern Production Management.* New York: John Wiley & Sons, 1965.

Chase, R. and Aquilano, N. *Production and Operations Management.* Homewood, Ill.: Richard D. Irwin, 1977.

Fabrycky, W. and Torgersen, P. *Operations Economy.* Englewood Cliffs, N.J.: Prentice-Hall, 1966.

Garrett, L. and Silver, M. *Production Management Analysis.* New York: Harcourt Brace Jovanovich, 1973.

Gaummitag, R. K. and Brownlee, O. H. "Mathematics for Decision-Makers." In *Harvard Business Review,* May–June 1956.

Hoffman, Thomas. *Production Management and Manufacturing Systems.* Belmont, Calif.: Wadsworth Publishing Co., 1967.

MacNiece, E. H. *Production Forecasting, Planning and Control.* New York: John Wiley & Sons, 1961.

Mayer, R. *Production and Operations Management.* 3rd ed. New York: McGraw-Hill, 1975.

Monks, J. *Operations Management: Theory and Problems.* New York: McGraw-Hill, 1977.

Olsen, Robert. *Manufacturing Management.* Scranton, Pa.: Intext, 1968.

Richards, M. and Greenlaw, P. *Managerial Decision Making.* Homewood, Ill.: Richard D. Irwin.

Roscoe, E. and Freak, D. *Organization for Production.* Homewood, Ill.: Richard D. Irwin, 1971.

Savage, L. J. "The Theory of Statistical Decision." In *Journal of the American Statistical Association,* March 1951.

Van Horne, J. *Financial Management and Policy,* 2nd ed. Englewood Cliffs, N.J.: Prentice-Hall, 1971.

Vandell, R. "Management Evolution in the Quantitative World." In *Harvard Business Review,* January–February 1970.

Vollman, T. *Operations Management.* Reading, Mass.: Addison-Wesley, 1973.

Weston, Frederick C. "Operations Research Techniques Relevant to Corporate Planning Function Practices: An Investigative Look." In *Academy of Management Journal,* September 1973.

Notes

Chapter 1

1. Peter Drucker, *Preparing Tomorrow's Business Leaders Today* (Englewood Cliffs, N.J.: Prentice-Hall, 1969), p. 81.

2. Committee for Economic Development, *Social Responsibilities of Business Corporations* (New York: Committee for Economic Development, June, 1971), pp. 14–15. Reprinted by permission.

3. Barbara J. Flower, *Business Amid Urban Crisis* (New York: Conference Board, 1968), p. 6. Reprinted by permission.

4. *Ibid.*, p. 7.

5. *Ibid.*, p. 11.

6. *Ibid.*, p. 47.

7. *Ibid.*, p. 27.

8. Grace J. Finley, *Mayors Evaluate Business Action on Urban Problems* (New York: Conference Board, 1968), p. 7.

9. Quoted in O. Thompson, *The Economics of Environmental Protection* (Cambridge, Mass.: Winthrop, 1973), p. 229.

10. *Business Week*, September 14, 1974, p. 103.

11. Quoted in H. Henry, *Pollution Control: Corporation Responses* (New York: American Management Association, 1974), p. 4.

12. Richard A. Hopkinson, *Corporation Organization for Pollution Control* (New York: Conference Board, 1970), p. 3.

13. "Job Description for Air and Water Conservation Advisor," Gulf Oil Corporation. Reprinted by permission.

14. Committee for Economic Development, *Social Responsibilities of Business Corporations*, p. 54.

15. Flower, *Business Amid Urban Crisis*, p. 41.

16. Flower, *Business Amid Urban Crisis*, p. 43.

17. For a more detailed view of product safety statistics see U.S. Consumer Product Safety Commission, *Consumer Product Hazard Index, Fiscal Year 1977* (Washington, D.C.: National Information Clearing House, 1977).

18. P. Weaver, "The Hazards of Trying to Make Consumer Products Safer," *Fortune*, July 1975, p. 140.

19. D. Aaker and G. Day, "A Guide to Consumerism," *Journal of Marketing* 34 (July 1970), 12–19.

20. Y. Furuhaski and E. McCarthy, *Social Issues of Marketing in the American Economy* (Columbus, Ohio: Grid, Inc., 1971), p. 68.

21. U.S. House of Representatives, Committee on Interstate and Foreign Commerce, 89th Congress, 2nd Session, "Public Policy Implications of Investment Company Growth," (Washington, D.C.: U.S. Government Printing Office, 1966), p. 721.

22. D. Aaker and G. Day, *Consumerism: Search for the Consumer Interest* (New York: Free Press, 1971), pp. 301–302.

23. J. Kolb, "The Price of Faulty Design Gets Steeper Every Day," in D. Aaker and G. Day, *Consumerism: Search for the Consumer Interest*, pp. 321–322.

24. "Whirlpool Warranty," Whirlpool Corporation. Reprinted by permission of the Whirlpool Corporation.

25. Adapted by permission of the publisher, from *The Economics of Affirmative Action* by James V. Koch, John F. Chizmar, Jr., pp. 10–42. (Lexington Books, D.C. Heath and Co. © 1976, D.C. Heath & Co.)

26. "Women at Work," *Newsweek*, December 6, 1976, p. 69.

27. *Ibid.*, p. 70.

28. *Ibid.*, p. 73.

29. J. Carson and G. Steiner, "Measuring Business Social Performance: The Corporate Social Audit," (New York: Committee for Economic Development, 1974), p. 61. Exhibit 1.3 (p. 28) reprinted by permission.

Chapter 2

1. George Cabot Lodge, "Top Priority: Renovating Our Ideology," *Harvard Business Review,* September–October 1970, p. 14.

2. "The Embattled Businessman," *Newsweek,* February 16, 1976, p. 56.

3. For a discussion of these activities see Susan Brown et al., "The Incredible Bread Machine" (Pasadena, Calif: The Ward Ritchie Press, 1975).

4. "Payoff Scandals," *Newsweek,* February 23, 1976, p. 30. Copyright 1976 by Newsweek, Inc. All rights reserved. Reprinted by permission.

5. "The Embattled Businessman," *Newsweek,* February 16, 1976, p. 56.

6. Ralph Nader and Mark Green, "What To Do About Corporate Corruption," *Wall Street Journal,* March 12, 1976, p. 8.

7. Archie Carroll, "Managerial Ethics: A Post Watergate View," *Business Horizons,* April 1975, p. 77. Excerpts and table reprinted by permission.

8. Quoted in Kenneth Andrews, "Toward Professionalism in Business Management," *Harvard Business Review,* March–April 1969, p. 90.

9. Adapted from Robert Austin, "Code of Conduct for Executives," *Harvard Business Review,* September–October 1961, p. 26.

10. S. Brenner and E. Molander, "Is the Ethics of Business Changing?" *Harvard Business Review,* January–February 1977, pp. 57–71. Copyright © 1977 by the President and Fellows of Harvard College; all rights reserved. Reprinted by permission.

11. *Ibid.,* p. 65.

12. "The Embattled Businessman," *Newsweek,* February 16, 1976, p. 59.

13. *Ibid.,* p. 59.

14. Brenner and Molander, "Is the Ethics of Business Changing?" p. 66.

15. "How Companies React to the Ethical Crisis," *Business Week,* February 9, 1976, p. 78.

16. This is a recurring complaint of business executives; see A. Newburg,

"Finding a Way Through the Tax Jungle," *Euromoney,* December 1977.

17. For a different perspective see "Why the SEC's Enforcer is in Over his Head: More and More Companies are Fighting SEC Changes in Court–and Winning," *Business Week,* October 11, 1976, p. 70ff.

18. The problems associated with antitrust interpretation are discussed in G. Thompson and G. Brady, *Antitrust Fundamentals* (St. Paul, Minn.: West Publishing, 1974).

19. Ralph Nader and Mark Green, "What To Do About Corporate Corruption," *Wall Street Journal,* March 12, 1976, p. 18.

Chapter 3

1. W. McQuade, "What Stress Can Do to You," *Fortune,* January 1972, p. 102.

2. *Ibid.,* p. 106.

3. H. Beric Wright, *Executive Ease and Dis-Ease* (New York: John Wiley & Sons, 1975), p. 19. Reprinted by permission of Gower Press (Teckfield Ltd.), Farnborough, England.

4. *Ibid.,* p. 25.

5. M. Friedman and R. Rosenman, *Type A Behavior and Your Heart* (Greenwich, Conn.: Fawcett, 1974).

6. R. Rosenman et al., "Coronary Heart Disease in the Western Collaborative Group Study: Final Follow-up Experience of 8½ years." *Journal of American Medical Association* (1975), 872–877.

7. Herbert Benson, "Your Innate Asset for Combating Stress," *Harvard Business Review,* July–August 1974, p. 90.

8. H. Selye, *Stress Without Distress* (Philadelphia: J. B. Lippincott, 1974), Chapter 1.

9. Quoted in McQuade, "What Stress Can Do to You," p. 134.

10. Abraham Zaleznick, "Management of Disappointment," *Harvard Business Review,* November–December 1967, pp. 59–70.

11. H. Livesey, "Second Acts," *Quest,* July–August 1977.

12. *Ibid.*

13. A further discussion of this and associated problems can be found in H.E.W. Special Task Force, *Work in America* (Cambridge, Mass.: MIT Press, 1974).

14. "Keeping Fit in the Company Gym," *Fortune*, October 1975, p. 136.

15. *Ibid.*, p. 136.

16. Carl Rogers and J. L. Wallen, *Counseling with Returned Service Men* (New York: McGraw-Hill, 1946).

17. Jack Gibb, "Meaning of the Small Group Experience," in *New Perspectives on Encounter Groups*, L. Solomon and B. Berzon, eds. (San Francisco, Calif.: Jossey Bass, 1972), p. 11.

18. *Ibid.*

19. Eli Goldston, "Executive Sabbaticals: About to Take Off," *Harvard Business Review*, September–October 1973.

20. L. DiCara and N. Miller, "Instrumental Learning of Systolic Blood Press Rats by Curarized Rats: Dissociation of Cardiac and Vascular Changes," *Psychosomatic Medicine* 30 (1968), 489–494.

21. McQuade, "What Stress Can Do to You," p. 252.

22. *Ibid.*, p. 53.

Chapter 4

1. There are those, however, who would look to the work of Charles Babbage as the true beginning of an orientation toward the management process. Babbage's main work, *On the Economy of Machinery and Manufacturers*, published in 1832, did contain a discussion of job specialization and time study as they applied to the manufacturing process.

2. Selected from Harold Koontz and Cyril O'Connell, *Principles of Management* (New York: McGraw Hill, 1964) and Lyndall Urwick, "Organization and Coordination Principles," in Joseph Litterer, *Organizations: Structure and Behavior* (New York: John Wiley & Sons, 1963).

3. Max Weber, "Bureaucracy," in *Max Weber: Essays in Sociology*, H. H. Gerth and C. Wright Mills, eds. (New York: Oxford University Press, 1967), p. 215.

4. *Ibid.*, p. 196.

5. *Ibid.*, p. 214.

6. F. Roethlisberger and W. J. Dickson, *Management and the Workers* (Cambridge, Mass.: Harvard University Press, 1939).

7. Harold Koontz, "The Management Theory Jungle," *Journal of the Academy of Management*, December 1961, pp. 174–188.

Chapter 5

1. James C. Worthy, "Organizational Structure and Employee Morale," in *Studies in Organizational Behavior and Management*, D. Porter and P. Applewhite, eds. (International Textbook Co., 1964), p. 31f.

2. Worthy, "Organizational Structure and Employee Morale," p. 33.

3. Thomas Burns, and G. M. Stalker, *The Management of Innovation* (London: Tavistock Publications, 1961).

4. Richard H. Hall, "Interorganizational Structural Variation: Application of the Bureaucratic Model," *Administrative Science Quarterly* 7 (December 1962), in *Readings in Organizational Behavior and Human Performance*, L. L. Cummings and W. E. Scott, eds. (Homewood, Ill.: Richard D. Irwin, 1969).

5. *Ibid.*, p. 398.

6. *Ibid.*, p. 396.

7. Joan Woodward, *Industrial Organization: Theory and Practice* (Oxford: Oxford University Press, 1965). Reprinted by permission.

8. P. R. Lawrence, and J. W. Lorsch, *Organization and Environment: Managing Differentiation and Integration* (Homewood, Ill.: Richard D. Irwin, 1969), p. 1.

9. *Ibid.*, p. 11.

Chapter 6

1. In later chapters, other models of human motivation will be discussed, including the theories of F. Herzberg, D. McClelland, B. F. Skinner and Victor Vroom.

2. Douglas McGregor, *The Human Side of Enterprise* (New York: McGraw-Hill, 1960).

3. Data (for diagram) based on Hierarchy of Needs in "A Theory of Human Motivation" in *Motivation and Personality,* 2nd edition by Abraham H. Maslow. Copyright © 1970 by Abraham H. Maslow. Reprinted by permission of Harper & Row, Publishers, Inc.

4. Adapted from Timothy W. Costello and Sheldon S. Zalkind, *Psychology in Administration: A Research Orientation* (Englewood Cliffs, N.J.: Prentice-Hall, 1963).

5. Chris Argyris, *Personality and Organization* (New York: Harper & Row, 1957).

6. Judson Gooding, "Blue Collar Blues on the Assembly Line," *Fortune,* July 1970, pp. 69–71.

7. *Ibid.,* p. 69.

Chapter 7

1. George Homans, *The Human Group* (New York: Harcourt Brace, 1950), p. 1.

2. Edgar Schein, *Organizational Psychology* (Englewood Cliffs, N.J.: Prentice-Hall, 1965), p. 67.

3. Leonard Sayles, "Work Group Behavior and the Larger Organization." In M. Richards and W. Nielander, eds., *Readings in Management* (Cincinnati: South-Western), pp. 431–44.

4. *Ibid.*

5. John Thibaut and Harold Kelley, *Social Psychology of Groups* (New York: John Wiley & Sons, 1961).

6. Bales' research results are found in a number of resources, including R. Bales, *Interaction Process Analysis* (Reading, Mass.: Addison-Wesley, 1950), and R. Bales and F. Strodtbeck, "Phases in Group Problem Solving," *Journal of Abnormal and Social Psychology,* 46 (1951), 485.

7. J. L. Moreno, "Contributions of Sociometry to Research Methodology in Sociology," *American Sociological Review,* June 1947, pp. 287–292.

8. J. L. Moreno and H. H. Jennings, "Statistics of Social Configurations," *Sociometry,* 1938, pp. 324–374.

9. Solomon Asch, "Effects of Group Pressure Upon the Modification and Distortion of Judgments," in *Group Dynamics: Research and Theory,* ed. D. Cartwright and A. Zander (New York: Harper & Row, 1960). Reprinted by permission of the publisher and the author.

10. Richard Crutchfield, "Conformity and Character," *American Psychologist* 10 (May 1955), 191, and Muzafer A. Sherif, "A Study of Some Social Factors in Perception," *Psychology,* 187, (1935).

11. Louis Allen, "Making Better Use of Committees," *Management Record,* December 1955.

12. R. Tillman, Jr., "Problems in Review: Committees on Trial," *Harvard Business Review,* May–June 1960.

13. Melville Dalton, *Men Who Manage* (New York: John Wiley & Sons, 1959). Reprinted by permission.

14. Leonard Sayles, *The Behavior of Industrial Work Groups* (New York: John Wiley & Sons, 1958). Reprinted by permission of the author.

Chapter 8

1. Ralph Stogdill, *Handbook of Leadership* (New York: Free Press, 1974), p. 7; Fred E. Fiedler, "Personality and Situational Determinants of Leadership Effectiveness," in *Group Dynamics: Research and Theory,* D. Cartwright and A. Zander, eds. (New York: Harper & Row, 1968); R. Tannenbaum, I. Weschler, and F. Massarik, *Leadership and Organization: A Behavioral Science Approach* (New York: McGraw-Hill, 1961), p. 24.

2. Edwin Ghiselli, "The Validity of Management Traits in Relation to Occupational Level," *Personnel Psychology* 16, No. 2. (Summer 1963). Adapted by permission of the publisher and author.

3. *Ibid.,* p. 112.

4. Stogdill, *Handbook of Leadership*, p. 63.

5. *Ibid.*, p. 81.

6. *Ibid.*, p. 81.

7. Keith Davis, *Human Relations at Work,* 3rd ed. (New York: McGraw-Hill, 1967), p. 99.

8. Ralph White and Ronald Lippitt, "Leader Behavior and Member Reaction in Three Social Climates," in *Group Dynamics: Research and Theory*, D. Cartwright and A. Zander, eds. (New York: Harper & Row, 1960).

9. R. Stogdill and A. Coons, eds., *Leader Behavior, Its Description and Measurement* (Columbus, Ohio: Ohio State University Bureau of Business Research, 1957).

10. *Ibid.*, pp. 11–12.

11. R. House, A. Filley, and S. Kerr, "Relation of Leader Consideration and Initiating Structure to R & D Subordinates Satisfaction," *Administrative Science Quarterly* (March 1971).

12. Robert Blake and Jane Mouton, *The New Managerial Grid* (Houston: Gulf Publishing Company, 1978), p. 11.

13. R. J. Tannenbaum and W. Schmidt, "How to Choose a Leadership Pattern," *Harvard Business Review,* March–April 1958.

14. Stogdill, *Handbook of Leadership*, p. 419.

15. J. R. P. French and B. Raven, "Bases of Social Power," in *Group Dynamics: Research and Theory*, D. Cartwright and A. Zander, eds. (New York: Harper & Row, 1968).

Chapter 8 Appendix

1. Victor Vroom, *Work and Motivation* (New York: John Wiley & Sons, 1964).

2. Robert House and T. Mitchell, "Path-Goal Theory of Leadership," *Journal of Contemporary Business*, Autumn 1974, p. 290.

3. *Ibid.*, p. 288.

4. A. Filley, R. House, S. Kerr, *Managerial Process and Organizational Behavior* (Glenview, Ill.: Scott-Foresman Co., 1976), pp. 254–262.

5. Fred Fiedler, "Personality and Situational Determinants of Leadership Effectiveness," in *Group Dynamics: Research and Theory*, D. Cartwright and A. Zander, eds. (1968).

6. Fred E. Fiedler, "Engineer the Job to Fit the Manager," *Harvard Business Review,* September–October 1965, p. 119. Copyright © 1965 by the President and Fellows of Harvard College; all rights reserved. Reprinted by permission.

Chapter 9

1. Lydia Strong, "Do You Know How to Listen?" in *Effective Communication on the Job*, M. Dooher and V. Marques, eds. (New York: American Management Association, 1956), p. 28.

2. M. Haire, "Role Perceptions in Labor-Management Relations: An Experimental Approach," *Industrial Labor Relations Review* 8 (1955).

3. J. Thibaut and Harold Kelley, *The Social Psychology of Groups* (New York: John Wiley & Sons, 1961), p. 76.

4. Solomon Asch, *Social Psychology* (Englewood Cliffs, N.J.: Prentice-Hall, 1952), pp. 208–211.

5. A. Bavelas, "Communication Patterns in Task Oriented Groups," *Journal of the Acoustical Society of America* 22 (1950), 725–730; H. J. Leavitt, "Some Effects of Certain Communication Patterns on Group Performance," *Journal of Abnormal and Social Psychology* 46 (1951); Harold Guetzkow and Herbert Simon, "The Impact of Certain Communication Nets Upon Organization and Performance in Task Oriented Groups," *Management Science* 329 (April–July 1955).

6. Alex Bavelas and Dermot Barrett, "An Experimental Approach to Organizational Communication," *Personnel*, March 1951.

7. Dale Level, "Communication Effectiveness Method and Situation," *Journal of Business Communication*, Fall 1972.

8. Norman R. F. Maier, L. Richard Hoffman, John J. Hooven, and William H. Read, "Superior-Subordinate Communication

in Management." *AMA Research Study 52,* ©
1961 by American Management Association,
Inc., p. 10.

9. Read, W. "Upward Communication in
Industrial Hierarchies," *Human Relations* 15
(1962).

10. *Ibid.*

11. Keith Davis, "Management
Communication and the Grapevine,"
Harvard Business Review,
September–October 1953, pp. 43–49.

12. A. K. Wickesberg, "Communication
Networks in the Business Organization
Structure," *Academy of Management Journal*
11, No. 3, (1968), 253–262. Reprinted by
permission of the publisher and the author.

13. D. Dearborn and H. Simon, "Selective
Perception: A Note on the Departmental
Identifications of Executives," *Sociometry* 21
(1958), 140–144.

14. Rensis Likert, *New Patterns of
Management* (New York: McGraw-Hill, 1961),
p. 105. Reprinted by permission of the
publisher.

15. F. J. Roethlisberger, "The
Administrator's Skill: Communication,"
Harvard Business Review,
November–December 1953, pp. 55–62.

Chapter 10

1. Frederick W. Taylor, *Scientific
Management* (New York: Harper & Row,
1947).

2. F. Roethlisberger and W. Dickson,
Management and the Worker (Cambridge,
Mass.: Harvard University Press, 1939).

3. F. Herzberg, B. Mausner, and D.
Snyderman, *The Motivation to Work* (New
York: John Wiley & Sons, 1959). Figure 10.2
reprinted by permission of the publisher.

Chapter 11

1. A. Graicunas, "Relationship in
Organization," *Papers on the Science of
Administration,* L. Gulick and L. Urwick, eds.
(New York: Institute of Public
Administration, 1937), pp. 183–187.

2. A. Hare, "A Study of Interaction and
Consensus in Different Sized Groups,"
American Sociological Review, June 1952, pp.
261–267.

3. George Miller, "The Magic Number
Seven; Plus or Minus Two: Some Limits on
Our Capacity for Processing Information,"
Psychological Review 63 (March 1956), 81–96.

4. Harold Stieglitz, "Optimizing Span of
Control," *Management Record* 24 (September
1962), 27.

5. *Ibid.,* p. 29.

Chapter 12

1. Alfred G. Larke, "Linear Responsibility
Chart: New Tool for Executive Control."
Reprinted with special permission from
Dun's Review, 1954. Copyright, 1954, Dun &
Bradstreet Publication Corporation.
Reprinted by permission of the publisher.

Chapter 13

1. R. Johnson, F. Kast, and J. Rosenzweig,
The Theory and Management of Systems
(New York: McGraw-Hill, 1963), and Jay
Forrester, "A New Corporate Design,"
Industrial Management Review 7 (1965).

Chapter 14

1. Lester Coch and John French,
"Overcoming Resistance to Change," *Human
Relations* 1 (1948), 512–533.

2. *Ibid.,* p. 514.

3. Peter Drucker, *The Practice of
Management* (New York: Harper & Row, 1954).

4. *Ibid.,* p. 129.

Chapter 15

1. William Guzzardi, Jr., "The Uncertain
Passage from College to Job," *Fortune,*
January–February 1976, p. 127.

2. Edgar Schein, "How to Break In the
College Graduate," *Harvard Business
Review,* November–December 1964, p. 147.

3. *Ibid.,* p. 147.

4. G. Dalton and P. Thompson,
"Accelerating Obsolescence of Older

Engineers," *Harvard Business Review,* September–October 1971, p. 111.

5. W. Dill, W. Crowston, and E. Elton, "Strategies for Self-Education," *Harvard Business Review,* November–December 1965.

6. "A Guide to Executive Education," *Business Week,* March 8, 1976, p. 80.

7. *Ibid.,* p. 81.

Chapter 16

1. See Chapter 5.

2. J. Woodward, *Industrial Organization* (Oxford: Oxford University Press, 1965).

3. P. Lawrence and J. Lorsch, *Organization and Environment: Managing Differentiation* (Boston: Graduate School of Business Administration, Harvard University, 1967).

4. J. Worthy, "Organizational Structure and Employee Morale," *American Sociological Review* 15 (1950), 169–179. S. Udy, "The Comparative Analysis of Organizations," *Handbook of Organizations,* J. March, ed. (Chicago: Rand McNally, 1965).

5. T. M. Burns and G. M. Stalker, *The Management of Innovation* (London: Tavistock Publications, 1961).

6. Douglas McGregor, *The Human Side of Enterprise* (see Chapter 6).

7. Sheldon A. Davis and Robert Tannenbaum, "Values, Man, and Organizations," *Sloan Management Review,*

Winter 1969, pp. 67–86. Adapted by permission.

8. W. French, "Organizational Development: Objectives, Assumptions, and Strategies," *California Management Review* 12, No. 2, p. 23.

9. W. Bennis, *Organizational Development: Its Nature, Origin and Prospects* (Reading, Mass.: Addison-Wesley, 1969), p. 2.

10. French, "Organizational Development: Objectives, Assumptions, and Strategies," p. 24.

11. C. Argyris, "T-Groups for Organizational Effectiveness," *Harvard Business Review,* March–April 1964, p. 60. Copyright © 1964 by the President and Fellows of Harvard College; all rights reserved. Reprinted by permission.

12. *Ibid.,* pp. 62–64.

13. R. Morton and B. Bass, "The Organizational Training Laboratory," *Training Directors Journal,* October 1964.

14. A. Filley, R. House, and S. Kerr, *Managerial Process and Organizational Behavior,* 2nd ed. (Glenview, Ill.: Scott Foresman & Co., 1976). Reprinted by permission.

Chapter 18

1. L. J. Savage, "The Theory of Statistical Decision," *Journal of the American Statistical Association,* March 1951.

Glossary

Acceptance theory of authority. Chester Barnard's view that a superior's authority is dependent upon a subordinate's acceptance of that authority.

Behavior modification. An approach to changing individual behavior by manipulating rewards to individuals.

Bounded discretion. The area in which managers are free to make decisions, determined by organizational and environmental norms, rules, policies, and sanctions.

Brainstorming. A group technique used to generate creative ideas by encouraging a free exchange of information and opinion without subjecting them to evaluation.

Bureaucracy. An organizational form characterized by (1) clearly defined duties for each position, (2) explicit chain of command, (3) specified rules, regulations, and procedures, (4) impersonal orientation, and (5) promotion based on technical competency.

Centralization. The extent to which control and decision making reside at the top levels of management.

Coercive power. The power of a leader to influence others based on the leader's ability to punish.

Communication. A process in which a message is transmitted by a sender and received and understood by a receiver.

Contingency theory. An approach to management which holds that there is no one best way to manage. Successful management consists of "fitting" organizational resources to the demands of the environment and technology.

Contingency theory of leadership. A leadership theory which holds that a task orientation works best in either very favorable or very unfavorable situations and that a human relations orientation works best in intermediate situations.

Control. The monitoring and measuring of variables associated with an activity for the purpose of detecting deviations.

Cost-benefit analysis. A quantitative technique used to evaluate the economic costs and the social benefits associated with a particular course of action.

Decision tree. A quantitative technique used to assess the expected value of problems that have several possible outcomes.

Decentralization. An organizational control system which has the effect of moving operating responsibility further down the hierarchy.

Departmentalization. The rational grouping of various individuals within an organization to ensure effective direction and coordination.

Differentiation. The degree to which organizational members working on different tasks hold different orientations toward goals, time horizons, and interpersonal relations.

Econometric models. A series of simultaneous equations which represent key economic variables designed to capture the essential relationships of a range of economic circumstances.

Economic order quantity (EOQ). A technique which provides a decision rule to aid managers in controlling costs associated with various inventory levels.

Emergent system. The activities, interactions, and sentiments of group members as a result of adapting to the required system.

Environment. All the factors which impact on the organization or unit being considered.

Exchange theory. A theory of group interaction based on the notion that individuals evaluate relationships in terms of rewards and costs.

Executive development. Programs designed to develop the skills and talents perceived as necessary for advancement of managers to more responsible positions. Areas covered include leadership development, behavioral concepts, planning and control techniques.

Expectancy theory. A theory of motivation which holds that motivation equals the expectation that behavior will lead to goal achievement (expectancy) times the desirability of the goal (valance).

Expected value. The conditional value (what the event is worth) multiplied by the probability of the event actually occurring.

Functional management. An approach to management emphasizing the administrative activities of a manager as they are performed at all levels of the hierarchy.

Functional structure. A form of organization in which sub-units are organized around the basic business functions (e.g., accounting, marketing, production).

Geographical structure. A form of organization in which sub-units are organized around geographical markets or regions served.

Grapevine. Informal communication routes within the organization.

Group. Any collection of individuals who interact, directly or indirectly, in order to achieve some common goals on the basis of command, task, friendship, or interest.

Group cohesiveness. The strength of attraction that exists among the members of a group.

Group norm. Patterns of behavior deemed acceptable by the group which define ways in which members *ought* to act.

Halo effect. The tendency for an individual's evaluation of another individual in a specific area, either negative or positive, to be transferred to an evaluation in another area.

Hawthorne studies. A series of experiments conducted at the Hawthorne Western Electric plant which revealed the impact of the "informal organization" on behavior in organizations.

Human relations school. An approach to management which emphasizes the effect of social needs and informal groups on the level of productivity.

Hygiene factors. Factors associated with a job that do not lead to satisfaction by their presence, but lead to dissatisfaction by their absence.

Index of centrality. A measure of the extent to which a given individual interacts with others.

Index of peripherality. A measure of the extent to which individuals are precluded from interacting with others.

Integration. The degree to which collaboration among individuals with differing time horizons, interpersonal relations, and goal orientations occurs within an organization.

Interaction. The mutual engagement of individuals in the course of carrying out activities at either a verbal or nonverbal level.

Interaction process analysis. A classification of interaction patterns, involving both task related and interpersonal processes, which is used when observing groups by focusing on the contents of who the sender and receiver are, and reactions to communications.

Job cycle. The entire sequence of activities that a worker must perform to complete a specific task.

Job enlargement. Programs designed to increase the horizontal scope of a job by allowing the employee to perform more operations in the job cycle.

Job enrichment. Programs designed to increase the vertical depth of a job by providing the employee with more responsibility for how the job cycle is completed.

Job shop. A department, or firm, in which an individual or small group is normally responsible for the complete asembly of a given component or product.

La Place criterion. A choice strategy which

uses the criterion of rationality. The manager assumes each outcome has an equal probability of occurring and acts accordingly.

Layering. The hierarchical formation of departments in pyramid fashion for the purpose of coordinating effort.

Leadership. Influencing the behavior of others to achieve some goal or task.

Leadership style. A consistent pattern of behavior along the dimensions associated with leader behavior (i.e., initiation, membership, representation, integration, etc.).

Line. Individuals and activities contributing directly to the accomplishment of the organization's primary objective.

Linear programming. A quantitative technique used to determine the optimal mix of limited resources for maximizing profits or minimizing costs.

Linear responsibility chart. A chart in matrix form in which each cell defines the responsibility relationship between an individual and a specific job or task.

Linking pin. An individual who is accepted as a legitimate member of two or more groups within an organization and serves as a means of coordination and communication between the two groups.

Maintenance role. Individual roles with a group that facilitate the performance of those functions necessary to keep the group functioning as a working unit.

Management by objectives (MBO). A technique to involve employees in the goal setting process through the following steps: (1) establishing mutually understood goals acceptable to both superior and subordinate, (2) setting up a specific action plan, (3) defining rewards that will result from achievement of goals, and (4) periodic review to monitor progress.

Managerial grid. An analysis of an individual's leadership style in terms of task versus person orientation, followed by a training program aimed at improving the individual's leadership style.

Manpower analysis. An assessment of the actual skills, aptitudes, and performance levels of current employees.

Maslow's need hierarchy. A theory of motivation which holds that human needs are arranged in a hierarchy (physiological, safety, love, esteem, self-actualization), and that a satisfied need no longer acts as a motivating force.

Mass production. A system in which large number of units are worked on simultaneously by workers who perform one or a few operations.

Matrix organization. An organizational structure which combines project management and functional departments. Project managers direct the flow of projects while the functional managers allocated resources to meet project needs.

Maximax. A choice strategy which uses a criterion of optimism. The manager assumes the best outcomes will occur and acts accordingly.

Maximin. A choice strategy which uses a criterion of pessimism. The manager assumes the worst will happen and acts accordingly.

Mechanistic structure. An organizational structure characterized by: coordination through the formal hierarchy, high level of job specialization, well-defined job descriptions, high value on individual loyalty to the organization, and emphasis on vertical interaction.

Method of least squares. A quantitative technique which defines a straight line through data points so that the sum of squared distances that each point lies off the line is minimized. This technique is an integral part of many forecasting procedures.

Minimax. A choice strategy which uses the criterion of regret. The manager acts to minimize the difference between the maximum payoff possible and the payoff for each individual alternative.

Monte Carlo simulation. A quantitative technique in which the variables included in the simulation take on values determined probabilistically for any particular run of the simulation.

Motivators. Factors associated with a job that must be present if a worker is to be satisfied.

Organic structure. An organizational structure characterized by: interactions concerned primarily with problem solving, network structure of control and communication, decisions based on expertise rather than formal position, and orientation toward using organizational skills wherever they are located.

Organizational development. A series of programs, or interventions, designed to facilitate change within the organization that results in more effective functioning.

Path-goal theory. A theory of leadership which holds that the effective leader selects a style based on the characteristics of subordinates and the environment, leading to a clear definition of goals, the removal of obstacles to those goals, and the tying of rewards to goal-achieving behavior.

Personal roles. Roles individuals assume within a group to satisfy their own needs, whether or not they are related to the goals of the group.

Position analysis. An assessment of the skills, aptitudes, and abilities required by each position within the company.

Power. A source of the ability of an individual to bring about some desired behavior on the part of others. Five such sources are reward, coercive, referent, expert, and legitimate.

Process production. A system in which a completed product results from a completely automated process in which workers monitor the process (e.g., oil refineries).

Product structure. A form of organization in which subunits are organized around products, or groups of products, produced by the organization.

Profit center concept. Each unit manager (project or department) is held responsible for quantity, quality, and cost considerations associated with his/her assignment.

Program evaluation and review techniques (PERT). A schematic model which uses the network concept to show the sequencing and timing of work activities associated with a project.

Project management. An organizational structure in which a single individual is held responsible for all activities associated with the project from its inception to its completion.

Unit production. A system in which products are made one at a time by workers who perform a wide range of tasks.

Relaxation response. A physiological response which is the opposite of the stress response. The relaxation response is induced by a relatively simple procedure emphasizing deep breathing and muscle relaxation.

Required system. The *formal* specification of the activities, interactions, and sentiments that organizational members *should* engage in.

Role. Behavior expected from an individual when he/she interacts with others.

Role playing. A learning technique in which participants assume the roles assigned in the exercise and act in accordance with those roles.

Scientific management. An approach to management which emphasizes finding the most efficient way to complete a task through the application of time and motion studies.

Selective perception. The tendency to perceive information through the "filter" of one's particular orientation.

Sensitivity training. A group experience designed to promote personal growth through the expression and acceptance of each member's feelings.

Sentiments. The feelings, attitudes, and values held by individuals within a group.

Slack analysis. An analysis of the amount of time a given event within the PERT network is ahead of or behind schedule and the impact this status will have on other events.

Sociometric analysis. A technique for analyzing group processes by observing the frequency of communications between individuals, the content of the communications, and sentiments of individuals about other group members.

Span of control. The number of subordinates that report directly to the same superior.

Staff. Individuals and activities supporting or facilitating the organization's primary objective through the application of specialized skills.

Stereotyping. A tendency to associate certain behavioral and personality attributes to particular individuals because of preconceived ideas one may have regarding age, appearance, ethnic background, etc.

Stress. The response of the body to any demand placed upon it. Normal usage of the term connotes a response that is experienced as negative.

Stressor. Environmental demands placed upon an individual which may lead to a stress response.

Task role. Individual roles within a group that facilitate the successful completion of a job or task.

Technical obsolescence. Outdating of an individual's knowledge, skills, or abilities by rapid changes in his/her chosen career area.

T-group. A training technique which focuses on building a trusting and open environment in which to explore personal insights and interpersonal relations.

Theory X. The notion that people inherently dislike work, need to be coerced and controlled, and will avoid responsibility whenever possible.

Theory Y. The notion that people take to work naturally, exercise self-control, and seek responsibility under proper conditions.

Type A behavior. A pattern of behavior that has been associated with a high probability of heart attacks. High ambition, competitiveness, aggressiveness, and working against time pressure characterize this pattern.

Type B behavior. A pattern of behavior that has been associated with a low probability of heart attacks. Patience, a leisurely pace, and lack of preoccupation with achievement characterize this pattern.

Unity of command. An early "principle of management" which holds that a particular individual should only be responsible to a single superior.

Worker participation. Involvement of workers in decisions that directly affect their work through a variety of techniques and programs (e.g., MBO).

Bibliography

Aaker, D. and Day, C. *Consumerism: Search for the Consumer Interest.* New York: Free Press, 1971.

Adams, J. "Inequity in Social Exchange." In *Advances in Social Psychology,* Vol. 2. L. Berkowitz, ed. New York: Academic Press, 1965.

Argyris, Chris. *Personality and Organization.* New York: Harper and Brothers, 1957.

———. "The Individual and Organization: Some Problems of Mutual Adjustment." *Administrative Science Quarterly* 2 (1957).

Asch, S. "Effects of Group Pressure Upon the Modification and Distortion of Judgments." In *Group Dynamics: Research and Theory,* D. Cartwright and A. Zander, eds. New York: Harper & Row, 1960.

Athos, A. and Coffey, R. *Behavior in Organizations: A Multi-Dimensional View.* Englewood Cliffs, N.J.: Prentice-Hall, 1968.

Bales, R. *Interaction Process Analysis.* Reading, Mass.: Addison-Wesley, 1950.

Barnard, C. *The Functions of the Executive.* Cambridge, Mass.: Harvard University Press, 1938.

Bennis, W. *Changing Organizations.* New York: McGraw-Hill, 1966.

Benson, H. "Your Innate Ability for Combating Stress." In *Harvard Business Review,* July–August 1974.

Blake, R. and Mouton, J. *The Managerial Grid.* Houston, Texas: Gulf Publishing Co., 1964.

Blau, P., and Scott, W. *Formal Organizations.* New York: Chandler, 1962.

Blauner, R. *Alienation and Freedom.* Chicago: University of Chicago Press, 1964.

Brenner, S. and Molander, E. "Is the Ethics of Business Changing?" In *Harvard Business Review,* January–February 1977.

Brown, S., et al. *The Incredible Bread Machine.* Pasadena, Calif.: Ward-Ritchie Press, 1974.

Buffa, E. *Modern Production Management.* New York: John Wiley & Sons, 1965.

Burns, T. and Stalker, G.M. *The Management of Innovation.* London: Tavistock Publications, 1961.

Campbell, J., et al. *Managerial Behavior, Performance and Effectiveness.* New York: McGraw-Hill, 1970.

Carlson, J. and Misshauk, M. *Management Decision Simulations.* New York: John Wiley & Sons, 1971.

Carroll, A. "Managerial Ethics: A Post Watergate View." In *Business Horizons,* April 1975.

Carroll, S. and Tosi, H. *Management by Objectives.* New York: Macmillan, 1973.

Cartwright, D. and Zander, A., eds. *Group Dynamics: Research and Theory.* New York: Harper & Row, 1960.

Coch, L. and French, J. "Overcoming Resistance to Change." *Human Relations* 1 (1948).

Corson, J. and Steiner, G. "Measuring Business' Social Performance: The Corporate Social Audit." New York: Committee for Economic Development, 1974.

Costello, T. and Zalkind, S., eds. *Psychology in Administration.* Englewood Cliffs: Prentice-Hall, 1963.

Cummings, L. and Schwab, D. *Performance in Organizations: Determinants and Appraisal.* Glenview, Ill., Scott, Foresman and Co., 1973.

Dale, E. *The Great Organizers.* New York: McGraw-Hill, 1961.

Dalton, M. *Men Who Manage.* New York: John Wiley & Sons, 1959.

Davis, K. *Human Behavior at Work,* 4th ed. New York: McGraw-Hill, 1972.

———. "Management Communication and the Grapevine." In *Harvard Business Review,* September–October 1953.

Drucker, P. *Managing for Results.* New York: Harper & Row, 1964.

———. *The Practice of Management.* New York: Harper & Row, 1954.

Dunnette, M. et al. "The Effect of Group Participation on Brainstorming: Effectiveness for Two Industrial Samples." In *Journal of Applied Psychology* 47 (1963).

Fabrycky, W. and Torgersen, P. *Operations Economy.* Englewood Cliffs, N.J.: Prentice-Hall, 1966.

Fayol, H. *Industrial and General Administration.* London: Sir Isaac Pitman & Sons, Ltd., 1949.

Fiedler, F. Personality and Situational Determinants of Leadership Effectiveness." In *Group Dynamics: Research and Theory.* A. Cartwright and D. Zander, eds. New York: Harper & Row, 1968.

Filley, A., House, R., and Kerr, S. *Managerial Process and Organizational Behavior.* Glenview, Ill.: Scott, Foresman and Co., 1976.

Forrester, J. "A New Corporate Design." In *Industrial Management Review* (Fall 1965).

———. *Industrial Dynamics.* New York: John Wiley & Sons, 1961.

French, J., et al. "Employee Participation in a Program of Industrial Change." In *Personnel,* Vol. 35 No. 3 (1958).

——— and Raven, B. "Basis of Social Power." *Group Dynamics: Research and Theory,* A. Cartwright and D. Zander, eds. New York: Harper & Row, 1964.

French, W. "Organizational Development: Objectives, Assumptions and Strategies." In *California Management Review,* Vol. 1 No. 2 (1969).

Friedlander, F. "Motivations to Work and Organizational Performance." In *Journal of Applied Psychology* 50 (1966).

Galbraith, J. *Designing Complex Organizations.* Reading, Mass.: Addison-Wesley, 1973.

Gantt, H. *Organizing for Work.* New York: Harcourt Brace Jovanovich, 1976.

Garrett, L. and Silver, M. *Production Management Analysis.* New York: Harcourt Brace Jovanovich, 1973.

Georgopouloulos, B. et. al. "A Path-Goal Approach to Productivity." In *Journal of Applied Psychology* 41 (1957).

Ghiselli, E. *Explorations in Managerial Talent.* Pacific Palisades, Calif.: Goodyear, 1971.

Gouldner, A. *Patterns of Industrial Bureaucracy.* New York: Free Press, 1954.

Greiner, L. "Antecedents of Planned Organizational Change." In *Journal of Applied Behavioral Science,* Vol. 3, No. 1 (1967).

———. "Patterns of Organizational Change." In *Harvard Business Review,* May–June 1967.

Guzzardi, W., Jr. "The Uncertain Passage from College to Job." In *Fortune,* January 1976.

Haire, M. "Role Perceptions in Labor-Management Relations: An Experimental Approach." In *Industrial Labor Relations Review* 8 (1955).

Hall, R. "Intraorganizational Structural Variation: Application of the Bureaucratic Model." *Administrative Science Quarterly* (December 1962).

Hampton, D. et al. *Organizational Behavior and the Practice of Management.* Glenview, Ill.: Scott, Foresman and Co., 1968.

Hare, P. et al. *Small Groups.* New York: Knopf, 1962.

Henderson, H. "Should Business Tackle Society's Problems?" In *Harvard Business Review,* July–August 1968.

Herzberg, F. *The Motivation to Work.* New York: John Wiley & Sons, 1959.

House, R. et al. "Relation of Leader Consideration and Initiating Structure to R&D Subordinates Satisfaction." In *Administrative Science Quarterly,* March 1971.

——— and Mitchell, T. "Path-Goal Theory of Leadership." In *Journal of Contemporary Business,* Autumn 1974.

Hulin, C. and Blood, M. "Job Enlargement, Individual Differences, and Worker Responses." In *Psychological Bulletin* 69 (1968).

Ivancevich, J. *Organizational Behavior and Performance*. Pacific Palisades, Calif.: Goodyear Publishing, 1977.

Johnson, R. et al. *The Theory and Management of Systems*. New York: McGraw-Hill, 1963.

Kahn, R. *Organizational Stress*. New York: John Wiley & Sons, 1964.

Katz, D. and Kahn, R. *The Social Psychology of Organizations*, 2nd ed. New York.: John Wiley & Sons, 1978.

"Keeping Fit in the Company Gym." In *Fortune*, October 1975.

Khare, R. et al. *Environmental Quality and Social Responsibility*. Madison, Wisconsin: University of Wisconsin Press, 1972.

Koch, J. and Chizmar, J. *The Economics of Affirmative Action*. Lexington, Mass. Lexington Books, 1976.

Koontz, H. and O'Donnell, C. *Principles of Management*. New York: McGraw-Hill, 1955.

Lawler, E. *Pay and Organizational Effectiveness*. New York: McGraw-Hill, 1971.

Leavitt, H. "Applied Organizational Change in Industry: Structural Technological and Humanistic Approaches." In *Handbook of Organizations*, J. March, ed. Skokie, Ill., Rand McNally, 1965.

Lewin, K. "Group Decision and Social Change." In *Readings in Social Psychology*, T.M. Newcomb and E.L. Hartley, eds. New York: Holt, Rinehart and Winston, 1958.

Likert, R. *New Patterns of Management*. New York: McGraw-Hill, 1961.

_____. *The Human Organization*. New York: McGraw-Hill, 1967.

Livesey, H. "Second Acts." In *Quest*, July–August 1977.

Locke, E. "The Nature and Causes of Job Satisfaction." In *Handbook of Industrial and Organizational Psychology*, M. Dunnette, ed. Chicago: Rand McNally, 1976.

Lorsch, J. and Morse, J. *Organizations and their Members: A Contingency Approach*. New York: Harper & Row, 1974.

Luthans, F. *Contemporary Readings in Organizational Behavior*, 2nd ed. New York: McGraw-Hill, 1972.

_____. *Organizational Behavior*. New York: McGraw-Hill, 1977.

_____. *Social Issues in Business*. New York: Macmillan, 1972.

Lyle, J. "Affirmative Action Programs For Women: A Survey of Innovative Programs." *EEOC Report*. Washington. D.C.: U.S. Government Printing Office, 1973.

Maier, N. et. al. "Superior-Subordinate Communication in Management." In *AMA Research Study, No. 52*, (1961).

March, J. and Simon, H. *Organizations*. New York: John Wiley & Sons, 1958.

Margules, N. and Raia, A. *Organizational Development: Values, Process and Technology*, New York: McGraw-Hill, 1972.

Maslow, H. *Eupsychian Management*. Homewood, Ill.: Richard D. Irwin, 1965.

_____. *Motivation and Personality*. New York: Harper and Brothers, 1954.

Mayo, E. *The Human Problems of an Industrial Civilization*. New York: Macmillan, 1933.

McClelland, D. *The Achieving Society*. New York. Van Nostrand Reinhold, 1961.

McGregor, D. *The Human Side of Enterprise*. New York: McGraw-Hill, 1960.

McQuade, W. "Doing Something About Stress." In *Fortune*, May 1973.

_____. "What Stress Can Do to You." In *Fortune*, January 1972.

Miles, R. *Theories of Management*. New York: McGraw-Hill, 1975.

Mintzberg, H. *The Nature of Managerial Work*. New York: Harper & Row, 1973.

Moreno, J. *The Sociometric Reader*. New York: Free Press, 1960.

Morse, N. and Reimer, E. "The Experimental

Change of a Major Organization Variable." In *Journal of Abnormal and Social Psychology* 52 (1956).

Murdick, R. and Ross, J. *Information Systems for Modern Management*. Englewood Cliffs, N.J.: Prentice-Hall, 1971.

Nader, R. and Green, M. "What to Do About Corporate Corruption." In *Wall Street Journal*, 12 March 1976.

Olmsted, M. *The Small Group*, New York: Random House, 1959.

Olsen, R. *Manufacturing Management*. Scranton, Pa.: International Textbook Co., 1968.

Ouchi, W. and Maguire, M. "Organizational Control: Two Functions." In *Administrative Science Quarterly* 4 (1975).

Porter, D. et. al. *Studies in Organizational Behavior and Management*, 2nd ed. Scranton, Pa.: Unitext Educational Publishers, 1971.

Porter, L. et. al. *Behavior in Organizations*. New York: McGraw-Hill, 1975.

Richard, M. and Greenlaw, P. *Management Decision-Making*, Homewood, Ill.: Richard, D. Irwin, 1966.

Riesman, D. *The Lonely Crowd*. New Haven, Conn.: Yale University Press, 1969.

Roethlisberger, F. "The Administrator's Sill: Communication." *Harvard Business Review*, November–December 1953.

———. *Management and Morale*. Cambridge, Mass. Harvard University Press, 1941.

——— and Dickson, W. *Management and the Worker*. Cambridge, Mass.: Harvard University Press, 1939.

Roscoe, E. and Freak, D. *Organization for Production*, Homewood, Ill.: Richard D. Irwin, 1971.

Ross, J. *Management by Information System*. Englewood Cliffs, N.J.: Prentice-Hall, 1970.

Savage, L. "The Theory of Statistical Decision." In *Journal of the American Statistical Association*, March 1951.

Sayles, L. *The Behavior of Industrial Work Groups*. New York: John Wiley & Sons, 1958.

———. "Work Group Behavior and The Larger Organization." In *Readings in Management*. M. Richards and W. Nielander, eds. Cincinnati, Ohio: South-Western Publishing Co., 1963.

Schein, E. "How to Break In the College Graduate." In *Harvard Business Review*, November–December 1964.

———. "The Individual, the Organization and the Career: A Conceptual Scheme." In *Organizational Psychology*, D. Kolb et. al., eds. Englewood Cliffs, N.J.: Prentice-Hall, 1974.

———. *Organizational Psychology*. Englewood Cliffs, N.J.: Prentice-Hall, 1965.

——— and Bennis, W. *Personal and Organizational Change Through Group Methods*. New York: John Wiley & Sons, 1966.

Schoderbek, P. *Management Systems*. New York: John Wiley & Sons, 1967.

Scott, W. "Activation Theory and Task Design." In *Organizational Behavior and Human Performance* 1 (August 1966).

———. *Organization Theory*. Homewood, Ill.: Richard D. Irwin, 1967.

Seashore, S. *Group Cohesiveness in the Industrial Work Group*, Ann Arbor, Mich.: Survey Research Center, Institute for Social Research, 1954.

Selznick, P. *T.V.A. and the Grass Roots*. Berkeley: University of California Press, 1949.

Sherif, M. and Sherif, C. *Reference Groups*, New York: Harper & Row, 1964.

Simon, H. *Administrative Behavior*. New York: Mcmillan, 1947.

Solomon, L. and Berzon B., eds. *New Perspectives on Encounter Groups*. San Francisco, Calif.: Jossey-Bass, 1972.

Stieglitz, H. "Optimization of Span of Control." In *Management Record* (September 1962).

Stogdill, R. *Handbook of Leadership*. New York: The Free Press, 1974.

———. *Individual Behavior and Group Achievement*. New York: Oxford University Press, 1959.

_____ and Coons, A., eds. *Leader Behavior: Its Description and Measurement.* Columbus, Ohio: Bureau of Business Research, 1957.

Tannenbaum, R. and Davis, S. "Values, Man and Organizations." In *Industrial Management Review* 10 (Winter 1969).

_____ and Schmidt, W. "How to Choose a Leadership Pattern." In *Harvard Business Review,* March–April 1958.

_____ et. al. *Leadership and Organization: A Behavioral Science Approach.* New York: McGraw-Hill, 1961.

Taylor, Frederick W. *The Principles of Scientific Management.* New York: Harper & Row, 1911.

Thibaut, J. and Kelley, H. *The Social Psychology of Groups.* New York: John Wiley & Sons, 1959.

Thompson, D. *The Economics of Environmental Protection.* Cambridge, Mass.: Winthrop, 1973.

Thompson, V. *Modern Organization.* New York: Knopf, 1961.

Tosi, H. and Carroll, S. "Management by Objectives." In *Personnel Administration,* July–August 1970.

Tracey, W. *Designing Training and Development Systems.* New York: American Management Association, 1971.

Trist, E. and Bamforth, K. "Some Social and Psychological Consequences of the Longwall Method of Coal-Getting." In *Human Relations* 4 (1951).

Trumbo, D. "Individual and Group Correlate of Attitudes Toward Work Related Change." In *Journal of Applied Psychology* 45 (1961).

Turkel, Studs. *Working.* New York: Avon Books, 1974.

Tyler, W. "Measuring Organizational Specialization: The Concept of Role Variety." In *Administrative Science Quarterly,* September 1973.

Van Horne, J. *Financial Management and Policy,* 2nd ed. Englewood Cliffs, N.J.: Prentice-Hall, 1971.

Vroom, V. *Work and Motivation.* New York John Wiley & Sons, 1964.

_____ and Yetton, P. *Leadership and Decision-Making.* Pittsburgh, Pa.: University of Pittsburgh Press, 1973.

Walker, C. "Life in the Automated Factory." In *Harvard Business Review* January–February 1958.

_____ and Guest, R. *The Man on the Assembly Line.* Cambridge: Harvard University Press, 1952.

Weaver, P. "The Hazards of Trying to Make Consumer Products Safer." In *Fortune,* July 1975.

Webber, R. *Management.* Homewood, Ill.: Richard D. Irwin, 1975.

Weston, F. "Operations and Research Techniques Relevant to Corporate Planning Function Practices: An Investigative Look." In *Academy of Management Journal,* September 1973.

White, R. and Lippitt, R. "Leader Behavior and Member Reaction in Three Social Climates." In *Group Dynamics: Research and Theory.* D. Cartwright and A. Zander, eds. New York: Harper & Row, 1960.

Woodward, J. *Industrial Organization: Theory and Practice.* London: Oxford University Press, 1965.

Worthy, J. "Organizational Structure and Employee Morale," In *American Sociological Review* 15 (1950).

Wright, H. *Executive Ease and Dis-ease.* New York: John Wiley & Sons, 1975.

Zaleznick, A. "Management of Disappointment." In *Harvard Business Review,* November–December 1967.

Zalkind, S. and Costello, T. "Perception: Some Recent Research and Implications for Administration." In *Administration Science Quarterly* 7 (1962).

Zimbardo, P. and Ebbesen, E. *Influencing Attitudes and Changing Behavior.* Reading, Mass.: Addison-Wesley. 1969.

Index